Client-Side Reporting
with Visual Studio in C#

Asif Sayed

Apress®

Client-Side Reporting with Visual Studio in C#

Copyright © 2007 by Asif Sayed

ISBN-13 (pbk): 978-1-59059-854-2

ISBN-10 (pbk): 1-59059-854-7

Printed and bound in the United States of America 9 8 7 6 5 4 3 2 1

Lead Editors: Jim Huddleston, Jeff Pepper
Technical Reviewer: Ty Anderson
Editorial Board: Steve Anglin, Ewan Buckingham, Gary Cornell, Jonathan Gennick, Jason Gilmore,
    Jonathan Hassell, Chris Mills, Matthew Moodie, Jeffrey Pepper, Ben Renow-Clarke,
    Dominic Shakeshaft, Matt Wade, Tom Welsh
Project Manager: Kylie Johnston
Copy Edit Manager: Nicole Flores
Copy Editor: Heather Lang
Assistant Production Director: Kari Brooks-Copony
Production Editor: Ellie Fountain
Compositors: Dina Quan and Linda Weidemann
Proofreader: Nancy Riddiough
Indexer: Carol Burbo
Artist: Kinetic Publishing Services, LLC
Cover Designer: Kurt Krames
Manufacturing Director: Tom Debolski

Distributed to the book trade worldwide by Springer-Verlag New York, Inc., 233 Spring Street, 6th Floor, New York, NY 10013. Phone 1-800-SPRINGER, fax 201-348-4505, e-mail orders-ny@springer-sbm.com, or visit http://www.springeronline.com.

For information on translations, please contact Apress directly at 2855 Telegraph Avenue, Suite 600, Berkeley, CA 94705. Phone 510-549-5930, fax 510-549-5939, e-mail info@apress.com, or visit http://www.apress.com.

The source code for this book is available to readers at http://www.apress.com in the Source Code/ Download section.

This book is dedicated to the late James Huddleston (the initial editor of this book) and to my loving family and friends who provided the support, love, and encouragement that made this endeavor possible.

Contents at a Glance

Contents

About the Author

ASIF SAYED has over fifteen years' experience in designing software solutions and business process architecture. A senior systems analyst with a leading energy services provider in Toronto, Canada, he also teaches .NET technologies as a part-time faculty member at Centennial College in Toronto.

About the Technical Reviewer

TY ANDERSON is a partner at Cogent Company in Dallas, Texas. He spends his time consulting and building software using Microsoft technologies. Ty writes frequently about Microsoft technologies including SharePoint, Office, and SQL Server, and his articles have been featured on several technology-focused web sites including CIO.com, Devx.com, and Simple-Talk.com. Look for him at any tech conference—he will be wearing his yellow Oakland Athletics hat. Say hello, and he will most likely buy you a beer.

Acknowledgments

I'd like to start by remembering the late James Huddleston, the initial editor on this book. James saw one of my articles on client-side reporting and approached me with the idea of writing a book on this topic. I remember James was even more excited than me with this book. I really wish James was alive today to see this book published. James will be always alive in my memories; rest in peace, James.

My sincere gratitude goes to all the folks who are associated with this book in any capacity. Some of you have spent countless hours working on this project. And some of you have given me your valuable time to look through the initial draft chapters and provided me with your valuable input.

I would like to sincerely thank Jeffrey Pepper. Jeff took over this project after James left us to begin his heavenly journey. I must say, you did a wonderful job of catching up with the project and provided me with the same level of guidance and support that I enjoyed from James.

I would like to thank my technical editor Ty Anderson. Ty, I don't know how to put in words how much I enjoyed your comments, and they have helped me to shape the content of each chapter. I wish and hope that I'll have you or someone like you for the role of technical editor for any other book I'll write in the future.

My sincere thanks to the team at Apress: Kylie Johnston, Heather Lang, Ellie Fountain, and all the other folks who took part in making this book. Kylie, I hope every author gets a project manager like you. Thank you for keeping me motivated and helping me meet the tight deadlines. A special thanks for your patience and e-mails full of encouragements.

A special thanks also goes to Diana May from SQL Server Magazine, Frank Beverdam of Dynamiczones.com, David Riggs of aspnetpro.com, and Steve Jones of sqlservercentral.com. I sincerely thank all of you for extending a helping hand to feature my book on your esteemed media resources.

Many other folks provided valuable feedback by unofficially reviewing the book or a chapter. I would like to specially name my maternal uncle Abdul Aziz, who has been in the field of journalism for the last three decades. Special thanks go to Mohammed Khan, professor and course supervisor at Centennial College in Toronto. Thank you, Mr. Khan, for introducing me to the wonderful field of teaching. My teaching assignments with the college over the years have helped greatly while writing this book. I also extend my sincere thanks to many of my dear students who volunteered to try out the examples from this book. I would especially like to thank one of my favorite students, Photis Castrounis.

I also wish to take this opportunity to thank my parents, my friends, my business partners, and my colleagues at work. I'd like to thank all the teachers who contributed to my life and every other person who contributed in any form or shape to help me be who I am today.

Finally, I like to thank my wife Aliya for always being there for me. I appreciate your understanding and patience. Like the saying goes, "Behind every successful man, there is a wise woman;" for me, that woman is Aliya. Although my son Jared is just one-and-a-half years old at the time of this writing, he too played his part by keeping me entertained and engaged in competition to see who hit more keys on our keyboard.

Introduction

My first interaction with client-side Reporting Services (RS) started with the release of the Visual Studio 2005, beta 2. RS was by far my favorite feature from the "what's new" list—and why not? Before RS, the only out-of-the-box client-side reporting alternatives were Crystal Reports or writing your own reporting solution using the .NET printing classes.

When the beta 2 release of Visual Studio 2005 appeared, I was working on a financial system for one of my clients. After spending some time with this tool, I was able to create some neat reports ranging from simple invoices to a complicated balance sheet.

One of the prime motivations for me to write this book was to share my experiences with you. I tried my best to bring in all sorts of different reporting scenarios to help you learn all the cool features of RS. I sincerely hope that this book will reduce your learning curve and that you can also bring the sample projects' functionality into your projects.

This book will take you step-by-step on a journey of report authoring by using practical examples from real-world business cases. You'll also learn how reports can be processed by various clients developed using Visual Studio.

This book will focus on the design of practical reporting projects using the Visual Studio IDE and on viewing the reports using the supplied ReportViewer control. This means that you, the reader, must be comfortable with the development methods of your favorite client.

The approach adopted in this book is simple: You'll learn hands on, while doing the examples. Major emphasis is applied to small details of report authoring, and when it comes to clients, minimal attention is given—they're covered only to the extent that they look good as hosts for our authored reports.

All reports in this book have some real-world touch associated with them; that is, you will not learn the dry way: "What is data grouping?" Instead, you will learn with a pinch of a spicy flavor, like this: "How does this regionwide sales report use the reporting technique called data grouping?"

Who Should Read This Book

On the level of expertise, this book is for everyone, so whether you're a beginner at reporting or an expert, you'll find something to learn and enjoy in report development. However, over 60 percent of the content is written with the prime focus on an audience that's beginner-level in reporting. The examples used in this book are in C#, so unless you are just looking for a general understanding of reporting techniques, understanding C# is a requirement.

The topics are diverse and descriptive, and there's something in here for everyone, whether you're a developer, a business intelligence (BI) practitioner, or a business analyst. As long as you've a sound base knowledge of Visual Studio IDE and relational databases in general, then this book will act as a tutorial to beginners and a best practices guide to experts using real-world examples.

What You Need to Know Before You Read This Book

This book assumes that you know the basics of software development using the Visual Studio IDE and are comfortable with the C# programming language. If you're completely new to the .NET framework, then I recommend that you read an introductory book on doing development with Visual Studio and C# before reading this book. In the body of this book, all the code samples are presented in C#.

Basic familiarity with SQL Server 2005 or 2008 is desirable to understand the data model that is used to generate reports. Any previous exposure to a report writing tool would be a plus in helping you to quickly grasp the report design concepts.

All of the examples through Chapter 13 are developed using the VS 2005 IDE. I've used the Visual Studio 2008 beta 1 release for Chapters 14 and 15. Developing reports with client-side RS remains similar between the Visual Studio 2005 IDE and the Visual Studio 2008 beta 1 IDE. Therefore, you can do all the reports, which I did, using either IDE. It would be worth the effort to redo the examples through Chapter 13 using the Visual Studio 2008 IDE.

How This Book Is Structured

This book is written in such a way that you can read through the book cover to cover or you can jump directly to your favorite topic. However, I'd strongly suggest reading Chapters 4 and 5, as many of the features of RS are covered in detail. The structure of the book is as follows.

Chapter 1: What Is Client-Side Reporting?

This chapter will start with briefly discussing client-side reporting and the architecture on which it is built. You'll see the new approach for accessing data and delivering reports using various local clients. You'll also explore the factors that come into play to get that perfect report! You'll get a detailed overview of how reports are structured and see various different reporting patterns and generic templates used to report real-world information.

Chapter 2: Client-Side Reporting Components

This chapter will raise the curtain and introduce you to the out-of-the-box local processing of Reporting Services (RS) functionality. You'll explore the details of the built-in report designer and all the available report controls. You'll also get an introduction to ReportViewer.

Chapter 3: Data Models, Datasets, and the ADO.NET Interface

The purpose of this book is to teach you RS using real-world reporting projects; this chapter will help you understand how to use the dataset to gather data using ADO.NET interface code from the RealWorld database. You'll also go through a step-by-step tutorial to learn how to get the dataset ready for the reporting project.

Chapter 4: Reporting with Windows Forms

You'll start with a "Windows Forms 101" tutorial in this chapter; this tutorial will teach you how to create a basic application that is capable of hosting ReportViewer. Different aspects of report authoring and local hosting will be demonstrated using real-world business cases, for example, a Customer Address List report using the multicolumn feature.

Chapter 5: Reporting with ASP.NET Web Forms

You'll move to Web Forms in this chapter. Here, we'll start with an "ASP.NET Web Sites 101" tutorial. This tutorial will teach you how to create a basic application to host reports inside your favorite browser. You'll learn to develop a few more exciting reporting projects, for instance, an Aged Accounts Receivables report.

Chapter 6: Reporting with Web Services and Mobile Devices

This chapter will guide you through the development of a simple web service. Further, in this chapter, you will see how you can create a Travel Itinerary in PDF format. You'll also learn how this PDF report can be consumed with a Windows Forms client. You'll learn how to expose the reporting capabilities of RS via a web service to various cross-platform clients. We'll also discuss how reports can be made available on demand to mobile clients in both offline and online modes.

Chapter 7: Reporting with a Console Application

In this chapter, you'll learn to make use of non-GUI clients to generate reports. We'll start with a quick step-by-step tutorial. This is followed by a reporting project that will save report output to a local drive on your PC. I'll also show you how to use FTP as a report delivery vehicle, and you'll see how to schedule automated report generation and delivery.

Chapter 8: Reporting with a Windows Service

In this chapter, you'll make use of a client that has no user interface. You'll see how to leverage the power of Windows Services to automate the delivery of reports. A simple "Windows Services 101" tutorial will guide you step by step through automating and scheduling report delivery. As an example, you will see how to develop reports that have nested groups of data.

Chapter 9: Reporting with Web Parts

This chapter will guide you to develop reports as web parts, which can be hosted with Share-Point services. You'll learn how easy it is to distribute practical real-world reports using the power of SharePoint technology. In the reporting project, you'll see the charting feature of RS in action.

Chapter 10: Reporting on Other Data Sources

RS is capable of reporting from a variety of different data sources. This book is primarily focused on using the data from SQL Server. However, this chapter will let you report on diverse data sources, such as Oracle, Access, and XML.

Chapter 11: Integrating Server-Side Reports

This book is focused on client-side RS. However, this chapter will provide insight on the other side, the server side. You'll get a brief overview of the mechanics required to manage reports hosted on the server side with your favorite client.

Chapter 12: Moving from Crystal Reports to Reporting Services

Although both Crystal Reports and Reporting Services are provided with Visual Studio as out-of-the-box local reporting solutions, they each adopt different styles and methodologies to produce reports. In this chapter, with the help of an example, you'll learn some basic differences and processes to remember for easy and successful transition from using Crystal Reports to using RS.

Chapter 13: Using Third-Party Tools and Having Fun with RS

This chapter will highlight the use of third-party tools integrated with client-side RS. You'll see how easy it is to create reports with graphical barcodes. Not all reports are a bunch of numbers or boxes and lines; this chapter will show you what else can be done using RS; for example, you'll learn how to create your very own personal dashboard.

Chapter 14: Reporting with Visual Studio 2008 Windows Forms

In this chapter, I'll show you how to develop reports using the Visual Studio 2008 IDE, and the client I'll target is Windows Forms. This chapter will also highlight how you can develop reports using the Report Wizard, which is new in Visual Studio 2008 for client-side RS.

Chapter 15: Reporting with Visual Studio 2008 Web Forms

Finally, I am using this last chapter to develop reports with a Visual Studio 2008 Web Forms client. This chapter will help you to see the similarity between Visual Studio 2005 and Visual Studio 2008 when it comes to developing reports.

Appendix: The Visual Studio IDE

Although I assume you are familiar with the workings of Visual Studio IDE in the examples from this book, in case you need a refresher on the workings of the IDE, this appendix provides a brief walk-through.

What You Need to Use This Book

To run the samples presented in this book, you'll need the following:

- *SQL Server 2005*: Most of the samples can be used with the Express Edition of SQL Server 2005. However, to use the server-side examples, you'll need to have the full version. An evaluation version of SQL Server and Reporting Services may be downloaded from Microsoft at `http://www.microsoft.com/sql`.

- *Windows 2000, Windows Server 2003, Windows XP Professional, or Windows Vista*: The examples in this book were developed on a machine running Windows XP.

- *Visual Studio 2005 Professional*: The professional version is required to use the samples presented in this book, up to Chapter 13. A trial version can be downloaded from Microsoft at `http://msdn.microsoft.com/vstudio/`.

- *Visual Studio 2008*: To run examples in Chapters 14 and 15, you'll need Visual Studio 2008, beta 1 onwards. By the time this book reaches you, the full release of Visual Studio 2008 will probably be available. Please consult the Microsoft site on how to get the trial version at `http://www.microsoft.com`.

- *Express Web Development*: ASP.NET web-based examples in this book (excluding the one in Chapter 15, which uses the Visual Studio 2008 IDE) can be done using Express Web Development. However, an additional Report add-in is required. The add-in can be downloaded from Microsoft at `http://msdn.microsoft.com/vstudio/express/vwd/download/`.

In addition, this book assumes that Visual Studio 2005, SQL Server 2005, and Visual Studio 2008 beta 1 are already configured and that you're ready to try the samples. Please follow the MSDN documents to set up the environment.

Source Code and Database

The entire sample source code and `RealWorld` database are available on this book's page in the Source Code/Downloads area of the Apress web site (`http://www.apress.com`). However, as you work through the examples in this book, you may decide that you want to type in code by hand. Many people prefer to type the code, because it is a good way to get familiar with the coding techniques, and it provides more interaction. However, if you don't like typing, downloading the source code from the Apress web site is a must! Either way, the code files will help you with updates and debugging.

Errata

Apress makes every effort to make sure that there are no errors in the text or the code. However, to err is human, and as such, we recognize the need to keep you informed of any mistakes as they're discovered and corrected. An errata sheet will be made available on this book's main page at `http://www.apress.com`.

If you find an error that hasn't already been reported, please let us know. The Apress web site acts as a focus for other information and support, including the code from all Apress books, sample chapters, previews of forthcoming titles, and articles on related topics.

Contacting the Author

You can contact Asif Sayed via his e-mail address at asif.blog@gmail.com. You can also visit his consultancy web site at http://www.feathersoft.ca.

■ ■ ■

CHAPTER 1

What Is Client-Side Reporting?

Client-side reporting is not a new phenomenon. No matter what platform you use for development, you need some way or other to produce reports. This chapter will explore the new client-side reporting features provided by Visual Studio (VS) 2005 and the forthcoming release of VS (Visual Studio 2008) and build a sound foundation for using them throughout this book. From here on, if you see a reference to "VS," I mean to say both VS 2005 and Visual Studio 2008.

In this chapter, the following topics will be covered:

- Characteristics of the client-side reporting architecture

- How client-side reporting supports various report users

- How clients can act as hosts for report delivery

- The three-step report-creation process

- Basic report structure (header, body, and footer)

- Extending the basic structure into subsections for complex reports

- Essentials for creating better reports

- Various industry-standard reporting patterns

- How different reporting patterns are used in the real world

Reporting Dynamics

Client-side reporting means producing reports on a local (client) computer rather than on a central server. When Microsoft (MS) introduced MS Access 1.0 in the early 1990s, producing reports simply and with minimal effort became possible. As we moved through the decade, the era of web reporting raised new challenges as the Web became ever more popular for delivering information. Although it was easy enough to produce reports and display them on web pages, other issues, such as printing attractive reports, were not easy to resolve. Visual Studio now has built-in support for creating professional-quality reports for various clients.

Before VS 2005, Microsoft provided various choices for client-side reporting. The most common is the Crystal Reports (CR) add-in from Business Objects. If you come from the world of Visual Basic 6, then you'll also know Data Report Designer. With the introduction of Reporting

Services (RS) at the client-side with VS 2005, Microsoft has given developers a serious tool for producing reports. Don't worry if you are already skilled with CR—in Chapter 12, we'll look at CR and RS in action side-by-side to help you transition to RS.

Efforts by Microsoft to provide an alternative to CR prior to VS 2005 were, at best, filling the blanks and were no serious challenge to the capabilities of CR. The .NET platform with Visual Studio came as a real opportunity to provide a simple architecture to produce client-side reports with access to all sorts of data.

This book teaches you how to use VS 2005 and Visual Studio 2008 RS for all your reporting needs through hands-on practice with the software. Before we start using RS, though, let's look at reporting architectures and environments in general.

Client-Side Architecture

The architecture of client-side reporting isn't rocket science. Everything revolves around your client application, as shown in Figure 1-1.

Your client application gathers data from your favorite data source and processes the report definition to produce a report. The ReportViewer presents the result to users. The interesting idea here is that all steps needed to produce a report are an integral part of the client. The steps needed to create the report definition and to collect data are identical for all supported clients.

VS 2005 and Visual Studio 2008 will create the report definition (as shown in Figure 1-1). ADO.NET is commonly used to collect data from the source. The last step is to bind the data with report definition using ReportViewer. The client application produces the report, with report definition technology embedded in the application or loaded from a disk.

Client-Side Architecture Characteristics

Let's briefly explore some of the characteristics of client-side reporting architectures and the terminology used to describe them.

Data Source

We know how important data is for creating reports. At times, getting hold of the data is easy, but at other times, it is a challenge. Let's keep it simple and say that data that ADO.NET can collect and load into a DataSet is a valid source.

But don't worry with terms such as ADO.NET and DataSet now. Just keep in mind that ADO.NET is a data interface provided with VS, and DataSet is a placeholder for the data that is used for reporting. ADO.NET is versatile enough to connect to a variety of data sources ranging from sophisticated relational databases to file-based text data. You can learn more about ADO.NET and DataSet in Chapter 3.

■**Note** It is a common misconception that VS Reporting Services is a SQL Server extension and can only report on SQL Server data. Both server-side and client-side RS report from a wide variety of data sources, including flat files and databases such as Oracle and MySQL.

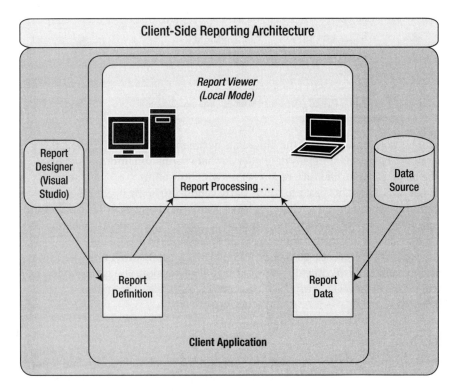

Figure 1-1. *Client-side reporting architecture*

Report Definition Language (RDL)

Report Definition Language (RDL) is an XML-based file. The report designer automatically produces the file, which has an .rdlc extension (the "C" stands for "client-side").

■**Note** You don't need to know XML or RDL to create reports. RS handles everything for you transparently.

All objects added to a report in the report designer are part of an RDLC file. Since XML is an open standard used by independent software vendors and custom solution developers, it is easy for them to create interface tools to interact with RS.

RDL also makes it easy for report designers and developers to open the report definition in a text editor to make changes outside the report designer. Here's a small snippet showing how a text box item is stored inside an RDLC file:

```
<Textbox Name="ProductNumber">
  <rd:DefaultName>ProductNumber</rd:DefaultName>
  <ZIndex>3</ZIndex>
  <Style>
    <PaddingLeft>2pt</PaddingLeft>
```

```
                    <PaddingBottom>2pt</PaddingBottom>
                    <PaddingRight>2pt</PaddingRight>
                    <PaddingTop>2pt</PaddingTop>
                </Style>
                <CanGrow>true</CanGrow>
                <Value>=Fields!ProductNumber.Value</Value>
            </Textbox>
```

So, you might be wondering, what is the difference between RDL and RDLC? Well, the main one is that RLDC files don't store any data query or data connation information. RDLC files can easily be hosted as RDL files on a report server with little effort.

Because RDL is XML based, it is easy for third-party vendors to come up with RS extensions. For example, how about printing a barcode? Well, that's easy enough with a component from Neodynamic. Watch out for a cool report based on a barcode component in Chapter 13. Or, you can get a trial version of Neodynamic's Barcode Professional software here: http://www.neodynamic.com/Products/BCRS/BarcodeRS.aspx?tabid=78&prodid=7.

If you think you would like to come up with your own RS extension, you can download the copy of the RDL specification at http://www.microsoft.com/sql/technologies/reporting/rdlspec.mspx.

Report Parameters

Report parameters are the key means of communication among report definitions and report requests. Most reports are designed to provide dynamic information based on criteria provided at run time. For example, if you had 50 employees in your organization, would you develop 50 different pay slip reports? No, you'd dynamically pass the Employee ID as a parameter to produce a report for each employee.

Previewing and Exporting

In VS, the most common way to display a report to users is the Preview feature. The Preview feature not only shows how a report looks but also lets users print reports. Besides preview and print capabilities, client-side reporting also offers the ability to export reports in Excel and PDF formats. You don't need separate software to render a report in PDF format.

Security

Client applications manage the security. Custom code used in reports must have permission to access the file system or network. For example, if your report is trying to read data from an XML file over a network, the application account must have proper rights to access that network.

Note RS has the same user interface in both VS and SQL Server. Client-side reports deploy as part of client applications; there's no need for a SQL Server license to use RS in VS.

Server-Side Reporting Architecture

This book is about client-side reporting, so why look at server-side reporting architecture? It is good to know both sides of the technology. Imagine if you need to port some of your client-side reports to the server-side? Also, it is interesting to make a contrast here, to better understand the client-side architecture by looking at the server-side counterpart. Figure 1-2 shows the server-side reporting architecture.

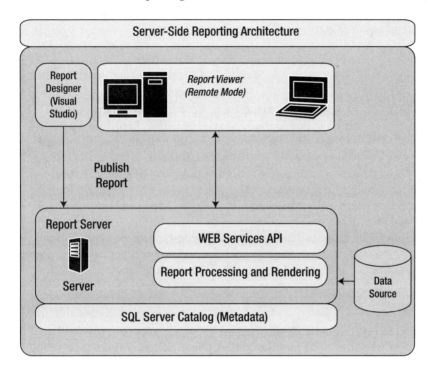

Figure 1-2. *Server-side reporting architecture*

There are a few differences between how the report gets produced by client-side and server-side RS architecture. Let's start with data. We can only report on data that is accessible through the reporting server, as opposed to getting everything that ADO.NET can bring for client-side reporting. The report server publishes the report on the server side.

ReportViewer manages user input to parameters on the server side; for a client-side report, you'll need custom user interface (UI) code. All export formats are supported by RS on the server side, including Excel, PDF, and MHTML. Client-side RS only supports Excel and PDF formats.

Users

People look at reports in a different ways, so a single report can have a different impact on various people. For example, a student progress report can say a lot to parents about a child's performance. On the other hand, the same report can help the school principal check the performance of teachers.

In almost all organizations, reporting perspectives vary in a hierarchical way. Executives mostly focus on summaries that help them decide about finances and future directions. Line-level managers and workers care about various details.

Informed decision making is important at all levels within an organization, and easy access to accurate information is also essential. It is of the utmost importance that developers understand both their users and their users' information needs, so they can design and produce effective reports.

It's not possible to describe every potential report user. However, a few generic classifications of the business-reporting audience are useful.

Customers

Developing reports to satisfy the needs of customers is a huge challenge. Customers come in various classifications, from one-time buyers to those who appear in a company's top ten list based on their sales volume. Trust me; both are easy to manage with a client-side reporting solution. You can easily develop a Sales Invoice report for one-time customers and an aged receivables report to track unpaid invoices for your regular customers.

You've probably heard the term business-to-consumer (B2C). So, how can client-side reporting communicate valuable information from business to consumers? Well, a common example is an Order Status report hosted on a corporate ASP.NET site to let customers track the shipping status of their orders.

Client-side reporting technology can help you develop reports to provide both current and historical information on demand to the customer. You can deliver reports through a web interface, e-mail, or mobile connectivity to improve the customer experience.

Vendors

Consumers deal with vendors primarily for two reasons: to buy a product or a service. This is often called business-to-business (B2B) communication. Client-side reporting supports both types of activities.

Vendors interact with businesses in different ways, according to the need. For example, you could develop a Stock Reorder report or a Fast-Moving Items report to share your stock consumption information for better handling of stock procurement.

The trend to automate business transactions is a common practice. For example, an automated Purchase Orders report can feed into a vendor's order system to speed up the purchasing process. Although business transactions carry lot of challenges, a properly done report can improve the interactivity among business and vendor partners.

Executives and Managers

Executives rely primarily on summary data and find graphical representations powerfully persuasive. For example, at the end of each fiscal year, executives may study a series of reports such as yearly sales analyses, budgeted versus actual expenses reports, and balance sheets to see how a business performed during the year.

Cool graphs and charts make the maze of numbers inherent in reports much more understandable. An intranet-based portal is a popular choice to deliver reports to executives, and it's supported by client-side reporting technology.

Line Managers

Line managers look for reports that are more detailed in nature. Reports that line mangers might need, like raw materials status or worker shift allocation reports, are easily handled on the client side.

Everyone Else

No matter what you do, some kind of information is useful. With VS RS, anyone can produce both detailed and summary reports from an extraordinarily wide set of data sources to meet virtually any information need.

■Note Report names, such as the Stock Reorder report, are mentioned in the previous section to tell you about what's available for use in various situations. You'll get a chance to practice the reports when we look at practical examples, starting in Chapter 4.

What Applications Are Supported?

In this book, we'll discuss four different kinds of client applications and develop various real-world examples with them. The client applications are based on the following technologies:

- Windows Forms
- Web Forms
- Web services
- Windows services

■Note Brief tutorials on how to use these client applications appear as they come up in this book, so don't worry if you're not an expert now.

Windows Forms

Windows Forms has improved a lot over the years. Better security features and ease of deployment have made this client a perfect host for client-side reporting solutions. Using VS RS, you'll develop a Windows Forms project and use the ReportViewer control to preview a report.

Which report is the best choice to host with the Windows Forms client? Well, it depends on what the report content is and who needs to see it. In Chapter 4, I'll guide you step-by-step through developing the most common reports in real-world desktop applications. For example, we'll create a Trial Balance report, which is a common feature of accounting applications.

Web Forms

ASP.NET Web Forms is a sound platform for reporting on both intranets and the Internet, and it's the easiest way to share reports with large numbers of users. In Chapter 5, you'll create an ASP.NET web site project with VS RS and host the report using the ReportViewer control on the page. With VS RS, you don't have to worry about application deployment to a client machine; all users need is browsing software, and they are ready to go.

The reach of the Web Forms application is much greater than Windows Forms applications. After going through the Web Forms tutorial in Chapter 5, I'll show you how some of the most common reports are developed using client-side reporting. For example, you'll create an order tracking report, and I'll show you some cool tricks on how to plot graphs in it.

Going wireless is getting increasingly popular among businesses. This trend has brought new challenges to the developer community as developers look for on-demand information-delivery solutions. Reports done with web pages can be easily shared with various smart devices, and therefore, give true meaning to concept of accessing information anywhere and any time.

Web Services

A web service is a technology designed to enable information sharing among the different systems over any given network, such as the Internet and an intranet. Web service can also help to eliminate the duplication of business functions that are commonly shared by more than one application.

If you are new to web service development, I'd strongly suggest you to go through the tutorial in Chapter 6. In that chapter, you'll also see how a report can be generated on demand by calling a web service method and sent across to the consumer client.

Windows Services

Windows services are a neat way to automate tasks that need to be performed on a predefined interval. Using VS RS, you can create a Windows service and automate it. Since this is a service, users will not be able to see the report preview; instead, the report will be exported to either Excel or PDF format.

Never developed a Windows service before? Not to worry, your friendly tutorial is standing by in Chapter 8. There are many opportunities to automate and deliver client-side reports using Windows services. I'll show you, among other things, step-by-step how to create a report called New Complaints report and send it to a customer service manager's e-mail box on a selected time interval.

The Report Creation Process

What if I said the report creation process is as simple as 1, 2, 3? Well, it may not be that easy, but I'm confident that you'll love the straightforward approach of creating reports in VS. Figure 1-3 shows the process, which is explained in more detail in the following sections.

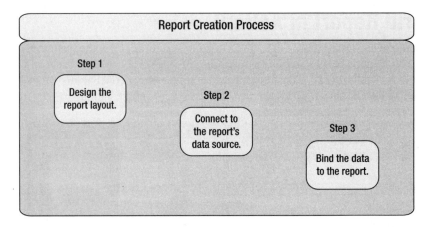

Figure 1-3. *The report creation process*

Designing the Report Layout

The best report layout is the one that reflects the nature of the data. Summary data is a good candidate for charts and graphs. Detail data often needs a list or drill-down approach. Industry-standard best practices are common for report layouts; ever wonder why all bank account statements look so similar?

Connecting to the Data Source

At times, data access is as simple as connecting to a local SQL Server or Access database. It becomes more challenging if we need access to a business application object or proprietary data source. How many different data sources can we use for a report? Typically one; however, for complex reports there can be more, and they can be of different types. For example, you can use data from both a SQL Server and another database in the same report.

■**Note** Data quality is another important issue. As the saying goes, "garbage in, garbage out." It's wise to always find out if we have any garbage to deal with and make sure it doesn't become a showstopper later.

Binding the Data to the Report

After taking care of the data source and designing your layout, all you need is to issue a few magical statements to pump life into your report. Binding data to the report programmatically is the same for every supported client, as mentioned earlier, and you can use any scripting language supported by VS to do it. We'll use C# for all the examples in this book.

A Real-World Report in Action!

I've made several references in this chapter to real-world report examples from the business world, and you'll practice many of these reports throughout the book. For now, let me show you what a real-world report looks like. Please see Figure 1-4 for a sample Trial Balance report that I've done for one of my clients (although the report is real, it uses mock data).

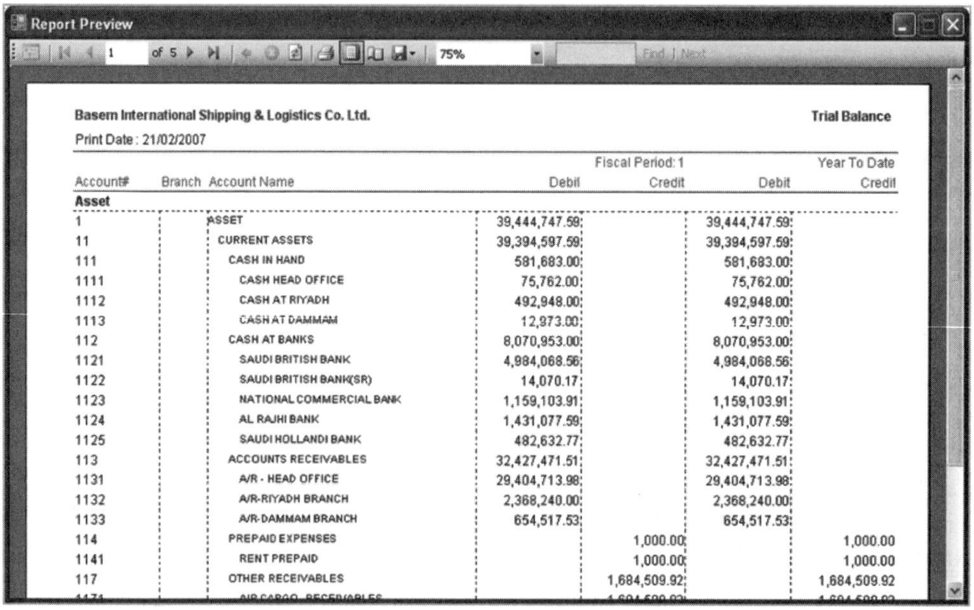

Figure 1-4. *A real-world report sample (Trial Balance)*

Let me also introduce you to one more cool feature of RS here. Do you think RS can develop reports only in English? How about reporting in other languages such as French or German? Well, you'll be glad to know that RS comes with strong support for developing international reports. Yes, that includes the languages that are read from right to left, such as Hebrew or Arabic. Figure 1-5 shows the Trial Balance report again. However, this time the report is in Arabic.

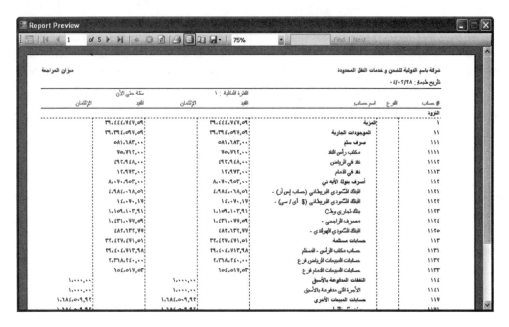

Figure 1-5. *A real-world report sample (Trial Balance) in Arabic*

A Hands-On Approach

When I started working on this book, I asked myself how I could make this book a guided tour for learning client-side reporting. Sure, I could've just asked you to click here, drag this, and change that to create a report. However, my goal is to teach you not only how to create a report but how to develop practical, professional, real-world reports. After much thought, I came up with the following approach, and I hope that it will be comfortable for you:

- *Challenge*: Define the reporting project.

- *Process*: Apply the three steps required in developing a report.

- *Practice*: Enhance your understanding with exercises; solutions are provided (but no peeking).

Challenge: Defining the Reporting Project

The most difficult decision for me was to decide which real-world report case study to present as a hands-on project throughout this book. By using a chart of accounts report, I would make accounting folks happy. However, what about folks who don't understand the language of debits and credits? What if you're an expert in human resources systems and hope to walk through a sample report in that field?

Covering each practical report out there in the world of business is not possible in this book. Therefore, I decided to pick the most common report type and one that has an easy-to-understand business case—the Chart of Accounts project. Even if you don't know accounting, I promise after going through the Chart of Accounts project, you'll sure learn a secret or two to brag about it in front of your accountant buddies.

I'll start with a general discussion of the business case for the report and show you a screen shot of what the finished report should look like. Your goal is to understand the underlying business case of the report and start the step-by-step guided tour of report development.

The business case will look like something you might have seen in a certification examination like the Microsoft Certified Professional (MCP) exam, for example, "You're a software developer with ABCD Pharmaceuticals, Inc. The company has ten profit centers in the United States and five in Canada. You need to develop a report that will show combined sales figures from all 15 profit centers on a quarterly basis."

Process: Applying the Three Steps in Developing a Report

The process of developing the report will be a bit challenging at first. However, as you move on from one project to another, you'll find yourself growing increasingly at ease. If you are at the beginner level, make sure you understand the business case thoroughly. Business cases can dictate a lot about what the report layout should look like and which report pattern is best to use. I'll show you how to develop the reporting project with the help of the three-step process shown in Figure 1-3.

I'd strongly advise you to start with the practical examples in Chapter 4, if you consider yourself at the beginner level; I've placed extra emphasis on explaining every detail to help you understand each step in the report creation process. While going through Chapter 4 and beyond, you'll notice that the complexity of examples will grow as you move through each chapter's content. All reporting projects discussed in this book will have many similarities among them. However, you'll also notice differences depending on the business case involved.

The process has the following three steps:

1. Create a dataset.

2. Design the report layout.

3. Write the C# code to gather the data and bind it to reporting engine.

Creating a Dataset

Can we create a report if we don't know what the content is? Obviously not—it is the data that helps in deciding about the report pattern. The first step is to create a typed dataset with one or more data tables inside.

Typically, the data table inside the dataset should use the same structure as the data source. However, the data table structure inside the dataset can have additional columns that are different than the data source. Such columns are manipulated and filled with data programmatically at run time before binding the report to the host. For example, a dataset can have the columns FirstName, LastName, and FullName, where FullName is an extra column that is filled in DataSet and not supplied by the data source.

I'll identify the data source to you from the RealWorld database, which has a variety of different business entities. You'll get a RealWorld database with the source code for this book, and I'll show you step-by-step how to map the data source to a data table inside the dataset. I've set aside Chapter 3 to discuss entities of the data model used with each report project; I'd advise you to use that chapter as a reference to the RealWorld data model.

■**Note** The dataset is a memory-resident representation of data that provides a consistent relational programming model regardless of the data source. The dataset page of MSDN can help you understand datasets in more detail: http://msdn2.microsoft.com/en-us/system.data.dataset.aspx.

Design the Report Layout

After taking care of the dataset, the next step is to make use of the report design surface. The nature of the data content is the first hint to deciding what report pattern to use. For example, if your data involves grouped items, the best choice is a tabular report pattern, while a graphical chart report is the best choice to present summary data.

You'll design the report step-by-step starting with the report structure, next picking relevant report items, and finally organizing them on the report design surface. You'll also learn how to give a professional look and feel to the report and see ways to beautify, such as setting its colors, shape, size, and fonts.

Writing the C# code

C# coding is the important final step to populate a dataset from one or more data sources. User input is sent across to the report using parameters. You'll get step-by-step guidance to get the data, work with parameters, and finally, bind the report to the client using the ReportViewer control.

■**Note** Although we will be using C# to interface with the ReportViewer control, RDL files only support VB.NET for scripting within the report.

Practice: Enhancing Your Understanding with Exercises

In Chapter 4, you'll see some exercise to practice and apply the basic report development knowledge you just learned. I'm preparing you for more challenging reports in Chapter 5 onward by offering you these exercises. Although solutions are provided, I'm sure there will be *no peeking*! First, try it out yourself.

Report Structure

Every report design assignment has its own challenges. Like a painter who changes the land-scape and colors in a painting to suit the subject, developers also change report structure to best suit reported data. The most basic report structure includes three sections, as shown in Figure 1-6:

- *Header*: Ideal place for items such as the report title and date

- *Body*: The details of the report, whether summary or detailed business transactions

- *Footer*: Ideal place for items such as page numbers and copyright information

---

■**Note** The body is also commonly called the details section.

Most real-world reports are developed using these three basic sections. However, some business cases bring additional complexity to reports. The most common adjustment is to add subsections to the default layout. In such cases, we will need to adjust the structure. Before we look into the details for each section of the report, let's examine the overall structure in Figure 1-6.

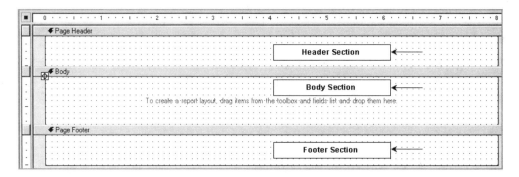

Figure 1-6. *The basic structure of a report*

VS RS offers this basic structure for you to start the design process. Notice in Figure 1-6 that the report design surface looks like a paper page; a page is like a drawing board or canvas. All you have to do is start putting your design skills to work and convert this blank canvas to a report with relevant information.

■**Note** When we add a report to a project, only the body section is automatically added; you'll need to manually add the header and footer later.

Header

The header section gives recognition to the report. How? Simple—the majority of the report's titles or names find a place in the header section.

So, what else goes into the header section apart from the report title? The following items qualify as good candidates to appear in the header section:

- Name of the organization

- Organization's logo

- Report date and time

- Drawing elements, such as a line or rectangle

- The supplied report parameter values (possibly)

- Page numbers (more commonly a footer section candidate though)

Please see Figure 1-7 for a simple illustration of what typically goes into the header section and how it helps the end user to understand the origin and subject of the report.

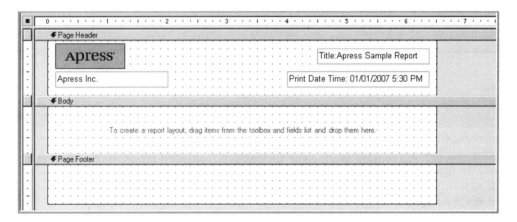

Figure 1-7. *Typical content for the header section*

Body

The body section is, by far, the most versatile of all three sections and is my favorite on the report design surface. I'd even go so far as to say that anything and everything can be placed here—from numbers to text to graphics, all information is welcome.

Out of the many different possibilities, the following most often appear as content in the body section:

- Summary totals

- Transaction details

- Grouping and sorting of data

- Multicolumn output

- Charts and graphs

- Links to other reports

- A specialty report, such as a promotional letter

Please see Figure 1-8 for a simple illustration of the body section; this one shows how the detail section uses payout detail transaction information to show bonus information.

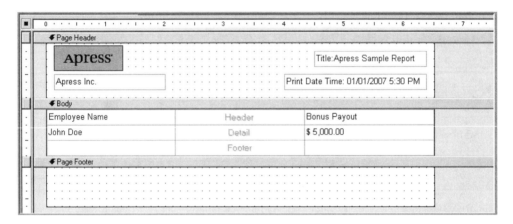

Figure 1-8. *Typical content for a body section*

I'm sure you've got a question for me now, "What are those additional header, detail, and footer labels doing inside the body section?" I know you're all excited to develop some cool reports with client-side reporting, so starting in Chapter 2, I'll show you each element of the Report Designer and Print Preview controls. I've used a table in the body section to show how a detail report can make use of this section to list column names, data details, and the total of all listed transactions.

Footer

The third and the final section in the report structure is the footer section. I've seen developers use the footer to show running page numbers in the report as a common practice. Developers enjoy the freedom VS offers in placing content in the header to footer according to user need. Other miscellaneous information, like copyright text, also makes it into this section. At times, even the physical file name of the report is displayed here for reference.

Please see Figure 1-9 for a simple implementation of the footer section, showing page numbers and a line separator.

Take a look at Figures 1-6 to 1-9 again. What you see is a gradual transition from the blank report design surface to a complete report. You, as a developer, will go through countless adventures like this one to produce stunning reports that I'm sure you'll be proud of.

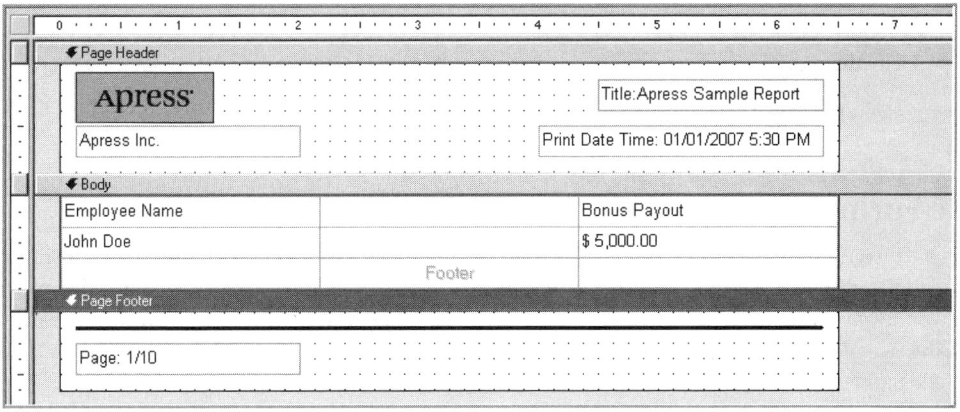

Figure 1-9. *Typical content for the footer section*

Creating Better Reports

How do you create those stunning reports? The following practices are widely used by report developers to come up with better report designs:

- Sketch the report layout on paper first.

- Decide on the page layout, paper size, and orientation (portrait or landscape).

- Determine the space allocations and formats for all data.

Once you've done this, you're ready to create the report with VS RS.

Report Patterns

The report design surface in RS is not like any other report designing tool you've used. In appearance, it's similar to Access or Active Report. However, you'll feel the difference once you start to develop reports. Let's imagine you've got a canvas; as you would mix and match different colors and brush strokes to fill the canvas, do the same with report items. Let your creative imagination run wild.

Naturally, with all this freedom on your side, you may want some patterns to focus your efforts. How many different reporting patterns can you use to design your reports? The most commonly used patterns in the real world follow:

- Form/page

- Tabular details

- Multicolumn

- Grouped data

- Matrix/pivot table

- Chart/graph

- Drill-through

- As you like it

The Form/Page Pattern

This pattern is largely popular in real-world report business cases to report data that is a single piece of information. The information could be anything, for example, a single record from a table or some static text. If you're developing a sales invoice or receipt voucher, you're already making use of this pattern.

Please see Figure 1-10 for a sample sales invoice report.

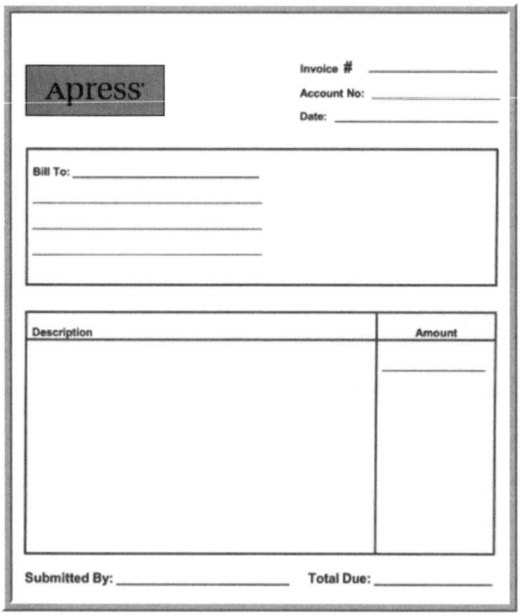

Figure 1-10. *An example of the form/page pattern*

The Tabular Details Pattern

The tabular pattern is the choice of many developers when it comes to reports with multiple lines of transaction details. Why is this pattern so popular? The content of this report presents detailed business transactions in a format like a spreadsheet, with rows and columns. In addition to transaction details, summary totals are also part of the report. Please see Figure 1-11 for an example of the Product List report, which displays product information and the total stock value.

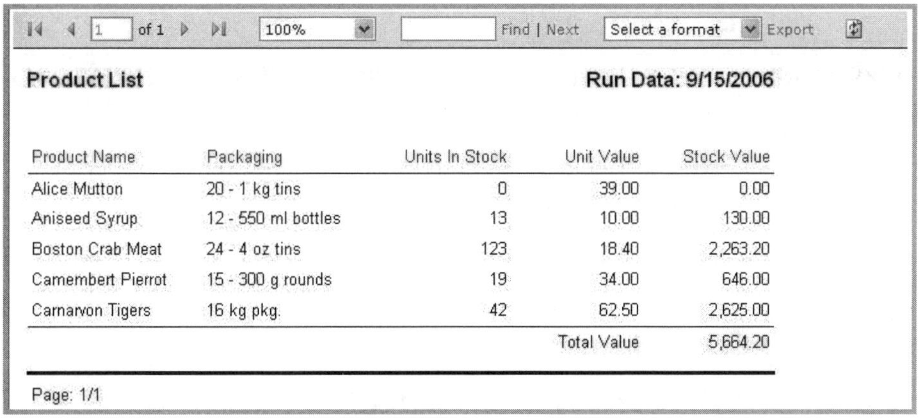

Product List **Run Data: 9/15/2006**

Product Name	Packaging	Units In Stock	Unit Value	Stock Value
Alice Mutton	20 - 1 kg tins	0	39.00	0.00
Aniseed Syrup	12 - 550 ml bottles	13	10.00	130.00
Boston Crab Meat	24 - 4 oz tins	123	18.40	2,263.20
Camembert Pierrot	15 - 300 g rounds	19	34.00	646.00
Carnarvon Tigers	16 kg pkg.	42	62.50	2,625.00
			Total Value	5,664.20

Page: 1/1

Figure 1-11. *An example report using the tabular details pattern*

The Multicolumn Pattern

Once, when I was developing a sales ordering system for one of my clients, I had to produce a report called Summary Price List. What made this report interesting to me was the user need: the user wanted to save large numbers of pages and still have a hard copy of the price list with only the Catalog ID, Cost Price, and Discount Factor columns.

The multicolumn pattern came to my rescue; I created a three-column report with a landscape page orientation and reduced the overall page count by ten percent, compared with the report with a single-column portrait format.

■ **Note** The multicolumn pattern is also a popular pattern to develop labels and contact cards for customers.

The Grouped Data Pattern

This pattern is similar to the tabular pattern. However, what makes it different is the ability to report data in a grouped and sorted manner. Let's look at this pattern with the help of an example. Please see Figure 1-12; this is typical tabular report with a list of orders as details. If you notice, all orders are listed as part of a group, and they appear under the heading of the customer name. Grouping information based on certain business criteria helps the user to access the information much easier.

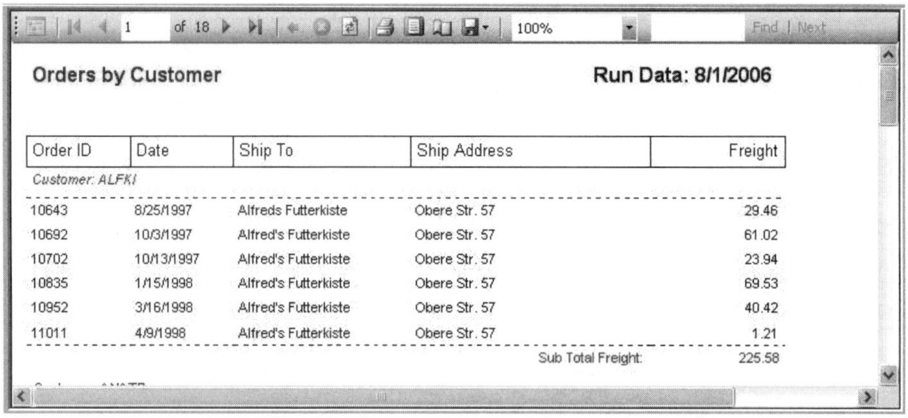

Figure 1-12. *An example of the grouped data pattern*

■ **Note** The drill-down report pattern is similar to the grouped pattern, but in addition, the user can collapse or expand the group information while previewing the report.

The Matrix/Pivot Pattern

The matrix/pivot report pattern, also referred as cross-tab, is widely used to report summary data by rolling up rows of details into columns. Being a developer, if you've ever tried to create a cross-tab report, you know how much of a serious effort it is. Some developers make use of SQL query or some write custom code to mimic the matrix pattern.

Good news! RS has made your life easy. All you have to do is drop the Matrix Report item onto the design surface and set the data source. You'll be surprised to see how easily your data is changed into a pivot table. Please check Figure 1-13 for an example of data with rows and columns converted into pivot output.

Order ID	Fruit Type	Quantity
1001	Apple	10
1002	Mango	2
1001	Apple	11
1003	Banana	55
1004	Mango	34
1005	Banana	11
1006	Apple	2
1006	Mango	3
1007	Mango	4
1001	Apple	6
1002	Banana	6
1005	Banana	10

Sum of Quantity	Fruit Type			
Order ID	Apple	Banana	Mango	Grand Total
1001	27			27
1002		6	2	8
1003		55		55
1004			34	34
1005		21		21
1006	2		3	5
1007			4	4
Grand Total	29	82	43	154

Figure 1-13. *A matrix/pivot pattern example*

The Chart/Graph Pattern

We often hear that a picture is worth a thousand words. Yes, at times instead of putting plain numbers on a report, it is better to present them using graphics. Executive and management users prefer this report pattern most often. Some of the most common chart types used in reporting are bar, column, pie, line, and area.

Please see Figure 1-14 for example of the chart/graph pattern.

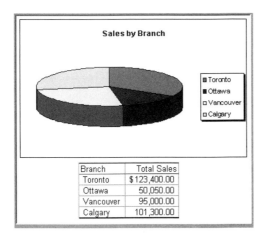

Figure 1-14. *An example using the chart/graph pattern*

The Drill-Through Pattern

The drill-through report pattern is unique in that any report can be a drill-through report. You might be wondering how. Well, it's possible because of something called a *link*; an embedded link allows the user to launch another report by clicking it. Any report that includes links is a drill-through report.

A typical example would be a receivables report, in which the user can click a highlighted link, such as an invoice ID, to launch the corresponding invoice report. You're running a report from within another report.

The "As You Like It" Pattern

Hmm, I can imagine that grin on your face. Like me, you will probably spend much of your time experimenting with this pattern. I've said a couple of times that the report design surface is like a canvas, and that's especially true of this pattern. Start from any direction; draw any control; mix and match any number of patterns; in short, have a fun time painting your ultimate creation.

How about developing a personal dashboard with an RSS feed from your favorite news channel? Yes, this all can be done. Look for your chance to practice this in Chapter 13.

The example figures in this section are just for you to get the concepts. The real work of designing using different patterns will be covered starting in Chapter 4.

Summary

In this chapter, we discussed the architecture of client-side reporting. We also looked at the typical users of client-side reports, the client applications we'll work with in this book, and the three steps for creating reports. I also touched on the report structure, real-world reporting patterns, and best practices for creating reports.

In the next chapter, we'll look at the client-side components offered by VS RS to produce stunning, powerful, professional reports.

CHAPTER 2

■ ■ ■

Client-Side Reporting Components

In Chapter 1, you learned about the architecture of client-side reporting. There was also a generic discussion about what constitutes a report. Now is a good time to look at the VS integrated development environment (IDE) and find out which components are offered to help you create great looking reports. Although I'm using VS 2005 for majority of this book, you'll see reporting examples with VS Visual Studio 2008 in Chapter 14 and Chapter 15.

To get an A+ for your reporting assignment, you need both a powerful reporting tool and clever, logical thinking. I'll stand with the development community here and assume the presence of logical thinking. However, most of the time, it is the lack of features of the tool that limits the reporting capabilities and makes the difference between a good report to a great one!

I was skeptical about VS Client-Side Reporting Service in the beginning. However, as I started churning out report after report, my confidence in this tool has grown by leaps and bounds. Imagine a reporting tool that is simple enough to use and fun to work with. I'm confident that after going through practical report projects from this book, you'll be able to produce stunning reports using all of its features.

This chapter will cover the following topics:

- Introduce of the report designer

- Examine the report designer surface

- Explore about various report items

- Explore formatting output

- Examine how report beautification works

- Explain how the expression editor works

- Examine the ReportViewer control

I'll start by introducing the report designer. Next, you'll learn about the report design surface. This introduction is essential for you to get to know the tool and prepare for the next chapters. I'll also brief you on each report item we'll use to develop our reports.

Using the report items and developing report looks are important. However, our work doesn't end there. I'll also show you some other important things, like formatting the report and beautifying the report output. Finally, I'll show you the Expression Editor, and we'll examine the ReportViewer control.

Report Designer

Let's begin the journey by learning about the report designer. Are you wondering how to get the report designer into your project? Well, the process is simple; all you have to do is add a report to your solution, and there you go: the report designer will appear in front of you.

If your VS 2005 IDE is not already started, you can launch the IDE by clicking the Windows Start button ➤ All Programs ➤ Microsoft Visual Studio 2005 ➤ the Microsoft Visual Studio 2005 icon.

Please create a new project or web site before you go through following steps to launch the report designer: Start by right-clicking the project name inside Solution Explorer. Next, click Add ➤ New Item, and select Report from Visual Studio's installed templates. Please see Figure 2-1 for an illustration of the steps.

▉**Note** The steps shown in Figure 2-1 only get you to the report designer. You'll see a detailed step-by-step of using it starting in Chapter 4.

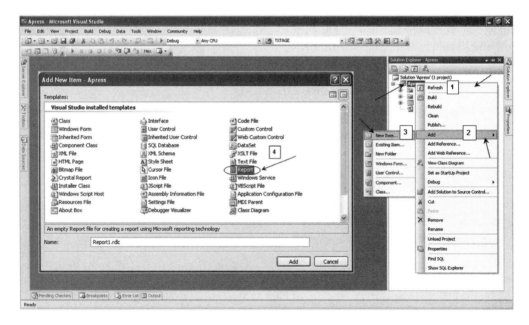

Figure 2-1. *Steps to add the report designer to a project*

After you finish the steps illustrated in Figure 2-1, you'll see the report added to the project, and the report designer window will open for you to start development. Figure 2-2 to shows the report designer layout.

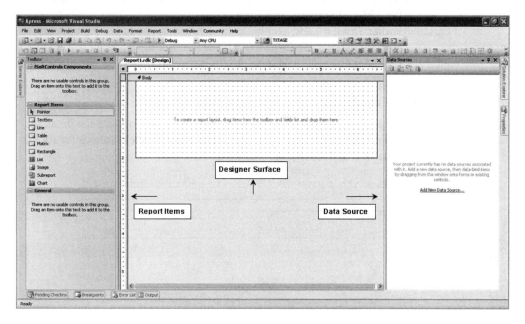

Figure 2-2. *The report designer layout*

■**Tip** The Data Source window is opened automatically every time you open the report in designer. If you don't see items in the toolbars as shown in Figure 2-2, you can access them by selecting View ➤ Toolbox from the IDE window or pressing Ctrl+Alt+X.

As you can see in Figure 2-2, the report designer consists of three important parts:

- Report design surface
- Report Items pane
- Report Data Source pane

All three parts play an important role in creating a report. The design surface is the place to lay out report items. Once report items are in place, we need to provide the data source for producing the report for the user. Let's look at all three parts in more detail now.

Report Design Surface

The report design surface is the real playground for you to show your skills in developing stunning reports. All you need to do to get started is to drag and drop the Report Items selections of your choice onto the surface to design the report.

As I mentioned earlier, when we add a report to the project, the body section appears automatically. Now, you can either start the design work by compiling the detail section or you can go ahead and add header and footer sections, according to report needs.

Adding Headers and Footers

Adding headers and footers is a breeze; all you need to do is right-click outside the detail section, and click Page Header or Page Footer in the menu that appears. Please check Figure 2-3 for a graphical representation of the process.

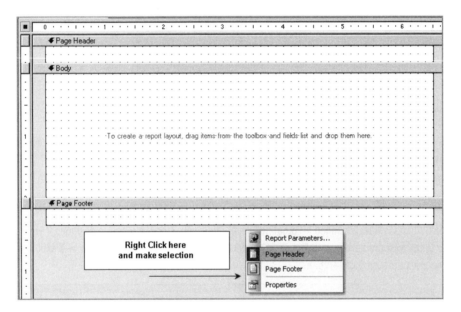

Figure 2-3. *Adding a header and footer to a report*

■**Tip** You can repeat the process shown in Figure 2-3 to reverse the effect, that is, to remove a header/footer.

Report Properties

The characteristics of a report are defined with the use of associated properties. You can access report properties in two ways. The first choice is to right-click outside any section of the report design and select Properties. You can also make sure the report is currently selected and look at the standard Properties toolbox of the VS 2005 IDE.

Please see Figure 2-4 for an illustration of the process.

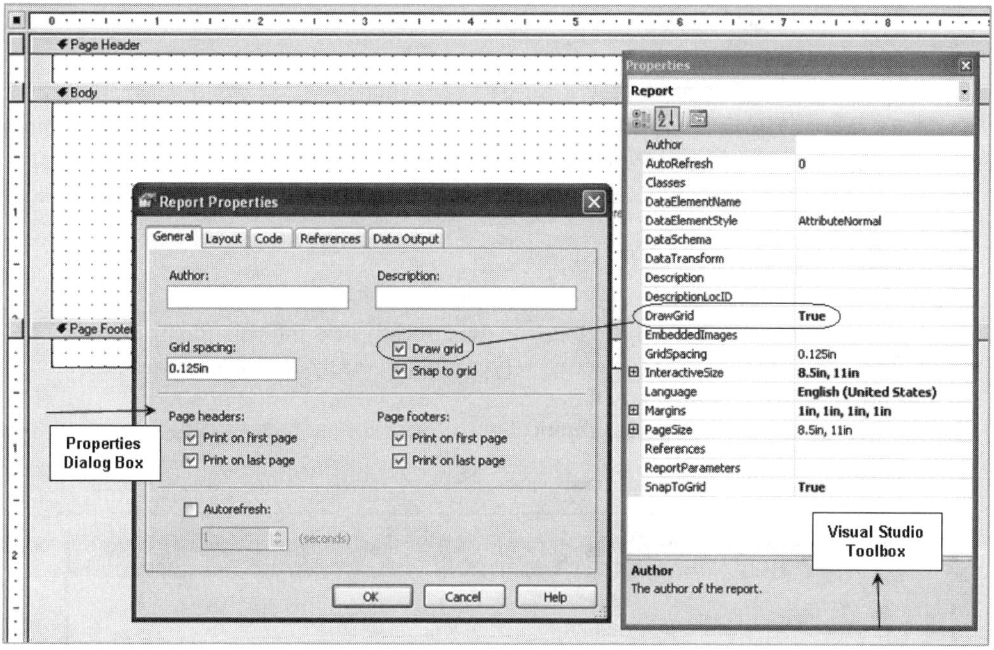

Figure 2-4. *Accessing the properties of a report*

Properties are grouped into five different tabs inside the Properties dialog box. The General properties tab has miscellaneous information about the report such as the author, a brief description, and settings to help make designing easy. You can also set, if you like, the page header to repeat on each page.

The Layout tab has all the choices to set up the page. You can specify top, bottom, left, and right margins. You can also set page width and height. One more interesting property here worth mentioning is the Column property. You need to change this to get the multicolumn report. The Code tab in the Properties dialog box is useful to specify custom code that is executed while a report is running.

The References section of the Properties dialog box is used to reference custom assemblies within the report. During compilation, references to assemblies such as Microsoft.VisualBasic, System.Convert, and System.Math get added automatically. The additional assemblies and functions that you specify can be used in code and expressions that you add to a report.

■**Note** The Properties dialog box doesn't contain all the properties related to report items. It is always better to look for the full list of properties in VS IDE Properties toolbox. For example, the Line Width property can be accessed only through the VS Properties toolbox (see Figure 2-9).

The Data Output section of the Properties dialog box is used to define XML data output options for the report. Setting the values in this tab adds metadata to the report definition (`.rdlc`) file that is used to render the report in XML.

■Note Because the XML rendering extension is only available in server-side reports, the data output properties are only effective if you later convert the `.rdlc` file to the `.rdl` format.

Report Parameters

Report parameters are used as a mechanism to dynamically pass information from the client to a report during run time. You can access report parameters by right-clicking outside any section and selecting Report Parameters.

Figure 2-5 presents the process graphically.

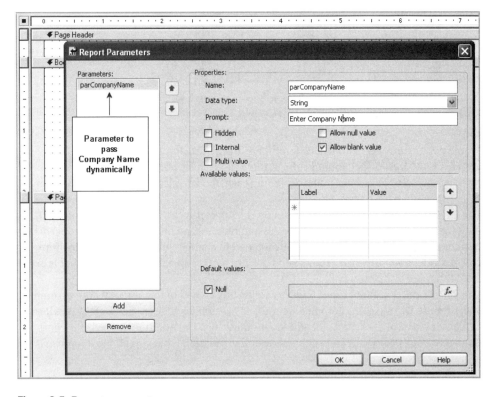

Figure 2-5. *Report parameters*

As you can see in Figure 2-5, instead of hard-coding Company Name, I'll be passing the relevant information from client to report using the CompanyName parameter. You can define parameters to support conditional formatting. You can also use them in expressions or code. The parameters properties that you specify in the Report Parameters dialog box become part of the report definition.

Note In contrast with server-side reports, a client-side report does not have a parameter input area used for selecting or typing parameter values. The client must take responsibility for providing an interface to accept input from the user. Look out for the reporting project in Chapter 4, which shows you how to create a UI to pass values to parameters.

Report Items

Report items are an important part of the report design; they act as a channel between the data source and the report structure. Each item is unique, displaying certain information from the attached data source.

I'll use this subtopic to give you a firsthand look at all of the options in the Report Items pane and what role they play in the report development process. Report items are simple objects; we have to know what properties they hold to make use of them.

Some properties are unique to the individual item. However, at times, a property is common to similar objects. For example, the Visibility property is applicable to all the items; even if there is variation, the difference is small.

Figure 2-6 shows the Report Items in Toolbox.

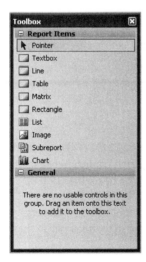

Figure 2-6. *Report Items Toolbox*

The Report Items supplied with the VS 2005 IDE are outlined in Table 2-1.

Table 2-1. *Report Items*

Report Item	Description
Pointer	Points to and selects report items
Textbox	The most often used report item; displays information from a data source
Line	Draws a line as a separator of information
Table	Show detailed transaction data in a table
Matrix	Displays data in cross-tabulation or pivot format
Rectangle	Groups related information
List	Lists detailed transaction data
Image	Displays images
Subreport	Launches another report from within the main report
Chart	Presents data in a graphical format

Pointer

The pointer item is used to point to and select report items. For example, if you have five text boxes on the designer surface, and you want to change the background color of the first text box, use the pointer item to mark the first text box as selected.

Once the selection is made, you change the background color of the text box using the Properties tool box. No report is complete without using the pointer item. It is no wonder that it comes as the first option in the list.

■**Tip** It is a good practice to switch back to selection mode by selecting the pointer item after dropping other report items on the designer surface.

Textbox

What would a report be without a text box? As far as I can tell, the Textbox item is always used in some way or other in a report. In RS, the Textbox selection enjoys much respect because of its versatile nature. You can use a text box to display the report title in the header section or use it to display running totals in the report body section.

Text boxes can display static text, text bound to a data source, calculations, and expressions. They can act like label controls to display static data and become dynamic as soon they get bound to a data source.

Please see Figure 2-7 to see an example using the Textbox item.

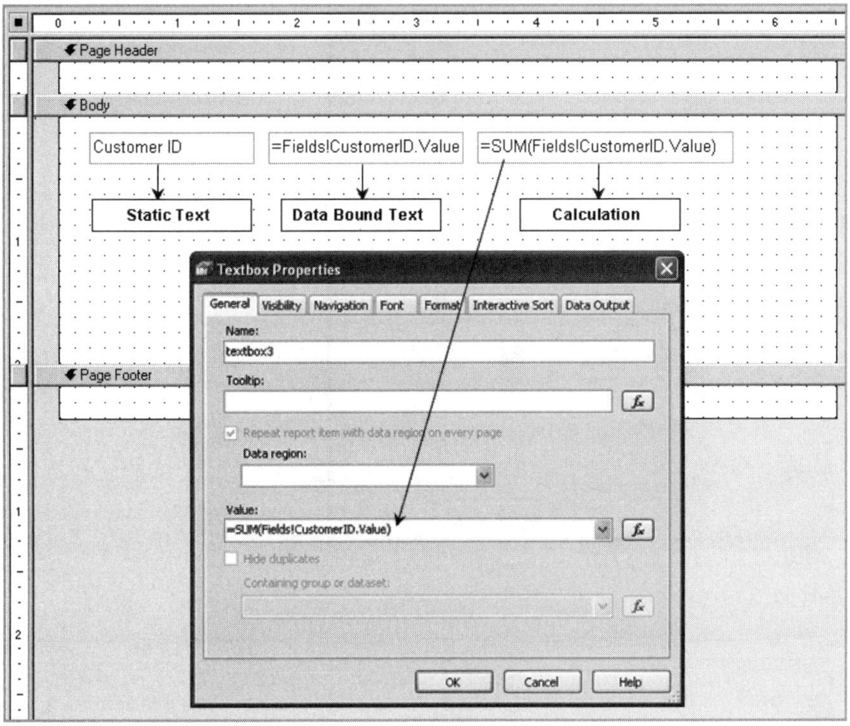

Figure 2-7. *A Textbox item example*

The Textbox Properties dialog box has seven tabs. You can also access these properties through the properties toolbox of the VS 2005 IDE. Use the General tab to define the name and value for the text box; you can also go ahead and define Tooltip text, which the user can see while the report is in preview mode. Use the Visibility tab to choose whether to display or not display the context of the text box. Use the Navigation tab to define the navigation options; for example, define how to jump to a given URL or to launch a subreport. The Font and Format sections are basically used to beautify the output.

The Interactive Sort tab allows the user to sort a text box when a report is in preview mode. When interactive sort is active, the user will see upward- and downward-facing arrows on column headings. To perform the sort action, the user simply needs to click either the up or down arrow. Figure 2-8 shows the Interactive Sort tabs options. In Chapter 13, you'll develop a reporting project with sorting enabled.

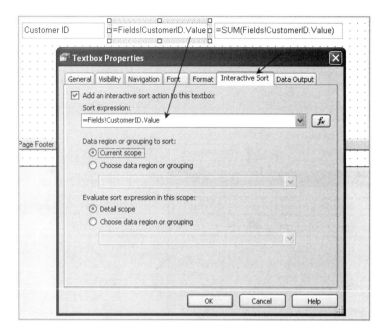

Figure 2-8. *Textbox sorting options*

Line

Trust me; the Line item is more than just a decoration to separate information; you can use it to highlight certain information on the report. You can choose from three different styles and set the width according to your report's needs. Another thing worth mentioning here is that you can draw lines in any direction. Please see Figure 2-9 for some sample uses of lines.

■**Note** In case of an ASP.NET client, lines are rendered as HTML, using techniques such as table borders or `div` tags using JavaScript and Virtual Reality Modeling Language (VRML) commands.

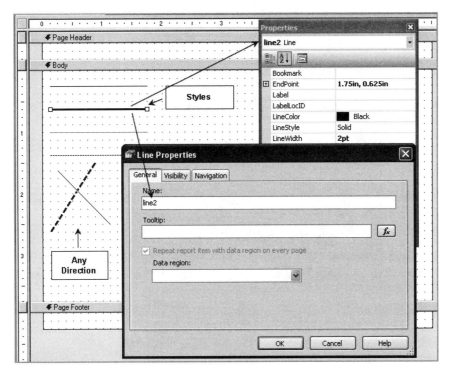

Figure 2-9. *A line item example*

Table

The Table option is the most useful item for reporting detailed transaction data. If you look at Figure 2-10, you'll notice that each table has its own structure with Header, Detail, and Footer sections. You should be careful not to mix up the table structure with your main report structure.

You can have more than one table in a report. Use the header section of a table to show column header names. The detail section provides a way to dynamically present one or more rows of information from the data source, and the footer section takes care of summarizing the transaction from the detail section.

Apart from regular properties like Visibility and Navigation, two important properties are worth mentioning here. The Groups tab lets you take care of all the grouping needed on a data source; a group is applicable to one or more data elements and can be dynamic also. Use the Filter tab to limit the data that the user can see and print when a report is executed.

There is lot more to this control; you'll see lots of it from Chapter 4 onward, so be ready.

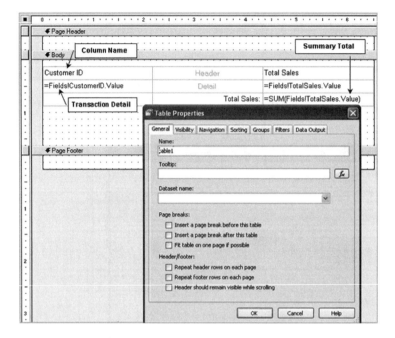

Figure 2-10. *A table item example*

Matrix

Now and then, we developers find ourselves in a situation that demands a cross-tab report. Well, that's nothing to worry about. You'll not even spend an hour to get your pivot report ready in VS 2005 and Visual Studio 2008. Please see Figure 2-11 for an example of the matrix item in action

All three sections in the matrix item need to be bound to a data source. You can simply drag and drop data fields from the data source on the Row, Column, or Details section according to the report's needs. A pivot report created using the matrix item also gives the user the ability to drill down for further detailed reported information. The value in the Detail section is aggregated for both Row- and Column-bound data.

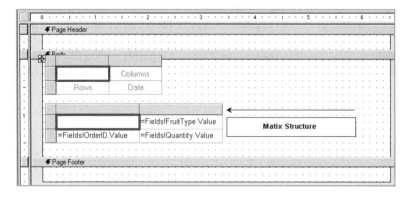

Figure 2-11. *A matrix item example*

Rectangle

The Rectangle option is similar to the GroupBox control in Windows Forms; you can use this item to arrange information in a report as groups. For example, you can put all the address-related report contents in a rectangle item, and then you can move all that information at once on the design surface as many times as you want. Figure 2-12 shows an example of a rectangle item. You'll also notice that I changed the BorderStyle property.

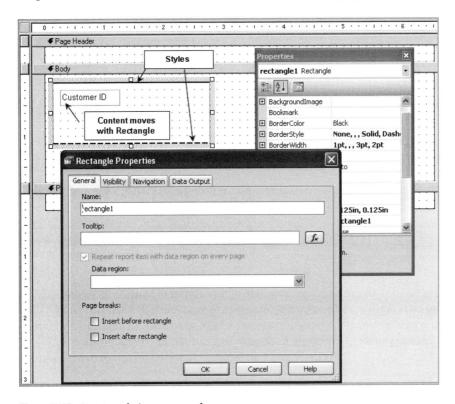

Figure 2-12. *A rectangle item example*

List

No doubt List is the simplest of all the Report Items options that use data regions: use it to list detailed transaction data. The list item doesn't come with header or footer options, as we get with tables. However, you can nest lists within each other; I call it the grouping effect (because if you nest one list inside another, it's like you created a group). Please see Figure 2-13 for an example of the list item.

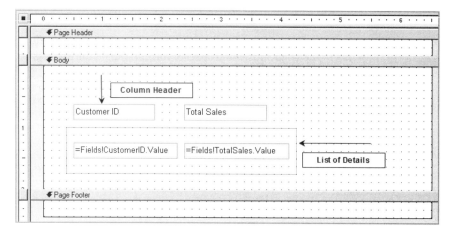

Figure 2-13. *A list item example*

Note Please make sure to put the column headers or titles outside the list's region; otherwise, they will be repeated for each detail item available from the data source.

Image

The Image option is used to get an image from one of three types of sources: External, Embedded, and Data Source. VS RS supports images in formats such as BMP, GIF, and JPG.

When putting an image on the designer surface, it is good to have an idea about the size of the image and how you want the image to display. You can set the Sizing property for images to AutoSize, Fit, FitProportional, or Clip. Figure 2-14 shows an image item example.

Tip Although you can use the AutoSize or Fit option, it is best to size the image before binding it to the report with the Image option.

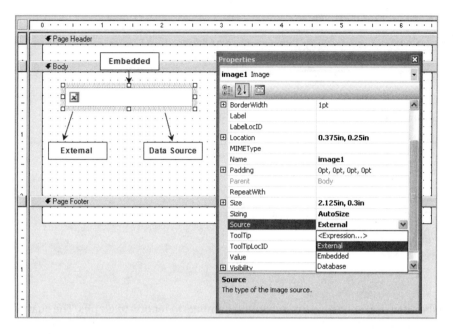

Figure 2-14. *An image item example*

Subreport

A report is called *subreport* when it is embedded inside another report, and a subreport is a full-fledged report like any other report created using reporting services. The subreport is the child report of the main (parent) report. Although subreports are a good feature, using them can potentially downgrade the performance of the parent report. Therefore, the decision to make use of a subreport is wise only where it is most suitable.

Let's take the master/detail relationship concept as an example. A subreport is used in such a relationship, obviously with the help of a link or data provided from the parent. A subreport can have its own, independent data source, though. Please see Figure 2-15 for a subreport example. In this example, the main report will have the grand total of receivables from the customer. A subreport with `CustomerID` as a link can bring in detail breakdown of receivables total in the form of individual invoices.

■**Note** Since the subreport is a separate report; the design is not visible in a parent report. Any changes needed for the subreport must be done outside the parent report; that means that the subreport must be modified like any other report.

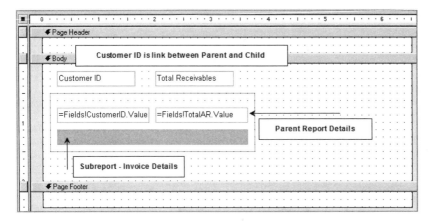

Figure 2-15. *A subreport example*

Chart

The Chart toolbox item is responsible for converting numbers in reports to graphs. The chart capabilities incorporated in RS are from Dundas Software. You'll have the popular chart types such as pie, bar, and column to use in your reports.

As you can see, in Figure 2-16, we have three pieces of information to produce a report of exports by country over the past five years. Country data is used as the series and years as the category. The detail data is the actual export amount. Illustrating this report with a graph is more appealing than just presenting a tabular report with five rows and two columns. It is also common practice to show tabular data with charts to bring more clarity to a report.

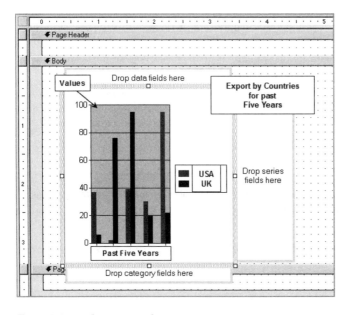

Figure 2-16. *A chart example*

Formatting Output

Formatting is an important aspect of a good report. Let's see: if your report could display total sales values as 2345453.552 or as $2,345,453.55, which output would you prefer? Naturally, you will prefer the formatted one, with the dollar sign and commas.

A typical report can have data of different types, such as decimal, data, or bit. It is important to know that each data type has the proper format applied to increase the visual appeal of the report. Please see Table 2-2 for a list of common SQL Server data types and their default output.

Table 2-2. *Default Output of Common SQL Server Data Types*

Data Type	Default Output
Float	123456789.123456 or 1.23456789012346E+19
Decimal	123456789.1234
Int, SmallInt, BigInt	123456789
Money	123456789.1234
Date	11/1/2003 3:34:26 PM
Bit	True or False

Format Dialog Box

The Format option appears as a tab selection when you select Textbox from the Report Item pane (please see Figure 2-7). The two data types that most often need formatting are the Numeric and Date types. For example, if you are developing a report for a North American user base, you will likely format the date as mm/dd/yyyy. Now, if the same report is for use in the United Kingdom, the format should be dd/mm/yyyy.

Figure 2-17 shows how the Choose Format dialog box will look if you're formatting a numeric data type with a dollar sign and thousands separator. You can also specify custom formatting which is commonly in use. If you specify format code as "C", it's equivalent to custom code "C" for currency.

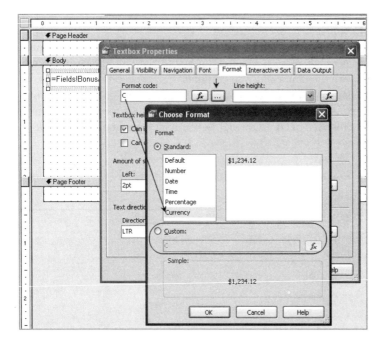

Figure 2-17. *Example of a numeric data type format*

What Are the Most Common Formats?

We can divide formatting into two main categories: standard and explicit. Standard formats are the most commonly used for numbers and dates. For example, you can use the Currency option to format a sales value, then if you do so, the format depends on the regional setting; for US/English, it'll show a dollar sign, or in the case of UK/English, it will show a pounds sterling symbol.

Please see Table 2-3 for a list of the most commonly used standard numeric formats.

Table 2-3. *Standard Numeric Formats*

Format	Description	Output
C	Currency	$123,456,789.12
D	Decimal	123456789.99
E	Scientific notation	1.234568e+008
F	Fixed point	123456789.12
P	Percentage	12.35%

■**Note** An optional additional level of precision can be specified in the case of numeric format; by adding a number to the format, you can specify the number of digits to include. For example specifying D12, instead of D, will produce output like the following: 000123456789. The length of output will be 12 digits.

Table 2-4 shows the most commonly used standard date formats.

Table 2-4. *Standard Date Formats*

Format	Description	Output
d	Short date	10/1/07
D	Long date	Thursday, January 18, 2007
t	Short time	4:45 PM
T	Long time	4:50:15 PM
f	Complete date and time	Thursday, January 18, 2007 4:45 PM
F	Complete date and time	Thursday, January 18, 2007 4:50:15 PM
g	General date and time	10/1/07 4:45 PM
G	General date and time	10/1/07 4:50:15 PM
M / m	Month	March 01
Y / y	Year and month	March, 2006

Explicit format means that, irrespective of your local regional setting, you can force a particular type of format to be applied. For example, if you always want to show the list price of a product in dollars, even though your business is based in Europe, you have to make use of an explicit format. Please see Table 2-5 for list of sample explicit formats.

Table 2-5. *Sample Explicit Formats*

Format	Description	Output
yyyy	Four-digit year	2007
yy	Two-digit year	07
MMMM	Month	March
MMM	Three-character month	Mar
MM	Two–digit month	03
dddd	Weekday, full name	Sunday
dd	Weekday, short name	Sun
HH	Hour, in 24-hour format	02 or 22
%	Percentage of numeric values	.75 will be displayed as 75%

■**Note** By setting Format property of the date type controls to MMMM d, yyyy the resulting output will appear as March 1, 2007, where MMMM=full name of month, d=1 and yyyy=2007.

Beautification

So, what makes a report look beautiful and attractive? Seems like a generic question right? How about this: if I asked a roomful of people, "What color do you think will look good on column headers?" I would see many hands in the air, and everyone would make a choice—dark blue, green, or medium aquamarine.

To make life easy, most companies have a standard color scheme selected, generally reflecting the corporate branding and image. For example, one of my clients has blue and dark orange as corporate colors, so all reports used some blue and dark orange colors. By making good use of fonts and colors, you can develop eye-catching reports. To make your report look attractive, you must pay attention to the color, font, and text attributes.

Fonts

As I mentioned in the previous paragraph, first see if you have any corporate policy for using a particular font. If not, select a font that is easy to read by all users. While making your font selection, it is important to make note of the size of the data for a given column.

You should also be considerate as to when to use a font attribute like bold or italics. Too much bold and italic type can prove negative, appearancewise. The Font tab is accessed by opening the Properties dialog box of the Report Item option or from the VS IDE Properties toolbox; please see Figure 2-18 for an illustration of how to access the font property settings in both locations.

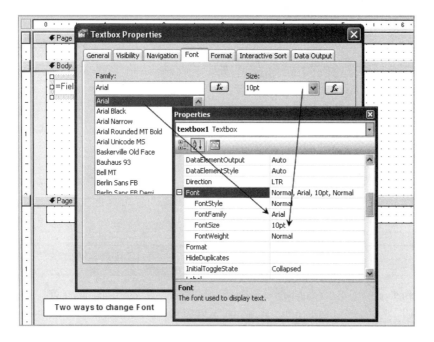

Figure 2-18. *Setting the font properties of the textbox item*

Colors

Colors can play an important role when the user is looking at the report. For example, in a customer receivables report, you can change the color of the receivables amount to red if an invoice is unpaid for more than 90 days; you'll get a chance to develop this receivables report as one of the hands-on examples Chapter 5.

Color is applicable to various attributes of report items. In the case of a textbox, you can specify what color the text will have and the background and border colors. Please see Figure 2-19 for a graphical illustration of how to access the font property and change the color of a selected report item.

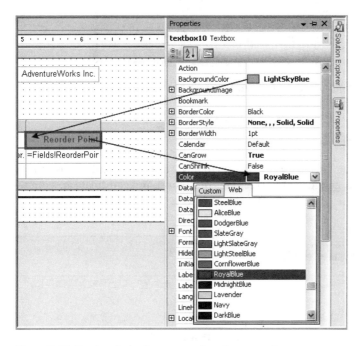

Figure 2-19. *Setting the color properties of a report item*

Text Alignment and Decoration

Sometimes even a small setting such as text alignment can do wonders for the appearance of your report. For example, imagine a report with the currency output left aligned; sure, it'll look weird. Sometimes, data looks best if it is centered inside the column. Figure 2-20 illustrates how to access the text alignment and the text decoration properties of a report item.

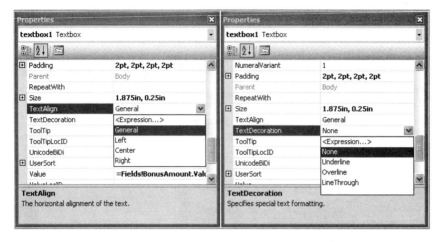

Figure 2-20. *Accessing the text alignment and decoration properties of a report item*

Expression Editor

The use of expressions is common in a report definition that will retrieve, calculate, display, group, sort, filter, parameterize, and format the contents of a report. You can create an expression manually, and some expressions are automatically created.

■Note All expressions must start with an equals sign.

A typical example of a manual expression follows:

```
="Page: " & Globals!PageNumber & "/" & Globals!TotalPages
```

This expression prints running page numbers. You can see the automatic expression example when you drag a field from the dataset window onto a table cell; an expression that retrieves the value of that field is displayed in the text box.

The following are some sample scenarios for which expressions can be created:

- Creating aggregates such as the sum, average, or percentage of a given business scenario

- Formatting text based on logic

- Dynamically changing a report title or the custom title of the company

- Producing a text string by concatenating data and constants

- Internal filtering of data while previewing a report

- Managing the content of parameters

- Supplying input to drill through reports

- Grouping and sorting of data

- Dynamically changing the look and feel of a report

■Note Expression Editor can only be used with the text box report item or a property in the Properties dialog box.

The Expression Editor includes a code window, a category tree, category items, and a Description pane. You can open the Expression Editor by right-clicking a text box or choosing <expression> in the values list of a property. Expressions are helpful to set many different properties, including color, font, and borders, to name a few. You can invoke the Expression Editor by clicking the "fx" button labeled next to each property value inside the properties window.

The Expression Editor is context sensitive; the category items and descriptions change in response to the expression category you are working with. It supports IntelliSense, statement completions, and syntax coloring so you can easily detect syntax errors. If you want a larger work surface, you can move and resize the Expression Editor's window (shown in Figure 2-21).

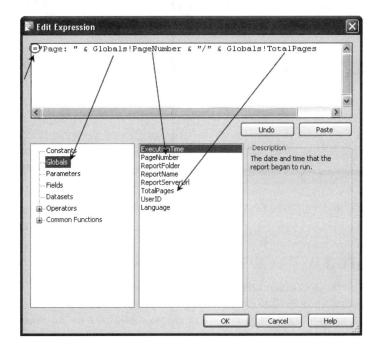

Figure 2-21. *Expression Editor*

As we go through various reporting projects in this book, you'll see many examples using the Expression Editor.

Conditional Formatting

You might be wondering what a formatting topic is doing here. Well, I purposely put this topic here because this type of formatting is dependent on the expression you're using. At times, certain pieces of information on a report are critical, and you, as the developer, want to call the attention of the user to these.

Let's take an example. Suppose you are developing a sales profitability report that displays all the invoices with sales values, costs, and profit/loss amounts. Now, to draw the attention of the user to all invoices that show a loss, you can change the text color of negative profit/loss values to red.

You can achieve this conditional formatting by writing the expression shown in Figure 2-22 for the profit/loss column.

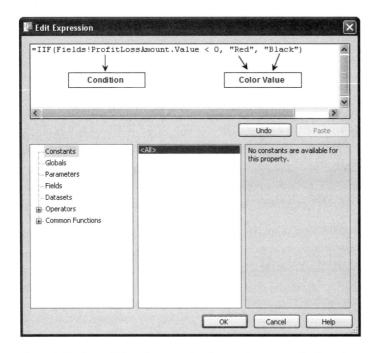

Figure 2-22. *A conditional expression formatting example that changes values less than zero*

Report Data Source

The report data source is the last piece in the puzzle of report development. This is the place for all the data we want the report to process and produce output. We'll cover this topic intensively in Chapter 3, since it correlates to the data model.

ReportViewer Control

The ReportViewer control is a key component of reporting services for client-side reporting. VS has different ReportViewer controls for Windows Forms and ASP. ReportViewer allows you to improve your application and provide a better report experience for users in the following ways:

- Create visually stunning reports by specifying fonts, colors, border styles, and images

- Provide easy data handling operations for developers such as filtering, sorting, grouping, and aggregation

- Dynamically change report data using custom embedded expressions

- Produce text by concatenating data and constants

- Support printing while previewing the report

- Export reports to Excel and PDF formats

- Present data as lists, tables, charts, and pivot tables

- Provide interactive end-user experience with navigation, document map, bookmarks and sorting

The control can process and render reports independently using a local mode, or it can display reports that are processed and rendered in a remote mode (report hosted on server-side). Figure 2-23 shows the use of the control with a Windows Forms client.

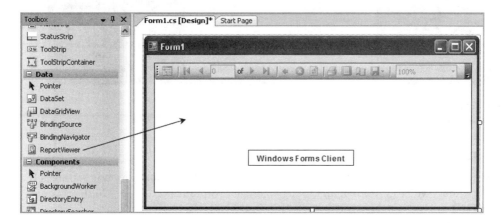

Figure 2-23. *The ReportViewer control used with a Windows Forms client*

Why Do We Need ReportViewer?

The report preview feature will commonly be the form of report delivery. However, occasionally, the output is sent directly to a printer. Sending a report as an e-mail attachment is also in wide practice. ReportViewer does more than just let you view the report; you can also print or save the output in either Excel or PDF format.

Figure 2-24 shows the ReportViewer control's Print Layout in action; the zoom mode is set to Whole Page. You'll also notice the navigation buttons in the toolbar. If your report is running into multiple pages, you can navigate to each page back and forth. You can also jump to a specific page number.

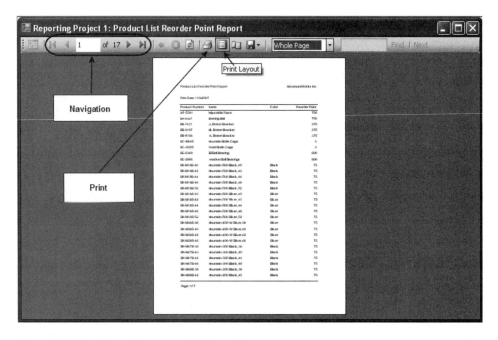

Figure 2-24. *The ReportViewer control in action*

Zoom Mode

A variety of zoom modes are available for previewing a report; the most common setting is 100 percent, though you can zoom in up to 500 percent. Or you can choose Page Width or Whole Page. Zoom can be a good feature, especially for users with visual disabilities.

Figure 2-25 shows the zoom settings provided by ReportViewer.

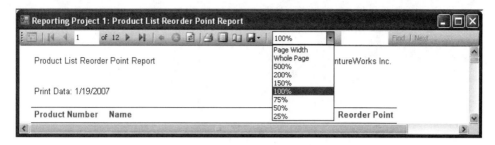

Figure 2-25. *Zoom settings in the ReportViewer control*

Report Export Choices

The ReportViewer control allows you to export reports in only two formats: Excel and PDF. A PDF file is commonly used as e-mail attachment. Output exported as an Excel file is commonly used to further analyze the data or do some calculations on it.

Figure 2-26 shows the export choices offered by ReportViewer.

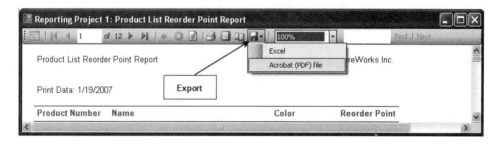

Figure 2-26. *Export options of the ReportViewer control*

Summary

In this chapter, we looked at the client-side components offered by the Visual Studio IDE. You also learned about different report items, which we will use to produce stunning, professional reports, and got an introduction to different aspects of the report designer and ReportViewer control.

In the next chapter, we'll start to look at our data model, the RealWorld database. This is a good time for users to know our data, so we'll get going with our hands-on report development efforts. You'll also learn about datasets and the ADO.NET interface to manage data and prepare it for reporting.

CHAPTER 3

∎∎∎

Data Models, Datasets, and the ADO.NET Interface

In Chapters 1 and 2, you were introduced to client-side RS and report controls. I'm sure you are eager to start putting this knowledge to the test by developing some reports now. Well, we will do just that starting in Chapter 4. So, what are you going to learn in this chapter? Before we move to the practical part of this book, let me introduce you to few key elements in the overall process of report development. We know the importance of data in producing reports. In this chapter, we will look at the process of gathering data and working with our `RealWorld` database.

This chapter will cover

- Working with a real-world sample database (`RealWorld`)

- Gathering data into a dataset

- The basics of the ADO.NET C# interface code to get the data into the dataset

Working with a Real-World Sample Database

I'm sure by this time you already have downloaded the code from the Apress site according to the instructions provided in this book's Introduction. If not, then I'd strongly advise you to do so before proceeding further. If you look at the downloaded code, you'll see two files, `RealWorld.mdf` and `RealWorld.ldf`, inside the database folder. What are these files? The `.mdf` file holds the data, and `.ldf` file holds the log information. Typically, a SQL Server database is made of an `.mdf` and an `.ldf` file. Therefore, our real-world database also has one of each of these files.

Understanding the Data Model

Let me ask you something. What is a real-world data model, and why do you need to know this to continue using this book and developing reporting projects? As you know, getting to know the source of the data is an important step in the report development process. Therefore, we must know which data model we are going to use. To put it simply, a data model helps us to understand the internals of how data is stored inside a database.

Whether you are a beginner or an expert in understanding data models, I'm confident that you will find this book's real-world data model simple and richly diverse. Richly diverse sounds interesting, doesn't it? Why not! How often do you find a data model that has entities belonging to several different business cases? For example, in the RealWorld database, you have an Itinerary table that holds travel-related data and another table that holds product pricing information for inventory. The simple reason for the diversity of information in this data model is my intention to cover as many different business cases as possible in the reporting projects coming in the following chapters.

To keep things simple, you'll find that a majority of the reporting projects in the book gather data from a single dedicated table in the RealWorld database. For example, the reporting project showing you how to create a Travel Itinerary report will use the data from the Itinerary table inside the RealWorld database. You don't have to worry about how data gets inside the table. Our goal here is to get the data out and publish it with RS.

Attaching the RealWorld Database

There are two common ways a database is distributed, as a backup or as physical files. In the case of a backup, you need to restore it. If a database is distributed as physical files, you need to attach it. I find attaching database files much simpler, especially if you're a new to databases—hence the .mdf and .ldf files in the downloaded code of the RealWorld database.

So, let's attach the database. As you know, the SQL Server database is needed for this book; it can be one of the full versions or the free express edition. Full versions of SQL Server come with the SQL Server Management Studio tool to manage the database. If you have the express edition of SQL Server, I'd suggest you download SQL Server Management Studio Express from here:

```
http://www.microsoft.com/downloads/details.aspx?FamilyId=➥
C243A5AE-4BD1-4E3D-94B8-5A0F62BF7796&displaylang=en
```

By the time this book reaches you, SQL Server 2008 may be on the market. If this is the case, please download the relevant tool from the download section of Microsoft's web site.

Attaching the database is a simple process. Once you make sure you have SQL Server Management Studio installed, please open it by accessing it from your Windows Start button, and use the following steps to attach the database; the instructions are the same for both the full and express releases of SQL Server 2005:

1. From the Connect to Server dialog box, select the proper credentials to connect to the server. I'm connecting using Windows authentication to my local instance of SQL Sever (localhost); see Figure 3-1. Please select the appropriate connection according to your SQL Server setup.

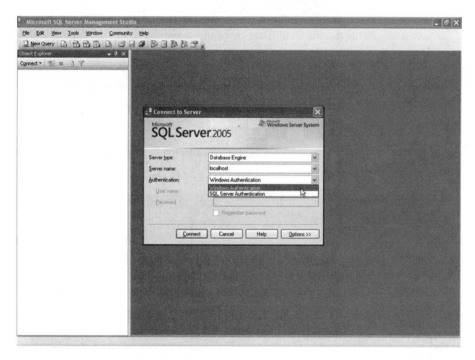

Figure 3-1. *Connecting to a SQL Server instance*

2. In Object Explorer, right-click the Databases node, and select Attach (see Figure 3-2).

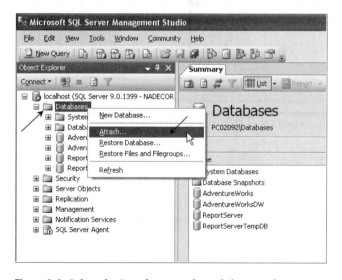

Figure 3-2. *Select the Databases node and the Attach menu option.*

3. You need to complete the following four steps in the Attach Database dialog box; please see Figure 3-3 for an illustration of the steps:

    a. Click the Add button.

    b. This action will open the Locate Database Files dialog; browse to the location of the `RealWorld.mdf` file in your PC.

    c. Select the file, and click the OK button.

    d. You'll see that `RealWorld.mdf` is selected and ready to attach; click the OK button to compete the process.

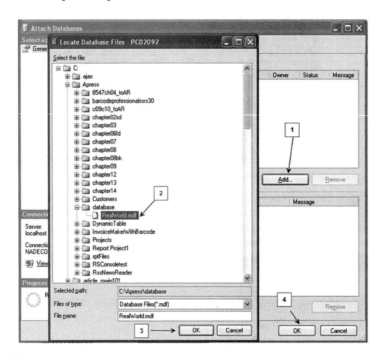

Figure 3-3. *Steps to browse and select RealWorld.mdf to attach*

This action will add a new node to the database tree on your SQL Server instance. Please make sure your database appears under the Databases tree node (see Figure 3-4). Now, you're all set to start reporting on your database. All right, with our database attached, let's move on now to learn some essentials of datasets.

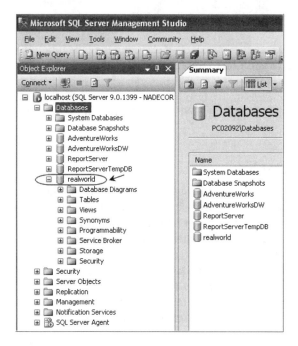

Figure 3-4. *Database node after attaching RealWorld sample database*

Gathering Data into a Dataset

As I explained to you in the Introduction, we have to gather data and store it temporarily for the RS reporting engine to use it. This temporary placeholder for our gathered data is called a dataset. For each report you develop, it is your responsibility as a developer to create a dataset.

What Is a Dataset?

Before we look into different ways to create a dataset, let me offer a quick insight into datasets! In simple words, a dataset is like a miniature relational database in memory, with tables, relationships, and constraints. A dataset is a very powerful component of the ADO.NET architecture. An in-depth analysis of a dataset is beyond the scope of this book; therefore, I'll discuss only the part that is required for us to know to develop reports.

■**Note** You can learn more on datasets here: `http://msdn2.microsoft.com/en-us/library/` `system.data.dataset(VS.71).aspx`.

What should you know about datasets? Well, all you have to know is how to create a dataset and a data table inside the dataset. Starting in Chapter 4, you'll notice that each reporting project makes use of a dataset. The data table inside the dataset is identical in structure to the underlying source table from the database. A dataset like this is also commonly known as a typed dataset.

We create a typed dataset by deriving it from the base dataset class. It has all the functionality that the base dataset class has to offer. In addition to this, a typed dataset provides strongly typed methods, events, and properties. To put it simply, this means you can access resources inside the dataset, such as tables and columns, by name. Another important benefit of a typed dataset is that any type mismatch is caught during the compilation, rather than at run time.

Creating a Typed Dataset Manually

This is an important section, as it explains how we are going to create the datasets for the rest of our reporting examples in this book. As you know, we are using different clients to report on, but no matter what the client, the process to add a dataset remains the same. For example, if you are creating a Windows Forms client or a Web Service client, you follow the same steps to add a dataset.

Let's make use of Windows Forms to create our example dataset. Before we go into creating an actual dataset, let's get our Windows Forms client ready. If you are new to the Visual Studio IDE, I'd advise you to go through this book's Appendix for a quick introduction.

Please open Visual Studio, and use the following steps, illustrated in Figure 3-5, to create a Windows application project:

1. Click File ➤ New ➤ Project, or press the hot keys Ctrl+Shift+N.

2. In the "Project types" pane of the New Project dialog box, select Visual C# ➤ Windows.

3. In the Templates pane, select Windows Application.

4. Please give the application a name; I've called the project TypedDataset. You may choose a different location for storing the application files according to your preference.

5. Click the OK button to finish the process. After you click OK, Visual Studio will create a new Windows application project. You'll also notice that a new form with the name Form1 is part of the project.

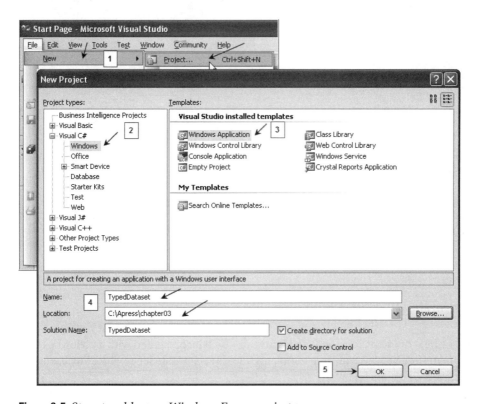

Figure 3-5. *Steps to add a new Windows Forms project*

Perfect! We have the Windows Forms project created now. Let's move on and see how a dataset is created with the VS IDE. Let's assume that you have a `CreditLimit` table in a SQL Server database with three columns inside: `CustomerID`, `CustomerName`, and `LimitAmount`. Now, our goal is to create a typed dataset with a data table inside that has a similar structure to the `CreditLimit` table.

What you are going to see now is the common method I'll use throughout the book to create the dataset. While trying any practical report from this book, if you face any difficulty in creating a dataset or data table, I'd advise you to revisit this section.

Adding a dataset is easy; here is how you can add a dataset to any client you will develop with the Visual Studio IDE. Start by selecting the project `TypedDataset` in Solution Explorer. Right-click it, and select Add ➤ New Item. Please see Figure 3-6 for an illustration of the steps.

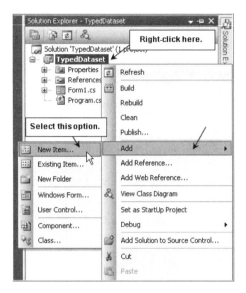

Figure 3-6. *Steps to add a new item to the project*

After finishing the steps illustrated in Figure 3-6, you'll be presented with a dialog box to pick a new item from various available templates. Please select DataSet as your choice, and name it dsCreditLimit; see Figure 3-7.

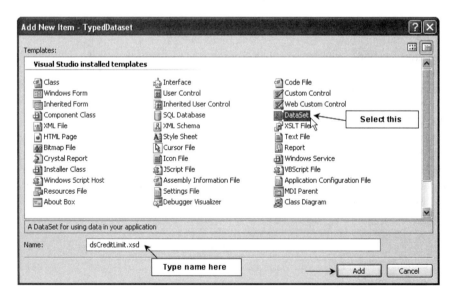

Figure 3-7. *Steps to add a new dataset to the project*

After you go through all the steps shown Figures 3-6 and 3-7, you'll notice that a new dataset is added to the project and a blank dataset designer is open for you to add a data table (see Figure 3-8).

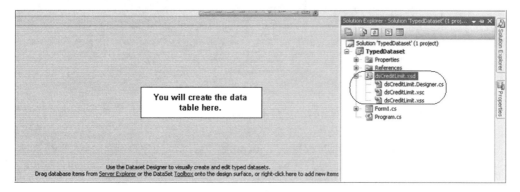

Figure 3-8. *Dataset design surface*

Creating a Data Table

Now that we've created the dataset, let's move on to add a data table to it. Use the following steps to add a data table inside the dataset:

1. You can go to the dataset designer in two ways: double-click dsCreditLimit inside Solution Explorer, or right-click the dsCreditLimit node and select View Designer (see Figure 3-9).

Figure 3-9. *Steps to launch the DataSet design surface*

2. Let's add the data table by right-clicking the design surface and selecting Add ➤ DataTable (see Figure 3-10).

Figure 3-10. *Steps to add a data table to dataset*

3. Click the header of the newly created data table, and name it dtCreditLimit. Let's start adding columns to dtCreditLimit by right-clicking the data table and selecting Add ➤ Column (see Figure 3-11).

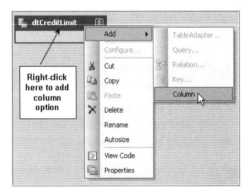

Figure 3-11. *Steps to add a column to a data table*

4. Please add the following columns into the data table (see Figure 3-12 to add columns and check DataType property, in the properties window); the data table should then look similar to the one shown in Figure 3-13:

   • CustomerID (System.String)

   • CustomerName (System.String)

   • LimitAmount (System.Double)

By default, when you add a column, the default DataType is System.String. In this case, make sure to change the DataType of LimitAmount to System.Double.

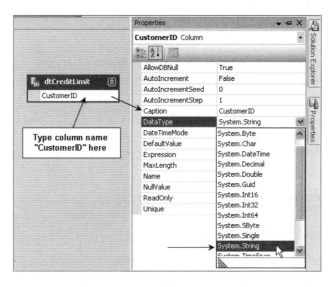

Figure 3-12. *Column name and properties view*

Figure 3-13. *Final look of data table inside the dataset*

That's it! That is all you need to do to get your typed dataset ready for use. With the dataset taken care of, now comes the job of gathering the data from a data source and temporarily holding it inside the dataset to be used by the report rendering engine.

Although we'll create datasets and data tables manually, as in this section, throughout the rest of this book, the Visual Studio IDE also has a wizard-based user interface to create a dataset and related data tables. You may choose either one of the methods to create datasets, but I suggest creating them manually for a better learning experience. Either approach will get the dataset ready to bind it with the reporting engine, though, so the next section explains how to use the wizard.

Creating a Typed Dataset Using the Wizard

To demonstrate the use of the wizard-based interface, let's make use of Windows Forms here. Please open Visual Studio, and use the following steps, illustrated in Figure 3-5, to create a Windows application project:

1. Click File ➤ New ➤ Project, or press the hot keys Ctrl+Shift+N.

2. In the "Project types" pane of the New Project dialog box, select Visual C# ➤ Windows.

3. In the Templates pane, select Windows Application.

4. Please give the application a name; I've called the project DatasetWizard. You may choose a different location for storing the application files according to your preference.

5. Click the OK button to finish the process. After you click OK, Visual Studio will create a new Windows application project. You'll also notice that a new form with the name Form1 is part of the project.

Now that you've created the project, let's see how we can use the wizard to create our dataset. Dataset Wizard can be accessed by two ways: You can click Data menu ➤ Add New Data Source, or you can click the Add New Data Source link inside the data source window. Please see Figure 3-14 for an illustration.

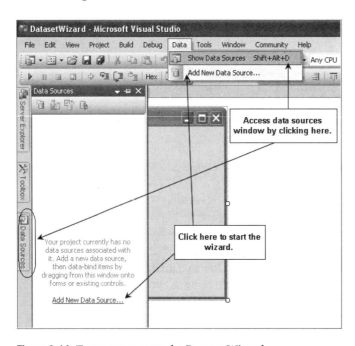

Figure 3-14. *Two ways to start the Dataset Wizard*

As soon you start the wizard, the first screen of wizard will give you three choices of data source types. Select Database, and click the Next button to move to the next screen of the wizard (see Figure 3-15). You can also select a web service or collection of objects as a data source. In later chapters, you will see how to use a collection of objects as a data source to develop a report.

The next screen will prompt you to choose the connection to the source database. Your database could be local or sitting on a remote server. In any case, proper connection to the database is a vital before moving to the next step of the wizard. It is possible that you might have created a connection before; in such a situation, your connection name will appear inside the list box on the left side of New Connection button. I don't have any connection set up yet; therefore, my list inside the wizard is empty. Please make sure your wizard screen looks similar to the one shown in Figure 3-16.

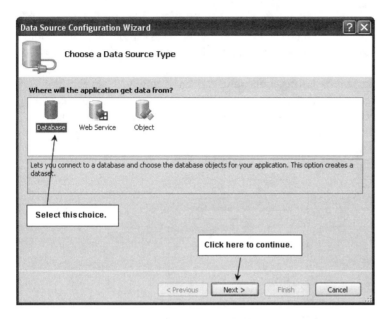

Figure 3-15. *The first screen of the wizard lets you choose a data type.*

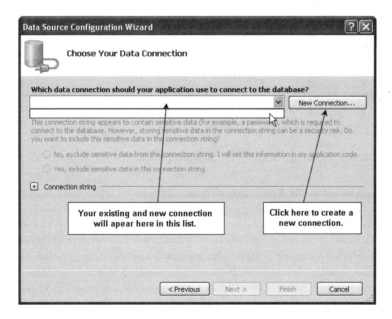

Figure 3-16. *The second screen of the wizard establishes the connection to the database.*

Let's create a new connection by clicking the New Connection button to open the
Add Connection dialog box. From this dialog box, select or type the server name. I selected
localhost as the server; you should select the server you have access to according to your
preference.

After selecting the service, choose either Windows or SQL Server authentication. I'm using the Windows authentication. Now, if your connection to the server is established, you should see the list of available databases on the server (I assume that you already have the RealWorld database attached to your server).

Please select the RealWorld database as your source database. Now, you can click the Test Connection button to see if everything works fine. Click the OK button the complete the process of creating a new connection. Please see Figure 3-17 for an illustration of steps to create new connection.

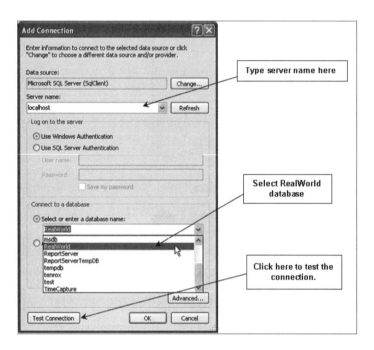

Figure 3-17. *Create a new connection and select RealWorld as the database.*

After you add the new connection, the newly created connection name will appear in the wizard screen; see Figure 3-18. In my case it is fsoft-server.RealWorld.dbo. The connection name consists of *servername.databasename.ownership*. fsoft-server is the name of the server, which is also referred to as localhost on my computer. In your case, the connection name will be your server name and RealWorld database. You can also see the connection string, which the wizard will use to eventually gather data into the dataset. Don't worry about the connection string here, as we are not going to use the TableAdapter, which the wizard generates to collect data; as usual, we will write our own C# code to get to data. If you would like to see how the connection string looks, just click the sign inside the circle. Click the Next button to move to the next step of the wizard; see Figure 3-18 for an illustration.

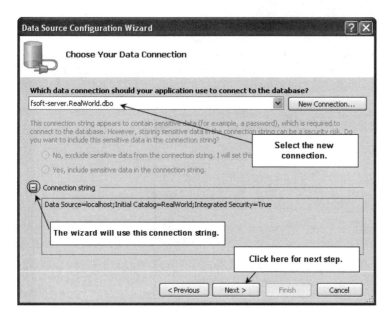

Figure 3-18. *The newly created connection inside the wizard screen's list of available connections*

After you click the Next button on the wizard screen, the next screen will ask you to save the connection string to the application configuration file (see Figure 3-19). We don't need to do anything on this screen; click the Next button to move to the next screen of the wizard.

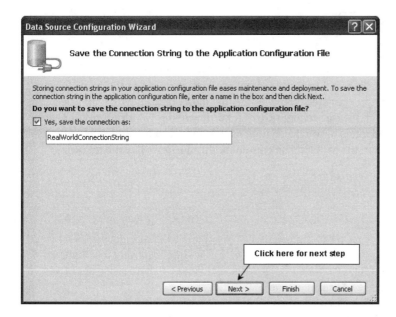

Figure 3-19. *Wizard screen to confirm saving the connection string*

After confirming the connection string, the next screen of the wizard will show you the objects from the `RealWorld` database. You'll see a tree structure of objects with Tables, Views, Stored Procedures, and Functions nodes. As you know, the `RealWorld` database has only tables, so let's expand the table section, and select the `BooksInfo` table to create our dataset. Please make sure the wizard screen looks similar to the one shown in Figure 3-20.

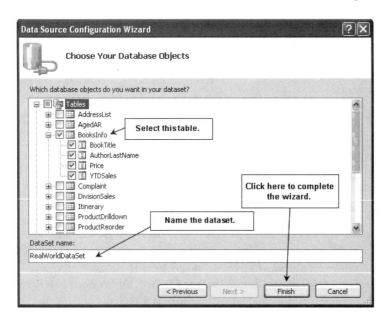

Figure 3-20. *Select the BooksInfo table to create a dataset.*

As you can see in Figure 3-20, this is the last screen in the wizard before generating the typed dataset for the `BooksInfo` table. Before you click the Finish button, make sure to give a meaningful name to your dataset; I kept the default `RealWorldDataset` as the name for the dataset. After you complete the last step, you'll notice that a new dataset with your selected name is added to the project. Please see Figure 3-21 for a view of the Solution Explorer window with the newly created dataset. You'll also notice that the wizard has added a configuration file named `app.config` to the project. The content of this file looks like the following:

```
<?xml version="1.0" encoding="utf-8" ?>
<configuration>
    <configSections>
    </configSections>
    <connectionStrings>
        <add name="DatasetWizard.Properties.Settings.RealWorldConnectionString"
            connectionString="Data Source=localhost;Initial Catalog=RealWorld;➥
                Integrated Security=True"
            providerName="System.Data.SqlClient" />
    </connectionStrings>
</configuration>
```

Do you remember the wizard asking you to save the connection string? This is where the wizard saved the connection string, in the app.config file. Since we are going to write our own C# code to gather the data, you might as well ignore this file or delete it from the solution if you wish.

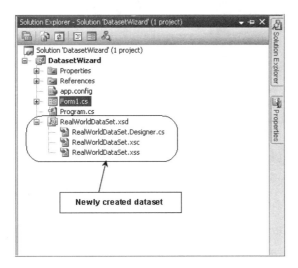

Figure 3-21. *Solution Explorer view with the newly created dataset*

For the last step before our dataset is ready to use in developing the reporting project, we need to delete the TableAdapter for this dataset. This table adapter is generated by the wizard to get the data from the data source. As I mentioned to you earlier, we will not need the help of the TableAdapter here, because we'll write our own ADO.NET interface code to connect to the database and get the data. All we want from the wizard is the dataset with the data table inside.

To delete TableAdatper, double-click the RealWorldDataSet icon in Solution Explorer to open the dataset designer. Once inside the dataset designer, select the table adapter, which is attached to the BooksInfo data table. Right-click it to access the pop-up menu, and select Delete. Figure 3-22 illustrates these steps.

After you delete the table adapter, all you will have left inside the dataset is a data table with the name BooksInfo. Your dataset designer screen will look similar to Figure 3-23 after getting rid of table adapter from the dataset.

And that's it for creating a dataset using the wizard. So, I leave it up to you to decide which way you like best for creating datasets. All projects in this book will show you the manual way, which I feel makes more sense, as you are learning. However, if you are one of those die-hard fans of wizards, you may go that way instead. Whether you work manually or use the wizard, the ultimate goal should be getting the dataset and data table ready.

I guess that's enough on dataset design; let's move on to the basics of the ADO.NET interface.

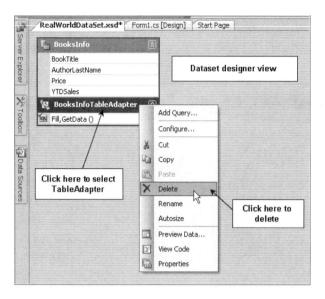

Figure 3-22. *Deleting the table adapter using the dataset designer*

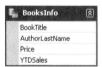

Figure 3-23. *Final look of the data table*

Creating the ADO.NET C# Interface Code

All right, we know the data source (CreditLimit table), and we have the dataset ready. Now, what do we need to do to populate the dataset with data from CreditLimit table? Well, let's look now at the last piece of the puzzle—the ADO.NET C# interface code. Before we start analyzing the C# code, let me give you a quick introduction to ADO.NET.

What Is ADO.NET?

In simple words, ADO.NET is a set of components to help developers access data and related data services. It comes as a base class library with the Microsoft .NET Framework. Both relational and nonrelational data sources can be accessed using ADO.NET.

A discussion of the full functionality of ADO.NET is beyond the scope of this book. Therefore, I'll stick to what is needed for you to get report development going. We'll look into two important parts of ADO.NET: data providers and datasets. To know more about ADO.NET, please visit the following link:

http://msdn2.microsoft.com/en-us/library/e80y5yhx(vs.80).aspx

Getting to Know the Data Provider

The data provider is a set of classes in ADO.NET that provide access to various data sources. Most of the examples in this book use SQL Server as a data source, but you will also see Oracle as a data source in Chapter 10.

Each data source has its own set of provider functionality. However, they share some common sets of utility classes as well. I am discussing three of them that we will use throughout this book:

- Connection: Needed to communicate with a data source

- Command: Needed to perform actions such as selecting, updating, and deleting data from a data source

- DataReader: Needed to read data from a data source, one record at a time

What is a Connection object? Simply put, the connection object is a must to get connected with the data source. All data providers have specific connection objects to use. If you are connecting to SQL Server, you need SqlConnection; if Microsoft Access is the data source, you need OledbConnection. The Connection class takes the connection string and offers the Open() and Close() methods to manage the connection with the data source.

After getting the connection established, we need to take the help of a Command object to set the command that will be sent to the data source. Similar to a connection object, Command objects also differ for each data provider. In the case of SQL Server, we need SqlCommand, and for Microsoft Access, we need OledbCommand. Among other tasks, the main jobs of Command are to take the SQL query from the client and pass it to the data source and make a call to ExecuteReader() to open the data reader stream for the DataReader object.

Finally, a DataReader object is used to get the data that is streaming from the data source into our dataset. Starting with ADO.NET 2.0, DataReader has a new method named Load(). This method can directly fill a dataset from the data reader.

Writing the C# Interface Code

It is time to share the C# code with you now. These lines of code are the instructions that do the job of collecting the data, storing it inside the dataset, and finally, passing it to the reporting engine to produce the report. The following is a typical example of C# code you'll see in the rest of the chapters:

```
using System;
using System.Collections.Generic;
using System.ComponentModel;
using System.Data;
using System.Drawing;
using System.Text;
using System.Windows.Forms;
using System.Data.SqlClient;
using Microsoft.Reporting.WinForms;
```

```csharp
namespace TypedDataset
{
    public partial class Form1 : Form
    {
        public Form1()
        {
            InitializeComponent();
        }

        private void Form1_Load(object sender, EventArgs e)
        {
            //declare connection string, please substitute
            //dataSource with your Server name
            string cnString = "Data Source=(local);Initial Catalog=RealWorld;➥
 Integrated Security=SSPI;";

            //declare Connection, command and other related objects
            SqlConnection conReport = new SqlConnection(cnString);
            SqlCommand cmdReport = new SqlCommand();
            SqlDataReader drReport;
            DataSet dsReport = new dsCreditLimit();

            try
            {
                //open connection
                conReport.Open();

                //prepare connection object to get the data
                //through reader and populate into dataset
                cmdReport.CommandType = CommandType.Text;
                cmdReport.Connection = conReport;
                cmdReport.CommandText = "Select * FROM CreditLimit";

                //read data from command object
                drReport = cmdReport.ExecuteReader();

                //load data directly from reader to dataset
                dsReport.Tables[0].Load(drReport);

                //close reader and connection
                drReport.Close();
                conReport.Close();

                //provide local report information to viewer
                rpvTypedDataset.LocalReport.ReportEmbeddedResource =➥
 "TypedDataset.rptTypedDatatset.rdlc";
```

```
                //prepare report data source
                ReportDataSource rds = new ReportDataSource();
                rds.Name = "dsCreditLimit_dtCreditLimit";
                rds.Value = dsReport.Tables[0];
                rpvTypedDataset.LocalReport.DataSources.Add(rds);

                //load report viewer
                rpvTypedDataset.RefreshReport();
            }
            catch (Exception ex)
            {
                //display generic error message back to user
                MessageBox.Show(ex.Message);
            }
            finally
            {
                //check if connection is still open then attempt to close it
                if (conReport.State == ConnectionState.Open)
                {
                    conReport.Close();
                }
            }
        }
    }
}
```

The preceding code listing is the complete code from Form1.cs. Now, let's break the code apart and analyze it. In this code listing, we are using SQL Server as the data provider. Our code is making reference to the following two namespaces in particular to access the data provider and dataset features of ADO.NET:

```
using System.Data;
using System.Data.SqlClient;
```

The first line is needed to make reference to the System.Data assembly, which has the dataset functionality. The second line of code is making reference to the System.Data. SqlClient assembly to access the functionally to work with the SQL Server as a data source.

■**Note** If you had Microsoft Access as a data provider here, you need to use using System.Data.OleDb; instead. For another data provider, such as Oracle or MySQL, please visit the manufacturer's web site.

The next section of code is making reference to the utility classes from the SQL Server data provider. The code looks like this:

```
string cnString = "Data Source=(local);Initial Catalog=RealWorld;➡
Integrated Security=SSPI;";

SqlConnection conReport = new SqlConnection(cnString);
SqlCommand cmdReport = new SqlCommand();
SqlDataReader drReport;
DataSet dsReport = new dsCreditLimit();
```

The first line here is a connection string. The connection string tells the data provider where the database server is and to which database to connect. It also has the security information related to the mode of connection. The next three lines are initializing the Connection, Command, and DataReader classes. The last instruction is to make reference to our typed dataset, which we created earlier in this chapter.

The section of the code which is inside the Try . . . Catch block is responsible for the actual job of connecting to the data source and reading the data. Here is the code:

```
conReport.Open();
cmdReport.CommandType = CommandType.Text;
cmdReport.Connection = conReport;
cmdReport.CommandText = "Select * FROM CreditLimit";
```

If you look at the code, it starts with calling the Open() method from the connection object. The following three lines provide the input to the command object. CommandType.Text means that the input is a text-based SQL query. The second line specifies the connection to the command, and the third line is the actual SQL query statement instructing the database to send all columns and all rows from the table CreditLimit.

The next two lines execute the command and return the data:

```
drReport = cmdReport.ExecuteReader();
dsReport.Tables[0].Load(drReport);
```

The first line makes a call to the command object's ExecuteReader() method. This instruction will return a data reader stream into the DataReader (drReport) object. The next line is a special call to the Load() method from the dataset. This call will read the data from DataReader to the table inside the dataset.

The following two lines of code make sure to close the connection to the data source:

```
drReport.Close();
conReport.Close();
```

The rest of the lines of code are basically used to supply the information to the reporting engine to generate the report. We'll discuss this in detail in the first practical report in Chapter 4. I'm sure you are ready to do some serious reporting now! So, what are we waiting for? Let's move on; the rest of the book is full of interesting reporting projects.

Summary

In this chapter, we looked at three topics. First, we learned how to get our `RealWorld` data model ready. Second, we looked at what is needed for us to get our typed dataset in place. Finally, we looked at the ADO.NET C# interface code.

Starting in the next chapter, you'll get into the world of developing reporting projects. The first client in line is Windows Forms, followed by AP.NET web forms and many more interesting reporting clients.

■■■

CHAPTER 4

Reporting with Windows Forms

So far, this book has covered the theory of client-side reporting services and various reporting patterns used in real-world situations. Since I feel you're eager to start with the practical part of this book, the rest of the book is hands-on in nature. There are many practical projects coming your way to help you master the craft of client-side reporting with Visual Studio.

Going through the chapters that discuss theory and provide a general introduction is different from going through the chapters with practical content. Before you start reading this chapter, I'd suggest that you get in front of your computer. Why? Because what I'm going to discuss here is not just narrative; it's a step-by-step walk-through designed to make you a report-developing champion.

I'm going to keep this hands-on approach as simple as possible. We'll start with the basic knowledge needed to build the host client, that is, a Windows Forms client. After that, we'll work on several real-world practical reporting projects. Each project targets a business case and is based on a reporting pattern, which we discussed in previous chapters.

This chapter will cover

- "Windows Forms 101," a step-by-step tutorial for using Windows Forms

- A variety of reporting projects

- Troubleshooting tips

- Exercises for you to practice

Windows Forms 101

Let's start the journey with a quick tutorial on Windows Forms. I know you might be thinking, "This book is about client-side reporting; why do I need to know Windows Forms?" Well, since we're going to host our reports with Windows Forms, it is important for you to know the minimum requirements to host your reports and present them to the user.

All right folks, the moment has arrived; let's roll up our sleeves to do some serious keyboarding and dragging and dropping. If you're comfortable with creating a Windows Forms project and know how to add the ReportViewer to a project, you may jump directly to the first project.

Please make sure you've properly installed Microsoft Visual Studio 2005 on your computer before you continue to the next section. If you are new to the Visual Studio IDE, I have created a brief introduction for you in Appendix A; please read it before moving forward.

Creating a Windows Forms Project

Please open Visual Studio, and use the following steps, illustrated in Figure 4-1, to create a Windows application project:

1. Click File ➤ New ➤ Project, or press the hot keys Ctrl+Shift+N.

2. In the "Project types" pane of the New Project dialog box, select Visual C# ➤ Windows.

3. In the Templates pane, select Windows Application.

4. Please give the application a name; I've called the project RSWin101. You may choose a different location for storing the application files according to your preference.

5. Click the OK button to finish the process. After you click OK, Visual Studio will create a new Windows application project. You'll also notice that a new form with the name Form1 is part of the project (see Figure 4-2).

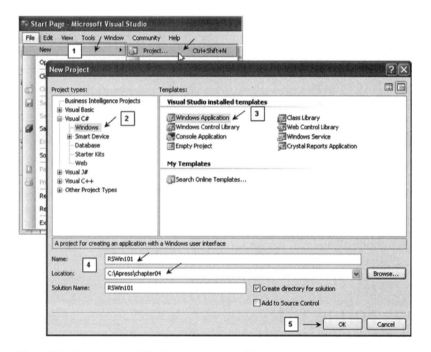

Figure 4-1. *Create a new Windows Forms application*

After you finish creating the project, you should see something similar to Figure 4-2. However, depending on your current IDE settings, you might see some toolboxes hidden or floating (please see the Visual Studio help files to learn how to customize the look and feel of the IDE). Anyway, you should see the blank Form1 created for you with the new project.

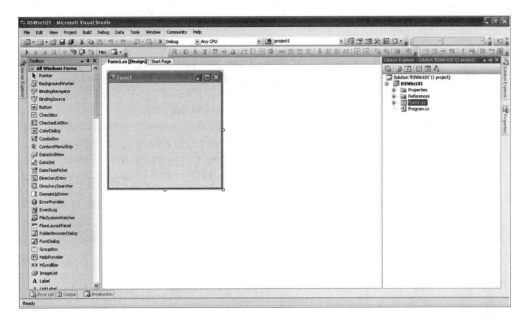

Figure 4-2. *The Visual Studio 2005 IDE with the RSWin101 project loaded*

■**Tip** You can always make the Toolbox window visible if you don't see it in the IDE by clicking View ➤ Toolbox or pressing Ctrl+Alt+X. To get the maximum amount of space on the design surface, you may want to use the auto-hide feature of toolboxes (see Appendix A to learn how to access the auto-hide feature).

Let's set the properties of Form1 according to the values in Table 4-1. We need to set the size property carefully to make sure we have enough space in Form1 for a complete view of the report; specifically, we need to make sure it's wide enough. While applying the property settings, if the property window is not visible in the IDE, you may press the F4 key to make it visible. Pease make sure to select Form1 before applying changes to properties using the property window.

Table 4-1. *Properties of Form1*

Property	Value
Text	Windows Forms Host Client
Size	750, 500

I'm assuming that you have at least 800 × 600 resolution set up on your computer. Therefore, I'm trying to get the maximum width of the form (750 pixels) available for viewing during run time. Please feel free to adjust or apply any other properties according to your needs.

Adding the ReportViewer to the Form

Why do we need a ReportViewer? Just as we need a DVD player to play a DVD, we need the viewer to preview the report. ReportViewer gives life to your reports.

ReportViewer not only allows you to preview the output but also helps you to produce the information in the various popular formats (e.g., PDF file and Excel spreadsheet). You can also print a hard copy of the report while you're viewing the output.

Let's start by dragging Data ➤ ReportViewer from the toolbox and dropping it onto the form (see Figure 4-5 for an illustration of the process). You might also like to use the shortcut method: double-click the ReportViewer icon. If you choose to use the double-clicking method, ReportViewer will appear in the top, left corner on the Form1 design surface.

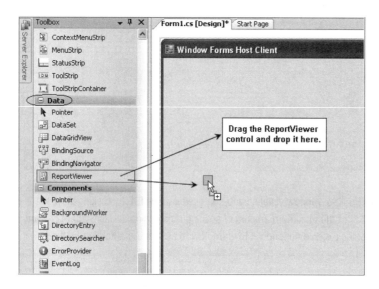

Figure 4-3. *Adding the ReportViewer to Form1*

As a result of this, a ReportViewer control will be added to the form with the name reportViewer1. Please set the properties of the ReportViewer control per Table 4-2. We are setting the Dock property to Fill, because we want the ReportViewer to fill the entire Form1 surface; that way, we provide the maximum amount of space to view report output. For all client-side processing of reports, we must make sure the processing mode is set to Local.

Table 4-2. *Properties of reportViewer1*

Property	Value
Dock	Fill
ProcessingMode	Local

After setting up properties for the ReportViewer, your form should look like the one shown in Figure 4-4. If it doesn't, I'd advise you to go through the instructions again and make sure you've not missed anything.

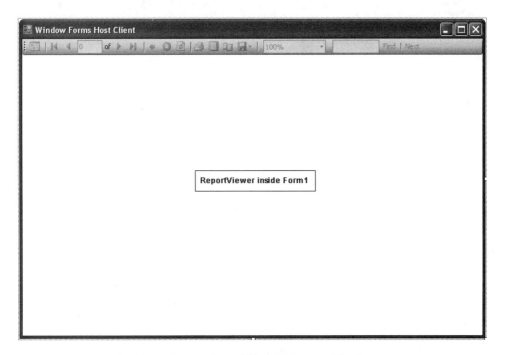

Figure 4-4. *Final look of form design after adding the ReportViewer*

Another interesting observation after adding the ReportViewer control to the form is that two new assembly references are part of the project now. What is an assembly? Simply put, an assembly is a compiled code library for use while developing the needed functionality. The two assemblies, `Microsoft.ReportViewer.Common` and `Microsoft.ReportViewer.WinForms`, are used to produce the report output for viewing and exporting. You can learn more about .NET assemblies here:

`http://msdn2.microsoft.com/en-us/library/hk5f40ct(vs.80).aspx`

Figure 4-5 shows the newly added assembly references.

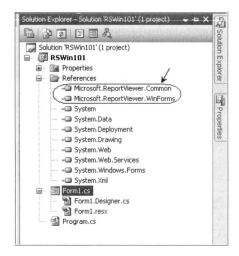

Figure 4-5. *Two new references are added as a result of adding the ReportViewer.*

Adding a Dataset to the Project

A dataset is very important part of developing a host client; and it should be, as it is holding the data from various sources that we'll use to prepare the reports.

Adding a dataset is easy: select the project RSWin101 in Solution Explorer; right-click it, and select Add ➤ New Item. Please see Figure 4-6 for an illustration of the steps.

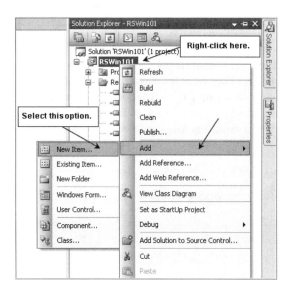

Figure 4-6. *Steps to add a new item to the project*

After completing the steps shown in Figure 4-6, you'll be presented with the Add New Item dialog box, where you can pick from various available templates. Please select DataSet as your choice, and name it dsRSWin101. Then, click the OK button. Figure 4-7 illustrates the steps.

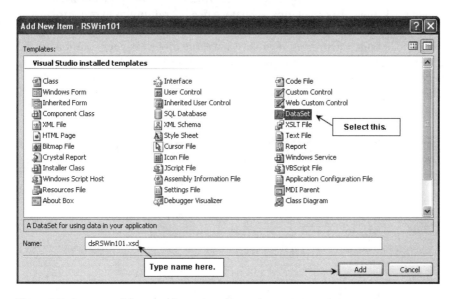

Figure 4-7. *Steps to add a new dataset to the project*

After you go through all the steps mentioned in Figures 4-6 and 4-7, you'll notice that a new dataset is added to the project and a blank dataset designer is open for you to add a data table (see Figure 4-8).

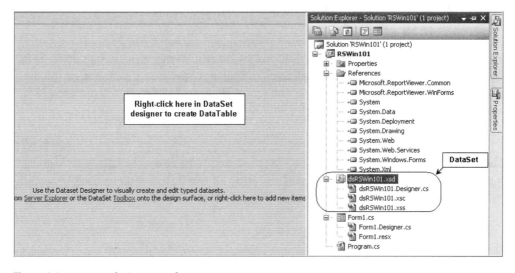

Figure 4-8. *DataSet designer surface*

Building the Project

That's it—we have completed the development steps required to get our Windows Form host client ready. I'd like to remind you that there is more to Windows Forms applications; what we did is just tip of the iceberg. However, this is what we need at minimum in order to host our report.

Now, it's the time to build the project. If you just have one project in your solution, by the way, building the solution and building the project are the same. You can build a project in a few ways: You can click the small, green play button in the main toolbox or press F5 on the keyboard to start the application in run-time mode. You can also select Build ➤ Build Solution from the main menu bar of the Visual Studio IDE (see Figure 4-9).

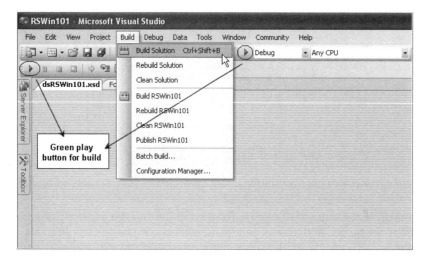

Figure 4-9. *Available options for building the project*

If all goes well, your project should compile without any issues, and you should be able to see it in run-time mode; it should look something like Figure 4-10. You'll notice that ReportViewer has the message "The source of the report definition has not been specified." The reason for this message is that we haven't bound any report to the viewer. For a quick explanation of messages like this one, see the troubleshooting section at the end of this chapter.

■**Note** Building is a process in which you compile your work and produce an executable, either in debug or release mode per your choice. By default, the Visual Studio IDE is set to build in debug mode; I'd suggest that you stay with the default settings of the IDE, unless you want to build a release version of the solution.

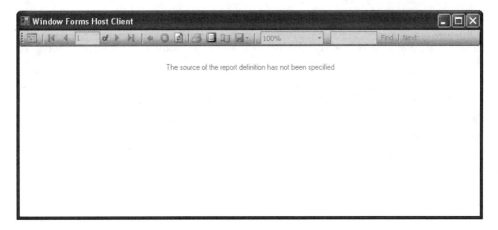

Figure 4-10. *The form in run-time mode*

Using This Project As a Template

You can use the RSWin101 project as a template for rest of the practical projects we're going to do in this chapter; that is, you can copy this project to a different folder and start changing it. This way, you don't need to create the project and add the ReportViewer, dataset, and so forth each time. From now on, I'll focus more on showing you the steps to design the reports and coding. We'll use same approach as this template to create the host client; if we have to put more controls on the client, I'll show you how to add them.

As you can see, in this tutorial, I have not shown you how to create the data table or add a report to the project. As both the data table and report are going to be different from project to project, you'll see different sets of instructions according to the demands of the reporting project.

■**Note** There are other ways to make use of datasets in our reporting projects. However, to be consistent, I'll use the approach mentioned in this tutorial. This approach is more hands-on, and for every project, you'll create a fresh dataset and related data tables from scratch.

Your First Reporting Project Is on Its Way . . .

Before we start the journey of learning report development, I'd like to say something here. The complexity of development efforts is different from project to project; I'll start with a simple List Report with no data grouping or summary totals. Why such a simple report? Well, I believe it is good idea to always take a simple approach in the beginning, and later, as your confidence grows, we'll do more complex reports.

As we move through the chapters, the projects will become more and more challenging. You should also keep in mind that there is more then one way of getting a report done. You can easily think that you would have done the same reports in different ways. The mechanics I'm selecting to do the reports in this book are chosen to use all possible functionality of client-side reporting.

So, what are we waiting for? Let's get the ball rolling with the Product List Reorder Point report!

Product List Reorder Point Report

Assume you're working for AdventureWorks Incorporated as a developer. You have been assigned the task of developing a report that will list all the products with their respective reorder points. The report should meet all characteristics described in Table 4-3, and the report output should match Figure 4-11.

Table 4-3. *Report Characteristics*

Characteristics	Value
Report title	Product List Reorder Point Report
Company title	AdventureWorks Inc.
Print date	Yes
Data source	ProductReorder
Columns to report	ProductNumber, Name, Color, ReorderPoint
Page size	Letter
Page orientation	Portrait
Page number	Yes (Page: n/n)

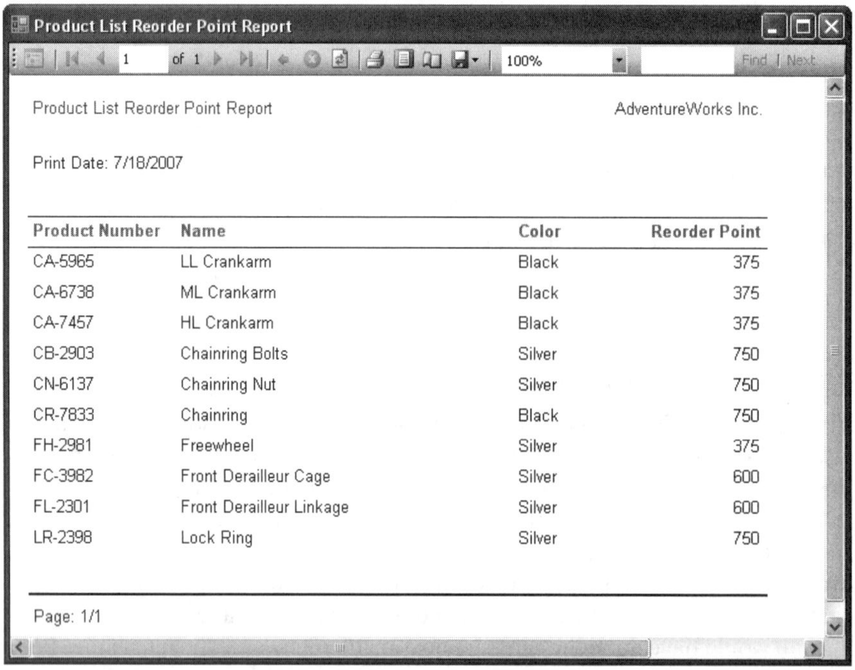

Figure 4-11. *Product List Reorder Point report output*

Business Case

It is good idea to get to know why we're doing this report. Developing a report is more than just dragging and dropping some report items and saying that it's all finished. A good understanding of the business case associated with a report usually helps you to decide how the report should be developed.

A reorder point report is common in industries in which inventory stock is kept. Businesses need to keep track of finished or unfinished inventory. Both retailers and manufacturers could use this report. This report helps the folks who keep an eye on the levels of stock inventory.

The level set as the reorder point is the indication that the current stock levels are lower than the levels that indicate reordering is necessary. The report also helps the purchasing folks: it tells them when the next purchase order must be placed to bring in more stock and cut the risk of being out of stock.

Selecting the Primary Report Items

As you can see in Figure 4-11, the output looks like a typical tabular format report. From what you have learned in the first two chapters on report items, what report item control is best suited to develop this kind of report? Well, I'd say, you can use either the table item or list item.

Questions like this will come again and again in your development efforts. Before selecting any report item, it is best to see which is most simple to use; your report should not be overkill. Let's use the table item this time; you'll see the list item in later projects.

Creating a Windows Forms Project

Open Visual Studio, and use the following steps to create a Windows application project; please refer to Figure 4-1 from the RSWin101 exercise for an illustration of this process:

1. Click File ➤ New ➤ Project, or you can press the hot keys Ctrl+Shift+N.

2. In the "Project types" pane of the New Project dialog box, select Visual C# ➤ Windows.

3. In the Templates pane, select ➤ Windows Application.

4. Please give a name to the application; I've called the project ProductReorder. You may choose a different location for storing the application files according to your preference.

5. Click the OK button to finish the process. Visual Studio will create a new Windows application project. You'll also notice that a new form with the name Form1 is part of the project.

Let's add the dataset and ReportViewer to the project. Select the project in Solution Explorer, right-click it, and select Add ➤ New Item ➤ DataSet. Please name the dataset dsProductReorder. Before you add the ReportViewer, please make sure Form1 is open in designer. Now, let's add the ReportViewer to the project by dragging and dropping Data ➤ ReportViewer from the toolbox. You may refer to RSWin101 tutorial for adding both the dataset and ReportViewer.

Set the properties as listed in Table 4-4.

Table 4-4. *Property Settings for the ProductReorder Project*

Object	Property	Value
Form1		
	Text	Product List Reorder Point Report
	Size	775, 500
reportViewer1		
	Dock	Fill

Step 1: Creating a Data Table

After creating the dataset, let's move on to add a data table to it. Use the following steps to add a data table inside the dataset:

1. You can go to the dataset designer in two ways: double-click dsProductReorder inside Solution Explorer, or right-click the dsProductReorder node and select View Designer (see Figure 4-12).

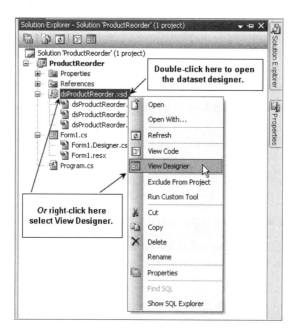

Figure 4-12. *Steps to get to dataset designer surface*

2. Let's add the data table by right-clicking the design surface and selecting Add ➤ DataTable (see Figure 4-13).

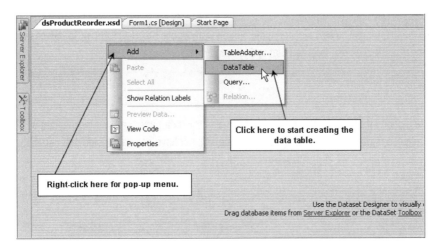

Figure 4-13. *Steps to add a data table to the dataset*

3. Click the header of the newly created data table, and name it dtProductReorder. Let's start adding columns to dtProductReorder by right-clicking the data table and selecting Add ➤ Column (see Figure 4-14).

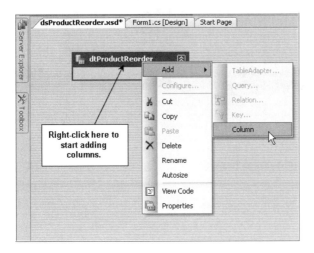

Figure 4-14. *Adding columns to the data table*

4. Please add the following columns into the data table and check the DataType properties (see Figure 4-15); the data table should then look similar to Figure 4-15:

   - ProductNumber (System.String)

   - Name (System.String)

   - Color (System.String)

   - ReorderPoint (System.Int32)

Note By default, when you add a column, the default DataType is `System.String`. In this case, make sure to change the DataType of ReorderPoint to `System.Int32`.

Note It is a good idea to keep the column names inside the data table the same as they are in the source database table. If a name does not match, the data table will not have any data inside that particular column.

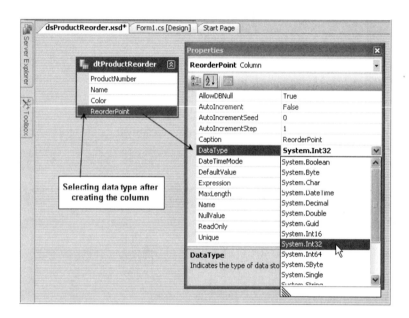

Figure 4-15. *Column name and properties view*

Figure 4-16. *Final look of data table inside the dataset*

Step 2: Designing the Report Layout

All right, we have our dataset in place with a data table and all the needed columns. We're all set to start designing the report layout, right? Wait a minute. Do we have the report added to our project yet? No.

Let's add the report. Select the project in Solution Explorer; right-click it, and select Add ➤ New Item. Then, select Report in the Add New Item dialog box. Please name the report rptProductReorder.rdlc, and click the Add button to complete the process. Figure 4-17 illustrates these steps.

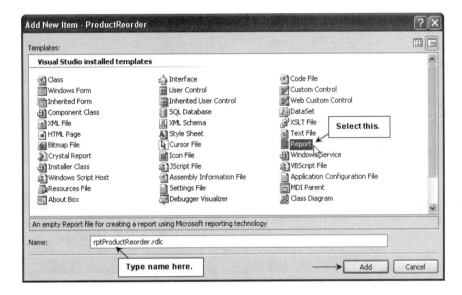

Figure 4-17. *Steps to add a report to the project*

As a result of clicking the Add button, a new report will be added to the project and opened in the report designer. You'll also notice that the Data Sources window is available with your dataset information inside (see Figure 4-18).

■**Note** The Data Sources window will be visible to you, based on your last setting, either on the right or left side of the report designer in Visual Studio's IDE. In case you don't see it, you can make the window visible by selecting Data ➤ Show Data Sources from the main menu or by pressing the hot keys Shift+Alt+D.

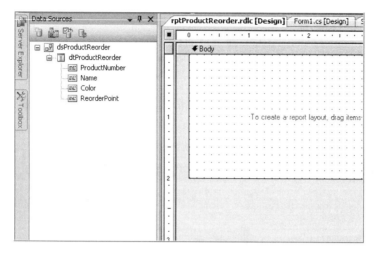

Figure 4-18. *Report designer with the newly added report and the Data Sources toolbox*

Adding the Header and Footer

Now, if you look closely at the report designer, you'll see that the newly added report has only a body section. The header and footer are missing. Since we need all three in our report, let's add the header and footer.

Adding these is simple; all you've got to do is right-click an open area (the gray part outside the body section) inside the report designer and select Page Header. Repeat the same process to select Page Footer. Afterward, your report design surface should more or less look like the one shown in Figure 4-19. Now, you can drag the edges of the body, header, or footer section's bands to meet your resizing needs.

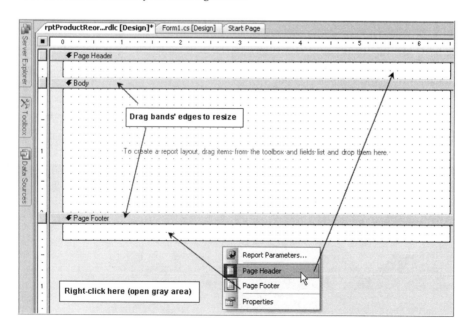

Figure 4-19. *The report designer with the header, body, and footer sections added*

If you look at Figure 4-19, the initial height of body section is 2 inches. And when you add the header and footer, each has its default height set to 0.25 inches. Now, you can increase or decrease the height of any band by simply dragging the band's edge. You can also set the size property of each band by clicking the band and changing it from the Properties dialog box.

For example, if you want your detail band's height set to 1.5 inches instead of the 2-inch default, simply change the Size property to 6.5in, 1.5in from 6.5in, 2in. The width of each band is always the same; initially, it is set to 6.5 inches, but you can change it to make use of maximum width available for the selected paper size.

Setting Up the Page

Our project demands are to have this report on a letter-size page and for the page orientation to be portrait. How do we know that the newly added report meets these criteria? Let's make sure that our report complies with requirements by examining the properties of the report.

Right-click the open gray area inside the design surface, as indicated in Figure 4-19, and select the Properties option. This will bring up the Report Properties dialog box. Make sure you select the General tab; your display should look similar to Figure 4-20.

Note You should always right-click an open gray area to access report properties. If you right-click inside any band, you'll get properties related to the selected band, not reports properties.

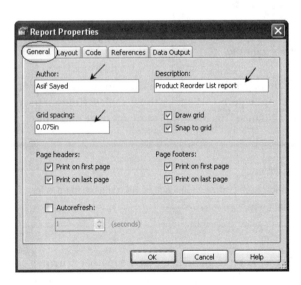

Figure 4-20. *General tab of the Report Properties window*

As you can see in Figure 4-20, I put my name as the Author and typed the report name in Description. You'll also notice that I changed the grid spacing from the default 0.125 inches to 0.075 inches; the reason for this change is that the finer the grid space, the better you can lay out the report control. From this report on, I'm setting the grid spacing to 0.075 inches.

The other settings determine how the grid will act and whether showing the page header and footer is necessary on each page of the report. For now, I'd advise you to let all other options stay at their defaults. For example, if you uncheck Draw Grid, you won't see gridlines inside the report designer. Gridlines helps you place report items; therefore, I'd suggest you keep the option as checked.

Before we continue to work on report design, let me tell you some important information about the Layout tab inside the Report Properties dialog box (see Figure 4-21). Click the Layout tab now.

Figure 4-21. *Layout tab of the Report Properties window*

The Layout tab is important for setting up pages. From here, you can control the layout of the output in terms of paper and page selection. Figure 4-21 shows the default settings of page width set to 8.5 inches and page height to 11 inches. This means a letter-size page and a portrait page orientation.

■**Tip** It is very simple to change the page orientation from portrait to landscape. All you have to do is to switch the values for the page width and page height.

You will also notice that all four margins are set to 1 inch. If you do the math, 6.5 inches width in body section plus 1 inch each for left and right margins makes the total 8.5 inches, the total width of a letter-size page.

■**Tip** You can set the top, bottom, left, and right margins to zero and set the band width in the report designer to 8.5 inches to use the maximum width available on the page.

Before we move on to design the header and footer, let's set the sizes of the header, body, and footer sections to 6.5in,1in, 6.5in,1in and 6.5in,0.5in respectively (please see Figure 4-22).

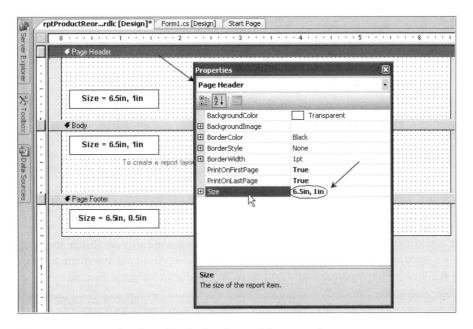

Figure 4-22. *Setting the sizes of body, header, and footer sections*

Designing the Page Header and Footer

Now, we have all three sections added to our report. You may decide to work on any of them first; however, I'd suggest setting the header and footer first, as they are not usually as complicated as the body section.

Adding report items to the report design surface is easy. All you need to do is select the report item you want from the Report Items toolbox and drag it to its destination on the design surface. The destination could be any band—header, body, or footer. Figure 4-23 shows an example of dragging and dropping a text box inside the header section.

Please make sure to drag and drop the following report items inside the header section:

- TextBox item for the report title

- TextBox item for the company title

- TextBox item for the print date

Please make sure to drag and drop the following report items inside the footer section:

- Line item for separation (for this item, you can draw from the left-side starting position and continue to draw until you reach the right-side position)

- TextBox item for the page number

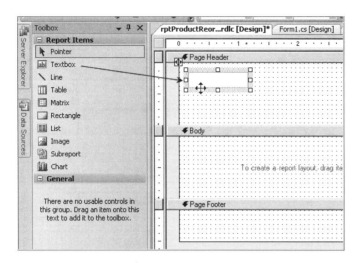

Figure 4-23. *Dragging report items from the toolbox to the design surface*

After adding the report items to the design surface, please make sure your design looks similar to my design in Figure 4-24. I dragged and dropped the report items in sequence, starting with the text box for report title and ending with text box for the page number.

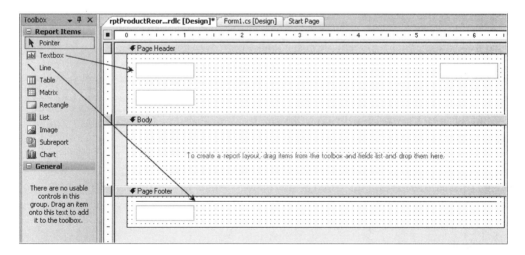

Figure 4-24. *Report designer after adding report items to the header and footer*

■**Note** When you drag and drop a text box to the design surface, the default size of the text box is 1 inch × 0.25 inches.

The text box report item is more or less the same as a standard text box control we'd use with Windows Forms or ASP.NET web forms. We can display both static and dynamic text using this report item. Each report control that we put onto our report designer surface is an object, and we all know objects have properties to define how they should look and behave. For example, when we added the series of text box items in the report designer, they were given the default name properties of textbox1 to textbox4.

Properties of report items can be changed in one of two ways: you can select the report item, right-click, and then select Properties (see Figure 4-25) or access the general properties toolbox (see Figure 4-26).

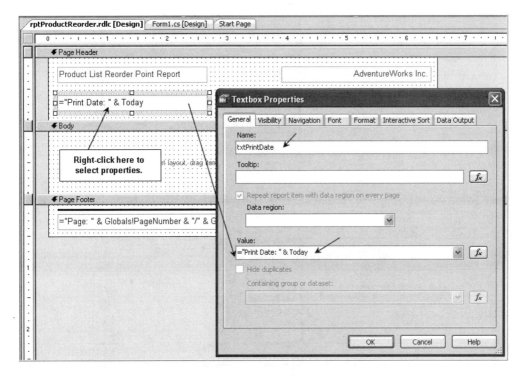

Figure 4-25. *Changing the properties of a report item using the reporting services Properties window*

In Figure 4-25 and Figure 4-26, I have shown you how to change properties, particularly the Value property of the print date text box item. All other properties like Color or Font are changed in a similar way. Let me show you how to set the Color property of the report title Textbox. You click the report title text box and change the Color setting from the VS IDE properties window (please see Figure 4-27).

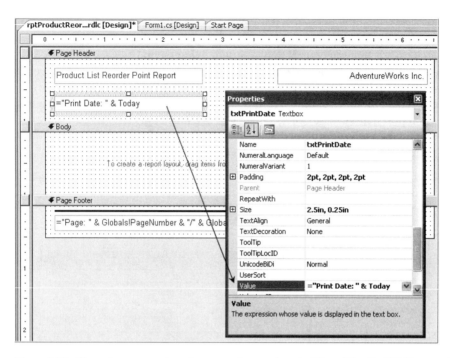

Figure 4-26. *Changing properties of a report item using the Visual Studio IDE Properties window*

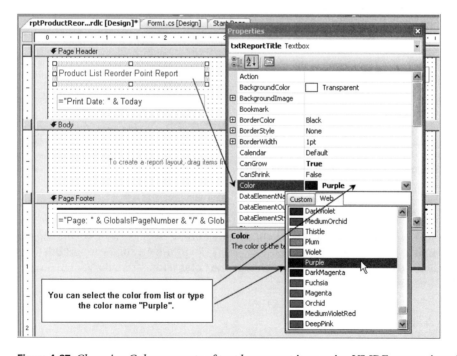

Figure 4-27. *Changing Color property of text box report item using VS IDE properties window*

Let's start changing properties. After selecting each text box, please specify its values according to Table 4-5.

Table 4-5. *Report Item Properties for the Header and Footer*

Report item	Property	Value
textbox1		
	Name	txtReportTitle
	Value	Product List Reorder Point Report
	Color	Purple
	Size	2.5in, 0.25in
textbox2		
	Name	txtCompanyTitle
	Value	AdventureWorks Inc.
	Color	Blue
	TextAlign	Right
	Size	2.5in, 0.25in
textbox3		
	Name	txtPrintDate
	Value	="Print Date: " & Today
	Size	2.5in, 0.25in
textbox4		
	Name	txtPageNumber
	Value	="Page: " & Globals!PageNumber & "/" & Globals!TotalPages
	Color	DarkBlue
	Size	3.75in, 0.25in
line1		
	Name	lineFooter
	LineWidth	2pt

Designing the Body Section

We have come about halfway to being able to see the results of our effort. Now is the time to work on the body section. You'll notice that the body section is a little different in all aspects than the header or footer. So far, we have used the text box and line items; now, let's say "hello" to the table item.

Let's start by dragging Report Items ➤ Table from the toolbox and dropping it inside the body section in the report designer. A new table item will be created for you, and it will have default name of table1. Please make sure your report designer resembles the one shown in Figure 4-28.

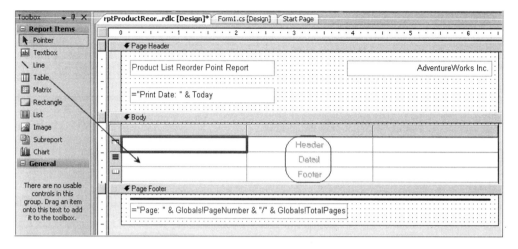

Figure 4-28. *Report designer after dropping a table item*

Dropping the table item will produce a table with three rows and three columns by default. You may also notice that the center column has been labeled: Header, Detail and Footer (wow, another set of header, detail (body), and footer sections!). Rows inside the table are given the names TableRow1 to TableRow3. Similarly, columns are given the names TableColumn1 to TableColumn3. Figure 4-29 points out the row, column, and cell information of a table item.

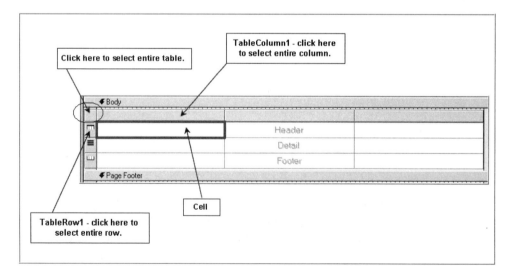

Figure 4-29. *Row, column, and cell information for a table report item*

Would you be surprised if I told you that a table item is nothing but bunch of text box items attached together? Yes, each and every cell in table item is like a text box item, which means you can either type static text in it or specify a dynamic expression. So, by adding a table item to our report, we have actually added nine text box items.

You might be wondering why can't I just put nine text boxes here instead of the table? Well, the simple reason behind this is that the table item acts like a data region and has binding information to the data table. On the other hand, a text box can only have static text or dynamic field-level values.

Before we start working on the table item, let's see how many columns we have inside the table. We have three, and the requirements say we need four. We can add as many columns as we want to the initial three columns, and columns can be deleted or can be cut and pasted to rearrange the order.

To add a column, right-click the right-most column header on the table, and select "Insert Column to the Right" (see Figure 4-30). The width of the report is changed as a result of adding a new column. We can resize all columns to fit the report width per report demand.

The rule about how much width each column should have is simple: Check the length of data the column carries. For example, if your column only produces "Yes/No", adjust the width so that it can accommodate three characters.

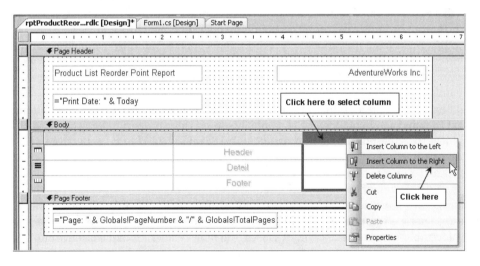

Figure 4-30. *Adding a new column to a table item*

After adding the new column, your report should look like the one shown in Figure 4-31. In Figure 4-31, you'll also notice that I've moved the table to the right side to align it with the report header text boxes. You can do this easily: click the left-most corner of the table to select the entire table (see Figure 4-29), and use the right arrow to move to the right. I've also set the Width properties of TableColumn1 to TableColumn4 to 1.24 inches, 3 inches, 1 inch, and 1 inch, respectively.

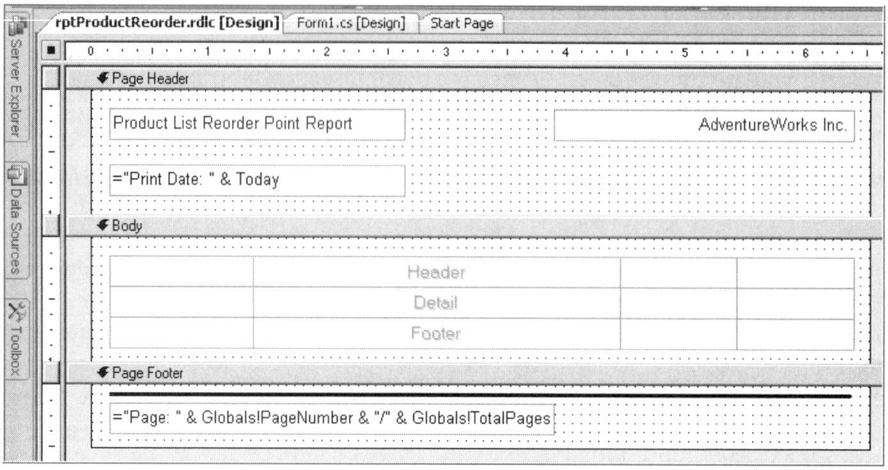

Figure 4-31. *Report layout after putting all the required report items*

We arrange the content of the table item similar to the way we do it with spreadsheet programs like Excel. We can drag the border to increase or decrease the size of each cell text box. Text boxes can be individually formatted and can have different looks and feels.

Previously, we have set the properties of report items, such as Value, by manually entering the text. We can do the same for a table item, too. However, as this is our first project, I say we take it easy and use a shortcut method that will do most of the work for us. We have plenty of projects coming our way to practice setting values manually.

What I meant by shortcut is this: for each column, we need to set two things—the column header and column value. Now, instead of manually setting Value properties for each them, we can achieve the same effect by simply dragging and dropping the column entity from the Data Source toolbox.

Let's start by dragging Data Source ➤ dsProductReorder ➤ ProductNumber and dropping it inside the first column of the table item's detail section. Please repeat this task for all the columns from dsProductReorder. While you are doing this, you'll also notice that the column header is automatically populated with the field name. For example, when you drag and drop ProductNumber into the details row of table1, the table header for that column automatically gets populated with the text "Product Number".

You'll also notice that as soon as you drag and drop ReorderPoint, the title "Reorder Point" is added, and the alignment set to Right. This is because, when you drag and drop, if the data field is numerical, it gets set to right alignment automatically.

Please make sure your report designer looks like the one shown in Figure 4-32. Also spend some time clicking each cell in the table to verify that it does have proper Values set according to Table 4-6.

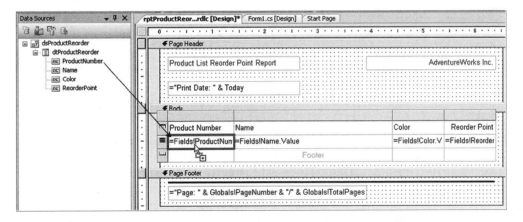

Figure 4-32. *Report layout after setting the table item with the content of the dataset*

Table 4-6. *Table Item Properties*

Report Item	Property	Value
textbox1	Value	ProductNumber
textbox2	Value	Name
textbox3	Value	Color
textbox10	Value	Reorder Point
textbox10	TextAlign	Right
ProductNumebr	Value	=Fields!ProductNumber.Value
Name	Value	=Fields!Name.Value
Color	Value	=Fields!Color.Value
ReorderPoint	Value	=Fields!ReorderPoint.Value
ReorderPoint	TextAlign	Right
ReorderPoint	Format	N
table1	DataSetName	dsProductReorder_dtProductReorder
TableRow1	Color	Green
TableRow1	Font	10pt, Bold
TableRow1	BorderStyle	None, , , Solid, Solid

You may notice some strange stuff in Table 4-6, and that is not surprising. As you may notice, when you drag a column from the dataset to table1, the process changes the Value property of the text box. However, the Name property stays as its default—that's why you see textbox1, textbox10, and so on. At the same time, both the Name and Value properties of the table1 detail row (TableRow2) are changed automatically for you. To set the last three properties that apply to TableRow1, see the next section, which talks about beautification.

> **■Note** The DataSetName property of the table Item is set automatically to the source dataset from which all the columns are dragged and dropped.

Beautification

Who doesn't like beauty? A good report is not just presenting information but also presenting it as a beautiful work of art. Some may not pay much attention to the appearance of a report, but the fact is that it is of equal importance to the reported data. Deciding what kind of font and color combination must be used to present data on the report is very important, and many organizations have set guidelines as to how reports should look and feel.

Before we start writing the C# code to populate the dataset and bind the report to the ReportViewer, let's apply some basic beautification to our first art work. Select the entire row of column names inside table1, and apply the format shown in Figure 4-33.

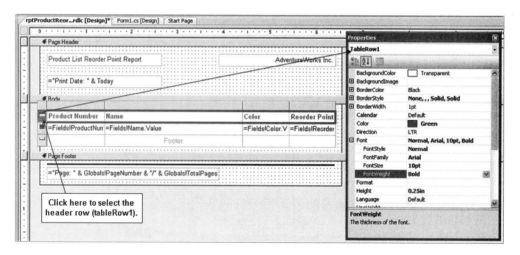

Figure 4-33. *Apply some formatting to the table item.*

Step 3: Writing C# Code

All right, we're 75 percent finished with the project. The final 25 percent is writing the code and running it to make sure your report looks as pretty as shown in Figure 4-11. So, for the absolute beginner, the million dollar question will be, "Where do I write the code?"

For most of the reporting projects we'll do in this book, the place to write code is under the load event. However, there are projects that take user input and pass it on to a report; in such cases, we'll end up writing code behind some other event, for example, a button click event.

Let's start by double-clicking Form1 inside the project. This should open Form1 in design mode. Right-click anywhere on Form1, and select View Code, as shown in Figure 4-34.

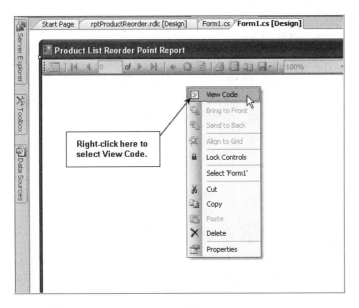

Figure 4-34. *Steps to access the load event of Form1*

Please get rid of any default code inside the form load event, and make sure the entire code behind the `Form1.cs` looks like following:

```
using System;
using System.Collections.Generic;
using System.ComponentModel;
using System.Data;
using System.Drawing;
using System.Text;
using System.Windows.Forms;
using System.Data.SqlClient;
using Microsoft.Reporting.WinForms;

namespace ProductReorder
{
    public partial class Form1 : Form
    {
        public Form1()
        {
            InitializeComponent();
        }

        private void Form1_Load(object sender, EventArgs e)
        {
```

```csharp
//declare connection string, please substitute
//DataSource with your Server name
string cnString = "Data Source=(local);➥
Initial Catalog=RealWorld;Integrated Security=SSPI;";

//declare Connection, command and other related objects
SqlConnection conReport = new SqlConnection(cnString);
SqlCommand cmdReport = new SqlCommand();
SqlDataReader drReport;
DataSet dsReport = new dsProductReorder();

try
{
    //open connection
    conReport.Open();

    //prepare connection object to get the data
    //through reader and populate into dataset
    cmdReport.CommandType = CommandType.Text;
    cmdReport.Connection = conReport;
    cmdReport.CommandText = "Select * FROM dbo.ProductReorder";

    //read data from command object
    drReport = cmdReport.ExecuteReader();

    //load data directly from reader to dataset
    dsReport.Tables[0].Load(drReport);

    //close reader and connection
    drReport.Close();
    conReport.Close();

    //provide local report information to viewer
    reportViewer1.LocalReport.ReportEmbeddedResource =➥
        "ProductReorder.rptProductReorder.rdlc";

    //prepare report data source
    ReportDataSource rds = new ReportDataSource();
    rds.Name = "dsProductReorder_dtProductReorder";
    rds.Value = dsReport.Tables[0];
    reportViewer1.LocalReport.DataSources.Add(rds);
```

```
                    //load report viewer
                    reportViewer1.RefreshReport();
                }
                catch (Exception ex)
                {
                    //display generic error message back to user
                    MessageBox.Show(ex.Message);
                }
                finally
                {
                    //check if connection is still open then attempt to close it
                    if (conReport.State == ConnectionState.Open)
                    {
                        conReport.Close();
                    }
                }
            }
        }
}
```

■**Note** Please make sure to properly set the connection string. You might have a different name for the data source.

In this example, we used the same ADO.NET interface that we discussed in Chapter 3. First, we must make sure that we make reference to the following assemblies:

```
using System.Data.SqlClient;
using Microsoft.Reporting.WinForms;
```

We need functionality from these assemblies to communicate with SQL Server and ReportViewer. As you can see, we start with connecting to the RealWorld database. Once the connection is established, we request all rows from the ProductReorder table.

After this, we collect the data into our typed dataset dsProductReorder and bind the dataset to the ReportViewer. Finally, we ask the reporting engine to process our report and produce the output.

Let the Show Begin

Hurray! We're finished with all the hard work; it's time to reap the fruit. Let's build the project and see if our report produces results similar to those shown in Figure 4-11. So, fingers crossed? Press F5 on your keyboard.

I assume at this moment that your code has no compile-level error, which will prevent the build from happening. Now, go ahead and check to see how the result looks. I can imagine two typical scenarios: either you're throwing your hands in the air and yelling "yes," or you're quietly whispering "oops."

In either case, I'm with you. If you said "Yes," then congratulations; you've done it. This is just the beginning; soon, you'll find yourself cracking very cool reports. Now, if you said "oops," then I'd advise you not to walk but to run to the "Troubleshooting" section of this chapter. If that is also not helpful, go over the steps again carefully or, if possible, do the steps again from scratch.

Moving On to the Next Project

Before we start with our next project, I'd like to discuss the mechanism we'll use. All projects from this point onward will not have screen shots for each and every step involved as you have seen in this first example. If you need to know, for example, how to add a dataset to a report later, you may revisit the first project of this chapter as many times you like to refer to the steps. Instead of repeating the same steps in every project, I'll bring in more techniques and screenshots to support them.

Are you ready? Any guess as to what the next project is? Well, I won't prolong the suspense here—the next project is another simple report called Customer Address List. What makes this report interesting is that we are going to use the multicolumn reporting feature of RS to develop this report.

Customer Address List Report

Assume you're working for AdventureWorks Incorporated as a developer; you've been asked to develop a Customer Address List report. This report should be done in two-column format to save space on paper. The report should list customer addresses in common mailing list format: customer name, address, city, state/province, postal code, and country. The report should meet all characteristics described in Table 4-7, and the report output should match Figure 4-35.

Table 4-7. *Report Characteristics*

Characteristics	Value
Data source	AddressList
Columns to report	CustomerName, AddressLine, City, StateProvince, PostalCode, Country
Page size	Letter
Page orientation	Portrait
Number of columns	2

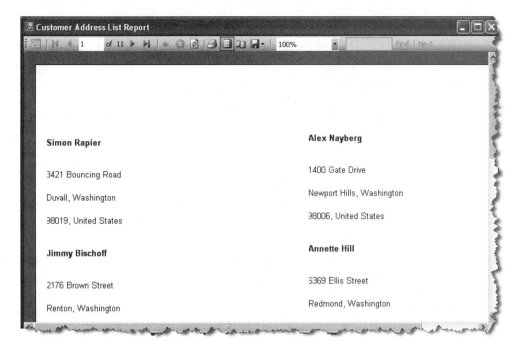

Figure 4-35. *The two-column Customer Address List report*

You might notice the some edges of the text in Figure 4-35 appear to be cut off; this only happens when previewing multicolumn report output. However, if you print the report, the report on paper comes out nice, without any cut-off edges.

Business Case

A customer address list is a common report used by small and large businesses alike. There are many uses for this report. For example, the output generated by this report can be used as address labels for mass mailings.

Using the Multicolumn Capabilities of RS

This report is one of the perfect cases to apply the multicolumn capabilities of RS. Imagine if you are dealing with a large customer base. Now, if you print five addresses on one page instead of ten addresses, as you can using multiple columns, you are wasting space; you could've used half the number of pages.

The multicolumn feature saves space on the report by making the data flow into the adjacent column, similar to a newspaper layout. You can define as many columns you want. Although you can use any report item in a multicolumn report, the best option is to make use of a report item that uses data regions, like a list item. For our report, we will make use of list and text box items to list the customer addresses.

Creating a Windows Forms Project

Please open Visual Studio, and use the following steps, illustrated in Figure 4-1, to create a Windows application project:

1. Click File ➤ New ➤ Project, or press the hot keys Ctrl+Shift+N.

2. In the "Project types" pane of the New Project dialog box, select Visual C# ➤ Windows.

3. In the Templates pane, select Windows Application.

4. Please give the application a name; I've called the project AddressList. You may choose a different location for storing the application files according to your preference.

5. Click the OK button to finish the process. After you click OK, Visual Studio will create a new Windows application project. You'll also notice that a new form with the name Form1 is part of the project.

Now it's time to add the dataset and ReportViewer to the project. Let's start by selecting the project in Solution Explorer. Right-click it, and select Add ➤ New Item ➤ DataSet. Please name the dataset dsAddressList. Before you add the ReportViewer, please make sure Form1 is open in the designer. Now, let's add the ReportViewer to the project from the drag and drop toolbox by selecting Data ➤ ReportViewer. Please make sure you set the properties listed in Table 4-8.

Table 4-8. *Property Settings for the Address List Project*

Object	Property	Value
Form1	Text	Customer Address List Report
Form1	Size	775, 500
reportViewer1	Dock	Fill

Step 1: Creating a Data Table

Since we already have the dataset in the project, it's time to add a data table to it. Please use the following steps to add a data table inside the dataset:

1. You can go to the dataset designer in two ways: double-click dsAddressList inside Solution Explorer, or right-click the dsAddressList node and select View Designer.

2. Let's add the data table by right-clicking the design surface and selecting Add ➤ DataTable.

3. Click the header of the newly created data table, and name it dtAddressList. Let's start adding columns to dtAddressList by right-clicking the data table and selecting Add ➤ Column.

4. Please add the following columns into the data table, which should then look similar to Figure 4-36:

- CustomerName (System.String)

- AddressLine (System.String)

- City (System.String)

- StateProvince (System.String)

- PostalCode (System.String)

- Country (System.String)

Figure 4-36. *Final look of the dtAddressList data table*

Step 2: Designing the Report Layout

As you know, we're going to use the multicolumn layout for this report. To list the details for customer addresses, we will use the list item. Each customer address consists of four lines of information. We will use four text box items to represent each customer address.

All right, we have our dataset in place, with the data table and all necessary columns. We're all set to start working on designing the report layout. Add the report by selecting the project in Solution Explorer and right-clicking it; select Add ➤ New Item, and select Report from the Add New Item dialog box. Please name the report rptAddressList.rdlc. Click the Add button to complete the process and make the new report part of the project.

Before we move to work on setting up the page, let me ask you to change the Size property of the body section to 3.25in, 2in, as shown in Figure 4-37. Why are we doing this? As you know, we are going to have two columns in this report; therefore, I am splitting the page into two sections of 3.25 inches each.

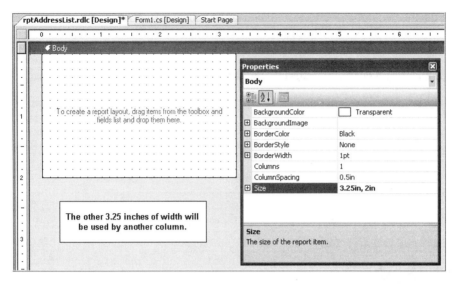

Figure 4-37. *Changing the size of the body section before setting up the multicolumn option*

Setting Up the Page

For this report, we need to pay a little extra attention to page setup. Right-click the open area inside the design surface, and select Properties. Once the Report Properties dialog box is visible, go to the Layout tab. From the Layout tab, we need to make sure the report is letter size and has a portrait page orientation. Please make sure the page width and height are set to 8.5 inches and 11 inches respectively.

To set up the report to have multiple columns, increase the Columns field to 2 (instead of the default of 1). Change the spacing to 0.25in. Finally, before clicking the OK button, make sure to set the right and left margins to 0. Please see Figure 4-38 for an illustration of the page layout setup.

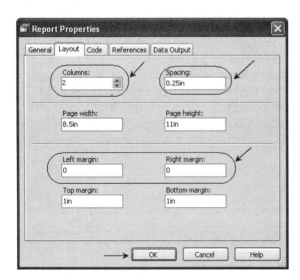

Figure 4-38. *Setting up page layout for a two-column report*

After you finish the steps shown in Figure 4-38, how does the report design surface look? If you are thinking the design surface will be split into two columns, you are right. However, to see the changed report design surface, you need to close and reopen the report designer. Please make sure your report design looks similar to the one in Figure 4-39.

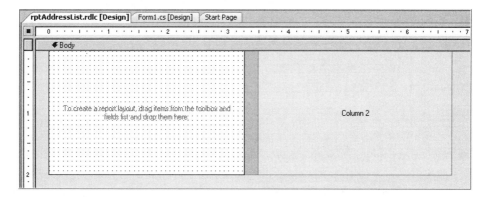

Figure 4-39. *Report design surface with two columns*

Designing the Body Section

Since we are going to put everything in the body section, this report doesn't need the header and footer. Let's start the design process now. Please drag and drop the following report items inside the body section (please make sure to drag and drop the text boxes inside the list):

- A List item for listing the address details
- A TextBox item for the customer name
- A TextBox item for the address line
- A TextBox item for the city and province/state
- A TextBox item for the postal code and country

Your report design should look similar to Figure 4-40 after adding all the needed report items.

Now that we have the report items ready, you may choose your favorite method to map the data table's columns to the text box report items: type an expression or drag and drop from the data source. I suggest dragging and dropping the first column's data source: drag Data Source ➤ dsAddressList ➤ CustomerName and drop it inside the first text box inside the list item.

For rest of the columns, I'd advise you to type inside the text boxes, as the last two values are expressions with a combination of values from different data columns. Please make sure you set the properties of all report items according to the information provided in Table 4-9. Your final report design surface should look similar to Figure 4-41.

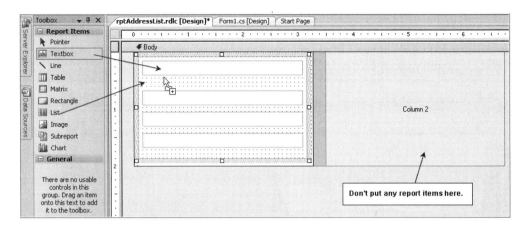

Figure 4-40. *The report design surface after adding report items*

Table 4-9. *Report Item Properties for the Header*

Report Item	Property	Value
list1		
	Size	3.075in, 1.8in
	DataSetName	dsAddressList_dtAddressList
textbox1		
	Value	=Fields!CustomerName.Value
	Font	Normal, Arial, 10pt, Bold
textbox2		
	Value	=Fields!AddressLine.Value
textbox3		
	Value	=Fields!City.Value + ", " + Fields!StateProvince.Value
textbox4		
	Value	=Fields!PostalCode.Value + ", " + Fields!Country.Value

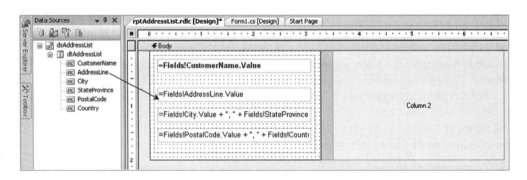

Figure 4-41. *The final look of the report design surface*

As you can see in Figure 4-41, we have four address lines. The first line lists the name of the customer, and I changed the style to bold so that the customer name is distinct. For the last two lines, I concatenated the data column values so that related information stays on the same line. All right, that's what we needed as a design for this report. Now, it's the time to move on to writing the C# code.

Step 3: Writing the C# Code

Since that's all we need on the front end of the report design, let's add the following code behind `Form1.cs` to see the address list report in action:

```
using System;
using System.Collections.Generic;
using System.ComponentModel;
using System.Data;
using System.Drawing;
using System.Text;
using System.Windows.Forms;
using System.Data.SqlClient;
using Microsoft.Reporting.WinForms;

namespace AddressList
{
    public partial class Form1 : Form
    {
        public Form1()
        {
            InitializeComponent();
        }

        private void Form1_Load(object sender, EventArgs e)
        {
            //declare connection string, please substitute
            //DataSource with your Server name
            string cnString = "Data Source=(local);Initial Catalog=RealWorld;➥
                    Integrated Security=SSPI;";

            //declare Connection, command and other related objects
            SqlConnection conReport = new SqlConnection(cnString);
            SqlCommand cmdReport = new SqlCommand();
            SqlDataReader drReport;
            DataSet dsReport = new dsAddressList();

            try
            {
                //open connection
                conReport.Open();
```

```
            //prepare connection object to get the data
            //through reader and populate into dataset
            cmdReport.CommandType = CommandType.Text;
            cmdReport.Connection = conReport;
            cmdReport.CommandText = "Select * FROM dbo.AddressList";

            //read data from command object
            drReport = cmdReport.ExecuteReader();

            //load data directly from reader to dataset
            dsReport.Tables[0].Load(drReport);

            //close reader and connection
            drReport.Close();
            conReport.Close();

            //provide local report information to viewer
            reportViewer1.LocalReport.ReportEmbeddedResource =➾
                    "AddressList.rptAddressList.rdlc";

            // you need to set this to show multi column output in report viewer
            reportViewer1.SetDisplayMode(DisplayMode.PrintLayout);

            // set the zoom mode of report viewer to 100%
            reportViewer1.ZoomMode = ZoomMode.Percent;
            reportViewer1.ZoomPercent = 100;

            //prepare report data source
            ReportDataSource rds = new ReportDataSource();
            rds.Name = "dsAddressList_dtAddressList";
            rds.Value = dsReport.Tables[0];
            reportViewer1.LocalReport.DataSources.Add(rds);

            //load report viewer
            reportViewer1.RefreshReport();
        }
        catch (Exception ex)
        {
            //display generic error message back to user
            MessageBox.Show(ex.Message);
        }
        finally
        {
            //check if connection is still open then attempt to close it
            if (conReport.State == ConnectionState.Open)
```

```
        {
            conReport.Close();
        }
      }
    }
  }
}
```

This code is almost the same as we had in our earlier example. The only change is that we get the data from a different table from the RealWorld database. Having said that, I'd like to bring your attention to the following lines of code:

```
// you need to set this to show multi-column output in report viewer
reportViewer1.SetDisplayMode(DisplayMode.PrintLayout);
// set the zoom mode of report viewer to 100%
reportViewer1.ZoomMode = ZoomMode.Percent;
reportViewer1.ZoomPercent = 100;
```

We need this code to make sure the report preview shows both the columns. Usually, we use the normal display mode. However, for this report we have set the display mode to PrintLayout. We have also set the zoom mode to percent, and set the percent value to 100. After applying these settings, you can see the report output in ReportViewer as it will appear on a printer or in a PDF and Excel file.

■**Note** A multicolumn report will not appear correctly if the ReportViewer display mode is set to normal (the default mode).

Building the Project

It's time to build the project now. You can click the small, green play button in the main tool-box or press F5 on the keyboard to start the application in run-time mode. If the program compiles without any errors, you will see the form with the report in preview mode. Please make sure the report looks similar to Figure 4-35.

■**Note** Multicolumn report render support is limited to PDF and Excel if you are using ASP.NET Web Forms as client.

So, how do you like the reporting projects so far? Easy reports, right? Well, I think so too. Let's develop a report that is a little bit more challenging now. How about a report that uses data with a master/detail relationship? In the next report, I'll show you not only how to report on master/detail data but also how to use the subreport feature of RS.

Stock Inventory Transfer Report

Assume you're working for AdventureWorks Incorporated as a developer; you've been asked to develop a Stock Inventory Transfer report. This report should gather data from two tables that have a master/details relationship. The report should meet all characteristics described in Table 4-10, and the report output should match Figure 4-42.

Table 4-10. *Report Characteristics*

Characteristics	Value
Report title	Stock Inventory Transfer Report (Header--Left)
Page number	Page: n/n (Header--Left)
Data source	TransferHeader, TransferDetail
Columns to report	TransferHeader: TransferID, DateOfTransfer, FromBranch, ToBranch TransferDetail: TransferID, ProductID, ProductName, UnitQuantity, UnitCost
Page size	Letter
Page orientation	Portrait
Subreport	rptTransferDetails

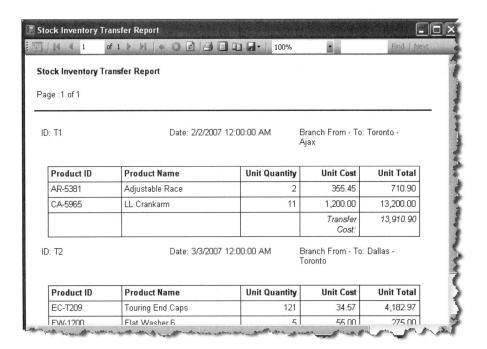

Figure 4-42. *Stock Inventory Transfer report*

Business Case

The Stock Inventory Transfer report is commonly used by various departments to keep track of stock movement among physical locations, as it is common for big companies to have multiple branches that keep stock. In this example, this report is helpful to find out how much stock is transferred from one branch to another.

Depending on sales, stock levels vary from branch to branch for any product. A company keeps track of stock levels as a whole for all the branches. And if any given branch is running low or out of stock for any product, the company can look for those products at other branches and perform an internal transfer of the stock. Transferring stock usually means that a certain quantity of a product is transferred between two branches. If there are any internal payables and receivables set up among branches, the total value of the stock transfer is also important.

Using the Subreport Feature

Subreport is a neat feature from RS to report on data that has master/details relationship. The master/details relationship is also commonly known as a parent/child or header/details relationship between two tables. In this example, our main report will list data from the header table and the subreport will list detail data. The key between these two tables is TransferID.

Simply put, the subreport feature of RS is an additional report that is embedded into a report. We can link the contents of the subreport with the main report using the parameters.

A subreport is also powerful in that it can gather data from a totally different source and link it up with the main report. For example, a main report can list employees' financial information from a SQL Server data source. With the help of a subreport, those same employees' payroll details can be gathered from an HR system that is an Oracle data source. The employee ID will be used as the key to link up the data.

Creating the Windows Forms Project

Please open Visual Studio, and use the following steps to create a Windows application project; refer to Figure 4-1 for an illustration of these steps:

1. Click File ➤ New ➤ Project, or you can press the hot keys Ctrl+Shift+N.

2. In the "Project types" pane of New Project dialog box, select Visual C# ➤ Windows.

3. In the Templates pane, select Windows Application.

4. Please give the application a name; I've called the project Transfer. You may choose a different location for storing the application files according to your preference.

5. Click the OK button to finish the process; Visual Studio will create a new Windows application project. Also notice that a new form with the name Form1 is part of the project.

Let's next add the dataset and ReportViewer to the project. Select the project in Solution Explorer, right-click it, and select Add ➤ New Item ➤ DataSet. Please name the dataset dsTransfer. Before you add the ReportViewer, make sure Form1 is open in the designer.

Now, add the ReportViewer to the project by selecting Data ➤ ReportViewer and dragging and dropping it onto the design surface.

Please set the properties in Table 4-11.

Table 4-11. *Property Settings for the Oracle Project*

Object	Property	Value
Form1		
	Text	Stock Inventory Transfer Report
	Size	790, 500
reportViewer1		
	Dock	Fill

Step 1: Creating the Data Tables

Usually, we need one data table; however, in this report we need two different data tables inside the dataset dsTransfer. We need one data table to store data related to the header (transfer information) and a second to store the data related to details (product details).

Creating the Header Table

Please use the following steps to add the header data table inside the dataset:

1. You can go to the dataset designer in two ways: double-click dsTransfer inside Solution Explorer, or right-click dsTransfer node and select View Designer.

2. To add the data table, right-click the design surface, and select Add ➤ DataTable.

3. Click the header of the newly created data table, and name it dsTransferHeader. Add columns to dsTransferHeader by right-clicking DataTable and selecting Add ➤ Column.

4. Add the following columns into the data table; your data table should look like Figure 4-43:

   • TransferID (System.String)

   • DateOfTransfer (System.DateTime)

   • FromBranch (System.String)

   • ToBranch (System.String)

Figure 4-43. *Final look of the data table dtTransferHeader*

Creating the Detail Table

Please use the following steps to add the detail data table inside the dataset:

1. You can go to the dataset designer in two ways: double-click dsTransfer inside Solution Explorer, or right-click dsTransfer node and select View Designer.

2. To add the data table, right-click the design surface, and select Add ➤ DataTable.

3. Click the Header of the newly created data table, and name it dsTransferDetail. Add columns to dsTransferDetail by right-clicking DataTable and selecting Add ➤ Column.

4. Add the following columns into the data table; your data table should look like Figure 4-44:

   • TransferID (System.String)

   • ProductID (System.DateTime)

   • ProductName (System.String)

   • UnitQuantity (System.Int32)

   • UnitCost (System.Decimal)

Figure 4-44. *Final look of the data table dtTransferDetail*

After adding both the data tables, please make sure your dataset design surface looks similar to Figure 4-45.

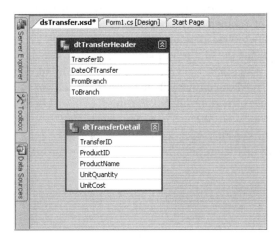

Figure 4-45. *Final look of the dataset dsTransfer*

Step 2: Designing the Report Layout

This report is like two reports in one; the subreport is embedded inside the main report. Let's call the main report the header report (which contains the transfer number, transfer date, and branch information) and the subreport the detail report (which contains the details for products that are being transferred). Both these reports have different layouts. Therefore, we will discuss them separately. Let's design the detail report first.

Designing the Layout for the Detail Report

If you look at Figure 4-42, the area that shows the product details is the result of our detail report. The layout of this report is simple; all we need to do is make use of the table report item. Since this report is going to be used as a subreport, we will need to do some special treatment, which I'll discuss later on.

Before we start designing the report layout, let's add the report to the project. As before, add the report by selecting the project in Solution Explorer, right-clicking it, and selecting Add ➤ New Item. Select Report from the Add New Item dialog box, and name the report rptTransferDetails.rdlc. Click the Add button to complete the process; a new report is now part of the project. We don't need any header or footer for this report. Stock transfer details are listed using the body section of the report.

Setting Up the Page

No special consideration is needed as far as page setup is concerned for this report. Just make sure the report is letter sized and has the portrait page orientation by right-clicking the open area inside the design surface and selecting Properties. Also, you may wish to put your name in the Author field and fill in the Description field.

Designing the Body Section

Recall that we will make use of a table report item here in the body section? Let's start working on this section by dragging Report Items ➤ Table and dropping it inside the body section in the report designer. A new table item is part of the report now, and it has the default name of table1. As usual, three columns are added for us, but we need two more columns. Please add two more columns to the right side (Figure 4-30 shows how to add columns), and make sure your report design surface looks similar to the one shown in Figure 4-46.

The table needs data mapping from our data tables; therefore, select Data Source ➤ dsTransfer ➤ ProductID and drag and drop it inside the first column of the table item's detail section (TableRow2). Repeat this task for ProductName, UnitQuantity, and UnitCost. How about the last column; what should its value be? Well, the last column will have the result derived by multiplying the UnitQuantity and UnitCost. The expression will look like this: =Fields!UnitQuantity.Value * Fields!UnitCost.Value. We also need the total cost of the transfer; for that, we will use the last two columns of the tabel1 footer (TableRow3).

After mapping the data, make sure to apply all the property settings of table1 according to Table 4-12.

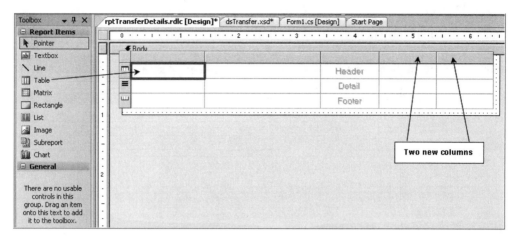

Figure 4-46. *Report design surface after adding a table report item*

Table 4-12. *Table Item Properties for the Body Section*

Table Item	Property	Value
table1	BorderStyle	Solid
All text boxes inside table1	BorderStyle	Solid
TableRow1	Font	Normal, Arial, 10pt, Bold
TableRow1 ➤ Column1	Value	Product ID
TableRow1 ➤ Column2	Value	Product Name
TableRow1 ➤ Column3	Value	Unit Quantity
TableRow1 ➤ Column3	TextAlign	Right
TableRow1 ➤ Column4	Value	Unit Cost
TableRow1 ➤ Column4	TextAlign	Right
TableRow1 ➤ Column5	Value	Unit Total
TableRow1 ➤ Column5	TextAlign	Right
TableRow1 ➤ Column5	Format	N
TableRow2 ➤ Column1	Value	=Fields!ProductID.Value
TableRow2 ➤ Column2	Value	=Fields!ProductName.Value
TableRow2 ➤ Column3	Value	=Fields!UnitQuantity.Value
TableRow2 ➤ Column3	Format	N0 (zero, 0, for no decimal)
TableRow2 ➤ Column4	Value	=Fields!UnitCost.Value
TableRow2 ➤ Column4	Format	N
TableRow2 ➤ Column5	Value	=Fields!UnitQuantity.Value * Fields!UnitCost.Value
TableRow2 ➤ Column5	Format	N
TableRow3	Font	Italic, Arial, 10pt, Normal
TableRow3 ➤ Column4	Value	Transfer Cost:
TableRow3 ➤ Column4	TextAlign	Right
TableRow3 ➤ Column5	Value	=SUM(Fields!UnitQuantity.Value * Fields!UnitCost.Value)

That's it. Our report design is ready now. Please make sure your final report design looks similar to the one shown in Figure 4-47.

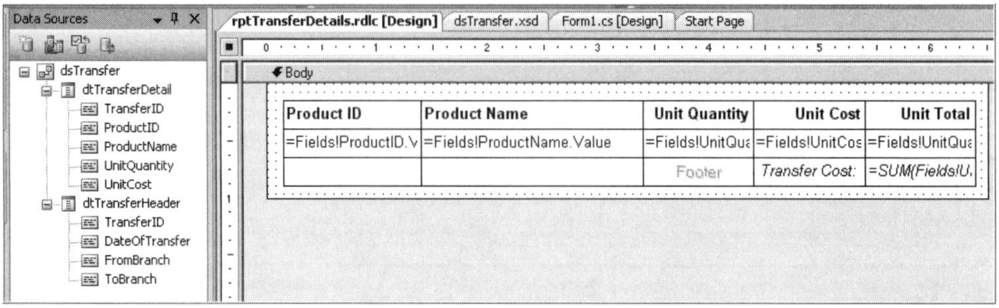

Figure 4-47. *Final look of report design*

The last step left here in this report design is to add a report parameter. Why do we need a report parameter? If you recall, I said in the introduction that report parameters are good mechanisms to pass dynamic information to the report. This dynamic information will be the TransferID in our case. We will pass the TransferID from the header report, which will be used to filter out only the needed products belonging to each transfer.

Adding a report parameter is easy. Let me show you how. Use the following steps to add a report parameter (see the illustration in Figure 4-48):

1. Right-click the gray open area in the report designer, and select Report Parameters.

2. Click the Add button from inside the Report Parameters dialog box.

3. Name the parameter parTransferID; for the prompt, type **Transfer ID**.

4. Click the OK button to complete the process.

All right, we've got the report parameter ready. Now what? Let's make use if it. We will use the report parameter to filter the data from the details table. We need to apply the filter on table1. To set up the filter, use the following steps (see Figure 4-49):

1. Right-click table1, and select Properties.

2. Select the Filters tab from the Table Properties dialog box.

3. Set the Filter List Express to =Fields!TransferID.Value. For Operator, select the equals sign (=), and set the Filter value to =Parameters!parTransferID.Value.

4. Click the OK button to complete the process.

That's it. We are finished with our detail report now. Let's move on to designing the header report, in which we will embed our detail report using a subreport report item.

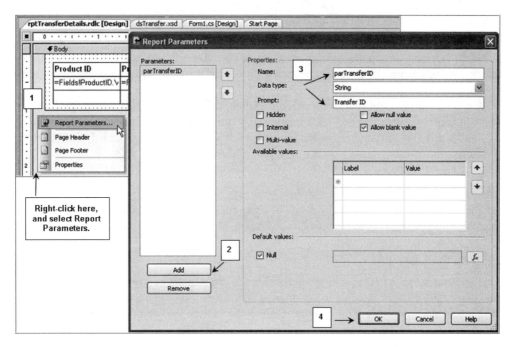

Figure 4-48. *Adding the report parameter*

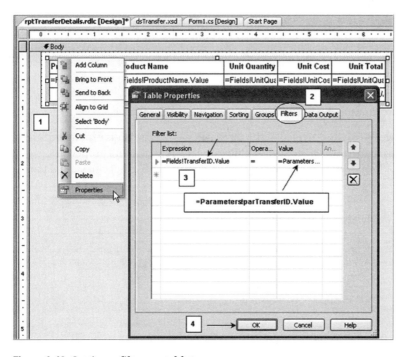

Figure 4-49. *Setting a filter on table1*

Designing the Layout for the Header Report

If you look at Figure 4-42, we have two report sections, a header and a body. The header section has the report title and page numbers. The body section will list the transfer information such as transfer ID, transfer date, and branch information. The product details will come from our subreport, which we have already designed.

Before we start designing the report layout, let's add the report to the project. Select the project in Solution Explorer, right-click it, and select Add ➤ New Item. Select Report from the Add New Item dialog box, and name the report rptTransferHeader.rdlc. Click the Add button to complete the process; a new report is now part of the project.

Adding a Header

Let's add the header to the report, as usual, by right-clicking the open area inside the report designer and selecting Page Header (refer to Figure 4-19).

Setting Up the Page

As in the other projects in this chapter, make sure the report is letter sized and has the portrait page orientation by right-clicking the open area inside the design surface and selecting Properties. As usual, you may wish to put your name in the Author field and fill in the Description field.

Designing the Page Header

We'll start working on the header now. Please drag and drop the following report items inside the header section:

- A TextBox item for the report title

- A TextBox item for the page number

- A Line item for separating the header section from the detail section

Report item properties can be changed in the same ways as the previous examples. Select each of the report items in turn, and specify the values for each report item's properties according to Table 4-13. Your report design surface, after completing the header, should look similar to Figure 4-50.

Table 4-13. *Report Item Properties for the Header*

Report Item	Property	Value
textbox1		
	Value	Stock Inventory Transfer Report
	Font	Normal, Arial, 10pt, Bold
textbox2		
	Value	="Page :" & Globals!PageNumber & " of " & Globals!TotalPages
line1		
	LineWidth	2pt

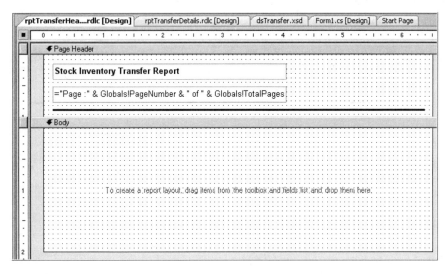

Figure 4-50. *Report design after adding the report header and related report items*

Designing the Body Section

We will introduce a new report item here in the body section. That report item is subreport. Please drag and drop the following report items inside the body section:

- A List item for transfer information

- A TextBox item for the transfer id (inside the list item)

- A TextBox item for the transfer date (inside the list item)

- A TextBox item for the branch from/to (inside the list item)

- A Subreport item for product details (inside the list item)

Select each of the report items in turn, and specify the values for each report item's properties according to Table 4-14. Your report design surface, after completing the detail section, should look similar to Figure 4-51.

Table 4-14. *Report Item Properties for the Details*

Report Item	Property	Value
textbox3		
	Value	= "ID: " & Fields!TransferID.Value
textbox4		
	Value	= "Date: " & Fields!DateOfTransfer.Value.ToString()
textbox5		
	Value	= "Branch From - To: " & Fields!FromBranch.Value & " - " & Fields!ToBranch.Value
ist1		
	DataSetName	dsTransfer_dtTransferHeader

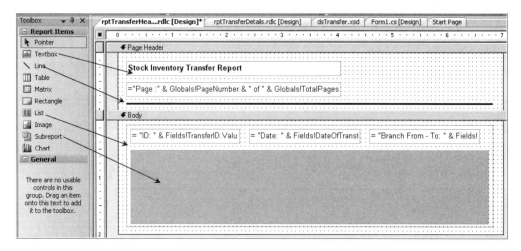

Figure 4-51. *Report Body section after adding all report items*

So far, we've just added the subreport item. Now, we need to configure it so that it takes the TransferID information and returns the product details accordingly. We also need to specify which report must be executed as a subreport.

First, we need to specify which report should be executed by subreport1. To set this, use the following steps (see Figure 4-52):

1. Select subreport1, right-click, and access the Properties dialog box.

2. Under the General tab, type or select Subreport: rptTrasnferDetails.

3. Click the OK button to complete the process.

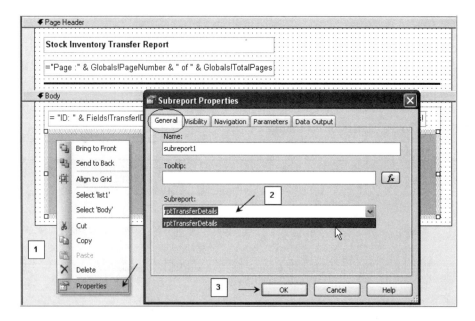

Figure 4-52. *Setting the subreport property*

We have reached the last step in setting up our report now. All we need to do is pass the TransferID as dynamic data to subreport1. If you recall, this information will be used by the table item inside the rptTransferDetails to filter the reported data. To set up passing of dynamic values to a parameter, use the following steps (see Figure 4-53):

1. Select subreport1, right-click, and access the Properties dialog box.

2. From the Parameters tab, set Parameter Name to partTransferID and Parameter Value to Fields!TransferID.Value.

3. Click the OK button to complete the process.

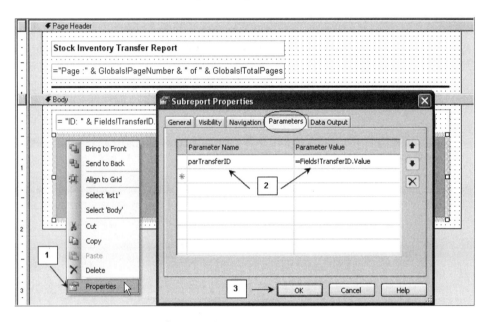

Figure 4-53. *Setting parameter's properties*

Step 3: Writing the C# Code

The code in this report is a little different from the previous examples; we will discuss how in the analysis section following this code. As usual, add the following code behind Form1.cs:

```
using System;
using System.Collections.Generic;
using System.ComponentModel;
using System.Data;
using System.Drawing;
using System.Text;
using System.Windows.Forms;
using System.Data.SqlClient;
using Microsoft.Reporting.WinForms;
```

```csharp
namespace Transfer
{
    public partial class Form1 : Form
    {
        public Form1()
        {
            InitializeComponent();
        }

        // data set at the class level to access by all methods
        DataSet dsReport = new dsTransfer();

        private void Form1_Load(object sender, EventArgs e)
        {
            // connection string
            string cnString = @"Data Source=(local);Initial Catalog=➥
                RealWorld;Integrated Security=SSPI;";

            SqlConnection conReport = new SqlConnection(cnString);
            SqlCommand cmdReport = new SqlCommand();
            SqlDataReader drReport;

            try
            {
                // open connection
                conReport.Open();

                cmdReport.CommandType = CommandType.Text;
                cmdReport.Connection = conReport;

                // get query string from string builder
                cmdReport.CommandText = "SELECT * FROM TransferHeader➥
                    ORDER BY TransferID; SELECT * FROM TransferDetail➥
                    ORDER BY TransferID";

                // execute query and load result to dataset
                drReport = cmdReport.ExecuteReader();

                dsReport.Load(drReport, LoadOption.OverwriteChanges,➥
                        dsReport.Tables[1], dsReport.Tables[0]);

                // close connection
                drReport.Close();
                conReport.Close();
```

```
            // prepare report for view
            reportViewer1.LocalReport.ReportEmbeddedResource =➥
                    "Transfer.rptTransferHeader.rdlc";

            // Add a handler for SubreportProcessing
            reportViewer1.LocalReport.SubreportProcessing➥
                += new SubreportProcessingEventHandler➥
                (SubreportProcessingEventHandler);

            ReportDataSource rds = new ReportDataSource();
            rds.Name = "dsTransfer_dtTransferHeader";

            rds.Value = dsReport.Tables[1];
            reportViewer1.LocalReport.DataSources.Add(rds);

            // preview the report
            reportViewer1.RefreshReport();
        }
        catch (Exception ex)
        {
            MessageBox.Show(ex.Message);
        }
        finally
        {
            if (conReport.State == ConnectionState.Open)
            {
                conReport.Close();
            }
        }
    }

    void SubreportProcessingEventHandler(object sender,➥
        SubreportProcessingEventArgs e)
    {
        e.DataSources.Add(new ReportDataSource("dsTransfer_dtTransferDetail",➥
            dsReport.Tables[0]));
    }
  }
}
```

As I mentioned earlier, this code has a little extra compared with previous examples. I define the dataset outside of the load event of the form to make it available to add the methods from the class.

Since we have two tables to fill in this example, I am sending two separate SQL select statements to the database, which are as follows:

```
cmdReport.CommandText = "SELECT * FROM TransferHeader➥
ORDER BY TransferID; SELECT * FROM TransferDetail➥
ORDER BY TransferID";
```

Next, I load the data from the data reader to the data set by calling the load method like this:

```
dsReport.Load(drReport, LoadOption.OverwriteChanges, dsReport.Tables[1],➥
dsReport.Tables[0]);
```

If you notice, I'm calling the load method and passing some extra parameters to first set the overwrite condition and then pass each table a reference from the dataset to fill. You might be wondering how the subreport manages to get the data. For that I have to create a handle, which looks like the following:

```
reportViewer1.LocalReport.SubreportProcessing +=➥
new SubreportProcessingEventHandler(SubreportProcessingEventHandler);
```

I add this event handler to the SubReportProcessing event of the main report. Then I add another method SubreportProcessingEventHandler, which responds to this event. The code behind my method takes care of getting the data for my subreport. The code inside my method looks like this:

```
e.DataSources.Add(new ReportDataSource("dsTransfer_dtTransferDetail",➥
dsReport.Tables[0]));
```

Excited to see our subreport in action? All right then, let's move on to building the report.

Building the Project

Again, build the project by clicking the small, green play button in the main toolbox or pressing F5. If the program compiles without any errors, you will see the form with the report in preview mode. Please make sure the report looks similar to Figure 4-42.

■**Note** Exporting to both Excel and PDF formats is supported for generating subreport output.

I hope that, as report complexity is growing by each reporting project, your appetite to get more complex stuff is increasing, right? So, let's continue and learn some more rich features of RS. The next example is about developing a cross tabulated report; also known as a pivot or matrix report.

Divisionwise Five Years' Sales Performance

Assume you're working for AdventureWorks Incorporated as a developer; you've been asked to develop a Divisionwise Five Years' Sales Performance report. This report should use the raw net sales data for the last five years for each division. The result should be a cross tabulation of net sales for the last five years (row) and respective divisions (column). The report should meet all characteristics described in Table 4-15, and the report output should match Figure 4-54.

Table 4-15. *Report Characteristics*

Characteristics	Value
Report title	`Divisionwise Five Years' Sales Performance (Body--Left)`
Data source	`DivisionSales`
Columns to report	`DivsionID, YearOfOperation, NetSalesAmount`
Page size	`Letter`
Report type	`Matrix`

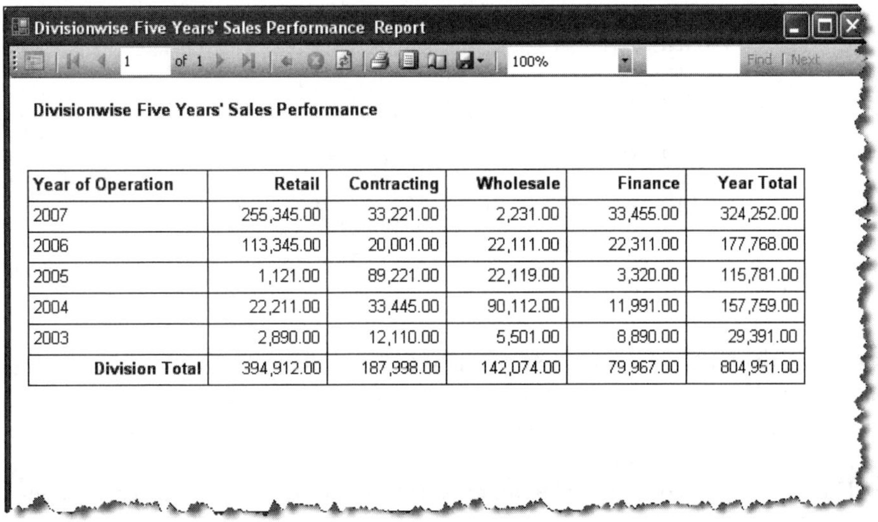

Year of Operation	Retail	Contracting	Wholesale	Finance	Year Total
2007	255,345.00	33,221.00	2,231.00	33,455.00	324,252.00
2006	113,345.00	20,001.00	22,111.00	22,311.00	177,768.00
2005	1,121.00	89,221.00	22,119.00	3,320.00	115,781.00
2004	22,211.00	33,445.00	90,112.00	11,991.00	157,759.00
2003	2,890.00	12,110.00	5,501.00	8,890.00	29,391.00
Division Total	394,912.00	187,998.00	142,074.00	79,967.00	804,951.00

Figure 4-54. *Divisionwise Five Years' Sales Performance report*

Business Case

All businesses want to grow with every passing year. An increase in net sales at the end of year means higher stock values and further chance of growth. Companies that cross-check the current year's data with historical data can better evaluate business trends.

A report like the Divisionwise Five Years' Sales Performance report helps especially the upper management to watch the sales trends for different divisions over time. This could allow them to see if any particular division is underperforming compared with previous years or performing better compared with previous years.

Using the Matrix Feature

Big companies usually keep historical data in data warehouse systems. Data from these kinds of data repositories are usually raw tables with data belonging to several years. For this report, the raw data consists of three columns, and each row is data for one year's worth of net sales for an individual division. Please see Figure 4-55 for a snapshot of the raw data.

DivisionID	YearOfOperation	NetSalesAmount
Retail	2007	255345.0000
Retail	2006	113345.0000
Retail	2005	1121.0000
Retail	2004	22211.0000
Retail	2003	2890.0000
Contracting	2007	33221.0000
Contracting	2006	20001.0000
Contracting	2005	89221.0000
Contracting	2004	33445.0000
Contracting	2003	12110.0000
Wholesale	2007	2231.0000
Wholesale	2006	22111.0000
Wholesale	2005	22119.0000
Wholesale	2004	90112.0000
Wholesale	2003	5501.0000
Finance	2007	33455.0000
Finance	2006	22311.0000
Finance	2005	3320.0000
Finance	2004	11991.0000
Finance	2003	8890.0000

Figure 4-55. *Snapshot of the raw data*

To make sense out of this data, RS has a cool feature of automatically cross tabulating it. We need to use a matrix report item to get this raw data into meaningful pivot table output. The matrix feature is simple to use; all you need is to identify two groups. One group's data becomes the rows and the other group's becomes the columns. In this example, the year of operation will be the rows and divisions the columns. The net sales figures will be cross-tabulated. Now, let me show you how simple creating this kind of report is with RS.

Creating a Windows Forms Project

Please open Visual Studio, and use the following steps, illustrated in Figure 4-1, to create a Windows application project:

1. Click File ➤ New ➤ Project, or press the hot keys Ctrl+Shift+N.

2. In the "Project types" pane of the New Project dialog box, select Visual C# ➤ Windows.

3. In the Templates pane, select Windows Application.

4. Please give the application a name; I've called the project DivisionSales. You may choose a different location for storing the application files according to your preference.

5. Click the OK button to finish the process. After you click OK, Visual Studio will create a new Windows application project. You'll also notice that a new form with the name Form1 is part of the project.

Just as we always do after creating the Windows application, let's add the dataset and ReportViewer to the project. Start by selecting the project in Solution Explorer; right-click it and select Add ➤ New Item ➤ DataSet. Please name the dataset dsDivisionSales. Before you add the ReportViewer, please make sure Form1 is open in the designer. Now, let's add the ReportViewer to the project from the drag and drop toolbox by selecting Data ➤ ReportViewer. Please make sure you set the properties listed in Table 4-16.

Table 4-16. *Property Settings for the Division Sales Project*

Object	Property	Value
Form1	Text	Divisionwise Five Years' Sales Performance Report
Form1	Size	775, 400
reportViewer1	Dock	Fill

Step 1: Creating a Data Table

Since we already have the dataset in the project, it's time to add a data table to it. Please use the following steps to add a data table inside the dataset:

1. You can go to the dataset designer in two ways: double-click dsDivisionSales inside Solution Explorer, or right-click the dsDivisionSales node and select View Designer.

2. Let's add the data table by right-clicking the design surface and selecting Add ➤ DataTable.

3. Click the header of the newly created data table, and name it dtDivisionSales. Let's start adding columns to dtDivisionSales by right-clicking the data table and selecting Add ➤ Column.

4. Please add the following columns into the data table, which should then look similar to Figure 4-56:

   • DivisionID (System.String)

   • YearOfOperation (System.String)

   • NetSalesAmount (System.Double)

Figure 4-56. *Final look of the dtDivisionSales data table*

Step 2: Designing the Report Layout

Let's start the report layout design. First, add the report by selecting the project in Solution Explorer and right-clicking it; select Add ➤ New Item, and select Report from the Add New Item dialog box. Please name the report rptDivisionSales.rdlc. Click the Add button to complete the process and make the new report part of the project.

Setting Up the Page

Nothing special is needed for the page setup in this report. Right-click an open area inside the design surface, and select Properties. Once the Report Properties dialog box is visible, make sure the report is letter sized and has a portrait page orientation. You may change any other properties of the page setup as you like. Since we'll have everything inside the body section for this report, let's jump directly to designing the body section.

Designing the Body Section

Let's start the design process now. Please drag and drop the following report items inside the body section:

- A TextBox item for the report title

- A Matrix item for the cross tabulation of the data

Your report design should look similar to Figure 4-57 after adding all needed report items.

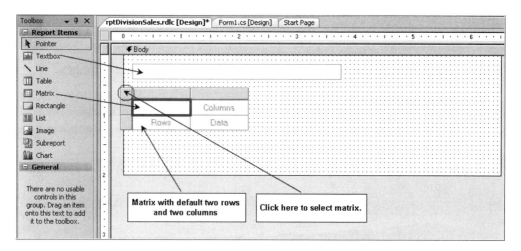

Figure 4-57. *Report design surface after adding report items*

Please take a look at the matrix item in Figure 4-57. Don't you think it has similarities compared with the table report item? I'd say they share many similarities. The main one is the tabular look; matrix report items also have rows and columns. By default, when you drag the matrix item onto the design surface, you get two rows and two columns with it, and a matrix item gets the default name of matrix1.

Unlike a table item, with a matrix item, we have fixed locations to drop the rows, columns, and data. You, as the developer, should know which data element from your data table needs to appear as a row or a column in the matrix. You can select an individual row, column, or a cell from a matrix, as you can with a table item. The cells inside the matrix act like text boxes as well; you can type any text as the value of a complex expression. Rows and columns are numbered in series beginning with MatrixRow1 and MatrixColumn1.

Let's do the data mapping from our data tables. Select Data Source ➤ dsDivisionSales ➤ YearOfOperation and drag and drop it inside the second row of the first column of the matrix, where it says "Rows". This takes care of rows.

Now, select Data Source ➤ dsDivisionSales ➤ DivisionID and drag and drop it inside the first row of the second column of the matrix, where it says "Columns". This takes care of columns.

Finally, select Data Source ➤ dsDivisionSales ➤ NetSalesAmout and drag and drop it inside the second row of the second column of the matrix, where it says "Data". This takes care of data, which will get tabulated for each row and column specified earlier. If you recall, we have one text box in the body section; set the value of this text box to "Divisionwise Five Years' Sales Performance". Also set the font of the text box to bold. After you do the mapping and set up the report title, your report design should look similar to the one shown in Figure 4-58.

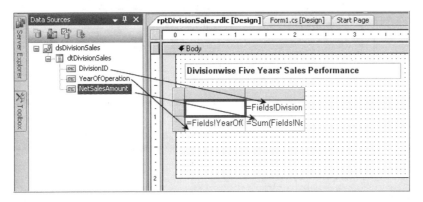

Figure 4-58. *Report design surface after mapping matrix with data columns*

If you notice in Figure 4-54, we have subtotals for both year of operation and division. How do we have these subtotals? Do we need to add additional rows and columns for them? Well, not to worry, even processing subtotals is easy with RS.

To add a subtotal for the division, select the first row of the second column, right-click, and select Subtotal from the pop-up menu. Figure 4-59 shows how the subtotal is done and how the matrix looks after you set the subtotal.

Now, to add a subtotal for the year of operation, the process is the same as for the division subtotal: select the second row of the first column, right-click, and select Subtotal from the pop-up menu. Figure 4-60 shows how the matrix looks after you set the subtotal for the year of operation.

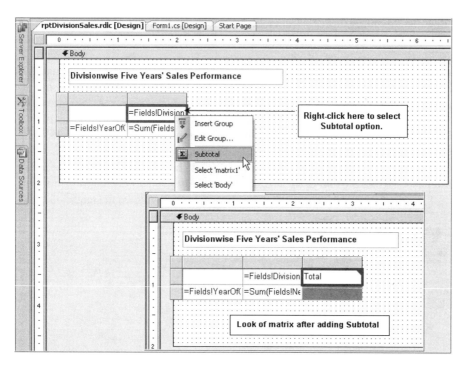

Figure 4-59. *Setting the subtotal for division*

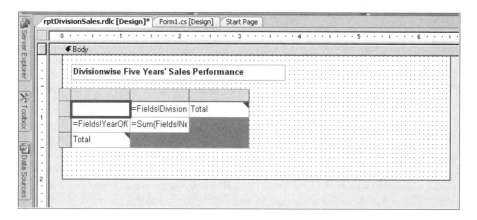

Figure 4-60. *Setting subtotal for year of operation*

You'll notice that, as a result of adding the subtotal, we have an additional row and an additional column for the matrix item. Now, let's do some beautification to our report by setting up various properties of matrix1. You can change the properties of matrix1 just like you change the properties of any other report item. Please make sure to apply all the properties settings in Table 4-17.

Table 4-17. *Matrix Item Properties for Body Section*

Table Item	Property	Value
MatrixRow1 ➤ Column1	Value	Year of Operation
MatrixRow1 ➤ Column1	Size	1.5in, 0.25in
MatrixRow1 ➤ Column2	Value	=Fields!DivisionID.Value
MatrixRow1 ➤ Column2	TextAlign	Right
MatrixRow1 ➤ Column2	Format	N
MatrixRow1 ➤ Column3	Value	Division Total
MatrixRow1 ➤ Column3	TextAlign	Right
MatrixRow1	Font	Normal, Arial, 10pt, Bold
MatrixRow1	BorderStyle	Solid
MatrixRow2 ➤ Column1	Value	=Fields!YearOfOperation.Value
MatrixRow2 ➤ Column2	Value	=Sum(Fields!NetSalesAmount.Value)
MatrixRow2 ➤ Column2	Format	N
MatrixRow2	BorderStyle	Solid
MatrixRow3 ➤ Column1	Value	Division Total
MatrixRow3 ➤ Column1	TextAlign	Right
MatrixRow3	BorderStyle	Solid

That's it. Our report design is ready now. Please make sure your final report design looks similar to the one shown in Figure 4-61.

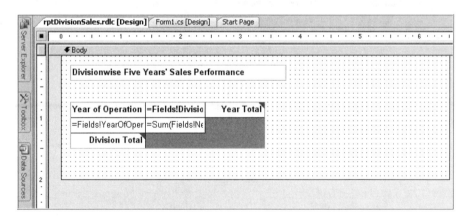

Figure 4-61. *Final look of report design*

All right, that's what we needed as a design for this report. Now, it's time to move on to writing the C# code.

Step 3: Writing the C# Code

As usual, make sure to have the following code behind Form1.cs:

```csharp
using System;
using System.Collections.Generic;
using System.ComponentModel;
using System.Data;
using System.Drawing;
using System.Text;
using System.Windows.Forms;
using System.Data.SqlClient;
using Microsoft.Reporting.WinForms;

namespace DivisionSales
{
    public partial class Form1 : Form
    {
        public Form1()
        {
            InitializeComponent();
        }

        private void Form1_Load(object sender, EventArgs e)
        {
            //declare connection string, please replace
            // DataSource with your Server name
            string cnString = "Data Source=(local);Initial Catalog=RealWorld;➥
                Integrated Security=SSPI;";

            //declare Connection, command and other related objects
            SqlConnection conReport = new SqlConnection(cnString);
            SqlCommand cmdReport = new SqlCommand();
            SqlDataReader drReport;
            DataSet dsReport = new dsDivisionSales();

            try
            {
                //open connection
                conReport.Open();

                //prepare connection object to get the data
                //through reader and populate into dataset
                cmdReport.CommandType = CommandType.Text;
                cmdReport.Connection = conReport;
                cmdReport.CommandText = "Select * FROM dbo.DivisionSales";
```

```
            //read data from command object
            drReport = cmdReport.ExecuteReader();

            //load data directly from reader to dataset
            dsReport.Tables[0].Load(drReport);

            //close reader and connection
            drReport.Close();
            conReport.Close();

            //provide local report information to viewer
            reportViewer1.LocalReport.ReportEmbeddedResource = ➥
                    "DivisionSales.rptDivisionSales.rdlc";

            //prepare report data source
            ReportDataSource rds = new ReportDataSource();
            rds.Name = "dsDivisionSales_dtDivisionSales";
            rds.Value = dsReport.Tables[0];
            reportViewer1.LocalReport.DataSources.Add(rds);

            //load report viewer
            reportViewer1.RefreshReport();
        }
        catch (Exception ex)
        {
            //display generic error message back to user
            MessageBox.Show(ex.Message);
        }
        finally
        {
            //check if connection is still open then attempt to close it
            if (conReport.State == ConnectionState.Open)
            {
                conReport.Close();
            }
        }
    }
  }
}
```

The code for this example is the familiar ADO.NET interface we are using. The process is the same. Connect to the database, and get the data into the dataset. Finally, bind the data to the reporting engine, and execute the report preview.

Building the Project

Let's build the project and see our matrix report in action. As usual, you can click the small, green play button in the main toolbox or press F5 on the keyboard to start the application in run-time mode. If the program compiles without any errors, you will see the form with the report in preview mode. The report will look like something similar to Figure 4-54.

Troubleshooting

Whether you're a new or seasoned professional, we all face development-related troubles (challenges) now and then. For your benefit, I thought a generic troubleshooting section would be a good addition. A few of the most common troubles you may encounter while going through the practical sessions are explained in the following sections.

Error: The Source of the Report Definition Has Not Been Specified

Although this does qualify as trouble, it is not something which qualifies as the mother of all troubles. Please refer to Figure 4-10; in that example, as soon we finished coding our Windows Forms template and ran it, the project ran successfully but the ReportViewer had this error message.

If you see this error, the report has not been assigned to the ReportViewer. Once you add a report to the project and bind it with C# code, you should not see this error.

■Note If you still get this error even after doing all the steps, make sure to the check the ProcessingMode property of the ReportViewer; it should be `Local`.

Error: The Report Definition of Report 'rptProductReorder.rdlc' Has Not Been Specified

This is a very common error, so my advice is: don't panic. The only mistake here is that the ReportViewer is unable to find the report, as you can see in the following code line:

```
reportViewer1.LocalReport.ReportEmbeddedResource =➡
"ProductReorder.rptProductReorder.rdlc";
```

We need to make sure that our report has a fully qualified project name. In our example, it is qualified with the name `ProductOrder`. At times, just a simple typo can lead you to this situation. Please see Figure 4-62 for an example of this error.

Figure 4-62. *Run-time error related to report not found*

Error: A Data Source Instance Has Not Been Supplied for the Data Source 'dsProductReorder_dtProductReorder'

This error sure causes a lot of annoyance, but it is not a big deal to fix it. However, the message is not very clear, so it's a challenge for beginners. As soon you see this error, make sure the following lines of code are correct:

```
ReportDataSource rds = new ReportDataSource();
rds.Name = "dsProductReorder_dtProductReorder";
```

The ReportDataSource.Name property must reflect the correct name as per the following pattern DataSet_DataTable. So, in our case, it is dsProductReorder_dtProductReorder. Please see Figure 4-63 for an example of this error.

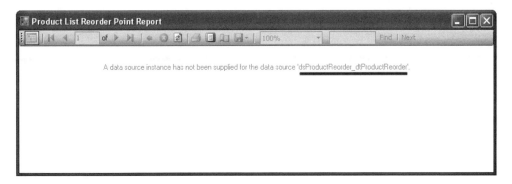

Figure 4-63. *Run-time error related to data source*

There's No Compile Error, But the Report Runs With No Output

If you did everything according to the steps and you don't see any compile or run-time error, why is the report output blank? Situations like this will almost certainly raise your panic level. However, to get normal again, all you have to do is make sure the following code appears at the end as the last instruction in the C# code:

```
reportViewer1.RefreshReport();
```

If you don't call the RefreshReport() method associated with the ReportViewer, no output will be generated. Please see Figure 4-64 for an example of this error.

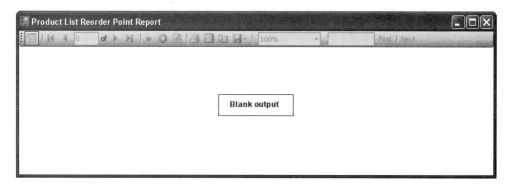

Figure 4-64. *Run-time error—no output*

Exercise 4-1

All right, it's exercise time now. As your first exercise, I want you to take the product reorder report and introduce data grouping based on the color for the project. The report should also list the number of products that fall in each color group. Your solution should be similar to the report output in Figure 4-65.

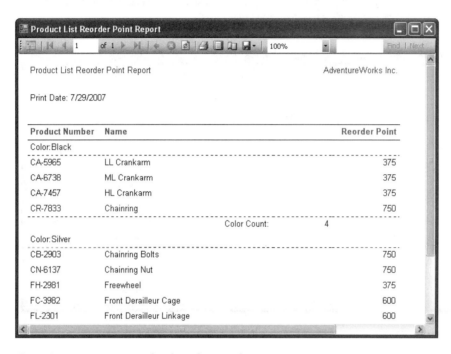

Figure 4-65. *Report output for the solution of Exercise 4-1*

Exercise 4-2

For this exercise, create a multicolumn report similar to what we did previously in the address list report. Unlike the address list report, though, your report will be letter sized and have a landscape page orientation. Why a landscape page orientation? Because you need to have three columns in this report. To have three columns, you need a wider page. Your report will only show the customer and postal code. After you are finished with this exercise, your report output should look similar to the report shown in Figure 4-66.

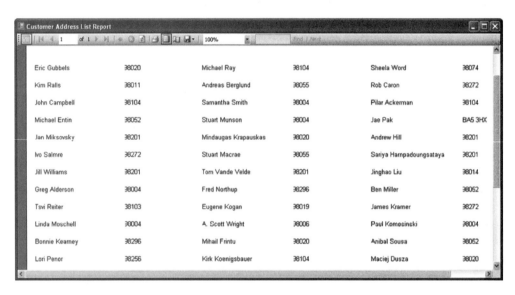

Figure 4-66. *The output of the solution of Exercise 4-2*

Exercise 4-3

For the last exercise, create a matrix report similar to the divisonwise sales comparison report. However, this time, flip the rows and columns in your matrix: show the years of operation as the columns' headings. After you are finished with your report, the output should look similar to the report shown in Figure 4-67.

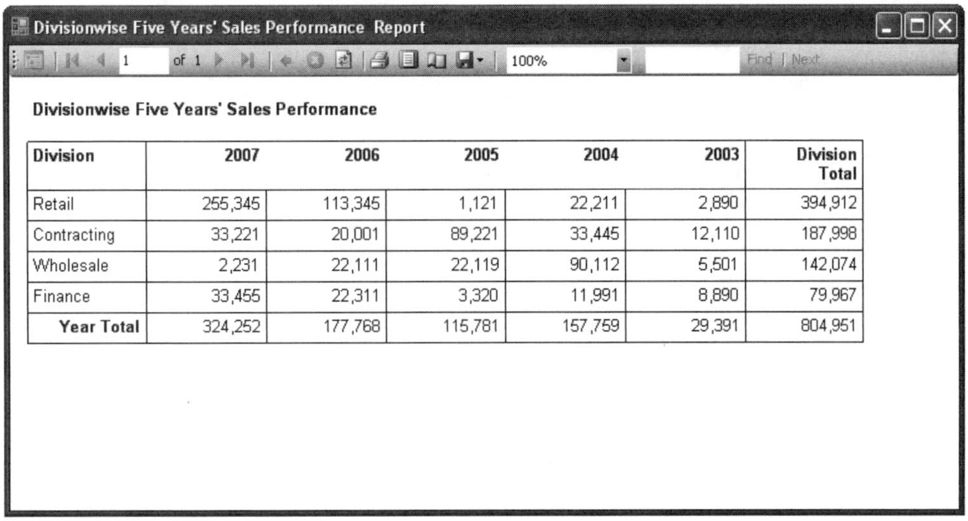

Divisionwise Five Years' Sales Performance Report

Divisionwise Five Years' Sales Performance

Division	2007	2006	2005	2004	2003	Division Total
Retail	255,345	113,345	1,121	22,211	2,890	394,912
Contracting	33,221	20,001	89,221	33,445	12,110	187,998
Wholesale	2,231	22,111	22,119	90,112	5,501	142,074
Finance	33,455	22,311	3,320	11,991	8,890	79,967
Year Total	324,252	177,768	115,781	157,759	29,391	804,951

Figure 4-67. *Output of the solution of Exercise 4-3*

Summary

In this chapter, you started your hands-on learning. You learned the steps to get your Windows Forms client up and running to host your reports, looked at a few reporting projects, and learned to apply client-side reporting functionality while going through the practical steps using real-world examples.

In the next chapter, we'll continue the same trend; however, next time our client will be an ASP.NET web form.

■ ■ ■

CHAPTER 5

Reporting with ASP.NET Web Forms

I am confident that you had fun and enjoyed developing reports with Windows Forms in the previous chapter. I promise to continue the same fun in this chapter. However, the reporting host client will be different—now, we'll develop reports for ASP.NET Web Forms.

Web Forms is a unique report delivery vehicle. By exposing your reports on the Web, you're reaching a far greater user base, in comparison to Windows Forms. All a user needs is access to an Internet browser and authorization to access your report. Reporting for the Web is always challenging for report developers, as the Web understands the language of HTML; for report developers, rendering complex output in HTML format is constantly a challenge.

Well, the good news is that now developers can breathe a sigh of relief, as client-side RS comes to the rescue. You just have to design the report; the ReportViewer takes care of everything else! You can see the same rich report output with Web Forms as you have seen with Windows Forms, and although Web Forms is a different report hosting client, developing reports remains the same.

This chapter will cover

- "ASP.NET Web Sites 101", a step-by-step tutorial for using web sites

- A variety of reporting projects

ASP.NET Web Sites 101

ASP.NET is a technology that developers can use to build dynamic web sites. It is a successor to Microsoft's Active Server Pages (ASP) technology. ASP.NET is part of .NET development platform, starting from its first release with the .NET framework. Like Windows Forms, ASP.NET Web Forms are built using the Common Language Runtime (CLR); therefore, they allow developers to code using their choice of any .NET scripting language. In this book, as usual, we'll use C#.

Similar to Windows Forms, ASP.NET helps you develop for the Web by making cool web controls available with rich design-time support. You'll be glad to see web controls such as buttons or text boxes function the same way as you have experienced while developing Windows Forms clients.

These web controls are rendered into HTML when a web page is delivered to a user's browser. You, as a developer, will also enjoy the event-driven GUI model to code against. Apart from this, you'll benefit from a lot of other cool stuff, such as view state management and support for AJAX.

Note AJAX (Asynchronous JavaScript and XML) is a web development technique used for creating interactive web applications. Its ability to reduce postback trips to the server makes it popular among many developers. You can learn more on ASP.NET AJAX here: `http://ajax.asp.net/`.

An ASP.NET web site needs Internet Information Services (IIS) as a host. The web site can be hosted with local IIS or on a remote machine. For our reporting project, you'll see the reports in action using the integrated web server of the Visual Studio IDE. This internal web server will act like IIS for use during the development phase. Covering everything offered by ASP.NET technology is beyond the reach of this book, so in this chapter, we'll use only the facilities that are needed to develop and host RS with web forms. You can learn more details about ASP.NET here:

`http://msdn2.microsoft.com/en-ca/asp.net/default.aspx`

Creating a Web Site Project

Please open Visual Studio, and use the following steps to create an ASP.NET web site project; see Figure 5-1 for a graphical representation of these steps:

1. Click File ➤ New ➤ Web Site.

2. In the Templates pane of the New Web Site dialog box, select ASP.NET Web Site.

3. From the Language drop-down menu, select Visual C#.

4. Please give the application a name; I've called the web site RSWebSite101. You may choose a different location for storing the application files according to your preference.

5. Click the OK button to finish the process. Visual Studio will create a new ASP.NET web site. Figure 5-2 shows the code that's produced and the files inside Solution Explorer.

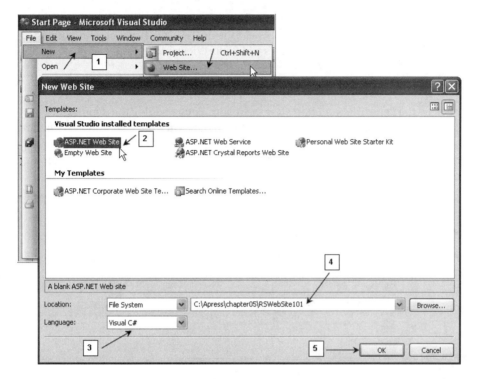

Figure 5-1. *Creating a new ASP.NET web site*

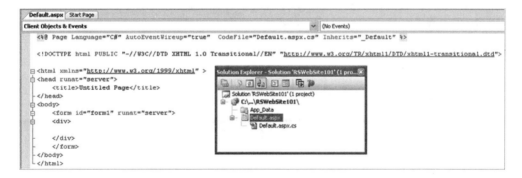

Figure 5-2. *The newly created ASP.NET web site*

As you can see in Figure 5-2, the project contains the App_Code folder and a blank web page Default.aspx. The generated code is a complete web site, ready to host with IIS. Does the generated code looks familiar to you? I'm sure your answer is "yes" if you know HTML. The HTML language makes use of tags to help the browser understand the pages' content. You can learn more about HTML here:

http://msdn2.microsoft.com/en-us/library/ms537623.aspx

Let's assume we hosted this web site with the local IIS. Now, what do you think this site is supposed to do? This site will appear as a blank page inside the user's browser with nothing to display. Therefore, before we build the site, let's add ReportViewer to it.

Adding ReportViewer to Default.aspx

We know we need the ReportViewer to preview the report. Before adding the ReportViewer, please make sure the Default.aspx page is open in the designer in source view mode (similar to the view in Figure 5-2). Let's add the ReportViewer now by dragging Data ➤ ReportViewer from the toolbox and dropping it between the <div> </div> tags; please see Figure 5-3 for an illustration of the process.

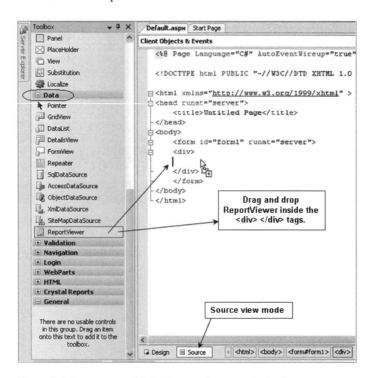

Figure 5-3. *Process to add the ReportViewer to Default.aspx*

■**Note** You can also add the ReportViewer to the Default.aspx page by switching to design view and dragging and dropping the ReportViewer control onto the design surface.

As a result of this, a ReportViewer control will be added to the Default.aspx page with the ID reportViewer1. After you add the ReportViewer, your generated HTML code should be similar to the following:

```
<%@ Page Language="C#" AutoEventWireup="true"➥
  CodeFile="Default.aspx.cs" Inherits="_Default" %>

<%@ Register Assembly="Microsoft.ReportViewer.WebForms,➥
 Version=8.0.0.0, Culture=neutral, ➥
   PublicKeyToken=b03f5f7f11d50a3a"
 Namespace="Microsoft.Reporting.WebForms" TagPrefix="rsweb" %>

<!DOCTYPE html PUBLIC "-//W3C//DTD XHTML 1.0 Transitional//EN"➥
 "http://www.w3.org/TR/xhtml1/DTD/xhtml1-transitional.dtd">

<html xmlns="http://www.w3.org/1999/xhtml" >
<head runat="server">
    <title>Untitled Page</title>
</head>
<body>
    <form id="form1" runat="server">
    <div>
        <rsweb:ReportViewer ID="ReportViewer1" runat="server">
        </rsweb:ReportViewer>
    </div>
    </form>
</body>
</html>
```

After you add the ReportViewer, extra lines of code are added: the first lines contain the registration information of the Microsoft.ReportViewer.WebForms assembly. The second new tag here, between the <div> tags, refers to our newly added ReportViewer.

So, are you curious to see how the ReportViewer looks on a Default.aspx page? Well, you have seen the ReportViewer in Windows Forms; it will look very similar in a web form. You can have a peek at it by making sure the Default.aspx page is open and switching to design mode from HTML source mode (see Figure 5-4). All right, we're all set to build the web site now.

Note You might be wondering why the Print button is missing in the ReportViewer! Well, the version with Visual Studio 2005 doesn't have it for web pages. However, the good news is that the ReportViewer that ships with Visual Studio 2008 has web page print functionality. To print from the Web in Visual Studio 2005, you have to save the report as an image, Excel, or PDF file.

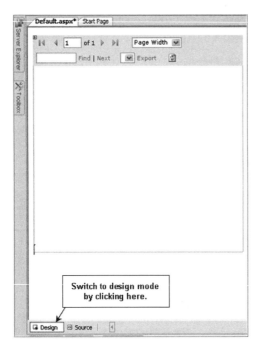

Figure 5-4. *ReportViewer in design mode on Default.aspx*

Building the Project

I'm sure you are ready to pump life into your web site. Sure, why not? After all, this is the time we can see our hard work in action. Building a web site is like any other project we build with the Visual Studio IDE. As you know, you can build a project by clicking the small, green play button in the main toolbox or pressing F5 on the keyboard to start the application in runtime mode.

If the Visual Studio IDE presents you with the Debugging Not Enabled dialog box, select the default choice of "Modify the Web.config file . . ." and click the OK button (see Figure 5-5).

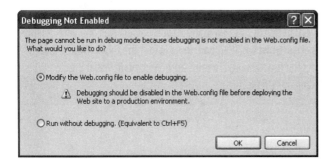

Figure 5-5. *Confirmation to enable debugging*

If you don't get any errors during the build, the web site will be automatically hosted with the internal web server of Visual Studio's IDE. Please see Figure 5-6 for the URL and port on which our web site is hosted. When my site is hosted with the internal web server, it uses port 3992 on my computer. However, if you build the site on your machine, you might get a different port number.

Figure 5-6. *The web site is hosted with the internal web server of the Visual Studio IDE.*

After the web service is successfully launched, a browser window will appear with a blank page, as in Figure 5-7 (which shows the page in Internet Explorer 7). Why still a blank page? Well, we just added the ReportViewer but have not yet developed a report to output.

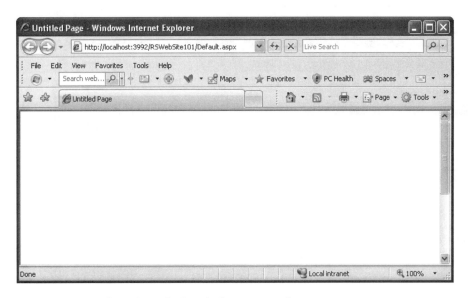

Figure 5-7. *The web site launched in the browser window*

All right, now it is time to move on to our reporting project. As our first reporting project, let's create the Aged Accounts Receivables report that I mentioned in Chapter 1.

Aged Accounts Receivables Report

Assume you're working for Modern Packaging Incorporated as a developer. You have the task of developing the Aged Accounts Receivables report. The report should highlight, using bold and italic font styles, any invoice that is 90 days old or older. The report should also provide the user with the ability to move to invoice details of any customers while viewing the report. The report should meet all the characteristics described in the Table 5-1, and the report output should match Figure 5-8.

Table 5-1. *Report Characteristics*

Characteristics	Value
Report title	Aged Accounts Receivables
Company title	Modern Packaging Inc.
Print date	Yes
Data source	AgedAR
Columns to report	InvioceNo, CustomerName, Amount, and InvoiceAge
Page size	Letter
Page orientation	Portrait
Page number	Yes (Page: n/n)
Layout design	Header and Body section
Document map	Yes (on Customer Name)

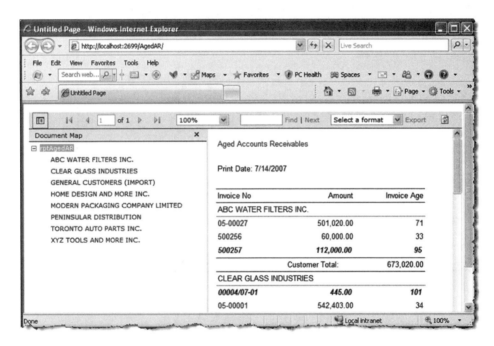

Figure 5-8. *The Aged Accounts Receivables report*

Business Case

We use a sales invoice once a product is sold or service is rendered to a customer. In a credit sale, it is a customer's duty to pay the invoiced amount before the due date. Different businesses have various policies of credit days that customers can enjoy before settling the invoice amount. The Aged Accounts Receivables report helps the collections department staff to look for the age of all outstanding sales invoices. In our example, highlighting the invoices that are overdue by 90 days or more helps the collections department take action.

Getting the Web Site Ready

Let's get the web site ready, similar to the way you have already learned earlier in this chapter. You can make use of the solution RSWebSite101 as a template for this project or create it from scratch. It is good idea to create the new project from scratch; you can always refer to steps mentioned in the tutorial if you get stuck.

Please use the following steps to create a web site project:

1. Click File ➤ New ➤ Web Site.

2. In the Templates pane of the New Web Site dialog box, select ASP.NET Web Site.

3. From the Language drop-down menu, select Visual C#.

4. Please give the application a name; I've called the web site AgedAR. You may choose a different location for storing the application files according to your preference.

5. Click the OK button to finish the process. Visual Studio will create a new ASP.NET web site.

Let's move on and add the dataset and ReportViewer to the project. Let's start by selecting the project in Solution Explorer. Right-click it, and select Add ➤ New Item ➤ DataSet. Please name the dataset dsAgedAR. You'll notice that Visual Studio will ask you to put the dataset inside the App_Code folder; go ahead click the Yes button. Select Cancel on the Table Adapter wizard dialog box; we'll create the data table later.

Its time to add the ReportViewer now; please repeat the steps from our "ASP.NET Web Sites101" tutorial earlier in this chapter to add the ReportViewer to the Default.aspx page (see Figure 5-3). Before continuing, please make sure the HTML code inside the Default.aspx page looks like the following:

```
<%@ Page Language="C#" AutoEventWireup="true" ➡
  CodeFile="Default.aspx.cs" Inherits="_Default" %>

<%@ Register Assembly="Microsoft.ReportViewer.WebForms, ➡
 Version=8.0.0.0, Culture=neutral, PublicKeyToken=b03f5f7f11d50a3a"
    Namespace="Microsoft.Reporting.WebForms" TagPrefix="rsweb" %>

<!DOCTYPE html PUBLIC "-//W3C//DTD XHTML 1.0 Transitional//EN"➡
 "http://www.w3.org/TR/xhtml1/DTD/xhtml1-transitional.dtd">

<html xmlns="http://www.w3.org/1999/xhtml" >
<head runat="server">
    <title>Untitled Page</title>
</head>
<body>
    <form id="form1" runat="server">
    <div>
        <rsweb:ReportViewer ID="ReportViewer1" runat="server"➡
        Width="775px">
```

```
        </rsweb:ReportViewer>
      </div>
      </form>
</body>
</html>
```

If you switch to the design view of the Default.aspx page, it should look similar to Figure 5-4, with the exception of the width of ReportViewer. In this example, we have set the width to 775 pixels.

Step 1: Creating a Data Table

Since we already have the dataset in the project, it's time to add a data table to it. Please use the following steps to add a data table inside the dataset:

1. You can go to the dataset designer in two ways: double-click dsAgedAR inside Solution Explorer, or right-click the dsAgedAR node and select View Designer.

2. Let's add the data table by right-clicking the design surface and selecting Add ➤ DataTable.

3. Click the header of the newly created data table, and name it dtAgedAR. Let's start adding columns to dtAgedAR by right-clicking the data table and selecting Add ➤ Column.

4. Please add the following columns into the data table, which should then look similar to Figure 5-9:

   - InvoiceNo (System.String)

   - CustomerName (System.String)

   - Amount (System.Double)

   - InvoiceAge (System.Int32)

Figure 5-9. *Final look of the dtAgedAR data table*

Step 2: Designing the Report Layout

Before we start with the layout design for the report, let's take a look at the report layout in Figure 5-8. What type of report items do you find in this report? Well, as you can see, the report has a table item to display the invoice and receivables information. You'll also see that we need the data grouping on CustomerName. We also need a group summary on total receivables for each customer.

All right, we have our dataset in place, with the data table and all necessary columns. We're all set to start working on designing the report layout. Add the report by selecting the project in Solution Explorer and right-clicking it; select Add ➤ New Item, and select Report from the Add New Item dialog box. Please name the report rptAgedAR.rdlc. Click the Add button to complete the process and make the new report part of the project. You'll also notice that a new toolbox called Data Sources is available with our dataset information inside.

Adding a Header

Let's add the header to the report. As usual, adding a header is simple: right-click the open area inside the report designer and select Page Header. Your report design surface should look similar to Figure 5-10.

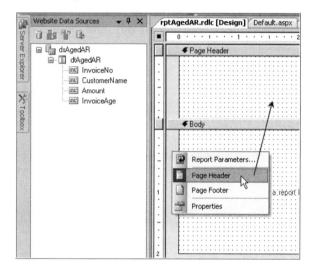

Figure 5-10. *The report design surface with header and body sections*

Setting Up the Page

According to the report's needs, let's set up the page. We need to make sure the report is letter sized and has a portrait page orientation. Right-click the open area inside the design surface, and select Properties, where you may wish to put your name in the Author field and add any information about the report in the Description field. I'd advise you to let all other choices stay at the defaults.

■**Note** Please make sure to set the properties Page Width to 8.5 inches and Page Height to 11 inches for a letter-sized, portrait report.

Designing the Page Header

Now, we have added the header and the body sections to our report. As we always do in this book, let's work on the header first. Please drag and drop the following report items inside the header section:

- A text box item for the report title
- A text box item for the report date
- A text box item for the company title
- A text box item for the page number

Report item properties are changed in one of the following two ways: by selecting the report item, right-clicking it, and selecting Properties or by accessing the general properties toolbox. Let's change the properties; select each of the text box items in turn, and specify the values for each report item's properties according to Table 5-2.

Table 5-2. *Report Item Properties for Header*

Report Item	Property	Value
textbox1		
	Value	Aged Accounts Receivables
	Color	Purple
textbox2		
	Value	Modern Packaging Inc.
	Color	Blue
	TextAlign	Right
textbox3		
	Value	="Print Date: " & Today
textbox4		
	Value	="Page: " & Globals!PageNumber & "/" & Globals!TotalPages
	TextAlign	Right

Designing the Body Section

Let's start working on this section by selecting dragging Report Items ➤ Table from the toolbox and dropping it inside the body section in the report designer. A new table item is part of the report now, and it has the default name of table1. Since we have three columns to use with the table, we'll stick with the default three added automatically (we don't need to add any more columns to the table).

Note If you face any difficulties working with the table report item, please refer to the first reporting project from Chapter 4.

I'm sure you have a favorite method to map the data table's columns to the text boxes by now. Is it drag and drop? Or the old-school way of typing the name of the column expression inside the text box? Either way, you can map the text box items inside table1 the way you like best.

Select Data Source ➤ dsAgedAR ➤ InvoiceNo and drag and drop it inside the first column of the table item's detail section. Repeat this task for InvoiceAge and Amount. For CustomerName, hold off for now; we need to use it in the group header later. Make sure your report design surface looks similar to the one shown in Figure 5-11.

You'll notice in the figure that I've selected the first row of table1. As you know, three rows are added by default when you add a table item to a report. Rows are referred to as TableRow1 to TableRow3 in sequence. We can add as many table rows as we need in addition to the default three initial rows.

■**Note** Selecting an entire table row is useful to apply formatting to all the text boxes that the row contains. For example, you can change the font of all text boxes in the selected row or apply top and bottom border styles.

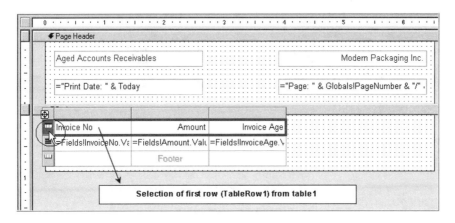

Figure 5-11. *The report designer after adding the header and body*

Even after adding the table item and mapping the text boxes, we haven't quite finished yet. We still need to work on the CustomerName data group. If you recall, one of the requirements of this report is to provide users a way to quickly jump to information pertaining to any customer. For this, we have to create a document map on CustomerName. As you can see in Figure 5-8, this document map will help the user to jump directly to records related to any given customer.

So, now is the time to add the data group and document map. Let's begin by adding a group. Select the Detail row (TableRow2), right-click it, and select Insert Group; the Grouping and Sorting Properties dialog box will appear. Please make sure to select the General tab, and type the following into the Expression field: **=LEFT(Fields!CustomerName.Value,1)**. On the same tab, select or type the same expression for "Document map label"—yes, the same expression for both the group and document map. Please see Figure 5-12 for an illustration of these steps.

Let me shed some light on the document map. What do you think a document map is? If I put it simply, it is a feature built into RS to help users navigate the report output. It has a familiar tree view UI; the information related to the document map appears on the left side of the report.

You can treat the tree as a table of contents, and when you click on any of the items, the report gets refreshed with the needed information. For example, in this case, all customers will appear as the table of contents, and if you select any customer from the tree view, the result on the right side will be refreshed with invoice information for that customer.

■**Note** A document map is only supported with Internet Explorer. For example, if you open this report with Firefox, you will not see the document map. Please check the following link for browser compatibility with the ReportViewer: http://msdn2.microsoft.com/en-us/library/ms251673(VS.80).aspx.

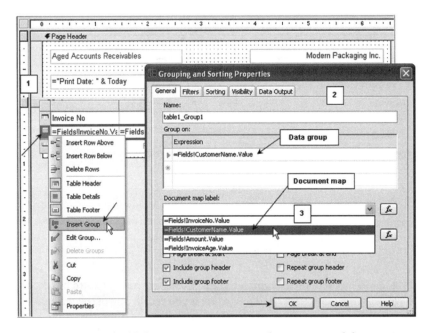

Figure 5-12. *Steps to add the CustomerName as a data group and document map*

After you add the data grouping and document map, you'll notice that two new rows have become part of table1 now. No matter if you add or remove row(s) from the table item, the row number is always assigned from top to bottom: if your table has five rows, the first row reference will be TableRow1 and the last row reference will be TableRow5. Please make sure your report design looks similar to Figure 5-13 after adding the data group and document map.

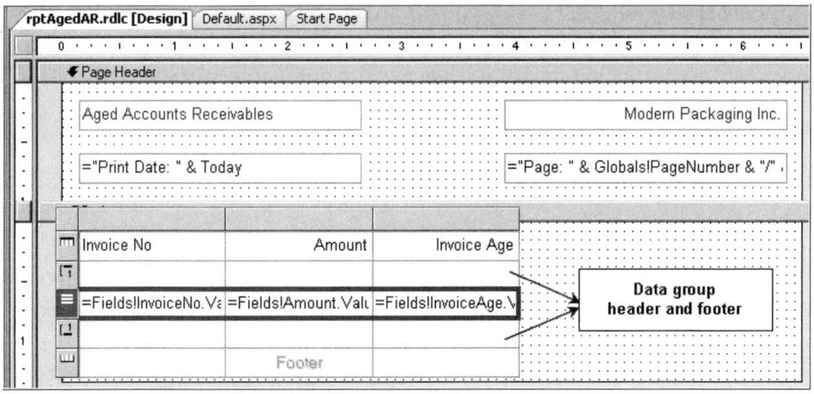

Figure 5-13. *Report design after adding data group and document map*

Let's take care of the data group header and footer now. For the header, we need to show the customer name. For the group footer, we need to show the total receivables of each customer. Before we add the customer name to the group header, let's merge all the text boxes (cells) in the group header row (TableRow2). As you know, the table item is like a worksheet with rows and columns; we can select two or more columns from the same row and merge them to look like a single cell.

We'll do this to TableRow2; please select all three columns (referred to as cells), right-click, and select Merge. After this, you can map the CustomerName from dtAgedAR or type the expression **Fields!CustomerName.Value**. For the data group footer (TableRow4), select column 2, and type **Customer Total:**. For column 3, we will use the SUM() function to calculate the total receivables for the customer. Please make sure to use the following expression for the calculation: = SUM(Fields!Amount.Value). Please see Figure 5-14 for an illustration of the steps.

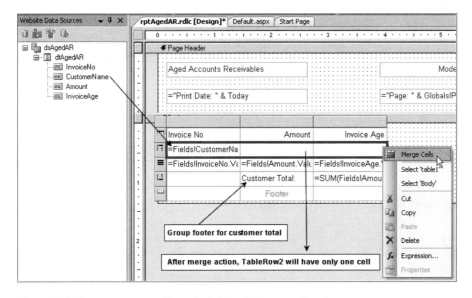

Figure 5-14. *Steps to merge cells and add the data group header*

We have one important step left; that is to highlight any invoice that is 90 or more days old. This is very simple to do. All we need to do is apply the FontStyle and FontWeight properties of the details row (TableRow3) inside table1. Please use the following FontStyle expression:

```
=IIF(Fields!InvoiceAge.Value >= 90,"Italic","Normal")
```

Similarly, use the following expression for FontWeight:

```
=IIF(Fields!InvoiceAge.Value >= 90,"Bold","Normal").
```

One last step before we say the design for the body section is complete—let's make the report look pretty. The properties are applicable to any selected row or column. Please make sure the report design properties for table1 are set according to Table 5-3.

Table 5-3. *Table Item Properties for the Body Section*

Table Item	Property	Value
TableRow1 ➤ Column1	Value	Invoice No
TableRow1 ➤ Column2	Value	Amount
TableRow1 ➤ Column2	TextAlign	Right
TableRow1 ➤ Column3	Value	Invoice Age
TableRow1 ➤ Column3	TextAlign	Right
TableRow1	BorderStyle	None, , , Solid, Solid
TableRow2 ➤ Column1	Value	=Fields!CustomerName.Value
TableRow2	BorderStyle	None, , , , Dotted
TableRow3 ➤ Column1	Value	=Fields!InvoiceNo.Value
TableRow3 ➤ Column2	Value	=Fields!Amount.Value
TableRow3 ➤ Column2	Format	N
TableRow3 ➤ Column3	Value	=Fields!InvoiceAge.Value
TableRow3 ➤ Column3	Format	N0 (=zero for no decimal)
TableRow3	FontStyle	=IIF(Fields!InvoiceAge.Value >= 90,"Italic", "Normal")
TableRow3	FontWeight	=IIF(Fields!InvoiceAge.Value >= 90,"Bold", "Normal")
TableRow4 ➤ Column2	Value	Customer Total:
TableRow4 ➤ Column2	Value	=SUM(Fields!Amount.Value)
TableRow4	BorderStyle	None, , , Solid, Solid

That's it. Our report design is ready to test with some C# code now. Before we move to the code section, make sure your final report design looks similar to the one shown in Figure 5-15.

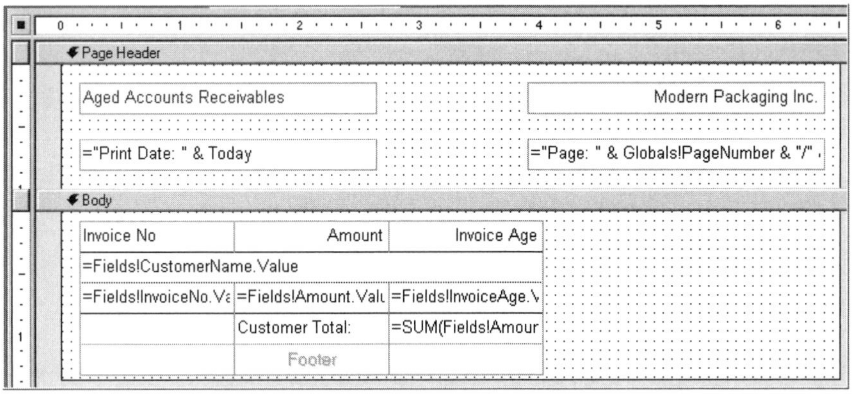

Figure 5-15. *The final look of the report design*

Step 3: Writing C# Code

Please make sure you have the following code inside the Default.aspx.cs file:

```csharp
using System;
using System.Data;
using System.Configuration;
using System.Web;
using System.Web.Security;
using System.Web.UI;
using System.Web.UI.WebControls;
using System.Web.UI.WebControls.WebParts;
using System.Web.UI.HtmlControls;
using Microsoft.Reporting.WebForms;
using System.Data.SqlClient;

public partial class _Default : System.Web.UI.Page
{
    protected void Page_Load(object sender, EventArgs e)
    {
        //Declare connection string
        string cnString = "Data Source=(local);➥
Initial Catalog=RealWorld;Integrated Security=SSPI;";

        //Declare Connection, command, and other related objects
        SqlConnection conReport = new SqlConnection(cnString);
        SqlCommand cmdReport = new SqlCommand();
        SqlDataReader drReport;
        DataSet dsReport = new dsAgedAR();
```

```
        try
        {
            conReport.Open();

            cmdReport.CommandType = CommandType.Text;
            cmdReport.Connection = conReport;
            cmdReport.CommandText = "Select * FROM dbo.AgedAR➥
    order by CustomerName, InvoiceNo";

            drReport = cmdReport.ExecuteReader();
            dsReport.Tables[0].Load(drReport);

            drReport.Close();
            conReport.Close();

            //provide local report information to viewer
            ReportViewer1.LocalReport.ReportPath = "rptAgedAR.rdlc";

            //prepare report data source
            ReportDataSource rds = new ReportDataSource();
            rds.Name = "dsAgedAR_dtAgedAR";
            rds.Value = dsReport.Tables[0];
            ReportViewer1.LocalReport.DataSources.Add(rds);
        }
        catch (Exception ex)
        {
            //display generic error message back to user
            Response.Write(ex.Message);
        }
        finally
        {
            //check if connection is still open then attempt to close
            if (conReport.State == ConnectionState.Open)
            {
                conReport.Close();
            }
        }
    }
}
```

The code here is a common ADO.NET interface similar to what you saw in Chapter 4. We start with connecting to our RealWorld database and gathering data from the table AgedAR. After that, we bind the data to the reporting engine. You may want to revisit Chapter 3 for a refresher on the C# ADO.NET interface code.

Building the Project

As usual, let's build the project. You can click the small, green play button in the main tool-box or press F5 on the keyboard to start the application in run-time mode. As you learned earlier, click OK when you build it for the first time to enable the debug mode setting. Assuming that you don't encounter any issue during the build, your report output should look similar to Figure 5-8.

As I mentioned in a note earlier, the document map is supported only by the Internet Explorer browser. Figure 5-16 shows you how our report looks with the Firefox browser (note the missing document map).

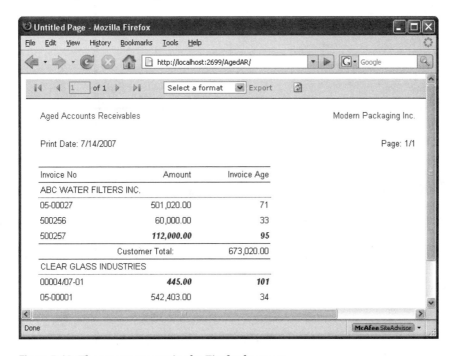

Figure 5-16. *The report output in the Firefox browser*

Let me ask you a question here. If we export this report to either Excel or PDF format, is the document map supported? Well, the answer is "yes;" both Excel and PDF files can show the document map.

In the case of Excel, the generated .xls file will have two sheets: one holds the document map, and the other is the actual report. If you click any of the items in the document map, you will be taken to the sheet that has the data for the selected customer. Please see Figure 5-17 for the document map and Figure 5-18 for the report data after it is exported to Excel format.

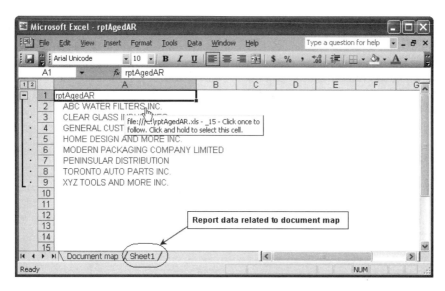

Figure 5-17. *Excel file view of the document map*

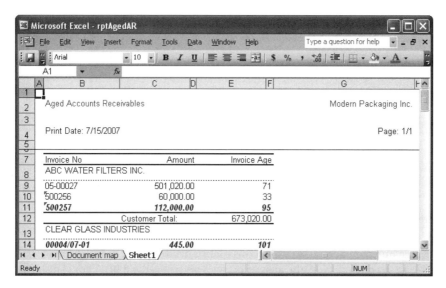

Figure 5-18. *Excel report data after selecting a customer from the document map*

In the case of exporting to PDF, the generated file will have the document map and report data in the same page. The document map is treated as a bookmark inside the PDF file. As you click customers, the report data is refreshed to reflect your customer selection. Please see Figure 5-19 for a view of the report inside Acrobat Reader.

■**Note** I'm using Acrobat Reader version 8.1.0. If you are using another version, your view will be a little bit different than what appears in Figure 5-19.

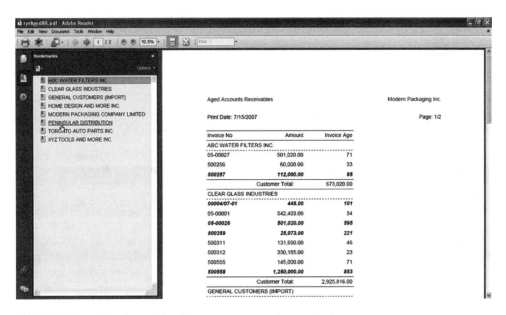

Figure 5-19. *PDF file view of the document map and report data*

I'm confident that you enjoyed this report and had fun with the document map feature. All right, let's move on to our next reporting project, where you will learn to make use of custom code and more conditional formatting.

Sales Profit Analysis Report

Assume you're working for A1 Financial Services Incorporated as a developer. You have the task of developing the Sales Profit Analysis report. The report should show sales information for individual invoices and determine the profit/loss ratio after taking cost into consideration.

The details of the invoices should appear in ledger format, and alternating rows should be colored light yellow. The report should make use of icons (Sad, Happy, and Come See Me) to reflect the position of each invoice. If the invoiced transaction made less than 10 percent profit, it should display the Sad icon; if it made a profit of 10 percent or better, it should display the Happy icon, and a loss should display Come See Me. Further, reports should meet all the characteristics described in Table 5-4, and the report output should match Figure 5-20.

Table 5-4. *Report Characteristics*

Characteristics	Value
Report title	Sales Profit Analysis
Company title	A1 Financial Services Inc.
Print date	Yes
Data source	SalesAnalysis
Columns to report	InvoiceNo, CustomerName, Amount, and Cost
Page size	Letter
Page orientation	Portrait
Page number	Yes (Page: n/n)
Layout design	Header and body sections

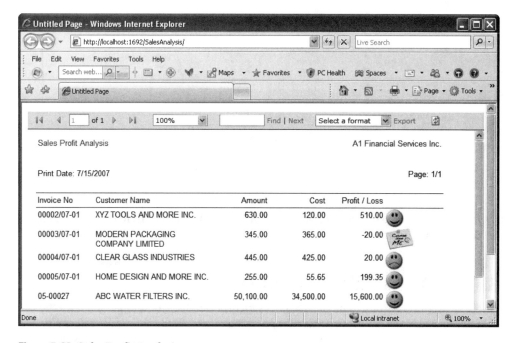

Figure 5-20. *Sales Profit Analysis report*

Business Case

How does a business determine if a profit was made on any given sale? The formula in simple: take the invoice value and subtract the cost, and you will end up with profit or loss. Generating more and more invoices is good for the business. However, each of those invoices should meet the profit expectations (or at least should not incur a loss).

A sales profit analysis report helps the sales department monitor the profit ratio. In this example, we will list all invoices with their individual profit or loss figures. You'll also see that an icon next to each invoice's details that will tell you how the profit looks. A happy face means all is good; a sad face means attention is required, and finally, the Come See Me icon is a message from the sales boss to start the fact finding process to figure out how come the transaction was a loss!

Getting the Web Site Ready

Please use the following steps to create a web site project:

1. Click File ➤ New ➤ Web Site.

2. In the Templates pane of the New Web Site dialog box, select ASP.NET Web Site.

3. From the Language drop-down menu, select Visual C#.

4. Please give the application a name; I've called the web site SalesAnalysis. You may choose a different location for storing the application files according to your preference.

5. Click the OK button to finish the process. Visual Studio will create a new ASP.NET Web site.

As usual, it is time to add the dataset and ReportViewer to the project. Start by selecting the project in Solution Explorer; right-click it, and select Add ➤ New Item ➤ dataset. Please name the dataset as dsSalesAnalysis. You'll notice that Visual Studio will ask you to put the dataset inside the App_Code folder; go ahead and click the Yes button. Select Cancel on the Table Adapter wizard dialog box; we'll create the data table later.

Let's take care of the ReportViewer now. Please repeat the steps from the Aged Accounts Receivables example to add the ReportViewer; refer to Figure 5-3 if you need help adding the ReportViewer. Before we move on, please make sure the HTML code inside the Default.aspx page looks like the following:

```
<%@ Page Language="C#" AutoEventWireup="true" ➥
 CodeFile="Default.aspx.cs" Inherits="_Default" %>

<%@ Register Assembly="Microsoft.ReportViewer.WebForms, !CCC
Version=8.0.0.0, Culture=neutral, ➥
 PublicKeyToken=b03f5f7f11d50a3a"
 Namespace="Microsoft.Reporting.WebForms" TagPrefix="rsweb" %>

<!DOCTYPE html PUBLIC "-//W3C//DTD XHTML 1.0 Transitional//EN"➥
 "http://www.w3.org/TR/xhtml1/DTD/xhtml1-transitional.dtd">

<html xmlns="http://www.w3.org/1999/xhtml" >
<head runat="server">
    <title>Untitled Page</title>
</head>
```

```
<body>
    <form id="form1" runat="server">
    <div>
        <rsweb:ReportViewer ID="ReportViewer1" runat="server" Width="775px">
        </rsweb:ReportViewer>
    </div>
    </form>
</body>
</html>
```

Step 1: Creating a Data Table

Our usual, step number one is to add a data table to the dataset. Please use the following steps:

1. You can go to the dataset designer in two ways: double-click dsSalesAnalysis inside Solution Explorer, or right-click the dsSalesAnalysis node and select View Designer.

2. Let's add the data table by right-clicking the design surface and selecting Add ➤ DataTable.

3. Click the header of the newly created data table, and name it dtSalesAnalysis. Let's start adding columns to dtSalesAnalysis by right-clicking the data table and selecting Add ➤ Column.

4. Please add the following columns into the data table, which should then look similar to Figure 5-21:

   - InvoiceNo (System.String)

   - CustomerName (System.String)

   - Amount (System.Double)

   - Cost (System.Double)

Figure 5-21. *Final look of the dtSalesAnalysis data table*

Step 2: Designing the Report Layout

Before we start with the layout design for the report, let's take a look at the report layout in Figure 5-20. What type of report items do you find in this report? Well, as you can see, the report has table items to display the sales profit analysis of individual invoices, and the little images are a unique way to state the profit status. Another point that is unique to this report is the ledger-style presentation; that means the background color alternates between white and light yellow for each invoice row.

In the last step, we took care of our dataset. We're all set to start working on designing the report layout now. Add the report by selecting the project in Solution Explorer and right-clicking it; select Add ➤ New Item, and select Report from the Add New Item dialog box. Please name the report `rptSalesAnalysis.rdlc`. Click the Add button to complete the process and make the new report part of the project.

Adding a Header

Let's add the header to the report. As usual, adding a header is simple: right-click the open area inside the report designer and select Page Header.

Setting Up the Page

We need to make sure the report is letter sized and has a portrait page orientation. Right-click the open area inside the design surface; select Properties, and set the page width to 8.5 inches and the page height to 11 inches.

Designing the Page Header

Let's begin to work on the page header now; please drag and drop the following report items inside the header section:

- A text box item for the report title
- A text box item for the report date
- A text box item for the company title
- A text box item for the page number

The report item properties are changed in one of the following two ways: by selecting the report item, right-clicking it, and selecting Properties; or by accessing the general properties toolbox. Let's change the properties; select each of the text box items in turn, and specify the values for each report item's properties according to Table 5-5.

Table 5-5. *Report Item Properties for the Header*

Report Item	Property	Value
textbox1		
	Value	Sales Profit Analysis
	Color	Purple
textbox2		
	Value	A1 Financial Services Inc.
	Color	Blue
	TextAlign	Right
textbox3		
	Value	="Print Date: " & Today
textbox4		
	Value	="Page: " & Globals!PageNumber & "/" & Globals!TotalPages
	TextAlign	Right

Designing the Body Section

Let's start working on this section by dragging Report Items ➤ Table from the toolbox and dropping it inside the body section in the report designer. A new table item is part of the report now, and it has the default name of table1. Since we need a total of six columns, we need to add three additional columns to table1. To add three more columns, right-click the right-most column header on the table item, and select Insert Column to the Right. Repeat the process two more times; you should have a total of six columns in table1.

Let's map the data table's column to the text boxes now. We need to map the first four columns. The fifth column will have the calculation expression, and the last column will display the image item display based on the result of a custom code function.

Select Data Source ➤ dsSalesAnalysis ➤ InvoiceNo and drag and drop it inside the first column of the table item's detail section. Repeat this task for CustomerName, Amount, and Cost. For the fifth column, type the following expression as the value: **=Fields!Amount.Value – Fields!Cost.Value**.

In sixth column of table1, we need to show the icon. As you know, to show any kind of image in a report, we need to make use of the image report item. Therefore, drag Report Items ➤ Image from the toolbox and drop it inside the sixth column of the tabel1 detail row (TableRow2). Type the following expression as its value:

```
=Code.GetImage(Fields!Amount.Value, Fields!Cost.Value)
```

Make sure your report design surface looks similar to the one shown in Figure 5-22.

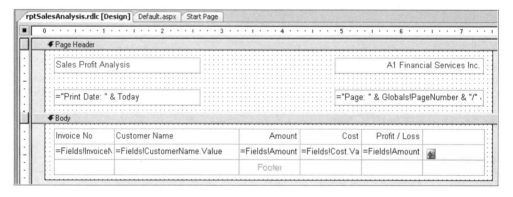

Figure 5-22. *The report designer after adding the header and body sections*

In case you are wondering what the GetImage() function is, it is the custom code function that we need to change the icon based on the profit ratio of each invoice. Before I show you how to work with custom code, let me tell you about expressions to calculate profit/loss ratios. As you have seen, we didn't use the drag and drop method to map the value of the profit/loss column; instead we typed the expression:

```
=Fields!Amount.Value - Fields!Cost.Value
```

One of the beauties of RS is that it allows us to perform calculations on data fields. In this case, by using subtraction, we can determine the amount of profit or loss.

Now, let me show you how to write custom code that is embedded within the report. Writing custom code is easy; right-click any open area inside the report designer and select Properties. From the Report Properties dialog box, select the Code tab (see Figure 5-23), and type the code for our custom function.

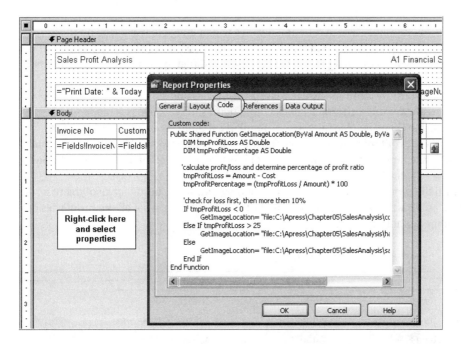

Figure 5-23. *The Code tab of the Report Properties window*

Make sure the custom code you typed inside the report properties code section is as follows:

```
Public Shared Function GetImageLocation(ByVal Amount AS Double,➥
 ByVal Cost AS Double) AS String
       DIM tmpProfitLoss AS Double
       DIM tmpProfitPercentage AS Double

      'calculate profit/loss and determine percentage of profit ratio
       tmpProfitLoss = Amount - Cost
       tmpProfitPercentage = (tmpProfitLoss / Amount) * 100

      'check for loss first, then more then 10%
       If tmpProfitLoss < 0
GetImageLocation= ➥
 "file:C:\Apress\Chapter05\SalesAnalysis\comeseeme.jpg"
       Else If tmpProfitLoss > 25
GetImageLocation= ➥
 "file:C:\Apress\Chapter05\SalesAnalysis\happy.jpg"
```

```
        Else
GetImageLocation= ➡
"file:C:\Apress\Chapter05\SalesAnalysis\sad.jpg"
        End If
End Function
```

Let me tell you how our custom function decides which image to use based on the invoice's profit ratio. First of all, our custom function takes two input parameters, Amount and Cost. It returns the path to the image file based on logic outlined in the report requirements earlier.

The function starts by temporarily calculating profit/loss and profit percentage figures. Once the figures are available, the logic checks these figures to see if a loss is made. If so, the function returns the Come See Me note image. Similarly, if there is not a loss, the function checks whether the profit margin ten percent or more. If so, it shows the Happy image. Finally, the last possible scenario here is of a profit ratio of less than ten percent. In this case, the Sad image is shown.

Let's finish the process of the report body design by setting the border style of the first row from table1 (TableRow1) to solid on the top and bottom. Make sure to set all the properties of table1 according to Table 5-6.

Table 5-6. *Table Item Properties for the Body Section*

Table Item	Property	Value
TableRow1 ➤ Column1	Value	Invoice No
TableRow1 ➤ Column2	Value	Customer Name
TableRow1 ➤ Column3	Value	Amount
TableRow1 ➤ Column3	TextAlign	Right
TableRow1 ➤ Column4	Value	Cost
TableRow1 ➤ Column4	TextAlign	Right
TableRow1 ➤ Column5	Value	Profit / Loss
TableRow1 ➤ Column5	TextAlign	Right
TableRow1	BorderStyle	None, , , Solid, Solid
TableRow2 ➤ Column1	Value	=Fields!InvoiceNo.Value
TableRow2 ➤ Column2	Value	=Fields!CustomerName.Value
TableRow2 ➤ Column3	Value	=Fields!Amount.Value
TableRow2 ➤ Column4	Value	=Fields!Cost.Value
TableRow2 ➤ Column5	Value	=Fields!Amount.Value - =Fields!Cost.Value
TableRow2 ➤ Column5	Format	N
TableRow2 ➤ Column6	Value	=Code.GetImageLocation (Fields!Amount.Value, Fields!Cost.Value)
TableRow2 ➤ Column1 to Column 5	BackgroundColor	=iif(RowNumber(Nothing) Mod 2, "LightYellow", "White")

Step 3: Writing the C# Code

Please make sure you have the following code inside the Default.aspx.cs file:

```csharp
using System;
using System.Data;
using System.Configuration;
using System.Web;
using System.Web.Security;
using System.Web.UI;
using System.Web.UI.WebControls;
using System.Web.UI.WebControls.WebParts;
using System.Web.UI.HtmlControls;
using Microsoft.Reporting.WebForms;
using System.Data.SqlClient;

public partial class _Default : System.Web.UI.Page
{
    protected void Page_Load(object sender, EventArgs e)
    {
        //Declare connection string
        string cnString = "Data Source=(local);➥
        Initial Catalog=RealWorld;Integrated Security=SSPI;";

        //Declare Connection, command, and other related objects
        SqlConnection conReport = new SqlConnection(cnString);
        SqlCommand cmdReport = new SqlCommand();
        SqlDataReader drReport;
        DataSet dsReport = new dsSalesAnalysis();

        try
        {
            conReport.Open();

            cmdReport.CommandType = CommandType.Text;
            cmdReport.Connection = conReport;
            cmdReport.CommandText = "Select * FROM dbo.SalesAnalysis";

            drReport = cmdReport.ExecuteReader();
            dsReport.Tables[0].Load(drReport);

            drReport.Close();
            conReport.Close();

            //provide local report information to viewer
            ReportViewer1.LocalReport.ReportPath = "rptSalesAnalysis.rdlc";
```

```
            //enable report's ability to read external images
            ReportViewer1.LocalReport.EnableExternalImages = true;

            //prepare report data source
            ReportDataSource rds = new ReportDataSource();
            rds.Name = "dsSalesAnalysis_dtSalesAnalysis";
            rds.Value = dsReport.Tables[0];
            ReportViewer1.LocalReport.DataSources.Add(rds);
        }
        catch (Exception ex)
        {
            //display generic error message back to user
            Response.Write(ex.Message);
        }
        finally
        {
            //check if connection is still open then attempt to close it
            if (conReport.State == ConnectionState.Open)
            {
                conReport.Close();
            }
        }
    }
}
```

The code here is a common ADO.NET interface similar to our example earlier in this chapter. We start with connecting to our RealWorld database and gathered data from the SalesAnalysis table. After that, we bind the data to the reporting engine.

Building the Project

The process to build the project remains the same. You can click the small, green play button in the main toolbox or press F5 on the keyboard to start the application in run-time mode. As you learned earlier, click OK when you build it for the first time to enable the debug mode setting. Assuming that you don't encounter any issues during the build, you should see report output that's similar to Figure 5-20.

In this report, you see how we can use the power features of RS by writing your own custom code. You can put images in the report to make it more advantageous by using icons to indicate the profit ratio and to make it look cool.

Ready for more fun and learning new things that RS has to offer? Why not? Let's move on and learn about one more interesting reporting project. What makes this next project interesting is that we are going to use the business object class as the source of data for this report. See, I told you it is going to be a lot of fun, and it will be a bit challenging too!

Net Income Comparison Report

You're working for Home Decorations Incorporated as a developer. Home Decorations has businesses in different countries. You have the task of developing a bar chart report that will display net income comparisons between the current year's and last year's data, by country of operation. The report should meet all characteristics described in Table 5-7, and the report output should match to Figure 5-24.

Table 5-7. *Report Characteristics*

Characteristics	Value
Report title	Net Income Comparison Current Vs Last Year
Company title	Home Decorations Inc.
Data source	Business Object Collection
Columns to report	Country, CurrentYear, and LastYear
Page size	Letter
Page orientation	Portrait
Layout design	No header or footer; all information should be in body section

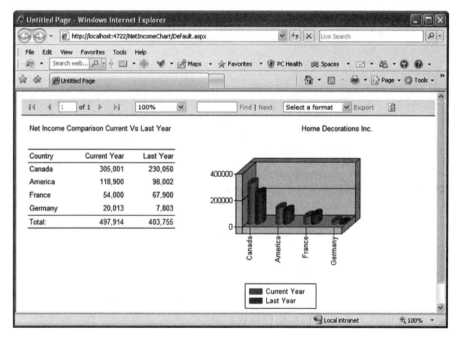

Figure 5-24. *The Net Income Comparison report*

Business Case

We know how important healthy net income figures are at the end of a fiscal year for any business. This becomes even more interesting in a business setup that operates in several countries. The upper management compares these figures with figures from the last year to know the strengths and weaknesses for different places of operation.

You'll routinely see reports like this appear in boardroom presentations and published to all stakeholders. This report also highlights if a particular underperforming country's business operation needs attention.

Getting the Web Site Ready

Please use the following steps to create a web site project:

1. Click File ➤ New ➤ Web Site.

2. In the Templates pane of the New Web Site dialog box, select ASP.NET Web Site.

3. From the Language drop-down menu, select Visual C#.

4. Please give the application a name; I've called the web site NetIncomeChart. You may choose a different location for storing the application files according to your preference.

5. Click the OK button to finish the process. Visual Studio will create a new ASP.NET web site.

After this step, usually we add the dataset to our project. For this project, since we are using the business object collection as a source of data, we will make use of the `ObjectDataSource` class. We will take care of the object data source later; first, let's take care of the ReportViewer. Please repeat the steps from the earlier example to add the ReportViewer, and refer to Figure 5-3 if you need help adding it. Before we move on, please make sure the HTML code inside the `Default.aspx` page looks like the following:

```
<%@ Page Language="C#" AutoEventWireup="true" ➥
 CodeFile="Default.aspx.cs" Inherits="_Default" %>

<%@ Register Assembly="Microsoft.ReportViewer.WebForms,➥
 Version=8.0.0.0, Culture=neutral, ➥
  PublicKeyToken=b03f5f7f11d50a3a"
  Namespace="Microsoft.Reporting.WebForms" TagPrefix="rsweb" %>

<!DOCTYPE html PUBLIC "-//W3C//DTD XHTML 1.0 Transitional//EN"➥
 "http://www.w3.org/TR/xhtml1/DTD/xhtml1-transitional.dtd">

<html xmlns="http://www.w3.org/1999/xhtml" >
<head runat="server">
    <title>Untitled Page</title>
</head>
```

```
<body>
    <form id="form1" runat="server">
    <div>
        <rsweb:ReportViewer ID="ReportViewer1" runat="server" Width="775px">
        </rsweb:ReportViewer>
    </div>
    </form>
</body>
</html>
```

Step 1: Creating Business Object Collections

Let's get started with creating the business object collections as our data source. We need to create two custom classes; the first class will hold the data for net income of the current and last year of all the countries. Adding a class to the project is easy. Start by selecting the project in Solution Explorer; right-click it, and select Add ➤ New Item ➤ Class. Please name the class NetIncome. You'll notice that Visual Studio will ask you to put the class inside the App_Code folder; go ahead click the Yes button to confirm this. Please make sure the code inside NetIncome.cs looks like the following:

```
using System;
using System.Data;
using System.Configuration;
using System.Web;
using System.Web.Security;
using System.Web.UI;
using System.Web.UI.WebControls;
using System.Web.UI.WebControls.WebParts;
using System.Web.UI.HtmlControls;

/// <summary>
/// Summary description for NetIncome
/// </summary>
public class NetIncome
{
    private string _country;
    private double _currentYear;
    private double _lastYear;

    public string Country
    {
        get
        {
            return _country;
        }
        set
```

```
            {
                _country = value;
            }
        }

        public double CurrentYear
        {
            get
            {
                return _currentYear;
            }
            set
            {
                _currentYear = value;
            }
        }

        public double LastYear
        {
            get
            {
                return _lastYear;
            }
            set
            {
                _lastYear = value;
            }
        }

        public NetIncome(string CountryName, double CurrentYear, double LastYear)
        {
            this._country = CountryName;
            this._currentYear = CurrentYear;
            this._lastYear = LastYear;
        }
    }
}
```

The code inside the class is simple. It has only three properties and one method. The three properties are like data columns to us: each one supplies the data for the columns Country, CurrentYear, and LastYear respectively.

Let's add our second class to the project. Please add the class as we did earlier in this report. However, this time, name the class IncomeByCountry. Please make sure the code inside IncomeByCountry.cs looks like the following:

```csharp
using System;
using System.Data;
using System.Configuration;
using System.Web;
using System.Web.Security;
using System.Web.UI;
using System.Web.UI.WebControls;
using System.Web.UI.WebControls.WebParts;
using System.Web.UI.HtmlControls;
using System.Collections.Generic;

/// <summary>
/// Summary description for IncomeByCountry
/// </summary>
public class IncomeByCountry
{
    private List<NetIncome> _netIncome;

    public IncomeByCountry()
    {
        _netIncome = new List<NetIncome>();
        _netIncome.Add(new NetIncome("Canada", 305001, 230050));
        _netIncome.Add(new NetIncome("America", 118900, 98002));
        _netIncome.Add(new NetIncome("France", 54000, 67900));
        _netIncome.Add(new NetIncome("Germany", 20013, 7803));
    }

    public List<NetIncome> GetNetIncomeData()
    {
        return _netIncome;
    }
}
```

The code inside this class is as simple as the code of NetIncome class. As you can see, it is creating a generic collection of NetIncome objects. Data for each country is loaded with details for all three columns (Country, CurrentYear, and LastYear). You can learn more about generic collections here:

http://www.microsoft.com/belux/msdn/nl/community/columns/wuyttersprot/generics.mspx

Step 2: Designing the Report Layout

This report has two main report items: the first is the table, and the second is the chart item. We will use the table item to display data in text format, and with the help of the chart, we'll display the same data as graphics.

From the last step, we have our classes ready to use with the object data source for data binding. In this report, we will bind our business object collection directly to the ReportViewer. However, before we do this, we need to add the report to the project and set ObjectDataSource.

All right then, let's add the report. Select the project in Solution Explorer, and right-click it; select Add ➤ New Item, and select Report from the Add New Item dialog box. Please name the report `rptNetIncomeChart.rdlc`. Click the Add button to complete the process and make the new report part of the project.

I'd like to ask a question here: if you look at the Website Data Sources window now, what will you see? Well, you might be pleasantly surprised to see our class appear as a data source with our three columns ready to use, as shown in Figure 5-25.

If you don't see the classes in the Website Data Sources window, make sure you properly created the custom classes. You can also try closing and reopening the data source window or clicking the refresh icon on the data source window.

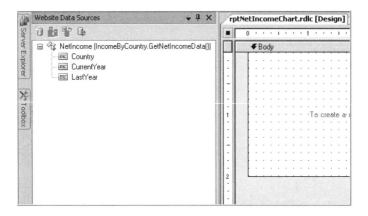

Figure 5-25. *The object collection as the data source*

Setting Up the Page

We need to make sure the report is letter sized and has a portrait page orientation. Right-click the open area inside the design surface; select Properties, and set the page width to 8.5 inches and the page height to 11 inches. Since we are putting everything inside the body section, please increase the height of the body section to 4 inches. You can do this by dragging the edge of the body section downwards or setting the Size property to `7in, 4in`.

Designing Body Section

It is interesting to see different pieces of information are part of the body section instead of divided among the header, footer, and body. This report is a perfect example of a freestyle report. You can see two powerful report items (table and chart) side-by-side. Please drag and drop the following report items inside the body section:

- A text box item for the report title

- A text box item for the company title

- A table item to display tabular data

- A chart item to display graphics

After adding the report items to the design surface, please arrange them according to the report's needs. As we always do now, let's take care of setting properties of various report items on the design surface. Please specify the values of each report item's properties according to Table 5-8.

Table 5-8. *Report Item Properties*

Report Item	Property	Value
textbox1	Value	Net Income Comparison: Current vs. Last Year
textbox2	Value	Home Decorations Inc.
textbox2	TextAlign	Right
TableRow1 ➤ Column1	Value	Country
TableRow1 ➤ Column2	Value	Current Year
TableRow1 ➤ Column2	TextAlign	Right
TableRow1 ➤ Column3	Value	Last Year
TableRow1 ➤ Column3	TextAlign	Right
TableRow1	BorderStyle	None, , , Solid, Solid
TableRow2 ➤ Column1	Value	=Fields!Country.Value
TableRow2 ➤ Column2	Value	=Fileds!CurrentYear.Value
TablcRow2 ➤ Column2	Format	N0
TableRow2 ➤ Column3	Value	=Fileds!LastYear.Value
TableRow2 ➤ Column3	Format	N0
TableRow3 ➤ Column1	Value	Total:
TableRow3 ➤ Column2	Value	=SUM(Fileds!CurrentYear.Value)
TableRow3 ➤ Column2	Format	N0
TableRow3 ➤ Column3	Value	=SUM(Fileds!LastYear.Value)
TableRow3 ➤ Column3	Format	N0
TableRow3	BorderStyle	None, , , Solid, Solid

After you're finished dropping report items on the design surface and setting up properties, your report design surface should look something similar to the one shown in Figure 5-26.

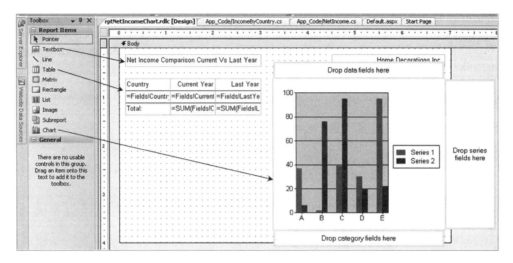

Figure 5-26. *The report designer with the body section*

Customizing the Chart Report Item

When you drag and drop the chart report item, it defaults to a column chart type, and we'll stick with this default choice. You'll also notice that you're guided to drag and drop data for chart plotting. In this example, we have two pieces of data to plot against.

Let's start by dragging Web Site Data Sources ➤ NetIncome ➤ Country and dropping it at the "Drop category fields here" prompt. Do the same for CurrentYear and LastYear, but drop these data sources at the "Drop data fields here" prompt. Please make sure your report design surface looks like the one shown in Figure 5-27 after you drop the plot data on the chart item.

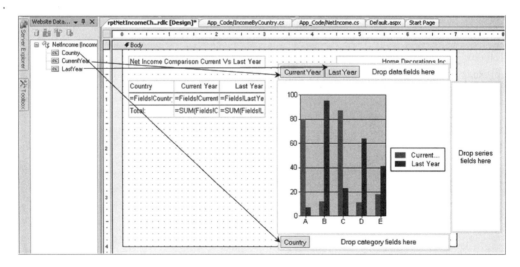

Figure 5-27. *The report designer after specifying plot data on the chart*

If you look at Figure 5-27, what you see is the default layout of the chart. Let's do some customization to this chart. For example, we'll bring the legend to the bottom center of the chart. Start by right-clicking the chart item and selecting Properties. Select the Legend tab, and make sure the "Show legend" check box is checked. Next, click the Position button in the center of the bottom row of options. Click the OK button to complete the legend setup. Please see Figure 5-28 for an illustration of the legend setup.

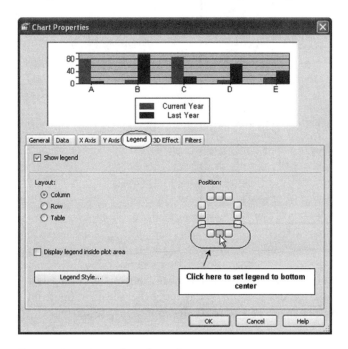

Figure 5-28. *Setting chart legend properties*

Next, let's make our chart look jazzy by changing the appearance to 3-D. Giving a 3-D effect to a chart is easy: right-click the Chart Item, and select Properties again. This time, select the 3D Effect tab and make sure the "Display chart with 3-D visual effect" check box is checked. Next, select the Realistic option from among the Shading radio buttons. Also, make sure to check the Orthographic and Cylinder check boxes. Click the OK button to complete the process; see Figure 5-29 for an illustration of these steps.

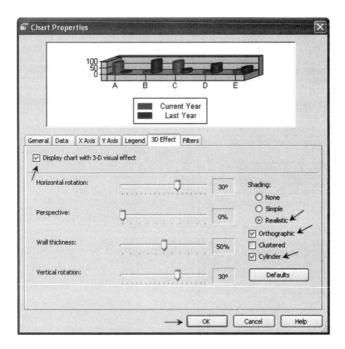

Figure 5-29. *Setting up the chart's 3-D visual effect*

After changing the position of the legend and introducing the 3-D effect, the chart gets a makeover and looks cool. As you make these alterations, you'll notice that the chart figure on the report design surface reflects your changes. Please make sure your report design looks similar to the one shown in Figure 5-30.

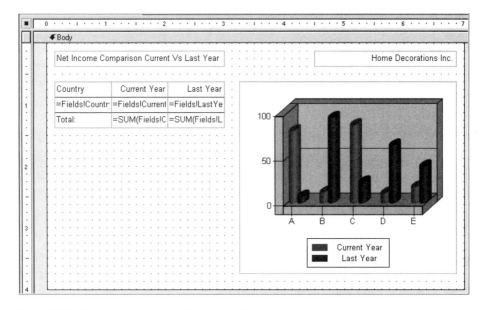

Figure 5-30. *The report designer after customizing the chart properties*

Getting ObjectDataSouce Ready

The last step before we can see our report in action here is using the `ObjectDataSource` class to bind the `NetIncome` collection object to the ReportViewer. The good news is that it is done transparently for us—all we need to do is tell the report name to the ReportViewer. This process automatically creates an instance of `ObjectDataSource` and gets our project ready for build.

Make sure the `Default.aspx` page is open in design view. Select the ReportViewer by clicking it once. As soon as you click it, you will see a small arrow-like icon in the right-most corner. Click the icon, and select our report, `rptNetIncomeChart.rpt`. This action will do the job of binding our object collection with the help of `ObjectDataSource`, and we are good to go to see the report in action. Please see Figure 5-31 for an illustration of the steps.

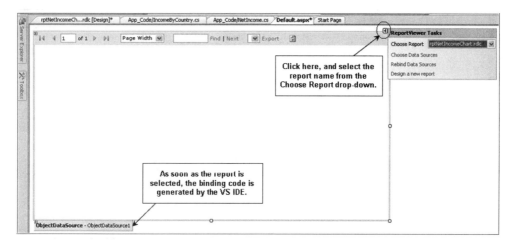

Figure 5-31. *Binding ObjectDataSource with the ReportViewer*

Step 3: Writing C# Code

All the code is taken care of for us by the VS IDE in this report. The only code we needed was to add two classes, which we have already done.

Building the Project

The data binding in this report is different compared with other reports we have done so far. It uses `ObjectDataSource` as the data provider and collection objects as the data source. Let's build the project; you can click the small, green play button in the main toolbox or press F5 on the keyboard to start the application in run-time mode.

If all goes well, you should see page in the default browser with a nice column chart. The output should match Figure 5-24.

Let's move on to another reporting project filled with challenges. This time, I'll show you how to use the drill-through feature of RS. This feature is often used to create a report that uses data from two tables with a master/details relationship. You'll also see how to provide user input to the report by passing in values from the GUI.

Product Information and Inventory Status Report

Assume you're working for AdventureWorks Incorporated as a developer; you've been asked to develop a Product Information and Inventory Status report. This report should gather data from two tables, which have a master/details relationship. Initially, the report will only display the product information. However, it should allow the users to click the product number to probe the inventory status. The UI on the web page should allow users to hide the price list information, if they choose not to see it on the report. Further, the report should meet all the characteristics described in Table 5-9, and the report output should match Figure 5-32.

Table 5-9. *Report Characteristics*

Characteristics	Value
Report title	`Product Information & Inventory Status` (Header Left)
Page number	Page: n/n (Header Right)
Note	`Click the Product Number to check the Inventory Status` (Header Left)
Data source	`ProductDrilldown, ProductLocation`
Columns to report	`ProductDrilldown: ProductNumber, ProductName, CategoryName` and `ListPrice` `InventoryStatus: ProductNumber, LocationName, Shelf, Bin` and `Quantity`
Page size	Letter
Page orientation	Portrait
Drill-through report	`rptInventoryStatus`

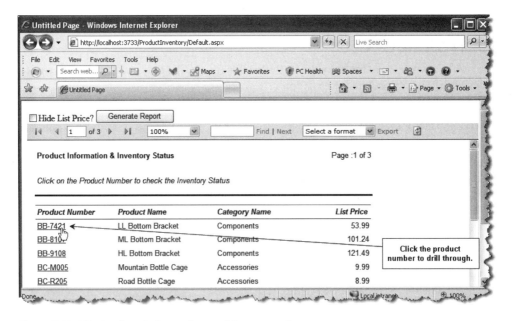

Figure 5-32. *The Product Information and Inventory Status report*

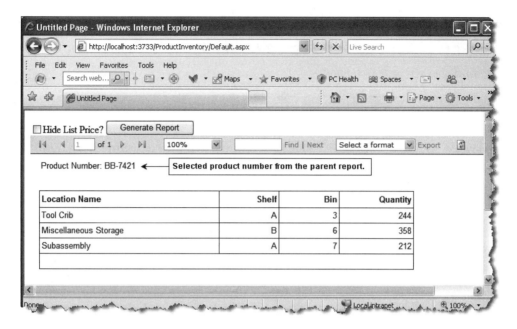

Figure 5-33. *Drill-through information for the selected product number*

The Product Information and Inventory Status report is a two-in-one report. Initially, the report will list the brief production information with the product list price. However, inventory status details can be viewed for any given product by clicking the product number.

Multitask reports like this are used by various departments in a company. Folks who just want to have a quick look at the product list can have what they want. A detailed inventory status with storage location information is helpful for others who use the information to carry on further business processes, for example, when the year-end physical count of inventory takes place for auditing purposes.

Using the Drill-through Feature

Drill-through is a neat feature from RS to report on data that has a master/detail relationship. Unlike the subreport feature we used in Chapter 4, the drill-through feature doesn't embed a child report inside the parent report; it simply jumps to any related report using a common piece of data that links the two reports. In this example, our main report will list the product information data. Using the drill-down feature, this main report will let a user jump to another report by clicking the product number. The link between the two reports is the product number, which is passed from the main report to the calling report with the help of report parameters.

The drill-through feature is also powerful in that it can gather data from totally different sources and link it up with the main report. An example would be a main report that can list employees' financial information from a SQL Server data source. With the help of the drill-through feature of RS, those same employees' payroll details can be gathered from an HR system that is an Oracle data source. The employee ID would be used as a key to link up the data.

Getting the Web Site Ready

Please open Visual Studio and use the following steps to create a web site project:

1. Click File ➤ New ➤ Web Site.

2. In the Templates pane of the New Web Site dialog box, select ASP.NET Web Site.

3. From the Language drop-down menu, select Visual C#.

4. Please give the application a name; I've called the web site ProductInventory. You may choose a different location for storing the application files according to your preference.

5. Click the OK button to finish the process. Visual Studio will create a new ASP.NET web site.

As usual, it is time to add the dataset and ReportViewer to the project. Start by selecting the project in Solution Explorer; right-click it, and select Add ➤ New Item ➤ DataSet. Please name the dataset `dsProductInventory`. As usual put the dataset inside the `App_Code` folder. Recall that we don't need the Table Adapter wizard dialog box, so cancel the process; we'll create the data table later.

As you know, the report should be dynamic in nature for the list price information. If users wish not to display the list prices in the report, they should have the power to indicate this in the GUI. One easy way to do this is by providing a check box that the user can check if they don't want to show the price list information. Therefore, drag CheckBox from the toolbox and drop it inside the `<div>` tags. In addition to the check box, we also need a button control to generate the report.

In this report, we will not put the code directly inside the page load event. We have to wait for the user to decide whether to hide the list price information in the report. Therefore, as you did with check box, drag a button from the toolbox and drop it inside the `<div>` tag after the check box entry.

After adding the button, add the ReportViewer inside the `<div>` tag. Before we go further, please make sure the HTML code inside the `Default.aspx` page looks like the following:

```
<%@ Page Language="C#" AutoEventWireup="false"➡
 CodeFile="Default.aspxcs" Inherits="_Default" %>

<%@ Register Assembly="Microsoft.ReportViewer.WebForms,➡
 Version=8.0.0.0, Culture=neutral,➡
 PublicKeyToken=b03f5f7f11d50a3a"
 Namespace="Microsoft.Reporting.WebForms" TagPrefix="rsweb" %>

<!DOCTYPE html PUBLIC "-//W3C//DTD XHTML 1.0 Transitional//EN"➡
 "http://www.w3.org/TR/xhtml1/DTD/xhtml1-transitional.dtd">

<html xmlns="http://www.w3.org/1999/xhtml" >
<head runat="server">
    <title>Untitled Page</title>
</head>
```

```
<body>
    <form id="form1" runat="server">
    <div>
        <asp:CheckBox ID="CheckBox1" Text="Hide List Price?" runat="server" />
            <asp:Button ID="Button1" runat="server" Text="Generate Report" />
            <rsweb:ReportViewer ID="ReportViewer1" runat="server" Width="800px">
            </rsweb:ReportViewer>
    </div>
    </form>
</body>
</html>
```

Please note that I changed the text from the default to "Hide List Price?" for the check box label. I also changed the text of the button to Generate Report and increased the width of ReportViewer to 800 pixels. Let's create the data tables now. Please change the page view to design mode, and make sure your Default.aspx page looks similar to the one shown in Figure 5-34.

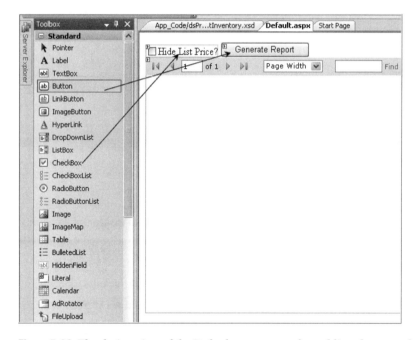

Figure 5-34. *The design view of the Default.aspx page after adding the controls*

Step 1: Creating the Data Tables

As this is two reports in one project, we need two separate data tables: we need one data table to store data related to product information and a second data table for the data related to inventory status.

Creating the Product Information Data Table

Please use the following steps to add the product information data table inside the dataset:

1. You can go to the dataset designer in two ways: double-click dsProductInventory inside Solution Explorer, or right-click dsProductInventory node and select View Designer.

2. To add the data table, right-click the design surface, and select Add ➤ DataTable.

3. Click the Header of the newly created data table, and name it dtProductInformation. Add columns to dtProductInformation by right-clicking DataTable and selecting Add ➤ Column.

4. Add the following columns into the data table; your data table should look like Figure 5-35:

   - ProductNumber (System.String)

   - ProductName (System.DateTime)

   - CategoryName (System.String)

   - ListPrice (System.Double)

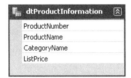

Figure 5-35. *Final look of the dtProductInformation data table*

Creating the Inventory Status Data Table

Please use the following steps to add the inventory status detail data table inside the dataset:

1. You can go to the dataset designer in two ways: double-click dsProductInventory inside Solution Explorer, or right-click dsProductInventory node and select View Designer.

2. To add the data table, right-click the design surface, and select Add ➤ DataTable.

3. Click the Header of the newly created data table, and name it dtInventoryStatus. Add columns to dtInventoryStatus by right-clicking DataTable and selecting Add ➤ Column.

4. Add the following columns into the data table; your data table should look like Figure 5-36:

   - ProductNumber (System.String)

   - LocationName (System.String)

   - Shelf (System. Int32)

- Bin (System.Int32)

- Quantity (System. Int32)

Figure 5-36. *Final look of the dtInventoryStatus data table*

After adding both the data tables, please make sure your dataset design surface looks similar to Figure 5-37.

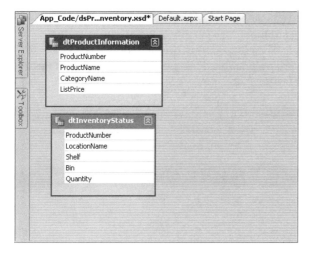

Figure 5-37. *Final look of the dsProductInventory dataset*

Step 2: Designing the Report Layout

Again, since this report is like two reports in one, the inventory status report can be drilled-through from the main product information report. Let's call the main one Product Information report and the drill-through report Inventory Status. Both of these reports have different layouts, so we will discuss them separately. Let's design the Inventory Status report first.

Designing the Layout for the Inventory Status Report

The layout of this report is simple; all we need to do is create a tabular report by using the table report item. Before we start designing the report layout, let's add the report to the project. As usual, add the report by selecting the project in Solution Explorer, right-clicking it, and selecting Add ➤ New Item. Select Report from the Add New Item dialog box, and name the report rptInventoryStatus.rdlc. Click the Add button to complete the process; a new report is now part of the project. We don't need any header and footer for this report; inventory status details are listed in the body section.

Setting Up the Page

No special considerations are needed as far as page setup is concerned. Just make sure the report is letter sized and has a portrait page orientation: right-click the open area inside the design surface, and select Properties to check. As usual, you may wish to put your name in the Author field and fill in the Description field.

Designing the Body Section

Recall that we will make use of a table report item here in the body section? Let's start working on this section by dragging Report Items ➤ Table from the toolbox and dropping it inside the body section in the report designer. A new table item is part of the report now, and it has the default name of table1. As usual, three columns are added for us, but we need one more column. Please add one more column to the right side.

As we don't want to repeat the product number on each row of the inventory status details, let's keep the product name outside of table1. For this, drag and drop a text box onto the report designer and make sure to place it over table1. Please make sure your report design surface looks similar to the one shown in Figure 5-38.

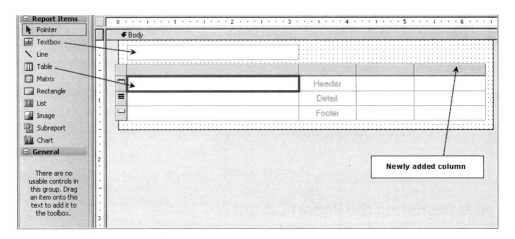

Figure 5-38. *The report design surface after adding the table and text box items*

The table needs data mapping from our data tables; therefore, select Data Source ➤ dsProductInventory ➤ LocationName and drag and drop it inside the first cell of the table item's detail section (TableRow2). Repeat this task for Shelf, Bin, and Quantity. How about the text box; what should the value be? Well, the text box will have the following expression to show the product number:

```
="Product Number: " &  Fields!ProductNumber.Value.
```

After mapping the data, make sure to apply all the properties settings of table1 according to Table 5-10.

Table 5-10. *Table Item Properties for the Body Section*

Table Item	Property	Value
table1	BorderStyle	Solid
All text boxes inside table1	BorderStyle	Solid
TableRow1	Font	Normal, Arial, 10pt, Bold
TableRow1 ➤ Column1	Value	Location Name
TableRow1 ➤ Column2	Value	Shelf
TableRow1 ➤ Column2	TextAlign	Right
TableRow1 ➤ Column3	Value	Bin
TableRow1 ➤ Column3	TextAlign	Right
TableRow1 ➤ Column4	Value	Quantity
TableRow1 ➤ Column4	TextAlign	Right
TableRow2 ➤ Column1	Value	=Fields!LocationName.Value
TableRow2 ➤ Column2	Value	=Fields!Shelf.Value
TableRow2 ➤ Column3	Value	=Fields!Bin.Value
TableRow2 ➤ Column4	Value	=Fields!Quantity.Value
TableRow1 ➤ Column2 to Column4	Format	NO

That's it. Our report design is ready now. Please make sure your final report design looks similar to Figure 5-39.

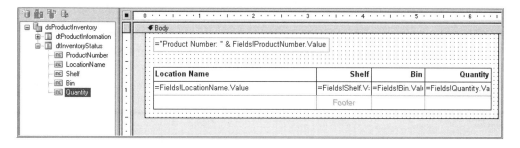

Figure 5-39. *Final look of the report design*

The last step left here in this report design is to add a report parameter. Why do we need a report parameter? We need the report parameter to pass on the product name dynamically to this report from the product information report. We will pass ProductNumber from the product information report, which will be used as a filter to show the inventory status of only the selected product.

Adding a report parameter is easy: use the following steps to add the report parameter (see the illustration in Figure 5-40):

1. Right-click the report designer's gray open area, and select Report Parameters.

2. Click the Add button in the Report Parameters dialog box.

3. Name the parameter `parProductNumber`; for the Prompt, type **Product Number**.

4. Click the OK button to complete the process.

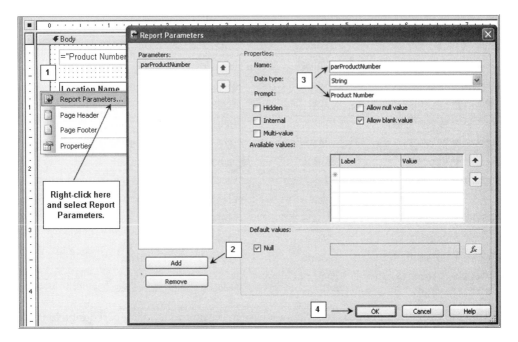

Figure 5-40. *Adding a report parameter*

All right, we've got the report parameter ready. Now what? Let's make use if it. We will use the report parameter to filter the data from the inventory status table. We need to apply the filter on `table1`. To set up the filter on `table1`, use the following steps (see Figure 5-41):

1. Right-click `table1`, and select Properties.

2. Select the Filters tab in the Table Properties dialog box.

3. Set the filter list Expression to `=Fields!ProductName.Value`. For Operator, select the equals sign (=), and set the Filter value to `=Parameters!parProductName.Value`.

4. Click the OK button to complete the process.

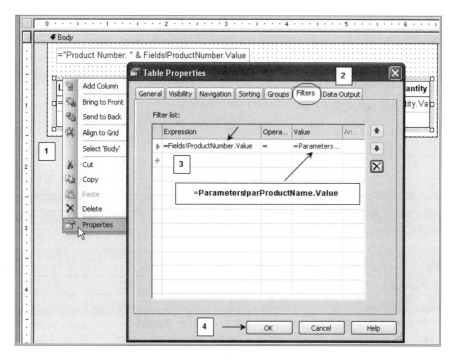

Figure 5-41. *Setting filter on table1*

We are finished with our inventory status report now. Let's move on to designing the product information report, which will drill through our Inventory Status report.

Designing the Layout for the Product Information Report

For the Product Information report, we need header and body sections. Recall that the header section has the report title, page numbers, and notes. The body section will be a tabular list with product information.

Before we start designing the report layout, let's add the report to the project. Select the project in Solution Explorer, right-click it, and select Add ➤ New Item. Select Report from the Add New Item dialog box, and name the report rptProductInformation.rdlc. Click the Add button to complete the process; a new report is now part of the project.

Adding a Header

Let's add the header to the report, as usual, by right-clicking the open area inside the report designer and selecting Page Header.

Setting Up the Page

As we always do, let's set up the page before working on the report design. Make sure the report is letter sized and has a portrait page orientation: right-click the open area inside the design surface, and select Properties to check. As usual, you may wish to put your name in the Author field and fill in the Description field.

Designing the Page Header

We'll start working on the header now. Please drag and drop the following report items inside the header section:

- A text box item for the report title

- A text box item for the page number

- A text box item for the note

- A line item for separating the header and detail sections

Report item properties can be changed in the same ways as the previous examples. Select each of the report items in turn, and specify the values for each report item's properties according to Table 5-11. Your report design surface, after completing the header, should look similar to Figure 5-42.

Table 5-11. *Report Item Properties for the Header*

Report Item	Property	Value
textbox1		
	Value	Product Information & Inventory Status
	Font	Normal, Arial, 10pt, Bold
textbox2		
	Value	="Page :" & Globals!PageNumber & " of " & Globals!TotalPages
	TextAlign	Right
textbox3		
	Value	Click on the Product Number to check the Inventory Status
	Font	Italic, Arial, 10pt, Normal
line1		
	LineWidth	2pt

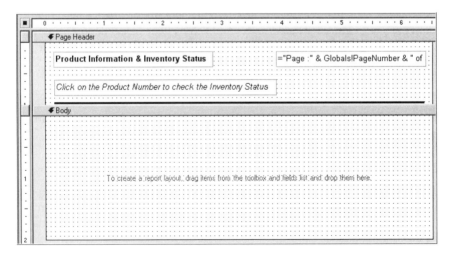

Figure 5-42. *The report designer after adding the report header and related report items*

Designing the Body Section

We'll make use of a table report item in this section to list product information. Let's start by dragging Report Items ➤ Table from the toolbox and dropping it inside the body section in the report designer. As usual, a new table item named table1 is part of the report now, and we have the three columns added for us. However, we need one more column, so please add one to the right side. Make sure your report design surface looks similar to the one shown in Figure 5-43.

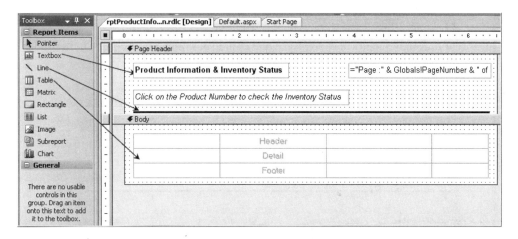

Figure 5-43. *The report design surface after adding the table item*

As usual, table1 needs to be mapped to our data tables; therefore, select Data Source ➤ dsProductInventory ➤ ProductNumber and drag and drop it inside the first cell of the table item's detail section (TableRow2). Repeat this task for ProductName, CategoryName, and ListPrice.

After mapping the data, make sure to apply all the properties settings of table1 according to the settings mentioned in Table 5-12. If you notice in the report output, the product number appears as an underlined link. This is achieved by setting TextDecoration property of the text box to Underline.

Table 5-12. *Table Item Properties for the Body Section*

Table Item	Property	Value
TableRow1	BorderStyle	Solid
TableRow1	Font	Italic, Arial, 10pt, Bold
TableRow1 ➤ Column1	Value	Product Number
TableRow1 ➤ Column2	Value	Product Name
TableRow1 ➤ Column3	Value	Category
TableRow1 ➤ Column4	Value	List Price
TableRow1 ➤ Column4	TextAlign	Right
TableRow2 ➤ Column1	Value	=Fields!ProductNumber.Value

Continued

Table 5-12. *Continued*

Table Item	Property	Value
TableRow2 ➤ Column1	TextDecoration	Underline
TableRow2 ➤ Column2	Value	=Fields!ProductNameValue
TableRow2 ➤ Column3	Value	=Fields!ProductCateogry.Value
TableRow2 ➤ Column4	Value	=Fields!ListPrice.Value
TableRow2 ➤ Column4	Format	NO

Our report design is ready now, so please make sure your final report design looks similar to Figure 5-44.

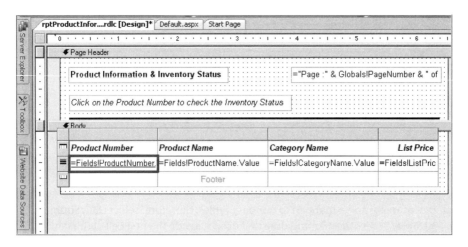

Figure 5-44. *Final look of the report design*

All right, our design is ready now, but how do we get the drill-through feature working? Well, it is easy. Recall that a user will click the product number to launch our Inventory Status report. To make this possible, we need to pass the product number from our parent report and provide instructions for jumping to the Inventory Status report. To set up the drill-through feature to accomplish that, use the following steps (see Figure 5-45):

1. Right-click the Product Number cell (TableRow2 ➤ Column1) to access the Textbox Properties dialog box.

2. From the Navigation tab, type or select rptInventoryStatus from the "Jump to report" drop-down menu.

3. Click the Parameters button, and set the following values (see Figure 5-46):

   - Parameter Name: parProductNumber

   - Parameter Value: =Fields!ProductNumber.Value

4. Click the OK button to complete the process.

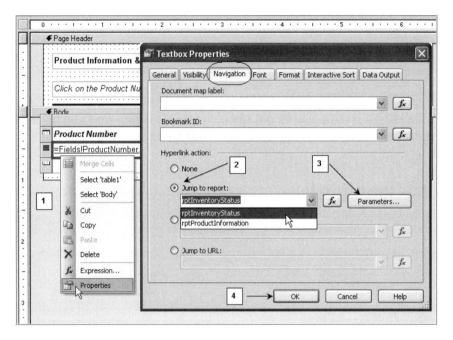

Figure 5-45. *Setting up the drill-through feature to jump to another report from the parent report*

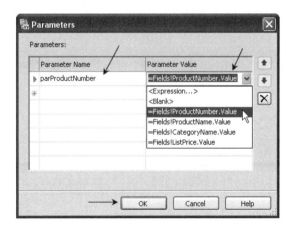

Figure 5-46. *Setting the drill-through parameter values*

We have reached to the last step to complete our report before we move on to writing the C# code. Recall that we need to provide the on-demand hide feature for the price list column. For this, we need to add a parameter to our report. We will use this parameter to get values from the GUI client, and based on the value, we will either hide or show the price list column.

Just like we added the parameter in the previous section for the inventory status report, let's add a parameter to this report now; use the following steps to add a report parameter (see Figure 5-40):

1. Right-click the report designer's gray open area, and select Report Parameters.

2. Click the Add button inside the Report Parameters dialog box.

3. Name the parameter `parHidePriceList`; for the Prompt, type `Hide Product List? Y/N`.

4. Click the OK button to complete the process.

This is what we needed as the design for this report. Let's move on to writing some cool C# code for dynamic communication between the client and reports and bring life to our drill-through report.

Step 3: Writing the C# Code

As usual, add the following code behind `Default.aspx.cs`:

```
using System;
using System.Data;
using System.Configuration;
using System.Collections;
using System.Web;
using System.Web.Security;
using System.Web.UI;
using System.Web.UI.WebControls;
using System.Web.UI.WebControls.WebParts;
using System.Web.UI.HtmlControls;
using System.Data.SqlClient;
using Microsoft.Reporting.WebForms;

public partial class _Default : System.Web.UI.Page
{
    protected void Page_Load(object sender, EventArgs e)
    {
        // Add a handler for drill-through report
        ReportViewer1.Drillthrough += new ➡
DrillthroughEventHandler(ReportViewer1_Drillthrough);
    }
    protected void Button1_Click(object sender, EventArgs e)
    {
        // connection string
        string cnString = @"Data Source=(local);Initial Catalog=➡
            RealWorld;Integrated Security=SSPI;";

        SqlConnection conReport = new SqlConnection(cnString);
        SqlCommand cmdReport = new SqlCommand();
        SqlDataReader drReport;
        DataSet dsReport = new dsProductInventory();
```

```
try
{
    // open connection
    conReport.Open();

    cmdReport.CommandType = CommandType.Text;
    cmdReport.Connection = conReport;

    // get query string from string builder
    cmdReport.CommandText = "SELECT * FROM ProductDrilldown➡
            ORDER BY ProductNumber; SELECT * FROM InventoryStatus➡
            ORDER BY ProductNumber";

    // execute query and load result to dataset
    drReport = cmdReport.ExecuteReader();

    dsReport.Load(drReport, LoadOption.OverwriteChanges,➡
            dsReport.Tables[1], dsReport.Tables[0]);

    // close connection
    drReport.Close();
    conReport.Close();

    Session["dsProductInventory"] = (DataSet)dsReport;

    // prepare report for view
    ReportViewer1.LocalReport.ReportPath = "rptProductInformation.rdlc";

    //pass user choice of hiding price list column to
    //report using the report parameters
    ReportParameter parHidePriceList = new➡
        ReportParameter("parHidePriceList", CheckBox1.Checked ? "Y" : "N");
    ReportViewer1.LocalReport.SetParameters(new ReportParameter[] ➡
            { parHidePriceList });

    ReportDataSource rds = new ReportDataSource();
    rds.Name = "dsProductInventory_dtProductInformation";

    rds.Value = dsReport.Tables[1];
    ReportViewer1.LocalReport.DataSources.Add(rds);
}
catch (Exception ex)
{
    Response.Write(ex.Message);
}
```

```
        finally
        {
            if (conReport.State == ConnectionState.Open)
            {
                conReport.Close();
            }
        }
    }
}

void ReportViewer1_Drillthrough(object sender,➥
    Microsoft.Reporting.WebForms.DrillthroughEventArgs e)
{
    DataSet ds = new DataSet();
    ds = (DataSet)Session["dsProductInventory"];

    LocalReport InventoryReport = (LocalReport)e.Report;
    InventoryReport.DataSources.Add(new ReportDataSource➥
        ("dsProductInventory_dtInventoryStatus", ds.Tables[0]));
}
}
```

This code has a few extra special instructions compared with previous examples. First, you'll see that there are page-load and button-click events. In the page-load event, I'm taking care of the drill-through event handler; I need to handle this event while the page loads, because when the user clicks the product number a postback happens. Due to this postback event, we need to handle the drill-through event again.

With the button-click event, I'm doing the bulk of the job. Since we have two tables to fill in this example, I sent two separate SQL SELECT statements to the database:

```
cmdReport.CommandText = "SELECT * FROM ProductDrilldown➥
ORDER BY ProductNumber; SELECT * FROM InventoryStatus➥
ORDER BY ProductNumber";
```

Next, I load the data from the data reader to the dataset by calling the Load method like this:

```
dsReport.Load(drReport, LoadOption.OverwriteChanges, dsReport.Tables[1],➥
dsReport.Tables[0]);
```

If you notice, I'm calling the Load method by passing some extra parameters; the first parameter sets the overwrite condition and the second passes in each table reference to fill from the dataset. You might be wondering how our drill-through report manages to get the data; for that, we have to create a handler, which looks like the following:

```
ReportViewer1.Drillthrough += new ➥
DrillthroughEventHandler(ReportViewer1_Drillthrough);
```

With the preceding lines added to code, we add an event handler to the Drillthrough event of the parent report. Next, we add another method, ReportViewer1_Drillthrough, that responds to this event. The code behind our method takes care of getting the data for our child report. The code inside our method looks like this:

```
DataSet ds = new DataSet();
ds = (DataSet)Session["dsProductInventory"];
LocalReport InventoryReport = (LocalReport)e.Report;
InventoryReport.DataSources.Add(new ReportDataSource➥
("dsProductInventory_dtInventoryStatus", ds.Tables[0]));
```

You'll also notice that I'm making use of a session to hold the dataset content intact for both the parent and drill-through reports. All right, it's time to see the magic of the drill-through report in action—let's move on to building the project.

Building the Project

Again, build the project by clicking the small, green play button in the main toolbox or pressing F5. If the program compiles without any errors, you will see the form with the report in preview mode. Please make sure the report looks similar to the ones shown in Figures 5-32 and 5-33 (this report varies depending on what product number you click in the parent report).

Recall that we built functionality to let the user decide if the price list should be displayed or not. Let's try this function and see how the report output looks. If you click the Hide List Price? check box and click the button to generate the report, your report output should look similar to Figure 5-47.

See how the entire price list column is hidden in the report output? This kind of dynamic control provides powerful interaction of the GUI and report rendering engine.

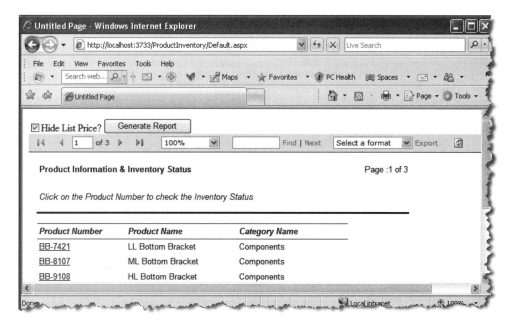

Figure 5-47. *Report output with the Hide Price List? option selected*

Recall in the first chapter that I showed you a real-world example of a Trial Balance report in Arabic? Well, let me show you now how you can create a report that is not in the English language. Further, you'll see how to handle a language that is written from right to left.

How about a Chart of Accounts report to demonstrate this feature of RS? We'll create the report in English, then in Arabic. I promise you will enjoy this example. I'm also including one more feature of RS here—reporting on hierarchical data.

Chart of Accounts Report in English

Assume you're working for Modern Freight and Logistics Limited as a developer; you're working on a financial system and creating a Chart of Accounts report. The report should list all the accounts' names in a hierarchical tree structure. For example, all Asset accounts must group together and trail down from Asset to Current Asset to Chat in Hand and so forth. Further, the report should meet all characteristics described in Table 5-13, and the report output should match Figure 5-48.

Table 5-13. *Report Characteristics*

Characteristics	Value
Report title	Chart of Accounts (Header Left)
Page number	Page: n/n (Header Right)
Data source	ChartOfAccounts
Columns to report	AccountID, AccountCode, AccountNameEng, AccountGeneralID, AccountGeneralCode, AccountType and AccountGroup
Page size	Letter
Page orientation	Portrait

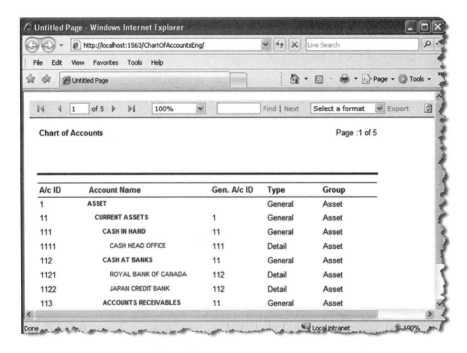

Figure 5-48. *The Chart of Accounts Report in English*

Business Case

I think a Chart of Accounts report is the heart of any financial system. Why is that? Well, this report shows the user how the financial structure of a company looks. All levels of users can benefit from this report. The account numbers and categorization could help a data-entry clerk. At the same time, this report tells a lot about the companywide financial structure, for example, how many banks the company operates and different cost accounts in use.

Getting the Web Site Ready

Please open Visual Studio, and use the following steps to create a web site project:

1. Click File ➤ New ➤ Web Site.

2. In the Templates pane of the New Web Site dialog box, select ASP.NET Web Site.

3. From the Language drop-down menu, select Visual C#.

4. Please give the application a name; I've called the web site ChartOfAccountsEng. You may choose a different location for storing the application files according to your preference.

5. Click the OK button to finish the process. Visual Studio will create a new ASP.NET web site.

By this time, I'm sure you know what our next step is after creating the web site. You got it right—we add the dataset and ReportViewer to the project. Start by selecting the project in Solution Explorer; right-click it, and select Add ➤ New Item ➤ DataSet. Please name the dataset dsChartOfAccounts, and put the dataset inside the App_Code folder. Recall that we don't need the Table Adapter wizard dialog box, so cancel the process; we'll create the data table later.

As usual, let's drag the ReportViewer from the toolbox and drop it inside the <div> tags. Before we move on, please make sure the HTML code inside the Default.aspx page looks like the following:

```
<%@ Page Language="C#" AutoEventWireup="true"➥
  CodeFile="Default.aspx.cs" Inherits="_Default" %>

<%@ Register Assembly="Microsoft.ReportViewer.WebForms,➥
 Version=8.0.0.0, Culture=neutral, ➥
  PublicKeyToken=b03f5f7f11d50a3a"
  Namespace="Microsoft.Reporting.WebForms" TagPrefix="rsweb" %>

<!DOCTYPE html PUBLIC "-//W3C//DTD XHTML 1.0 Transitional//EN"➥
 "http://www.w3.org/TR/xhtml1/DTD/xhtml1-transitional.dtd">

<html xmlns="http://www.w3.org/1999/xhtml" >
<head runat="server">
    <title>Untitled Page</title>
</head>
```

```
<body>
    <form id="form1" runat="server">
    <div>
        <rsweb:ReportViewer ID="ReportViewer1" runat="server" Width="800px">
        </rsweb:ReportViewer>
    </div>
    </form>
</body>
</html>
```

You'll notice that I added Width="800px" in the code to increase the width of
ReportViewer. Let's create the data table now.

Step 1: Creating the Data Table

Please use the following steps to add the data table inside the dataset:

1. You can go to the dataset designer in two ways: double-click dsChartOfAccounts inside
   Solution Explorer, or right-click dsChartOfAccounts node and select View Designer.

2. To add the data table, right-click the design surface, and select Add ➤ DataTable.

3. Click the Header of the newly created data table, and name it dtChartOfAccounts. Add
   columns to dtChartOfAccounts by right-clicking DataTable and selecting Add ➤
   Column.

4. Add the following columns into the data table; your data table should look like
   Figure 5-49:

   - AccountID (System.Int32)

   - AccountCode (System.String)

   - AccountNameEng (System.String)

   - AccountType (System.String)

   - AccountGroup (System.String)

   - AccountGeneralID (System.Int32)

   - AccountGeneralCode (System.String)

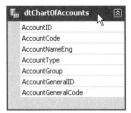

Figure 5-49. *Final look of the dtChartOfAccounts data table*

Step 2: Designing the Report Layout

This report has a simple tabular layout; what makes the output interesting is the hierarchical tree of account names. You'll also see some conditional formatting in action in this report. We will use our familiar table report item, but before we start designing the layout, let's add the report to the project. I'm sure you know how to add a new report by now: select the project in Solution Explorer, right-click it, and select Add ➤ New Item. Select Report from the Add New Item dialog box, and name the report `rptChartOfAccountsEng.rdlc`. Click the Add button to complete the process; a new report is now part of the project. We don't need any footer for this report, so let's begin the design by adding the header.

Adding a Header

Add the header to the report, as usual, by right-clicking the open area inside the report designer and selecting Page Header.

Setting Up the Page

Nothing's different here in the page setup. Before we start to work on the report design, make sure the report is letter sized and has a portrait page orientation by right-clicking the open area inside the design surface and selecting Properties. As usual, you may wish to put your name in the Author field and fill in the Description field.

Designing the Page Header

We'll start working on the header now. Please drag and drop the following report items inside the header section:

- A text box item for the report title

- A text box item for the page number

- A line item for separating the header and detail sections

The next step is to set the properties of the report items. Select each report item in turn, and specify the values for each item's properties according to Table 5-14. Your report design surface, after completing the header, should look similar to Figure 5-50.

Table 5-14. *Report Item Properties for the Header*

Report Item	Property	Value
textbox1		
	Value	Chart of Accounts
	Font	Normal, Arial, 10pt, Bold
textbox2		
	Value	="Page :" & Globals!PageNumber & " of " & Globals!TotalPages
	TextAlign	Right
line1		
	LineWidth	2pt

Figure 5-50. *The report designer after adding the report header and related report items*

Designing the Body Section

As I told you already, we'll make use of the table report item in this section to list account information. Let's start working on this section by dragging Report Items ➤ Table from the toolbox and dropping it inside the body section in the report designer. As usual, a new table item is part of the report now, with the name table1. As you can see in Figure 5-48, we need a total of five columns in the report output. This means we need to add two extra columns apart from the default generated three columns. Please add two more columns to the right side. Please make sure your report design surface looks similar to Figure 5-51. Notice that I have adjusted the width of the second column so that I can accommodate account names easily.

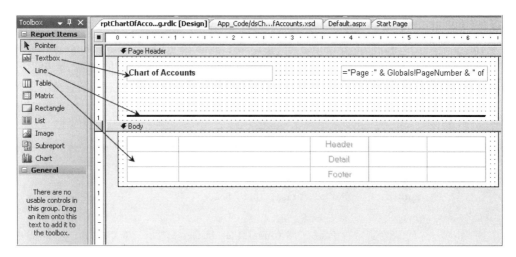

Figure 5-51. *The report design surface after adding the table item*

As usual, table1 needs data to be mapped from our data tables; therefore, select Data Source ➤ dsChartOfAccounts ➤ AccountCode and drag and drop it inside the first column of the table item's detail section (TableRow2). Repeat this task for AccountNameEng and AccountGeneralCode. How about the account type and account group? Well, for both of those, we will need to type an expression. For the account type, the column contains data as 1 and 2. However, in the report, we need to translate this and display "General" and "Detail" instead. We can achieve this dynamically by using the Switch() function in the expression. Please type the following expression for the account type:

```
=Switch(Fields!AccountType.Value = "1", "General", ➡
   Fields! AccountType.Value = "2", "Detail")
```

As you can see, the Switch() function replaces the values in the account type column with the values we want the report to display based on the original values. In other words, for every account entry that has account type "1", the report will display the value as General. Please make sure to type the following expression for the account group:

```
=Switch(Fields!AccountGroup.Value = "1", "Asset",➡
 Fields! AccountGroup.Value = "2",➡
 "Liabilities", Fields! AccountGroup.Value = "3", ➡
 "Capital", Fields! AccountGroup.Value = "4",➡
 "Revenue", Fields! AccountGroup.Value = "5", "Expense")
```

After mapping the data, make sure to apply all the properties settings of table1 according to Table 5-15. You'll notice that I have replaced the default column names with shorter versions; for example, instead of the default "Account Code", I changed the name to "A/c ID".

Table 5-15. *Table Item Properties for Body Section*

Table Item	Property	Value
TableRow1	BorderStyle	Solid
TableRow1	Font	Italic, Arial, 10pt, Bold
TableRow1 ➤ Column1	Value	A/c ID
TableRow1 ➤ Column2	Value	Account Name
TableRow1 ➤ Column3	Value	Gen. A/c ID
TableRow1 ➤ Column4	Value	Type
TableRow1 ➤ Column5	Value	Group
TableRow2 ➤ Column1	Value	=Fields!AccountCode.Value
TableRow2 ➤ Column2	Value	=Fields!AccountNameEng.Value
TableRow2 ➤ Column3	Value	=Fields!AccountGeneralCode.Value
TableRow2 ➤ Column4	Value	=Switch(Fields!AccountType.Value = "1", "General", Fields!AccountType.Value = "2", "Detail")
TableRow2 ➤ Column5	Value	=Switch(Fields!AccountGroup.Value = "1", "Asset", Fields!AccountGroup.Value = "2", "Liabilities", Fields!AccountGroup.Value = "3", "Capital", Fields!AccountGroup.Value = "4", "Revenue", Fields!AccountGroup.Value = "5", "Expense")

That's it; our report design is ready now. Please make sure your final report design looks similar to the one shown in Figure 5-52.

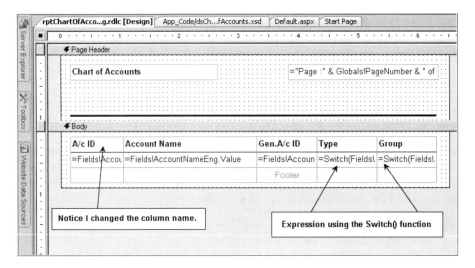

Figure 5-52. *Final look of the report design*

Recall that I mentioned earlier that the account name column will show the hierarchy. For example, as Figure 5-48 shows, the Cash in Hand account reports to the Current Assets account, which reports to the Asset account. This hierarchy is established by creating a parent/child relationship between `AccountID` and `AccountGeneralID` where each `AccountID` has a reporting `AccountGeneralID`.

With this parent/child relationship, we can use RS to create levels of hierarchy for account names. Further, we can display this information in a report. So, are you ready to see how hierarchical data is so easily taken care of by RS? All right, let me show you how to make use of this parent/child relationship.

To set up a hierarchical relationship, please use the following steps (see Figure 5-53):

1. Select the detail row (`TableRow2`), right-click it, and select Edit Group.

2. From the General tab, type or select `=Fields!AccountID.Value` for the Group on Expression.

3. Type or select `=Fields!AccountGeneralID.Value` in the "Parent group" drop-down.

4. Click the OK button to complete the process.

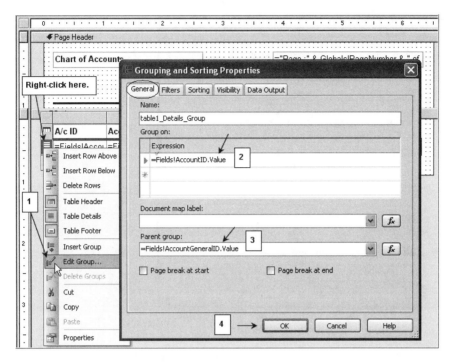

Figure 5-53. *Setting up a hierarchical relationship*

In Figure 5-53, a parent/child relationship is established between AccountID and AccountGeneralID. This relationship is formed as a group with the default name table1_Details_Group. We will make use of this group later to format the report output to show the account name hierarchy.

As you can see in the report output, depending on the hierarchy level, the account name shifts to the left. You'll also notice that all accounts that are of the General type appear in a bold font. Both of these settings are easy to apply.

Let's first take care of the bold font for all the General accounts. Please make sure to have the following expression set for the FontWeight property of TableRow2 ➤ Column2:

```
Normal, Arial, 8pt, =iif(Fields!AccountType.Value = "1", "Bold", "Normal")
```

Now, let's take care of the hierarchical display of account names. Recall that, depending on the hierarchy, the account name leaves some space to its left side. We can achieve this by setting up the Padding(Left) property with the following expression:

```
=Level("table1_Details_Group") * 10 & "pt", 2pt, 2pt, 2pt
```

As you can see here, we make use of the Level() function to find out the group level and multiply it by 10 pixels. Therefore, as the group level increases, so does the space on the left side of the account name, making the display look truly hierarchical.

Figure 5-54 shows the Properties window with FontWeight and Padding set up.

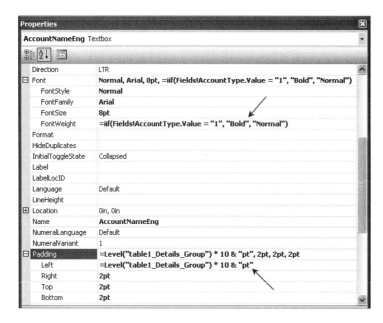

Figure 5-54. *Property setups for FontWeight and Padding*

We have reached the last step to complete our report now. Let's get our C# code ready to pump life into our report.

Step 3: Writing the C# Code

As usual, add the following code behind `Default.aspx.cs`:

```
using System;
using System.Data;
using System.Configuration;
using System.Web;
using System.Web.Security;
using System.Web.UI;
using System.Web.UI.WebControls;
using System.Web.UI.WebControls.WebParts;
using System.Web.UI.HtmlControls;
using System.Data.SqlClient;
using Microsoft.Reporting.WebForms;

public partial class _Default : System.Web.UI.Page
{
    protected void Page_Load(object sender, EventArgs e)
    {
        // connection string
        string cnString = @"Data Source=(local);Initial Catalog=➡
            RealWorld;Integrated Security=SSPI;";
```

```
SqlConnection conReport = new SqlConnection(cnString);
SqlCommand cmdReport = new SqlCommand();
SqlDataReader drReport;
DataSet dsReport = new dsChartOfAccounts();

try
{
    // open connection
    conReport.Open();

    cmdReport.CommandType = CommandType.Text;
    cmdReport.Connection = conReport;

    // get query string from string builder
    cmdReport.CommandText = "SELECT * FROM ChartOfAccounts➥
            ORDER BY AccountCode";

    // execute query and load result to dataset
    drReport = cmdReport.ExecuteReader();

    dsReport.Tables[0].Load(drReport);

    // close connection
    drReport.Close();
    conReport.Close();

    // prepare report for view
    ReportViewer1.LocalReport.ReportPath = "rptChartOfAccountsEng.rdlc";

    ReportDataSource rds = new ReportDataSource();
    rds.Name = "dsChartOfAccounts_dtChartOfAccounts";

    rds.Value = dsReport.Tables[0];
    ReportViewer1.LocalReport.DataSources.Add(rds);
}
catch (Exception ex)
{
    Response.Write(ex.Message);
}
finally
{
    if (conReport.State == ConnectionState.Open)
    {
        conReport.Close();
    }
}
    }
}
```

Much of the fancy work for this report was done during the report design. The C# code for this report is simple; as we have seen in some earlier examples, we're getting the connection, firing the query, and binding the dataset to the reporting engine. Let's move on to build the report now.

Building the Project

As usual, build the project by clicking the small, green play button in the main toolbox or pressing F5. If the program compiles without any errors, you will see the form with the report in preview mode. Please make sure the report looks similar to the one shown in Figure 5-48.

So, you see how easy it is to report on data that is hierarchical in nature! Let's continue the fun with our last report in this chapter. Yes, you guessed it; we will develop the same Chart of Accounts report, but now the report will be in the Arabic language. This is your chance to explore the international language support capabilities of client-side RS.

Chart of Accounts Report in Arabic

Assume that your financial application is bilingual in nature. That is, your system works in English and Arabic. To meet this criterion, you need to create the Arabic version of the Chart of Accounts report.

Keep all the functionality the same as the English version; you have to make sure all cosmetic changes are in place including the right-to-left interface of the Arabic language. Your report should meet all characteristics described in Table 5-16, and the report output should match Figure 5-55.

Table 5-16. *Report Characteristics*

Characteristics	Value
Report title	مخطط حسابات (Header—Right)
Page number	Page: n/n (Header—Left)
Data source	ChartOfAccounts
Columns to report	AccountID, AccountCode, AccountNameEng, AccountGeneralID, AccountGeneralCode, AccountType and AccountGroup
Page size	A4
Page orientation	Portrait

As you can see in Table 5-16, I've used the translation of "Chart of Accounts" to Arabic for the title. I'm using the beta version of Google Translate to translate from English to Arabic for this example. And the data for the report is a mockup of one of the systems I developed for a client based in the Middle East.

You can translate your English text with help of the Google site and then cut and paste the Arabic text to use it in the report design. Here is the link for the Google Translate tool:

```
http://translate.google.com/translate_t?langpair=en|ar
```

You'll also notice that, instead of our regular letter-size page, this time we'll use A4 as the page size; A4 is the common page size in most European and Middle Eastern countries.

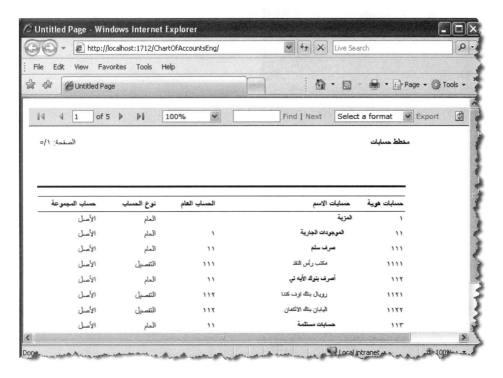

Figure 5-55. *Chart of Accounts Report in Arabic*

Getting the Web Site Ready

To get Arabic support, you need to make sure your current Windows setup is properly configured. You can set up Arabic language support easily by clicking Start ➤ Control Panel ➤ Regional and Language Options. From the Languages tab, make sure the "Install files for complex script and right-to-left languages" check box is selected. Figure 5-56 shows the Regional and Language options dialog box for Windows XP; for non-XP systems, please consult Microsoft's help documents.

After you make sure Arabic language support is properly installed, you can select one of the regions that support Arabic. For this example, I selected Arabic (U.A.E). Altering this setting will show you how the report designer screen changes according to regional settings of your PC. This setting is also important to see the Arabic numerals properly displayed in the report. Figure 5-57 shows the regional options setup.

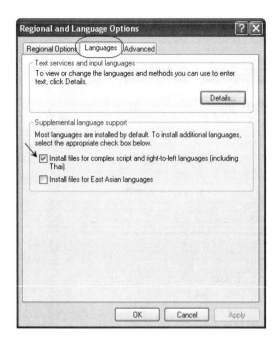

Figure 5-56. *Installing Arabic language support in Windows XP*

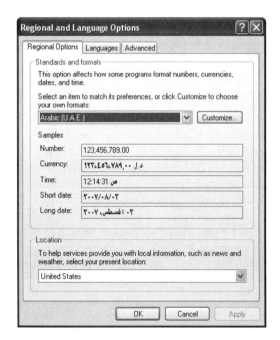

Figure 5-57. *Setting up regional options to support Arabic language*

As you can see in Figure 5-57, as soon as you select any region that supports Arabic, you'll see how Windows will interpret various types of information, for example, the currency or time formats. We are all set to create the Arabic-enabled Chart of Accounts report now. Let's move on and create the web site.

Please open Visual Studio, and use the following steps to create a web site project:

1. Click File ➤ New ➤ Web Site.

2. In the Templates pane of the New Web Site dialog box, select ASP.NET Web Site.

3. From the Language drop-down menu, select Visual C#.

4. Please give the application a name; I've called the web site ChartOfAccountsArb. You may choose a different location for storing the application files according to your preference.

5. Click the OK button to finish the process. Visual Studio will create a new ASP.NET Web site.

As we did for the English version of this report, add the dataset and ReportViewer to the project. Start by selecting the project in Solution Explorer; right-click it, and select Add ➤ New Item ➤ dataset. Please name the dataset dsChartOfAccounts. As usual, put the dataset inside the App_Code folder. Again, we don't need the Table Adapter wizard, so cancel the process; we'll create the data table later.

As usual, drag the ReportViewer from the toolbox and drop it inside the <div> tags, and please make sure the HTML code inside the Default.aspx page looks like the following:

```
<%@ Page Language="C#" AutoEventWireup="true"➡
  CodeFile="Default.aspx.cs" Inherits="_Default" %>

<%@ Register Assembly="Microsoft.ReportViewer.WebForms,➡
 Version=8.0.0.0, Culture=neutral, ➡
PublicKeyToken=b03f5f7f11d50a3a"
 Namespace="Microsoft.Reporting.WebForms" TagPrefix="rsweb" %>

<!DOCTYPE html PUBLIC "-//W3C//DTD XHTML 1.0 Transitional//EN"➡
 "http://www.w3.org/TR/xhtml1/DTD/xhtml1-transitional.dtd">

<html xmlns="http://www.w3.org/1999/xhtml" >
<head runat="server">
    <title>Untitled Page</title>
</head>
<body>
    <form id="form1" runat="server">
    <div>
        <rsweb:ReportViewer ID="ReportViewer1" runat="server" Width="800px">
        </rsweb:ReportViewer>
    </div>
    </form>
</body>
</html>
```

Step 1: Creating the Data Table

Creating the data table for this report is similar to creating it for the English version—the only change is that instead of the data column AccountNameEng, we'll use AccountNameArb. Please use the following steps to add the data table inside the dataset:

1. You can go to the dataset designer in two ways: double-click dsChartOfAccounts inside Solution Explorer, or right-click dsChartOfAccounts node and select View Designer.

2. To add the data table, right-click the design surface, and select Add ➤ DataTable.

3. Click the Header of the newly created data table, and name it dtChartOfAccounts. Add columns to dtChartOfAccounts by right-clicking DataTable and selecting Add ➤ Column.

4. Add the following columns into the data table; your data table should look like Figure 5-58:

   - AccountID (System.Int32)

   - AccountCode (System.String)

   - AccountNameArb (System.String)

   - AccountType (System.String)

   - AccountGroup (System.String)

   - AccountGeneralID (System.Int32)

   - AccountGeneralCode (System.String)

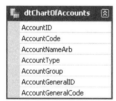

Figure 5-58. *Final look of the dtChartOfAccounts data table*

Step 2: Designing the Report Layout

The layout of this report stays the same as the earlier English version of the report. We will discuss the required cosmetic changes to introduce to the Arabic support, but before we start designing the report layout, let's add the report to the project. As usual, start by selecting the project in Solution Explorer, right-clicking it, and selecting Add ➤ New Item. Select Report from the Add New Item dialog box, and name the report rptChartOfAccountsArb.rdlc. Click the Add button to complete the process; a new report is now part of the project. We don't need any footer for this report. Therefore, let's begin the design by adding the header.

Adding a Header

Let's add the header to the report, as usual, by right-clicking the open area inside the report designer and selecting Page Header.

Setting Up the Page

Page setup is important for this report, as we want an A4-sized page. The good news is that, as soon as you change the regional settings, the report designer adapts to the new setup; it should switch the report to A4 for you. Before we start to work on the report design, let's make sure the report is A4-sized and has the portrait page orientation by right-clicking the open area inside the design surface and selecting Properties. You'll see that the page size is automatically adjusted to A4 size and the scale is changed from inches to centimeters (see Figure 5-59).

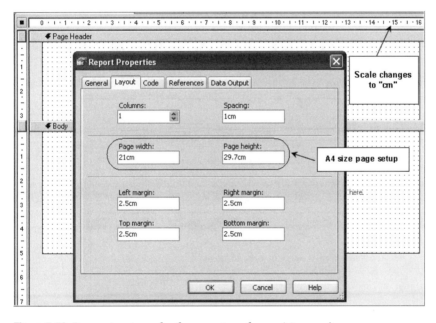

Figure 5-59. *Page setup to make the report render on A4 page size*

As usual, you may wish to put your name in the Author field and fill in the Description field.

Designing the Page Header

We'll start working on the header now. Please drag and drop the following Report Items inside the header section:

- A text box item for the report title

- A text box item for the page number

- A line item for separating the header and detail sections

The next step is to set the properties of the report items. Select each of the report items in turn, and specify the values for each item's properties according to Table 5-17. Your report design surface, after completing the header, should look similar to Figure 5-60. Please make note of the TextAlign property that's used to set the right-to-left display of the report title.

Table 5-17. *Report Item Properties for the Header*

Report Item	Property	Value
textbox1		
	Value	مخطط حسابات
	Font	Normal, Arial, 10pt, Bold
	TextAlign	Right
textbox2		
	Value	=" "="الصفحة : " : " & Globals!PageNumber & "/" & Globals!TotalPages
	TextAlign	Left
line1		
	LineWidth	2pt

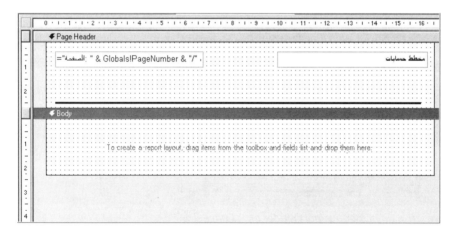

Figure 5-60. *Report design after adding report header and related report items*

Designing the Body Section

As we did in the English version, let's add the Table report item by selecting Toolbox ➤ Report Items ➤ Table and dragging and dropping it inside the body section in the report designer. As usual, a new table item with the name table1 is part of the report now. As with the English report, please make sure you have five columns in table1.

Let's take care of the mapping now. Drag Data Source ➤ dsChartOfAccounts ➤ AccountCode and drop it inside the last column of the table item's detail section (TableRow2). Repeat this task for AccountNameEng and AccountGeneralCode in reverse order.

As we did for the account type and account group expressions in the English version, please type the following Arabic expression for the account type (use the Google link I gave to you earlier for translation):

```
=Switch(Fields!AccountType.Value = "1", " "العام"","", ➥
  Fields!AccountType.Value = "2", " "التفصيلي"") ")
```

Similarly, please make sure to type the following Arabic-enabled expression for the account group:

```
=Switch(Fields!AccountGroup.Value = "1", " "الأصل"","", Fields!AccountGroup.Value = "2"➥
, " "المسؤوليات"","", Fields!AccountGroup.Value = "3", " "رأس المال"","", ➥
Fields!AccountGroup.Value = "4"➥
, " "دخل"","", Fields!AccountGroup.Value = "5", " "نفقة"") ")
```

After mapping the data, make sure to apply all the properties settings in Table 5-18 to table1.

Table 5-18. *Table Item Properties for the Body Section*

Table Item	Property	Value
TableRow1	BorderStyle	Solid
TableRow1	Font	Italic, Arial, 10pt, Bold
TableRow1	TextAlign	Right
TableRow1 ➤ Column1	Value	حساب المجموعة
TableRow1 ➤ Column2	Value	نوع الحساب
TableRow1 ➤ Column3	Value	الحساب العام
TableRow1 ➤ Column4	Value	حسابات الاسم
TableRow1 ➤ Column5	Value	حسابات هوية
TableRow2	TextAlign	Right
TableRow2 ➤ Column1	Value	=Switch(Fields!AccountGroup.Value = "1", " "الأصل"", ", Fields!AccountGroup.Value = "2", " "المسؤوليات"","", Fields!AccountGroup.Value = "3", " "رأس المال"","", Fields!AccountGroup.Value = "4", " "دخل"","", Fields!AccountGroup.Value = "5", " "نفقة"") ")
TableRow2 ➤ Column2	Value	=Switch(Fields!AccountType.Value = "1", " "العام"","", Fields!AccountType.Value = "2", " "التفصيلي"") ")
TableRow2 ➤ Column3	Value	=Fields!AccountGeneralCode.Value
TableRow2 ➤ Column4	Value	=Fields!AccountNameArb.Value
TableRow2 ➤ Column5	Value	=Fields!AccountCode.Value

Notice, in Table 5-18, that I have rearranged the data from right to left when mapping it. Usually, we start mapping from the first column on the right; in this report, I started mapping form the first column on the left to create the right-to-left effect.

Our report design is ready now. Please make sure your final report design looks similar to Figure 5-61.

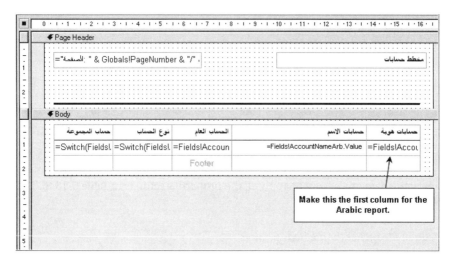

Figure 5-61. *Final look of the report design*

As in the English version, we need to set up the group to handle the parent/child relationship of account IDs in the Arabic version too; please use the following steps to do so (see Figure 5-53):

1. Select the detail row (TableRow2), right-click, and select Edit Group.

2. From the General tab, type or select =Fields!AccountID.Value for the Group on Expression.

3. Type or select =Fields!AccountGeneralID.Value in the "Parent group" drop-down.

4. Click the OK button to complete the process.

Let's take care of applying the bold font for all the General accounts. Please make sure to set the following expression for the FontWeight property of TableRow2 ➤ Column2:

```
Normal, Arial, 8pt, =iif(Fields!AccountType.Value = "1", "Bold", "Normal")
```

Next, we'll set up the hierarchical display of the account names. Recall that, depending on the hierarchy, the account name leaves some space to its right side (we had this space on the left side in the English version). We can achieve this by setting up the Padding(Right) property with the following expression:

```
2pt; =Level("table1_Details_Group") * 10 & "pt"; 2pt; 2pt
```

All right, we have reached the last step in completing our report now; it's time to write some C# code.

Step 3: Writing the C# Code

As usual, add the following code behind Default.aspx.cs:

```csharp
using System;
using System.Data;
using System.Configuration;
using System.Web;
using System.Web.Security;
using System.Web.UI;
using System.Web.UI.WebControls;
using System.Web.UI.WebControls.WebParts;
using System.Web.UI.HtmlControls;
using System.Data.SqlClient;
using Microsoft.Reporting.WebForms;

public partial class _Default : System.Web.UI.Page
{
    protected void Page_Load(object sender, EventArgs e)
    {
        // connection string
        string cnString = @"Data Source=(local);Initial Catalog=➡
            RealWorld;Integrated Security=SSPI;";

        SqlConnection conReport = new SqlConnection(cnString);
        SqlCommand cmdReport = new SqlCommand();
        SqlDataReader drReport;
        DataSet dsReport = new dsChartOfAccounts();

        try
        {
            // open connection
            conReport.Open();

            cmdReport.CommandType = CommandType.Text;
            cmdReport.Connection = conReport;

            // get query string from string builder
            cmdReport.CommandText = "SELECT * FROM ChartOfAccounts➡
                ORDER BY AccountCode";

            // execute query and load result to dataset
            drReport = cmdReport.ExecuteReader();

            dsReport.Tables[0].Load(drReport);

            // close connection
            drReport.Close();
            conReport.Close();
```

```
        // prepare report for view
        ReportViewer1.LocalReport.ReportPath = "rptChartOfAccountsArb.rdlc";

        ReportDataSource rds = new ReportDataSource();
        rds.Name = "dsChartOfAccounts_dtChartOfAccounts";

        rds.Value = dsReport.Tables[0];
        ReportViewer1.LocalReport.DataSources.Add(rds);
    }
    catch (Exception ex)
    {
        Response.Write(ex.Message);
    }
    finally
    {
        if (conReport.State == ConnectionState.Open)
        {
            conReport.Close();
        }
    }
    }
}
```

The code used here is exactly the same, processwise, as the code we used in the English version of this report. No special instructions are needed at the code level to do the conversion from English to Arabic.

Building the Project

As usual, build the project by clicking the small, green play button in the main toolbox or pressing F5. If the program compiles without any errors, you will see the form with the report in preview mode. Please make sure the report looks similar to the one shown in Figure 5-55.

You see how easy it is to develop a report that needs a non-English interface. You can try this with other right-to-left languages, such as Hebrew or Farsi. Apart from right-to-left languages, you can develop all sorts of non-English report outputs by properly using the correct regional settings.

Summary

In this chapter, we looked at two topics. First, you learned how to make use of a web site to deliver a report to various clients via the Internet and an intranet. Secondly, we looked at how we can make use of business object collections as data sources to report on. You also learned along the way how RS can help you to develop non-English reports.

In the next chapter, we will look at how we can generate reports with web services.

CHAPTER 6

Reporting with Web Services and Mobile Devices

Chapters 4 and 5 discussed using the Windows Forms and the Web Forms clients to host our reports. Starting with this chapter, we'll look at the rest of the clients that can host reports. First in line are web services and mobile devices. In later chapters, you'll see console applications, Windows services, and web parts in action as delivery vehicles for reports.

Both the web services and the mobile device clients are uniquely positioned to deliver the reports. By exposing your report with a web service, you are reaching a far greater user base, because a web service can be consumed by a variety of clients and is accessible across platforms. Similarly, providing report access with mobile devices can help users to get the information on demand. More and more organizations are moving toward service-oriented architecture (SOA) to manage information, and web services are an important part of SOA.

This chapter will cover

- What is a web service?

- "Web Services 101," a step-by-step tutorial for using web services

- Creating a report using web services

- Reporting with mobile devices

What Is a Web Service?

A *web service* is a technology designed to enable machine-to-machine interoperability over any given network. Web services are popularly used as web APIs and accessed over a network such as the Internet and intranets. Web services can also help to eliminate duplicate business functions by allowing them to be shared by more than one application. For example, a credit check web service can serve both billing and web enrollment applications. Web services can also be executed from a remotely hosted system.

In simple words, the common use of a web service is to communicate information using XML messages. The SOAP standard is used to communicate these messages. Functionality built with web services is ready to use by any potential client. For example, a financial institution can build a web service to provide currency exchange rates in which a client can consume this service to execute a web method to get the necessary exchange rate.

■**Note** Simple Object Access Protocol (SOAP) is a protocol for exchanging XML-based messages over computer networks, normally using the HTTP protocol. You can find more information on SOAP here: http://msdn2.microsoft.com/en-us/library/ms950803.aspx.

So, how does the client (consumer) requesting the service know about the available service functionality? Well, this information is provided by the service as a Web Services Description Language (WSDL) file. A WSDL file contains interface information that is needed for communication among web service producers and consumers. It allows a client to utilize a web service's capabilities without knowledge of the implementation details of the web service. You can get more information on WSDL here:

http://msdn2.microsoft.com/en-us/library/ms996486.aspx.

Once you develop a web service, it is available to consume by a variety of clients. These services are also shared across platforms; that means that a service hosted in the UNIX environment can be consumed using a .NET-based Windows client. Covering all the aspects of web services is beyond the reach of this book. I would suggest you to go through the Microsoft Help to know more; you can start here:

http://msdn2.microsoft.com/en-ca/webservices/default.aspx.

In the Windows environment, web services need Internet Information Services (IIS) as the host, either locally or on a remote machine. For our reporting project, we'll host the report generation service with local IIS and consume it with the Windows Forms application. Before we go on and develop the web service to produce a report in PDF format, let's learn to create a simple web service.

Web Services 101

Creating a web service is somewhat similar to creating an ASP.NET web site. Both the web site and the web service need IIS for the hosting. However, when it comes to behavior, they differ: web sites serve HTML pages to the user, and web services send XML messages. In this tutorial, we'll create a function to send a "Welcome to Web Service 101" message back to the client.

Creating a Web Service Project

Please open Visual Studio, and use the following steps to create an ASP.NET web service project; see Figure 6-1 for a graphical representation of these steps:

1. Click File ➤ New ➤ Web Site.

2. In the Templates pane of the New Web Site dialog box, select ASP.NET Web Service.

3. From the Language drop-down menu, select Visual C#.

4. Please give the application a name; I've called the web service RSWebService101. You may choose a different location for storing the application files according to your preference.

5. Click the OK button to finish the process. VS 2005 will create a new ASP.NET web service. Figure 6-2 shows the code that's produced and the files inside Solution Explorer.

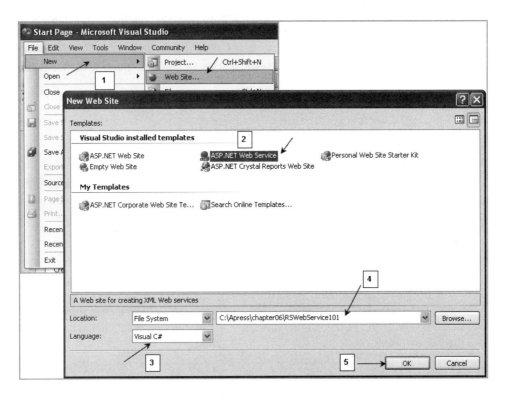

Figure 6-1. *Creating a new ASP.NET web service*

```
using System;
using System.Web;
using System.Web.Services;
using System.Web.Services.Protocols;

[WebService(Namespace = "http://tempuri.org/")]
[WebServiceBinding(ConformsTo = WsiProfiles.BasicProfile1_1)]
public class Service : System.Web.Services.WebService
{
    public Service () {

        //Uncomment the following line
        //InitializeComponent();
    }

    [WebMethod]
    public string HelloWorld() {
        return "Hello World";
    }
}
```

Figure 6-2. *The newly created ASP.NET web service*

As you can see in Figure 6-2, the project contains the App_Code folder containing the C# code and the Service.asmx file as part of the project. The generated code is a complete web service, ready to host with IIS.

Let's assume we hosted this service with local IIS. Now, what do you think this service is supposed to do? This service will simply return a "Hello World" message to the client application that consumes it.

Before we build and host this web service with local IIS, let's pay attention to the following important things:

- The namespace

- The Service.asmx file

- The web method

A namespace is needed to uniquely identify the web service. As you can see in Figure 6-2, VS gives the default name http://tempuri.org/. It is your responsibility to change it; you can use any name as long as you feel it is unique. The best practice here is to use a convention like http://ServiceName.CompanyName.org. In practice, this could translate to http://CalculateAnnualSales.BestHomeConstructions.org/, where ServiceName is CalculateAnnualSales and CompanyName is BestHomeConstructions.

Now, you know about the namespace, so what about the Service.asmx file? The main use of this file is to display the information about the various methods that are part of this web service. It also provides the WSDL information. You might be wondering if all this information is stored inside the file. Well, no. If you open the Service.asmx file, you'll notice that it only contains the following text:

```
<%@ WebService Language="C#" CodeBehind="~/App_Code/Service.cs" Class="Service" %>
```

As you can see, all it has is the scripting language information and location of the code behind the file. When you request the ASMX page through IIS, ASP.NET uses this information to generate the content displayed in the web browser (the web methods and their descriptions).

Let's move on to learn about web methods. I'm sure most of you have already guessed that this is the function part of the web service. As you can see in Figure 6-2, Visual Studio generates a default web method called HelloWorld. You can add as many web methods as you like to your web service.

Adding a Web Method to Service.cs

Let's add our own web method to send the "Welcome to Web Service 101" message to the consumer client. Adding the web method is simple; it is similar to writing your own C# method. The only difference here is that each web method you write must have the tag [WebMethod]. Please make sure that code behind the Service.cs file looks like the following after adding our web method:

```
using System;
using System.Web;
using System.Web.Services;
using System.Web.Services.Protocols;
```

```
[WebService(Namespace = "http://MyHelloWorld.Apress.com/")]
[WebServiceBinding(ConformsTo = WsiProfiles.BasicProfile1_1)]
public class Service : System.Web.Services.WebService
{
    public Service () {

        //Uncomment the following line if using designed components
        //InitializeComponent();
    }

    [WebMethod]
    public string HelloWorld() {
        return "Hello World";
    }

    [WebMethod]
    public string MyHelloWorld()
    {
        return "Welcome to Web Service 101";
    }
}
```

You can see that the new web method is called MyHelloWorld, and its scope is public. You'll also notice that this method returns our message as a string and that I changed the default namespace from http://tempuri.org/ to http://MyHelloWorld.Apress.com/. All right, now we're ready to build our web service and host it with the local IIS.

Building the Project

I'm sure you are ready to breathe life into your web service to see your hard work in action. Building a web service is like building any other project with the VS IDE. As you know, you can click the small, green Play button in the main toolbox or press F5 on the keyboard to start the application in run-time mode.

■**Note** If you're building the project for the first time in debug mode, click OK at the Debugging Not Enabled prompt.

Assuming that you don't encounter any errors during the build, the web service will be automatically hosted with the VS IDE's internal web server. Please see Figure 6-3 for the URL and port on which our web service is hosted.

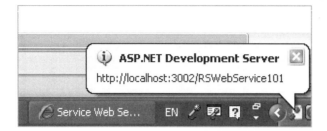

Figure 6-3. *The web service is hosted with the internal web server of the VS IDE.*

■Note You may get a different port number from the internal web server. As you can see in Figure 6-3, I got 3002 as the port number.

After the web service is successfully launched, a browser window will appear with our two web methods inside. Take a look at Figure 6-4. Does the URL in the address bar seem familiar to you? Well, as I mentioned earlier in this chapter, the browser window is launched with our ASMX file, which shows the functions of the web service to the user.

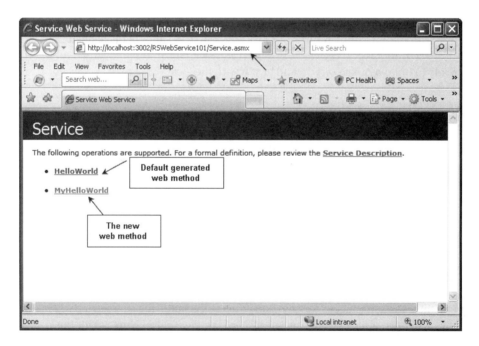

Figure 6-4. *Web service with default generated and newly created web methods*

How Does the Web Service Work?

As you can see in Figure 6-4, the web methods appear as links. So, what happens when we click them? Simply put, think of the web service as a sort of server waiting to provide the business function needed by the client. So far, we know we have the web service, ready to serve! As all web methods in a web service perform some business function, we need a client request to invoke them. So, where is the client?

It is common practice to build a test client in the same solution as the web service for testing. However, it is possible to test a web method without creating a test client. As you can see in Figure 6-4, the browser window acts like a client to let you invoke the web method and do some basic functionality testing. A user can make this browser window the client and execute a web method by clicking the link. So, if you click MyHelloWorld, you should see the browser window content change to include an Invoke button (see Figure 6-5).

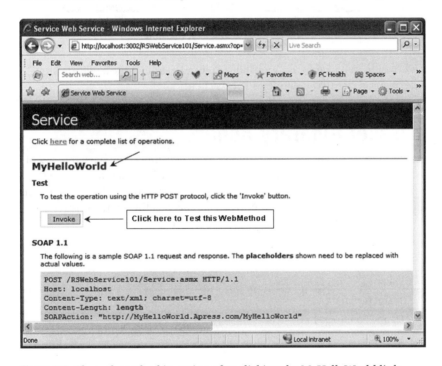

Figure 6-5. *The web method in action after clicking the MyHelloWorld link*

Now your browser window acts like a consumer client. What do you think the result will be if you click the Invoke button? As the button's name suggests, the MyHelloWorld web method will be invoked and return the greeting message as XML, as shown in Figure 6-6.

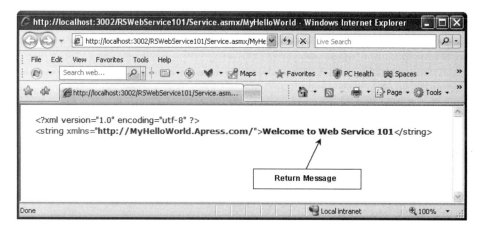

Figure 6-6. *The XML message is displayed after invoking the web method.*

All right, now it's time to move on to our reporting project. Let's generate a report using the web service and consume it with the Windows Forms client.

Creating a Travel Itinerary Report

Assume you're working for Happy Landings, Incorporated as a developer. You have the task of developing a web service to generate an on-demand travel itinerary. The itinerary should be sent across to the client in PDF format. To test the web site, you'll also create a Windows Forms client as the consumer of this web service. The report should meet all the characteristics described in Table 6-1, and the PDF report output should match Figure 6-7.

Table 6-1. *Report Characteristics*

Characteristics	Value
Report title	Travel Itinerary
Company title	Happy Landings, Inc.
Logo	Yes
Data source	Itinerary
Page size	Letter
Page orientation	Portrait
Layout design	All information should be in the body section (no header or footer).

HAPPY LANDINGS INC.

Itinerary for:

MR. JOHN DOE

Reservation code:MQY121

Friday, April 13 : AIR CANADA, AC 1234

From:	TORONTO, CANADA (YYZ)	Departs:	10:40am
To:	PARIS, FRANCE (CDG)	Arrives:	12:55pm
Departure Terminal:	TERMINAL 1	Duration:	8 hour(s) and 20 minute(s)
Arrival Terminal:	AEROGARE 2B	Class:	Economy
Seat(s):	Check-In Required	Status:	Confirmed
Gate:	N/A	Confirmation #:	ABC123
Aircraft:	AIRBUS A343 JET	Mileage:	3754
Meal:	Meals, Snack	Frequent Flyer #:	N/A
Smoking:	No		* *Please verify flight times prior to departure*

Notes: Meals: Low Salt

Figure 6-7. *Solution of the reporting travel itinerary report*

Business Case

When did you last have an itinerary? We know the importance of travel, especially air travel. Air travel has made this world a global village; we can quickly reach one part of the world from another. So, as you can see, an itinerary is a common form of report.

In this case, Happy Landings Incorporated wants to provide this report as a web service to empower its business partners. This web service can be used by individual travelers or by agents. Because this is a web service, all sorts of clients can benefit.

Getting the Web Service Ready

You learned how to create an ASP.NET web service earlier in this chapter; now it's your turn to practice getting the web service ready. You may make use of the solution RSWebService101 as a template for this project or create it from scratch. Creating the new project from scratch is good practice; you can always refer to the steps mentioned in the tutorial if you get stuck.

Please use the following steps to create an ASP.NET web service project (see Figure 6-1 for an illustration of the steps):

1. Click File ➤ New ➤ Web Site.

2. In the Templates pane of the New Web Site dialog box, select ASP.NET Web Service.

3. From the Language drop-down menu, select Visual C#.

4. Please give the application a name; I've called the web service Itinerary. You may choose a different location for storing the application files according to your preference.

5. Click the OK button to finish the process. VS will create a new ASP.NET web service project named Itinerary.

VS will create a default `HelloWorld` web method. Please delete the following code to remove this web method:

```
[WebMethod]
public string HelloWorld() {
    return "Hello World";
}
```

Let's add a new dataset to the project and name it `dsItinerary`. You'll notice that VS will ask you to put the dataset inside the `App_Code` folder; go ahead and click the Yes button. Select Cancel in the Table Adapter wizard dialog box; we'll create the data table later. Before continuing, please make sure your solution looks similar to the one shown in Figure 6-8.

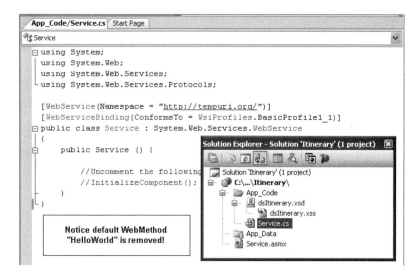

Figure 6-8. *Web Service–generated code with default WebMethod removed*

Step 1: Creating a Data Table

We've already added the dataset to the project, so now its time to add the data table to it. Please use the following steps to add the data table inside the dataset:

1. You can go to the dataset designer in two ways: double-click the dsItinerary node inside Solution Explorer, or right-click the dsItinerary node and select View Designer.

2. Start adding the data table by right-clicking the design surface and selecting Add ➤ DataTable.

3. Click the header of the newly created data table, and name it dtItinerary. Add the columns to dtItinerary by right-clicking DataTable and selecting Add ➤ Column.

4. Please add the following columns to the Data Table; your data table should look like Figure 6-9:

   - ReservationCode (System.String)

   - CustomerName (System.String)

   - DateOfTravel (System.String)

   - Airline (System.String)

   - TravelFrom (System.String)

   - TravelTo (System.String)

   - DepartsTime (System.String)

   - ArrivesTime (System.String)

   - DepartureTerminal (System.String)

   - ArrivalTerminal (System.String)

   - Seats (System.String)

   - GateInfo (System.String)

   - Aircraft (System.String)

   - Meal (System.String)

   - Smoking (System.String)

   - Duration (System.String)

   - Class (System.String)

   - Status (System.String)

   - AirlineConfirmation (System.String)

   - Mileage (System.String)

   - FrequentFlyerCode (System.String)

   - Notes (System.String)

Figure 6-9. *The final look of the dtItinerary data table*

Step 2: Designing the Report Layout

All right, we have our dataset in place with the data table and all the necessary columns, so we're all set to start working on designing the report layout. Add the report by selecting the project in Solution Explorer, right-clicking it, and selecting Add ➤ New Item; select Report from the Add New Item dialog box. Please name the report `rptItinerary.rdlc`. Click the Add button to complete the process.

Once you click the Add button, a new report is added to the project and opened in the report designer. If you look at the report output in Figure 6-7, you'll see that we don't need a header and footer here. All information present in the itinerary can be easily placed inside the body section. We'll make use of two rectangle report items: the first rectangle will have the logo and customer name, and the second will have the travel details.

Setting Up the Page

Let's set up the page to meet our needs. We need to make sure the report is letter-size and has a portrait page orientation. Right-click the open area on the design surface, and select Properties; you may wish to put your name in the Author field and add information about the report to the Description field. I'd advise you to let all other choices stay at their defaults.

Designing the Body Section

For this report, we need two rectangle items, one image item, and a total of forty text boxes. Let's start the design by dragging the two rectangle items from the Report Items toolbox and dropping them on to the report design surface. In the first rectangle, drag and drop the image and four text boxes.

We're going to embed the company logo in the report. Embedding an image is a two step process. First, you need to embed the logo in the report by setting the `EmbeddedImages` property. Next, you need to browse to the physical path of the image and embed it within the report. After you embed the image in the report, just set the Value property of the image report item to the image name.

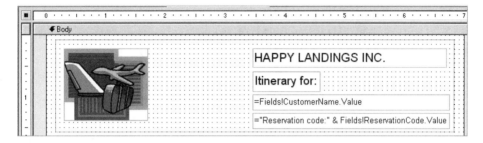

Figure 6-10. *The first rectangle report item with its content: the logo image, company name, "Itinerary for" label, customer name, and reservation code*

■**Note** If you move a rectangle report item, all content inside moves with it, because all report items contained inside the rectangle act as a group. Therefore, when the rectangle is moved, the entire group of items moves with it.

The report title and company name font sizes are set to 14 pt. You'll also notice that "Reservation Code" is concatenated with the information from the ReservationCode field of the dataset.

As usual, drag and drop the rest of the text box report items from the Report Items toolbox. Some text boxes are used as labels, and some are used to display values from the dataset. Please set up the text boxes as explained in Table 6-2.

Table 6-2. *Text Box Values, Labels, and Expressions*

Prompt	Value
From:	=First(Fields!TravelFrom.Value)
To:	=First(Fields!TravelTo.Value)
Departure Terminal:	=First(Fields!DepartureTerminal.Value)
Arrival Terminal:	=First(Fields!ArrivalTerminal.Value)
Seat(s):	=First(Fields!Seats.Value)
Gate:	=First(Fields!GateInfo.Value)
Aircraft:	=First(Fields!Aircraft.Value)
Meal:	=First(Fields!Meal.Value)
Smoking:	=First(Fields!Smoking.Value)
Departs:	=First(Fields!DepartsTime.Value)
Arrives:	=First(Fields!ArrivesTime.Value)

Continued

Table 6-2. *Continued*

Prompt	Value
Duration:	=First(Fields!Duration.Value)
Class:	=First(Fields!Class.Value)
Status:	=First(Fields!Status.Value)
Confirmation #:	=First(Fields!AirlineConfirmation.Value)
Mileage:	=First(Fields!Mileage.Value)
Frequent Flyer #:	=First(Fields!FrequentFlyerCode.Value)
Message1:	* Please verify flight times prior to departure
Message2:	="Notes: " & Fields!Notes.Value

After you set up the textbox items, your report design layout should look similar to the one shown in Figure 6-11.

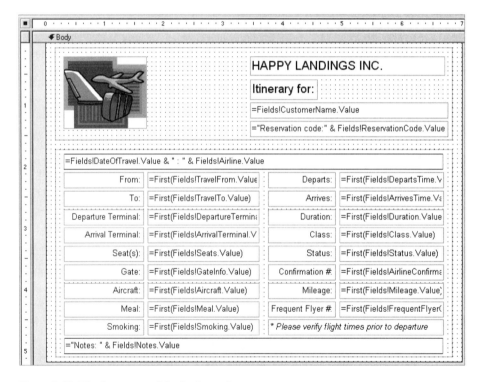

Figure 6-11. *Final content of the body section*

Beautifying the Report

As for the formatting, you need to make sure the label text boxes are right aligned. Also, check to see that the first and the last text box items have the top and the bottom borders, respectively, set to Solid. This will give the effect of using the line report item (of course, without using it). Did you notice that the font style of one of the text boxes (the one with the "Please verify . . ." message) is set in italics? In this example, setting the font style to italics helps draw the user's attention to that particular information on the report. As always, I want to stress the importance of good formatting: a report with poor formatting will not get the attention it deserves.

■**Note** The expressions =First(Fields!TravelTo.Value) and =Fields!TravelTo.Value have the same the effect in this report, because we have just one row from the dataset to deal with. The function First() is used to display the first value available from the first row of the data table.

Step 3: Writing the C# Code

Before we start with the code, we need to add a reference to Microsoft.Reporting.WebForms. Add the reference by selecting References under Itinerary Project, right-clicking, and selecting Add Reference. Under the .NET tab in the Add Reference dialog box, scroll down to Microsoft.Reporting.WebForms, and click the OK button. Please sure you have the following code inside the Service.cs file:

```
using System;
using System.Web;
using System.Web.Services;
using System.Web.Services.Protocols;
using System.Data;
using System.Data.SqlClient;
using Microsoft.Reporting.WebForms;

[WebService(Namespace = "http://tempuri.org/")]
[WebServiceBinding(ConformsTo = WsiProfiles.BasicProfile1_1)]
public class Service : System.Web.Services.WebService
{
    public Service () {

        //Uncomment the following line if using designed components
        //InitializeComponent();
    }

    [WebMethod]
    public byte[] GenerateItinerary()
    {
        LocalReport rpvItinerary = new LocalReport();

        //declare connection string
        string cnString = "Data Source=(local);➠
Initial Catalog=RealWorld;Integrated Security=SSPI;";
```

```csharp
//declare connection, command and other related objects
SqlConnection conReport = new SqlConnection(cnString);
SqlCommand cmdReport = new SqlCommand();
SqlDataReader drReport;
DataSet dsReport = new dsItinerary();

try
{
    //open connection
    conReport.Open();

    //prepare connection object to get the data from
    //the reader and populate the dataset
    cmdReport.CommandType = CommandType.Text;
    cmdReport.Connection = conReport;
    cmdReport.CommandText = "Select TOP 1 * FROM Dbo. Itinerary";

    //read data from command object
    drReport = cmdReport.ExecuteReader();

    //load data directly from reader to dataset
    dsReport.Tables[0].Load(drReport);

    //close reader and connection
    drReport.Close();
    conReport.Close();

    //provide local report information to viewer
    rpvItinerary.ReportPath = "rptItinerary.rdlc";

    //prepare report data source
    ReportDataSource rds = new ReportDataSource();
    rds.Name = "dsItinerary_dtItinerary";
    rds.Value = dsReport.Tables[0];
    rpvItinerary.DataSources.Add(rds);

    Warning[] warnings;
    string[] streamids;
    string mimeType;
    string encoding;
    string filenameExtension;

    byte[] bytes = rpvItinerary.Render(
        "PDF", null, out mimeType, out encoding, out filenameExtension,
        out streamids, out warnings);
```

```
            return bytes;
        }
        catch
        {
            return null;
        }
        finally
        {
            //check if connection is still open, then attempt to close it
            if (conReport.State == ConnectionState.Open)
            {
                conReport.Close();
            }
        }
    }
}
```

The code inside the web method is similar to what we have been coding so far—connecting to the database and supplying the required information to our local report. However, one piece of code I'd like to discuss is this:

```
            byte[] bytes = rpvItinerary.Render(
                "PDF", null, out mimeType, out encoding, out filenameExtension,
                out streamids, out warnings);
            return bytes;
```

We'll use the Render() method of the local report object to produce the report output. This output will be stored inside the array of bytes. Notice that our web method returns the bytes[] array; we'll retrieve this information from the client side and store it as a PDF file in a local resource.

I'd also like to mention the SQL statement used to retrieve the itinerary information from the database. As you can see, the SQL statement Select TOP 1 * FROM Dbo.Itinerary retrieves the first row from the requested table. Since there's only one record in the table, I used TOP 1, but in other cases, the record can be retrieved by providing the reservation code.

Building the Itinerary Web Service

You can click small, green Play button in the main toolbox or press F5 on the keyboard to start the application in run-time mode. After the web service is successfully launched, a browser window will appear with the link to the GenerateItinerary web method inside. If you click the GenerateItinerary link, the browser window will take you to the page with the web method's Invoke button. Finally, if you click the Invoke button, you will get the report in XML message form. Figure 6-12 shows the steps from launching of the web service to getting the XML message.

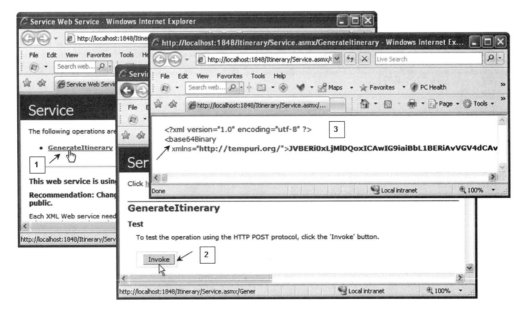

Figure 6-12. *Testing the itinerary web service after the build*

You can also see that the XML message is returned as base64Binary type. This can be easily read by the client application as a stream of bytes and saved as a physical file on the desired resource—so far, so good. Now, let's move on to create a Windows Forms client to consume this GenerateItinerary service and save the result as a PDF file.

Consuming the Web Service with a Windows Forms Client

You've now seen how we create the web service and check to make sure it is functional. But the real benefit of this service is when different clients interact with it. A variety of clients, such as an ASP.NET web site or a Windows Forms application, can access this web service. In case you are wondering, this service can also be accessed by clients that reside in the UNIX world, but this example will demonstrate the interaction of this service with a Windows Forms client.

We don't need to start a fresh solution here. All we need to do is add a new project to our existing solution. Please use the following steps to add a new Windows Forms project to this solution, which already has our web service as the project; please see Figure 6-13 for an illustration of the steps:

1. Right-click Itinerary, and select Add ➤ New Project.

2. In the Add New Project dialog box, select Visual C# ➤ Windows.

3. From the Templates pane, select Windows Application.

4. Please give a name to the application; I've called the project WinFormClient. You may choose a different location for storing the application files according to your preference.

5. Click the OK button to finish the process. VS will create a new Windows application project. You'll also notice that a new form with the name Form1 is part of the project.

Figure 6-13. *Steps to add a new Windows Forms project*

If you look at the solution now, you'll find the two projects: the web service and the project we just added. Let me ask you this: if you build and run the solution, which project will run? The web service will run, as it is the default startup project.

What if we want the newly added Windows Forms project to run? Well, that's easy; we need to set our Windows Forms client as the startup project. You can set the startup project by right-clicking the WinFormClient project and selecting "Set as Startup Project". Now, if you run the build, the Windows Forms project will run first.

Adding the Web Reference to the WinFormClient Project

What is a web reference? Why do we need this? Well, recall that we add references of different namespaces to use their functions. Similarly, to invoke specific web methods from a web service, we need to make references to them inside the client.

Adding web reference is relatively easy. Please use the following steps to add a web reference to Itinerary's web service to WinFormClient; Figure 6-14 illustrates these steps:

1. Right-click the WinFormClient project, and select Add Web Reference.

2. From Add Web Reference dialog box, select "Web services in this solution".

3. The Add Web Reference dialog box will refresh to show the Service link; please click it.

4. The Add Web Reference dialog box will show the GenerateItinerary web method. Please change the web reference name to WinGenItinerary, and click the Add Reference button.

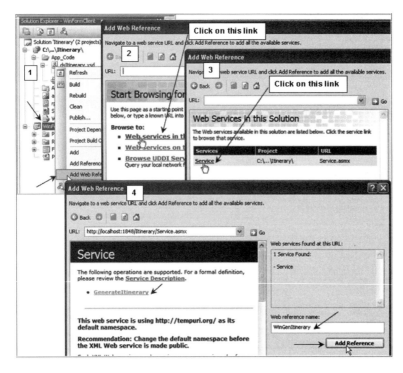

Figure 6-14. *Steps to add a web reference to the Windows Forms project*

Once you click the Add Reference button, a new section with the name Web References will become part of the WinFormClient project. Please see Figure 6-15 for the tree structure of the Windows Forms project; your project should look similar.

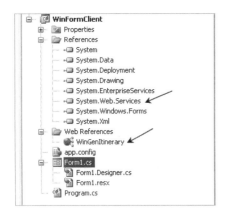

Figure 6-15. *Project tree after adding the web reference*

Creating the C# Code to Invoke the Web Service

Let's put a button control on Form1. Why do we need the button? Well, I'd like to use this button in the same way as the Invoke button that you saw earlier in this chapter. The code behind this button will invoke the web service and save the result as a PDF file.

All right, are you ready to create our Invoke button? Please make sure Form1 is open in design mode. If it is not, you can easily do this by double-clicking Form1 in Solution Explorer. Drag a button from the main toolbox and drop it onto the Form1 design surface. You'll see that a new button called button1 will be added to Form1. Please change the Text property of button1 from button1 to Invoke.

Now, we are ready to write some C# code to invoke the web method and save the result as a PDF file. Please make sure the code behind Form1.cs looks like the following:

```csharp
using System;
using System.Collections.Generic;
using System.ComponentModel;
using System.Data;
using System.Drawing;
using System.Text;
using System.Windows.Forms;
using System.IO;

namespace WinFormClient
{
    public partial class Form1 : Form
    {
        public Form1()
        {
            InitializeComponent();
        }

        private void button1_Click(object sender, EventArgs e)
        {
            try
            {
                WinGenItinerary.Service GenerateItinerarySrv➥
= new WinGenItinerary.Service();

                // call web method and store the result
                byte[] GenItineraryResult =➥
GenerateItinerarySrv.GenerateItinerary();

                // read through bytes arry and generate PDF file
                using (FileStream fs =➥
new FileStream(@"c:\Itinerary.pdf", FileMode.Create))
                {
                    fs.Write(GenItineraryResult, 0, GenItineraryResult.Length);
                }
```

```
        MessageBox.Show(@"Itinerary saved as c:\Itinerary.pdf");
    }
    catch (Exception ex)
    {
        MessageBox.Show(ex.Message);
    }


    }
  }
}
```

Before we move on to build our client and test the web service, let's look briefly at the code and discuss how a client interacts with a web service. As you can see in the code, we start by making reference to WinGenItnerary.Service(). After this, we execute the GenerateItinerary web method and store the result into a byte[] array. Finally, using System.IO, we convert the byte[] result set into a PDF file and store it to the local C drive.

Building the WinFormClient Project

As usual, you can click the small, green Play button in the main toolbox or press F5 on the keyboard to start the application in run-time mode. Assuming that you don't encounter any issues during the build, you should see the file generated on the C drive. After the file is generated, you will get the confirmation message box. Your confirmation should look similar to the one shown in Figure 6-16.

Figure 6-16. *Confirmation after saving the result as a PDF file*

Reporting with Mobile Devices

Client-Side RS has taken information reporting to the next level: information can be accessed any time, from any place, and on any device. As more and more people are going wireless, it is important for them to be able to access vital business data remotely.

Client-side reporting plays a big part here too. Reports developed with the use of this technology can be accessed by a variety of different mobile devices. You might be thinking, "And how it is done?" Well, reports can be designed using custom page sizes and rendered specifically to suit the display capabilities of the mobile devices.

As the web is gaining maturity, this phenomenon has fueled the new generation of mobile devices. These devices are evolving and getting smarter with every passing day. Now, users can go wireless and still have access to all their corporate resources, such as e-mail, databases, and documents, using devices ranging from laptops to handhelds—even some that can be worn on your wrist!

Mobile Devices Supported by VS 2005

As you saw in Chapters 4 and 5, VS 2005 provides us the tools to create cool Windows Forms applications and ASP.NET web sites. However, don't you think that VS 2005 should be equally good at providing tools to develop cool applications for mobile devices? Yes, you can create three types of mobile device applications: Pocket PC 2003, Smartphone 2003, and Windows CE 5.0; mobile devices are also referred as smart devices by Visual Studio. Please see Figure 6-17 for the New Project dialog box with these three choices.

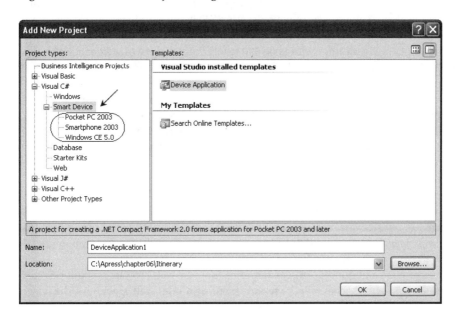

Figure 6-17. *Choices of smart device applications*

Now, before we discuss more about how to make use of mobile devices for reporting purposes, I'd like to share an important piece of information with you: the ReportViewer cannot be used directly by the mobile device applications. Why is that? Well, the ReportViewer is not supported by the .NET Compact framework.

■**Note** The .NET Compact framework is a scaled down version of the .NET framework. You can learn more about the .NET Compact framework here: `http://msdn2.microsoft.com/en-us/netframework/aa497273.aspx`.

If the .NET Compact framework is not supported to display or export reports, then how can we use these devices to deliver the reports? Well, we can do this in two ways. First, develop the reports as web pages so that mobile devices can display them using their built-in web browsers. Second, we can display reports in the offline mode, as PDF files. From these two options, the most common is to use the web browsers of smart devices.

Now, we know that our best bet for delivering reports to mobile devices is through ASP.NET web sites. Let's move forward and learn some design considerations to make sure that reports appear readable and professional on these devices.

Report Design Considerations for Mobile Devices

The most important consideration when designing reports to view with mobile devices is the screen size. Why this is such an important consideration? Well, the simple reason is that mobile devices come in all sorts of shapes and sizes. It is not like designing a report for a web site, where you can plan on a monitor with 800×600 resolution and be worry free in assuming most of users' PCs can support this resolution and the report will look presentable.

Before you start designing a report to be viewed with a mobile device, consider the specifics of your target device and offline viewing capabilities. For example, is your target device a Windows-CE-powered Pocket PC, or is it Windows Mobile Smartphone?

If your target is a Pocket PC, you typically have better screen resolution (240×300 pixels) to show report content. If your choice is a Smartphone, you have relatively little screen space (176×220 pixels) at your disposal.

Almost all next generation mobile devices have some sort of web browsing capabilities. If your report needs to be generic and available to all devices, you have to put a lot of emphasis on what to report and how to report it.

To prove that screen size does matter, let's assume that our Travel Itinerary report can be accessed via a web page. Now, if we pull this web page with a mobile device as it is, it might look something like the page shown in Figure 6-18.

If we want to provide a better reporting experience than the web browser capabilities of the mobile devices, how about accessing the report in offline mode? Well, even here, the way a report is delivered to mobile devices is important. Many mobile devices support offline viewing of documents in PDF format. Both client- and server-side RS can deliver reports to mobile devices with the help of the web browser.

Figure 6-18. *The itinerary report viewed from the web with a mobile device*

Summary

In this chapter, you learned what a web service is and how to make use of web services to deliver reports to various clients. After that, we looked at how we can empower users to get hold of reports using mobile devices.

In the next chapter, we will consider how we can generate reports with console applications, which have no GUI.

■■■

CHAPTER 7

Reporting with a Console Application

So far, we've covered various clients with visual interface capacities to host our reporting projects. Now, if I ask you to host a report with a client with no GUI interface, how would you respond? Naturally, you might be thinking that preview mode is ideal for the report delivery, and you're right. However, in the real world, there are many cases where we have to automatically produce reports without any human intervention (like clicking a print button or exporting to Excel).

This chapter will start with explaining how to build a console application. You'll see how to automate report delivery with console applications without a GUI. After that, we'll work on real-world practical reporting projects.

In this chapter, I'll cover

- "Console Applications 101," a step-by-step tutorial for using console applications

- Producing a report in Excel format on a local drive

- Producing a report in PDF format and delivering it using File Transfer Protocol (FTP)

- Scheduling the delivery of a report

Console Applications 101

Let's begin with the question, "What is a console application?" Well, the answer is simple: an application that doesn't have any GUI elements and runs at a DOS or command prompt. You have probably interacted with console applications in some way or other.

You might be wondering why we need console applications, in these days of modern GUI interfaces. Well, wait until you practice the reporting projects in this chapter; you'll see how much power is packed in this client. It's no wonder that VS 2005 and the forthcoming VS 2008 application have this project type available.

Console applications are built to do a variety of batch processing jobs like archiving old database logs or backing up data drives' content to a secure location. We're going to focus on a console application's ability to host reports and deliver them to various targets, like a file server and an FTP folder.

Console applications can start from a command prompt by typing the program's name or by using the Run dialog box. Another common way to start a console application is to browse for it in Windows Explorer and double-click it. Most of the time, a console application doesn't need any user input, but if necessary, users can pass in data using text-based input.

We can use the Windows Task Scheduler to run a console application at certain predefined intervals. This technique is commonly used to automate the delivery of reports on the client-side of reporting services.

Creating a Console Application Project

Open Visual Studio, and use the following steps to create a console application project; see Figure 7-1 for a graphical presentation of these steps:

1. Click File ➤ New ➤ Project, or press the hot key Ctrl+Shift+N.

2. In the "Project types" pane of the New Project dialog box, select Visual C# ➤ Windows.

3. In the Templates pane, select Console Application.

4. Let's give a name to the application; I've called the project RSConsole101. You may choose a different location for storing the application files according to your preference.

5. Click the OK button to finish the process; Visual Studio will create a new console application project. Figure 7-2 shows the produced code and files inside Solution Explorer.

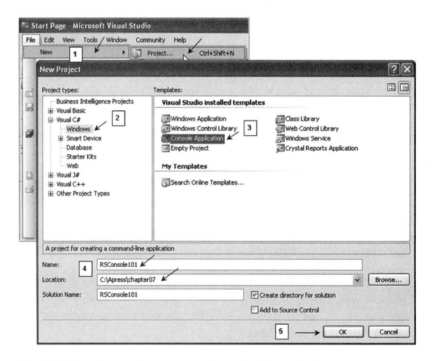

Figure 7-1. *Steps to create a new console application project*

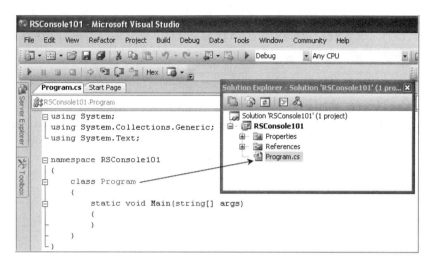

Figure 7-2. *The newly created console application*

Should we add the ReportViewer to the project now? Well, as you know, the ReportViewer is a GUI component, and this console application has no GUI, so we will not use the ReportViewer control here. Instead, we'll use a different approach to produce the reports with the console application client.

How about the dataset? Yes, the console application does need the dataset like any other client, to act as the data provider for reports.

User Interaction with a Console Application

Typically, a console application has little user interaction. When I say *user interaction*, I mean providing user input in run-time mode or overseeing the progress of the report. Most console applications run in a batch and produce application logs, which are examined in the case of a failure or to confirm success.

Let's say you want to create a console application that tells you about the progress of the application process and looks for input at the same time. We can use the following four methods to just do that:

- Read(): Returns the integer value of a character supplied through standard input

- ReadLine(): Returns all the characters supplied through standard input as a string

- Write(): Writes the provided expression as standard output to the console window

- WriteLine(): Same as Write() but the expression is terminated by a new line

> **Note** The Console class is part of the System Namespace and is responsible for handling standard input and output streams.

There is more to learn about console applications; I'm only touching base on functions that are important for you to know to produce reports. Let's add some input/output instruction and see how it looks in run-time mode. To start, please make sure the code inside Program.cs looks like the following:

```
using System;
using System.Collections.Generic;
using System.Text;

namespace RSConsole101
{
    class Program
    {
        static void Main(string[] args)
        {
            Console.Title = "Console Application 101";
            Console.Write("Please enter some text followed by Enter: ");
            String strInput = Console.ReadLine();
            Console.WriteLine("You entered: " + strInput);
            Console.WriteLine("Press any key to exit!");
            Console.Read();
        }
    }
}
```

Building the Project

The code used in this tutorial is simple: The user will enter some text, and that entered text will be output to the user. The program ends after the user presses any key on the keyboard. If you don't include the last line, Console.Read();, the program will automatically close as soon as the user enters the text.

That's it. This is what you'll need to get your console application ready to produce client-side reports. Now, let's build the project. You can click the small, green Play button in the main toolbox or press F5 on the keyboard to start the application in run-time mode.

If all goes well, your project should compile without any issues, and you should be able to see the console application in the command window, which should look somewhat similar to Figure 7-3.

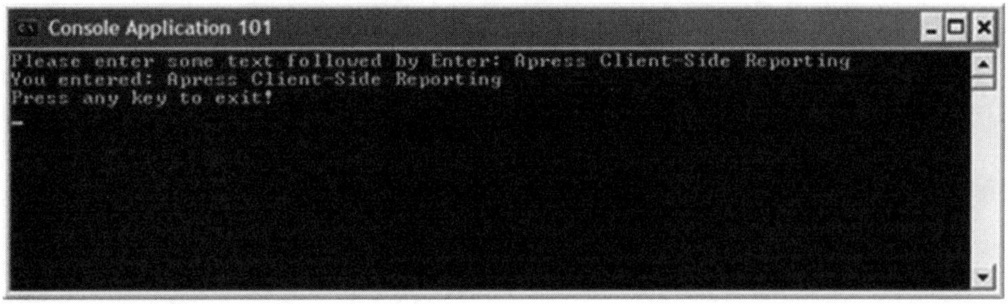

Figure 7-3. *The console application in run-time mode*

Customer E-mail List by Country Report

Assume you're working for Home Decorations, Incorporated as a developer with the task of creating a report that must list all the e-mail addresses of the customers by the customer's country of origin. The report should have all the characteristics described in Table 7-1.

Table 7-1. *Report Characteristics*

Characteristics	Value
Report title	Customer E-mail List by Country Report (Header, aligned center)
Company title	Home Decorations Inc. (Header, aligned center)
Logo	No
Print date	Yes (Header, aligned center)
Data source	tblCustomerEmail
Columns to report	CustomerID, FirstName, LastName, EmailAddress, CountryRegionName
Page size	Letter
Page orientation	Portrait
Page number	Page: n/n (Header, aligned Left)
Grouping	CountryRegionName
Page footer	No
Output format	Excel

The Customer E-mail List by Country report output in Excel format should look similar to Figure 7-4.

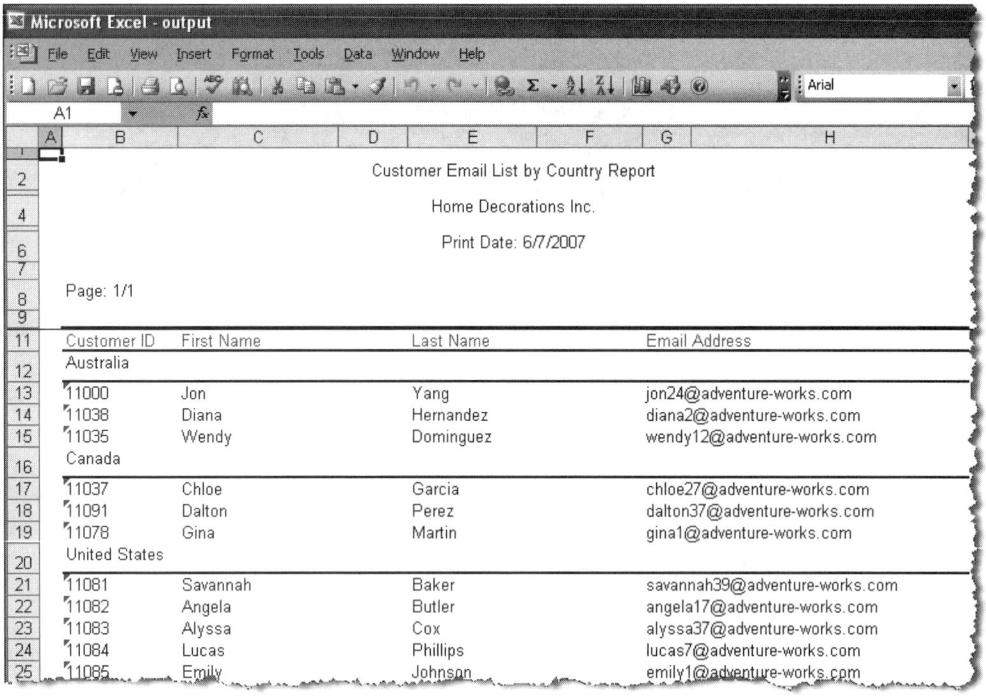

Figure 7-4. *The Customer E-mail List by Country report*

Business Case

We know how important the customer is to a business; naturally, lots of business transactions are related to the customers. It is common practice in the real world to produce various special reports to help workers to deal better with the customer base.

The Customer E-mail List by Country report is one such special report, and it is commonly used by marketing department folks to communicate breaking news, such as the newest production line, through e-mail. Since the output is produced in Excel, the information is easily shared and accessible by other departments too.

Getting the Host Client Ready

I showed you how to create a console application client earlier in this chapter; now it's your turn to practice getting the client ready. You may make use of the solution RSConsole101 as a template for this project or create the client from scratch. It is good idea to create the new application from scratch; you can always refer to steps mentioned in the tutorial if you get stuck.

Please use the following steps to create a console application project; refer to Figure 7-1 for an illustration of the steps:

1. Click File ➤ New ➤ Project, or press the hot key Ctrl+Shift+N.

2. In the "Project types" pane of the New Project dialog box, select Visual C# ➤ Windows.

3. In the Templates pane, select Console Application.

4. Give a name to the application; I've called the project CustomerEmail. You may choose a different location for storing the application files according to your preference.

5. Click the OK button to finish the process; Visual Studio will create a new console application project with name CustomerEmail.

You might be wondering about the dataset. Well, let's take care of that now. Please add a new dataset to the project, and name it dsCustomerEmail (You may always revisit Chapter 3 for detailed instructions for adding the dataset). Before continuing, please make sure your solution looks similar to the one shown in Figure 7-5.

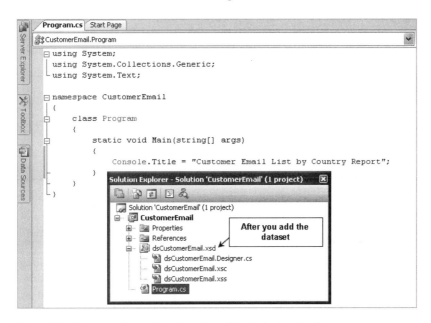

Figure 7-5. *The console application viewed in Solution Explorer*

Step 1: Creating a Data Table

As we do in each reporting project, let's arrange to gather and store data before supplying it to the reporting engine. As you know, the last step we did to get the host client ready was adding the dataset; now, its time to add a data table to it. We need five columns in the data table as identified in the report characteristics Table 7-1.

Please use the following steps to add the data table inside the dataset:

1. You can go to the dataset designer in two ways: double-click dsCustomerEmail inside Solution Explorer, or right-click the dsCustomerEmail node and select View Designer.

2. Add a data table by right-clicking the design surface and selecting Add ➤ DataTable.

3. Click the header of the newly created data table, and name it dtCustomerList. Start adding the columns to dtCustomerList by right-clicking the data table, and selecting Add ➤ Column.

4. Please add the following columns into the data table: your data table should look like Figure 7-6:

- CustomerID (System.String)

- FirstName (System.String)

- LastName (System.String)

- EmailAddress (System.String)

- CountryRegionName (System.String)

Figure 7-6. *Final look of data table dtCustomerList*

■**Note** If you face any issues with adding the dataset or data table, please refer to Chapter 3.

Step 2: Designing the Report Layout

Al lright, we have our dataset in place with the data table and all the necessary columns. We're all set to start designing the report layout. Add the report by selecting the project in Solution Explorer, right-clicking it, and selecting Add ➤ New Item. Then, select Report from the Add New Item template, and name the report rptCustomerEmail.rdlc. Click the Add button to complete the process.

Once you click the Add button, a new report is added to the project and opened in the Report Designer. You'll also notice that a new toolbox called Data Sources is available; it has our dataset's information inside.

■**Note** You can always go to the Data Sources toolbox by pressing the hot key Shift+Alt+D.

Adding a Header

I'm sure that you know by this time that when we add a new report, the body section is automatically created, but we do need to add the header to the report (remember, we don't need a footer in this report).

As usual adding the header is simple; all you've got to do is right-click the open area inside the report designer and select Page Header. After completing the action your report design surface should look similar to Figure 7-7; you may also notice that I've resized the Page Header and Body bands.

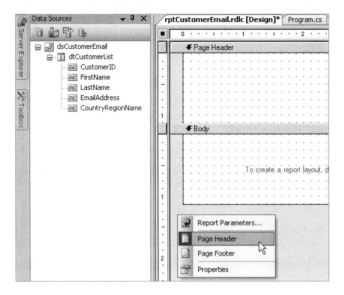

Figure 7-7. *The report designer with Page Header and Body sections*

Setting Up the Page

Let's set up the page so that the report is letter-sized and has a portrait page orientation. Right-click an open area on the design surface, and select Properties. You may wish to put your name as Author and add information about the report to the Description field. I'd advise you to let all other choices stay at defaults.

■**Note** Please make sure to set the properties Page Width to 8.5 inches and Page Height to 11 inches for a letter-sized, portrait report.

Designing a Page Header

Now, we have the header and body sections added to our report. As we do always, let's work on the header first. Please drag and drop the following report items inside the header section:

- A text box item for the report title

- A text box item for the company name

- A text box item for the print date

- A text box item for the page number

When you drag and drop, have you thought about the ideal location to drop the report items on the designer surface? Well, I'd say go with your own flow. I typically just drop them on the top-right corner of the design surface and later move them according to the report design. Make sure to align all text boxes to center except the text box that will hold page numbers.

After adding the report items to the design surface, you'll see that the header section is ready with the look and feel. It is important to check with the requirements often to help you reduce the number of design errors.

Let's change the properties of the report items to make them work. By this time, you know that, as you drop report items onto the design surface, they assume default names like TextBox1 or TextBox5. It is good to give them some meaningful names, so later, it'll be easy to make a reference to them.

Report item properties are changed in one of these two ways: select the report item, right-click it, and select Properties or access the general properties toolbox.

Let's start changing properties; after selecting each text box, please specify the values according to Table 7-2.

Table 7-2. *Report Item Properties for the Header*

Report Item	Property	Value
textbox1		
	Name	txtReportTitle
	Value	Customer E-mail List by Country Report
textbox2		
	Name	txtCompanyTitle
	Value	Home Decorations Inc.
textbox3		
	Name	txtPrintDate
	Value	="Print Date: " & Today
textbox4		
	Name	txtPageNumber
	Value	="Page: " & Globals!PageNumber & "/" & Globals!TotalPages
	Color	DarkBlue
line1		
	Name	lineHeader
	LineWidth	1pt

After you're finished with the header section, your report design surface should look something similar to the one shown in Figure 7-8.

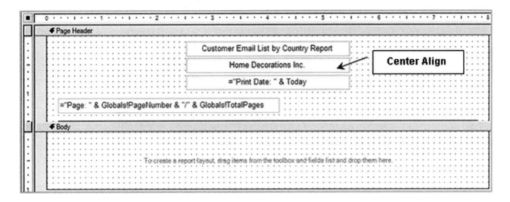

Figure 7-8. *The report designer with the completed header section*

Designing the Body Section

Let's start by dragging Report Items ➤ Table from the toolbox and dropping it inside the Body section in the report designer to create a new table item with the default name of table1. To add one more column, right-click the right-most column header in the table and select "Insert Column to the Right". Adjust the width of the columns suitably, for example, we should give more space to the E-mail Address column.

Now, we have our four columns inside the table, so let's map the data table columns to the text box report items. You may choose your favorite method to add mapping: either type an expression or drag and drop from the data source.

For this example, let's drag Data Source ➤ dsCustomerEmail ➤ CustomerID and drop it inside the first column of the table item detail section. Repeat the task for the rest of the columns from dsCustomerEmail except CountryRegionName. You might be wondering what'll happen to CountryRegionName. Well, you'll add it to the report, not as a column but as a group. Adding a group to a table item is simple, all you need to do is to select the detail row, right-click, and select Insert Group. Please see Figure 7-9 for graphical presentation of these steps.

When you add a new group to a table item, the group is added with its own header and footer. For this report, we'll make use of the group header, but you'll need to delete the group footer. After adding the group, drop CountryRegionName on to the group header. Then, please make sure your design surface looks like Figure 7-10.

■Note If you don't want to add the group header and footer, you may uncheck the "Include group header" and "Include group footer" check boxes (see Figure 7-9).

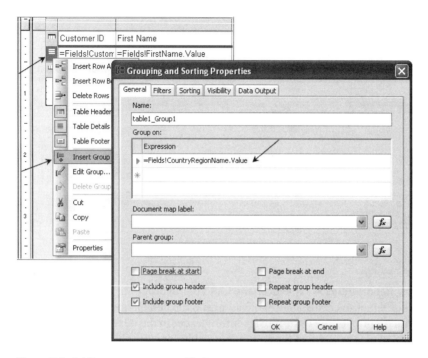

Figure 7-9. *Adding a group to a table item*

Figure 7-10. *Report designer after adding the fields in the body*

Please make sure you've mapped all columns correctly inside the table. You can refer to Figure 7-10 and Table 7-3 to confirm. You may also notice that we have small width for the Group header. To get more data displayed in the group header, merge all the cells in the group header row.

Table 7-3. *Table Item Properties*

Report Item	Property	Value
textbox1	Value	Customer ID
textbox2	Value	First Name
textbox3	Value	Last Name
textbox10	Value	E-mail Address
CustomerID	Value	=Fields!CustomerID.Value
FirstName	Value	=Fields!FirstName.Value
LastName	Value	=Fields!LastName.Value
EmailAddress	Value	=Fields!EmailAddress.Value
CountryRegionName	Value	=Fields!CountryRegionName.Value
table1	DataSetName	dsCustomerEmail_dtCustomerList
table1.TableRow1	RepeatOnNewPage	True (To display columns headers on every page)

Beautifying the Report

Even though we're not viewing this report in preview mode, that doesn't mean it should not look beautiful. We should keep in mind that when a user opens this report in Excel, the experience must remain good.

Before we start writing the C# code, let's apply some basic beautification to our report. The most important to me will be, of course, changing colors and adding borders to the column and group headers (you may refer to examples in Chapter 4 for instructions to apply colors and fonts).

Step 3: Writing the C# Code

We'll need to write the code inside Program.cs, which is generated automatically when we create the console application project. So, how does the code in a console application client compare to other clients? Well, you won't see the ReportViewer here; instead, you'll make reference to the Microsoft.ReportViewer.WinForms namespace and use the LocalReport() object.

Adding a Reference

Adding a reference is easy. Start by right-clicking References under the Project node and then selecting Add Reference. Under the .NET tab in the Add Reference dialog box, scroll down, and select Microsoft.ReportViewer.WinForms; you need to click the OK button to complete the action. You'll see the newly added reference in Solution Explorer. See Figure 7-11 for an illustration of all the steps needed to add a reference to the project.

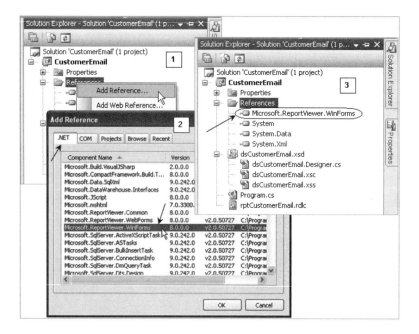

Figure 7-11. *Adding the Microsoft.ReportViewer.WinForms reference to the project*

Please make sure the code inside Program.cs looks like the following:

```
using System;
using System.Collections.Generic;
using System.Text;
using System.Data;
using System.Data.SqlClient;
using Microsoft.Reporting.WinForms;
using System.IO;

namespace CustomerEmail
{
    class Program
    {
        static void Main(string[] args)
        {
            Console.Title = "Customer E-mail List by Country Report";

            LocalReport rpvCustomerEmail = new LocalReport();

            //declare connection string
            string cnString = "Data Source=(local);Initial Catalog=RealWorld; ➥
Integrated Security=SSPI;";
```

```
//declare Connection, command and other related objects
SqlConnection conReport = new SqlConnection(cnString);
SqlCommand cmdReport = new SqlCommand();
SqlDataReader drReport;
DataSet dsReport = new dsCustomerEmail();

try
{
    //open connection
    conReport.Open();

    //prepare connection object to get the data through reader and
    //populate into dataset
    cmdReport.CommandType = CommandType.Text;
    cmdReport.Connection = conReport;
    cmdReport.CommandText = "Select * FROM tblCustomerEmail ➥
                    Order By CountryRegionName";

    //read data from command object
    drReport = cmdReport.ExecuteReader();

    //load data directly from reader to dataset
    dsReport.Tables[0].Load(drReport);

    //close reader and connection
    drReport.Close();
    conReport.Close();

    //provide local report information to viewer
    rpvCustomerEmail.ReportEmbeddedResource = ➥
    "CustomerEmail.rptCustomerEmail.rdlc";

    //prepare report data source
    ReportDataSource rds = new ReportDataSource();
    rds.Name = "dsCustomerEmail_dtCustomerList";
    rds.Value = dsReport.Tables[0];
    rpvCustomerEmail.DataSources.Add(rds);

    Warning[] warnings;
    string[] streamids;
    string mimeType;
    string encoding;
    string filenameExtension;

    byte[] bytes = rpvCustomerEmail.Render(
        "Excel", null, out mimeType, out encoding, out filenameExtension,
        out streamids, out warnings);
```

```
            using (FileStream fs = new FileStream("output.xls", FileMode.Create))
            {
                fs.Write(bytes, 0, bytes.Length);
            }
        }
        catch (Exception ex)
        {
            Console.WriteLine("Initial Error Message: " + ex.Message);

            string FinalErrorMessage = string.Empty;

            Exception innerError = ex.InnerException;

            while (!((innerError == null)))
            {
                FinalErrorMessage += innerError.Message;
                innerError = innerError.InnerException;
            }

            Console.WriteLine("Final Error Message:" + FinalErrorMessage);
            Console.WriteLine("Press any key to exit");

            //Wait for user action of press any key
            Console.ReadKey();
        }
        finally
        {
            //check if connection is still open then attempt to close it
            if (conReport.State == ConnectionState.Open)
            {
                conReport.Close();
            }
        }
    }
  }
}
```

■**Note** Please make sure to reference System.Data.SqlClient and System.IO; otherwise, the code will not compile properly.

In this report, we're adding functionality like creating an output file using System.IO. We achieve this by making use of the FileStream() object. First, we create a file stream by providing the file output name and which mode to use to create the file. The actual writing of the file is done by calling the Write() method by supplying bytes of an array that the report rendering engine has generated for us. You can experiment with producing PDF output instead of Excel by making the following changes to the code:

```
byte[] bytes = rpvCustomerEmail.Render(
    "PDF", null, out mimeType, out encoding, out filenameExtension,
    out streamids, out warnings);

using (FileStream fs = new FileStream("output.pdf", FileMode.Create))
{
    fs.Write(bytes, 0, bytes.Length);
}
```

If you build the application with this code change, your PDF output should look like Figure 7-12.

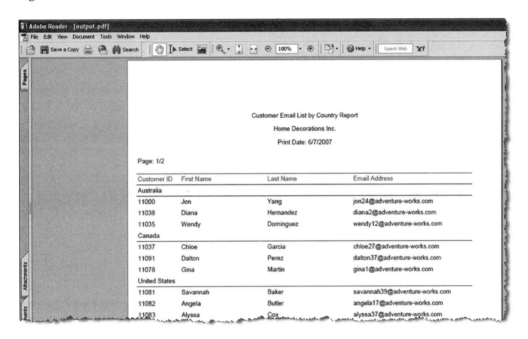

Figure 7-12. *Report in PDF format*

The other interesting piece of code is the code to investigate the InnerException. Most of the time, when we get an error in the code, try . . . catch responds with the error details. However, at times, this primary error information is not enough. Therefore, it is better to also probe the InnerException to pinpoint the exact source.

Building the Project

This console application is simple; it allows a user to produce the report when required. Let's build the project. You can click the small, green Play button in the main toolbox or press F5 on the keyboard to start the application in run-time mode.

If the program complies without any errors, Visual Studio will generate CustomerEmail.exe based on your build choice (debug or release). See Figure 7-13 for the location of the generated console application executable.

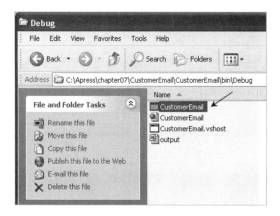

Figure 7-13. *The location of CustomerEmail.exe on the local drive*

You can double-click the CustomerEmail.exe file to generate the report and examine the output using Excel. If all goes well, the generated Excel file, output.xls, should have content similar to Figure 7-13.

■**Note** The code used to produce the PDF file, by default, will store the file inside the BIN build folder. If you wish the output to appear in the root of the C drive, change the code as follows: FileStream fs = new FileStream(@"c:\output.pdf", FileMode.Create).

Daily Vendor Purchase Order Summary Report

Assume that you're working for MyFirm Dairy Products, Incorporated as a developer, and the purchasing department is seeking a better way to communicate with all vendors, who want a daily summary report of all purchase orders (POs) issued to purchasing department.

To serve the vendors' needs, you'll produce a Daily Vendor PO Summary report. The report is to be delivered to the vendor FTP site by 9 p.m. each day. All characteristics described in Table 7-4 should be met, and report output in PDF format should match Figure 7-14.

Table 7-4. *Report Characteristics*

Characteristics	Value
Report title	Daily Vendor PO Summary Report (Header, align left)
Company title	MyFirm Diary Products Inc. (Header, align right)
Vendor title	Vendor : Value passed using Parameter
Print date	Yes (Header, align left)

Characteristics	Value
Data source	`tblVendorPO`
Columns to report	`PurchaseOrderID, OrderDate, SubTotal, TaxAmt, TotalDue, OrderPlaceByName`
Page size	`Letter`
Page orientation	`Portrait`
Page number	`Page: n/n` (Footer, align left)
Output format	`PDF`

Daily Vendor PO Summary Report   MyFirm Dairy Products Inc.

Print Date: 6/8/2007

Vendor Name: ABCD1234 Inc.

PO ID	Order Date	Sub Total	Tax Amt	Total Due	Order Place By
24	1/15/2002	4,215.75	337.26	4,658.40	Reinout Hillmann
103	4/9/2002	3,407.25	272.58	3,765.01	Eric Kurjan
182	7/24/2002	4,215.75	337.26	4,658.40	Fukiko Ogisu
261	11/12/2002	3,407.25	272.58	3,765.01	Erin Hagens
864	10/11/2003	4,215.75	337.26	4,658.40	Linda Meisner
947	10/22/2003	3,407.25	272.58	3,765.01	Mikael Sandberg
1046	11/15/2003	7,623.00	609.84	8,423.42	Reinout Hillmann
1110	12/9/2003	7,623.00	609.84	8,423.42	Frank Pellow
1189	12/20/2003	7,623.00	609.84	8,423.42	Arvind Rao
1268	12/29/2003	7,623.00	609.84	8,423.42	Linda Meisner
1347	1/6/2004	7,623.00	609.84	8,423.42	Mikael Sandberg
1426	1/14/2004	7,623.00	609.84	8,423.42	Reinout Hillmann
1505	1/24/2004	7,623.00	609.84	8,423.42	Eric Kurjan
1584	2/1/2004	4,215.75	337.26	4,658.40	Fukiko Ogisu
1663	2/9/2004	3,407.25	272.58	3,765.01	Erin Hagens
1742	2/18/2004	4,215.75	337.26	4,658.40	Annette Hill
1821	2/28/2004	3,407.25	272.58	3,765.01	Ben Miller
3954	9/1/2004	4,215.75	337.26	4,658.40	Fukiko Ogisu
		95,691.75			

Figure 7-14. *Output of the Daily Vendor PO Summary report*

Business Case

Every business has customers and vendors. MyFirm buys raw material from the vendors and sells the finished dairy products to customers. It is important for the firm to be on the top of the purchasing activities to make sure manufacturing folks are not short on supplies of raw materials.

Sending a daily summary of purchase orders to vendors is a key part of the communication strategy. This summary information can give a head start to the vendors in preparing and completing the purchase orders in a timely manner.

Automatically delivering the report to the vendor FTP site saves the purchasing department a lot of the manual effort to produce the report. PDF is an ideal document format, as it's widely used in all business environments for exchanging information. So, what is an FTP site?

FTP is an abbreviation for File Transfer Protocol. As the name suggests, FTP is used to transfer files. It is common practice among business partners to share information over an FTP site.

Getting the Host Client Ready

Please use the following steps to create a console application project; see Figure 7-1 for an illustration of these steps:

1. Click File ➤ New ➤ Project, or press the hot keys Ctrl+Shift+N.

2. In the "Project types" pane of the New Project dialog box, select Visual C# ➤ Windows.

3. In the Templates pane, select Console Application.

4. Give a name to the application; I've called the project VendorPO. You may choose a different location for storing the application files according to your preference.

5. Click the OK button to finish the process; Visual Studio will create a new console application project with the name VendorPO.

6. Add the dsVendorPO dataset to the project.

7. Add the Microsoft.ReportViewer.WinForms reference to the project (see Figure 7-11).

Before going further, please make your solution looks something like Figure 7-5. Please refer to either the "Console Applications 101" tutorial or the CustomerEmail projects earlier in this chapter if you need further details about how to add controls.

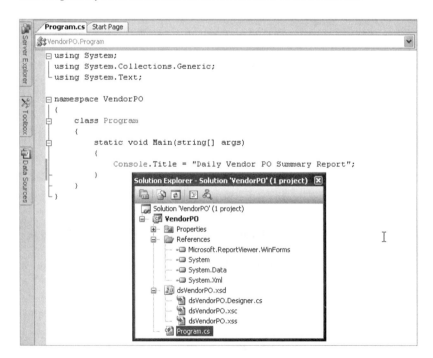

Figure 7-15. *The console application viewed in Solution Explorer*

Step 1: Creating a DataTable

As we know a data table is the key to our data, it is important to design the data table to match the data types returned from the database. Let's add a new data table to dsVendorPO. The data table will have all the columns identified in the report characteristics in Table 7-4.

Please use the following steps to add data table inside the dataset:

1. Go to the dataset designer by double-clicking dsVendorPO inside Solution Explorer or by right-clicking the dsVendorPO node and selecting View Designer.

2. Add a data table by right-clicking the design surface and selecting Add ➤ DataTable.

3. Click the header of the newly created data table, and name it dtPOList. Add columns to dtPOList by right-clicking the data table and selecting Add ➤ Column.

4. Please add the following columns into the data table; your data table should look like Figure 7-16:

   - PurchaseOrderID (System.String)

   - OrderDate (System.DateTime)

   - SubTotal (System.Double)

   - TaxAmt (System.Double)

   - TotalDue (System.Double)

   - OrderPlaceByName (System.String)

Figure 7-16. *Final look of the data table dtPOList*

Step 2: Designing a Report Layout

As we know, a report must be part of the project before we start working on the report's design. Therefore, let's add the report by selecting the project in Solution Explorer, right-clicking it, and selecting Add ➤ New Item. Select Report from the Add New Item template, and name the report rptVendorPO.rdlc. Click the Add button to complete the process; a new report will be added to the project and opened in the report designer.

Adding the Header and Footer

As usual, we'll add the header and footer to the report by right-clicking an open area inside the report designer and selecting Page Header; repeat the process and select Page Footer. Now, you'll see all three sections (header, body, and footer) added to the report and ready to host report items.

Setting Up the Page

We need to make sure the report is letter-sized and has a portrait page orientation. Right-click an open area on the design surface, and select Properties. You may wish to put your name as Author and fill in the Description of the report. Please make sure Page Width is set to 8.5 inches and Page Height to 11 inches.

■**Note** What if you need more space for data output? You can set the left and right margins to 0 inches.

Designing the Page Header

Please drag and drop the following report items inside the header section:

- A text box item for the report title
- A text box item for the company title
- A text box item for the print date

Please drag and drop the following report items inside the footer section:

- A text box item for the page number
- A line item for a separator

After adding the report items to the design surface, the header and footer section are ready. Please make sure to align the text boxes according to the design requirements.

Again, report item properties can be changed in one of two ways: select the report item, right-click it, and select Properties, or access the general properties toolbox. After selecting each text box item, please specify the values for each report item's property according to Table 7-5.

Table 7-5. *Report Item Properties for the Header*

Report Item	Property	Value
textbox1		
	Name	txtReportTitle
	Value	Daily Vendor PO Summary Report
textbox2		
	Name	txtCompanyTitle
	Value	MyFirm Daily Products Inc.

Report Item	Property	Value
textbox3		
	Name	txtPrintDate
	Value	="Print Date: " & Today
textbox4		
	Name	txtPageNumbers
	Value	="Page: " & Globals!PageNumber & "/" & Globals!TotalPages
line1		
	Name	lineFooter
	LineWidth	2pt

Designing the Body Section

Let's start by dragging Report Items ➤ Table from the toolbox and dropping it inside the Body section in the report designer. A new Table Item with the default name of table1 will be created. Add two more columns by right-clicking the right-most column header and selecting Table Item ➤ Insert Column to the Right. Adjust the width of column suitably to fit all five columns; allow extra space for the ShipMethodName column.

Select Data Source ➤ dsVendorPO ➤ PurchaseOrderID, and drag and drop it inside the first column of the table item in the detail section. Repeat the task for the rest of the columns from dsVendorPO.

This report is typically produced separately for each vendor. Therefore, we will send the Vendor Name to the report as a report parameter. Please use the following steps to add a report parameter:

1. Right-Click an open area inside the report designer, and select Page Header.

2. Click the Add button.

3. Give the report parameter the name parVendorName. In the Prompt field, type **Enter Vendor Name**.

4. Give a name to the application; I've called it VendorPO. You may choose a different location for storing the application files according to your preference (see Figure 7-1).

5. Click the OK button to complete the process. Please see Figure 7-17 for an illustration of the steps.

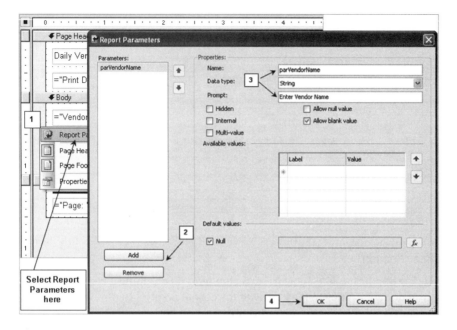

Figure 7-17. *Adding a report parameter*

Now we need use parVendorName to supply the Vendor Name from the console application to the report. Please select the text box txtVendorName, and enter following expression:

```
="Vendor Name: " & Parameters!parVendorName.Value.
```

Please make sure your report design surface looks like the one shown in Figure 7-18.

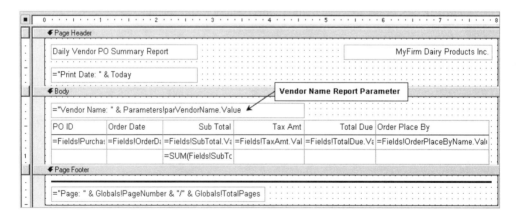

Figure 7-18. *The report designer after adding the header, footer, and body*

Please make sure you've included all the columns correctly inside the table item. You can refer to Figure 7-18 and Table 7-6 to confirm.

Table 7-6. *Table Item Properties*

Report Item	Property	Value
textbox1	Value	PO ID
textbox2	Value	Order Date
textbox3	Value	Sub Total
textbox10	Value	Tax Amt
textbox13	Value	Total Due
textbox4	Value	Shipment Method
PurchaseOrderID	Value	=Fields!PurchaseOrderID.Value
OrderDate	Value	=Fields!OrderDate.Value
SubTotal	Value	=Fields!SubTotal.Value
TaxAmt	Value	=Fields!TaxAmt.Value
Freight	Value	=Fields!TotalDue.Value
ShipMethodName	Value	=Fields!ShipMethodName.Value
Textbox9	Value	=SUM(Fields!SubTotal.Value)
table1	DataSetName	dsVendorPO_dtPOList
table1.TableRow1	RepeatOnNewPage	True (To display columns headers on every page)
txtVendorTitle	Value	="Vendor Name: " & Parameters!parVendorName.Value

Beautifying the Report

As usual, let's apply some formatting to our report. As you can see in the report output in Figure 7-14, the column header has top and bottom borders set. You can achieve this by selecting table1.TableRow1 and setting the top and bottom borders to solid. Next, format the order date: select the Order Date text box, select Properties, and set the format to d. Similarly, you can set the numeric format setting of N to SubTotal, TaxAmt, Freight and textbox9.

Step 3: Write the C# Code

Please make sure the code inside Program.cs looks like the following:

```
using System;
using System.Collections.Generic;
using System.Text;
using System.Data;
using System.Data.SqlClient;
using Microsoft.Reporting.WinForms;
using System.IO;
using System.Net;

namespace VendorPO
{
```

```
class Program
{
    static void Main(string[] args)
    {
        Console.Title = "Daily Vendor PO Summary Report";

        LocalReport rpvVendorPO = new LocalReport();

        //declare connection string
        string cnString = "Data Source=(local);Initial Catalog=RealWorld; ➥
                          Integrated Security=SSPI;";

        //declare Connection, command and other related objects
        SqlConnection conReport = new SqlConnection(cnString);
        SqlCommand cmdReport = new SqlCommand();
        SqlDataReader drReport;
        DataSet dsReport = new dsVendorPO();

        try
        {
            //open connection
            conReport.Open();

            //prepare connection object to get the data through reader and
            //populate into dataset
            cmdReport.CommandType = CommandType.Text;
            cmdReport.Connection = conReport;
            cmdReport.CommandText = "SELECT * FROM tblVendorPO ➥
            ORDER BY PurchaseOrderID";

            //read data from command object
            drReport = cmdReport.ExecuteReader();

            //load data directly from reader to dataset
            dsReport.Tables[0].Load(drReport);

            //close reader and connection
            drReport.Close();
            conReport.Close();

            //provide local report information to viewer
            rpvVendorPO.ReportEmbeddedResource = "VendorPO.rptVendorPO.rdlc";

            //setup report parameter to pass vendor name
            ReportParameter[] Param = new ReportParameter[1];
            Param[0] = new ReportParameter("parVendorName", "ABCD1234 Inc.");
```

```
    rpvVendorPO.SetParameters(Param);

    //prepare report data source
    ReportDataSource rds = new ReportDataSource();
    rds.Name = "dsVendorPO_dtPOList";
    rds.Value = dsReport.Tables[0];
    rpvVendorPO.DataSources.Add(rds);

    Warning[] warnings;
    string[] streamids;
    string mimeType;
    string encoding;
    string filenameExtension;

    byte[] bytes = rpvVendorPO.Render(
        "PDF", null, out mimeType, out encoding, out filenameExtension,
        out streamids, out warnings);

    using (FileStream fs = new FileStream("output.pdf", ➥
            FileMode.Create))
    {
        fs.Write(bytes, 0, bytes.Length);
    }

    //upload file to FTP site
    UploadToFTP("output.pdf");
}
catch (Exception ex)
{
    Console.WriteLine("Initial Error Message: " + ex.Message);

    string FinalErrorMessage = string.Empty;
    Exception innerError = ex.InnerException;
    while (!((innerError == null)))
    {
        FinalErrorMessage += innerError.Message;
        innerError = innerError.InnerException;
    }

    Console.WriteLine("Final Error Message:" + FinalErrorMessage);
    Console.WriteLine("Press any key to exit");

    //Wait for user action of press any key
    Console.ReadKey();
}
finally
{
```

```
                //check if connection is still open then attempt to close it
                if (conReport.State == ConnectionState.Open)
                {
                    conReport.Close();
                }
            }
        }


        static void UploadToFTP(string FileToUpload)
        {
            FileInfo FileInformation = new FileInfo(FileToUpload);
            string FTPUri = "ftp://localhost/" + FileInformation.Name;
            FtpWebRequest FTPRequest;

            //Create FtpWebRequest object and passing Credentials
            FTPRequest = (FtpWebRequest)FtpWebRequest.Create ➥
                            (new Uri("ftp://localhost/" + FileInformation.Name));
            //FTPRequest.Credentials = new NetworkCredential(ftpUserID,
            //ftpPassword);
            FTPRequest.Credentials = new NetworkCredential();

            //Close request after command is executed
            FTPRequest.KeepAlive = false;

            //Specify the command to be executed and mode
            FTPRequest.Method = WebRequestMethods.Ftp.UploadFile;
            FTPRequest.UseBinary = true;

            //File size notification
            FTPRequest.ContentLength = FileInformation.Length;

            int buffLength = 2048; //2kb
            byte[] buff = new byte[buffLength];
            int contentLen;

            //Open the file stream
            FileStream FTPFs = FileInformation.OpenRead();

            try
            {
                // Stream to which the file to be uploaded is written
                Stream StreamRequest = FTPRequest.GetRequestStream();

                // Read from the file stream 2kb at a time
                contentLen = FTPFs.Read(buff, 0, buffLength);
```

```
            // Until Stream content ends
            while (contentLen != 0)
            {
                // Write Content from the file stream to the
                // FTP Upload Stream
                StreamRequest.Write(buff, 0, contentLen);
                contentLen = FTPFs.Read(buff, 0, buffLength);
            }

            // Close the file stream and the Request Stream
            StreamRequest.Close();
            FTPFs.Close();
        }
        catch (Exception ex)
        {
            Console.WriteLine(ex.Message);
            Console.WriteLine("Press any key to contine...");
            Console.Read();
        }
    }
  }
}
```

Note Please make sure to reference System.Net and System.IO; otherwise, the code will not properly compile.

The highlight of the code in this report project is the delivery of the report to the FTP site. FTP sites can be securely accessible with a user ID and password; anonymous access is also widely used where security is not a major concern.

For this example, we're using a local FTP site (ftp://localhost) with anonymous access. You can access FTP site configuration on a Windows XP machine from Start ➤ Control Panel ➤ Administrative Tools ➤ Internet Information Services. FTP site properties are accessed by right-clicking Default FTP Site. You can get more information on how to work with FTP sites here:

http://msdn2.microsoft.com/en-us/library/6ws081sa(VS.80).aspx

You may also notice that I've set the local path to C:\ftpdata. The report will produce output.pdf and transfer it to C:\ftpdata using FTP. See Figure 7-18 to for graphical presentation of accessing a local FTP site.

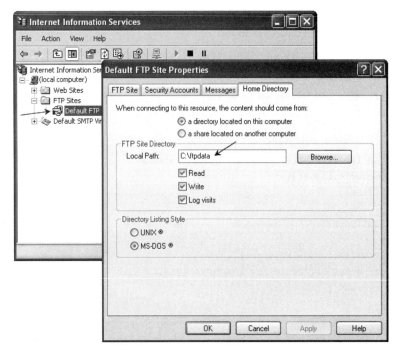

Figure 7-19. *Setting FTP properties*

Note To test a remote FTP site, replace `ftp://localhost/` with `ftp://IP Address`.

Building and Scheduling the Project

Let's start with building the project. You can click the small, green Play button in the main toolbox or press F5 on the keyboard to start the application in run-time mode. If the program complies without any errors, Visual Studio will produce `VendorPO.exe` based on your build option (debug or release).

Now, to run this report daily, we need to schedule it. I'm using Windows XP's scheduler; please consult the Microsoft help documents for scheduling on non-XP machines. Use the following steps to schedule `VendorPO.exe`:

- Click Start ➤ All Programs ➤ Accessories ➤ System Tools ➤ Scheduled Tasks.

- Double-click Add Scheduled Task to start the Scheduled Task Wizard, and click the Next button.

- Browse to `VendorPO.exe`, and add it to the scheduler.

- Select the Daily task.

- Set "Start time" to 9 PM, and "Perform this task" to Every Day.

- Specify the user account and password to finish the wizard.

Please see Figure 7-20 for a graphical presentation of the steps required to configure the scheduled task.

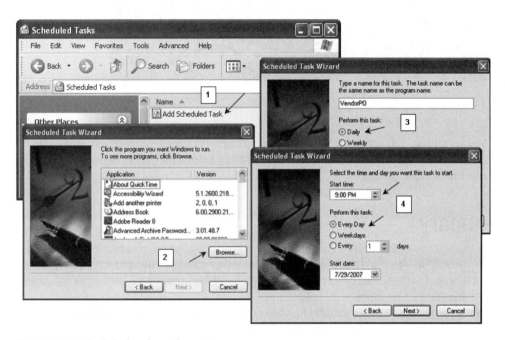

Figure 7-20. *Scheduled task configuration*

Troubleshooting Console Applications

Console applications also deserve a troubleshooting section. As with any other client, if you make mistakes while coding or fail to issue a proper instruction, you'll have trouble. As you build your knowledge throughout this book, you'll be able to fix most troubles. Let me show you what issues you'll learn to fix here.

You might receive an error message saying, "An error occurred during local report processing." That's a good, meaningful error that's tells us a lot about the issue, right? I know it is easy to get frustrated when you see an error like this; it seems like a perfect reason to start pulling out your hair. Don't panic; like most others, this scenario has a work-around.

Notice that the catch section has a few extra lines of code inside Catch() that are trapping the inner error. This trap will lead us to a more specific error message. Let's see what happens if I purposely introduce the following mistake in code:

```
rpvCustomerEmail.ReportEmbeddedResource = "zzCustomerEmail.rptCustomerEmail.rdlc";
```

As you can, see I've added zz in front of the project name. Now, if you run the code this way, you'll surely see the two errors—the generic one first and the detailed one second. Figure 7-21 shows the errors in run-time mode.

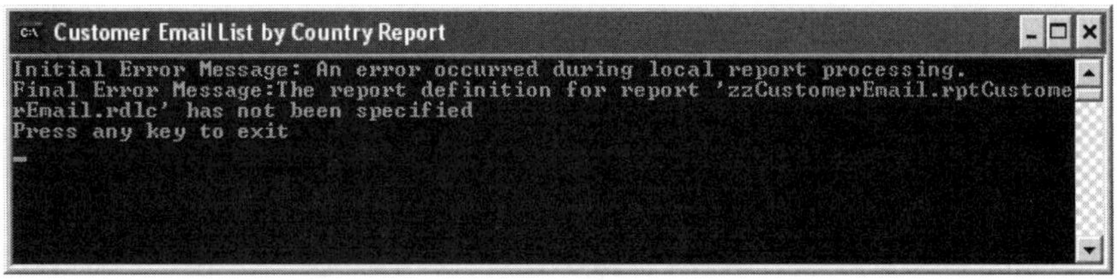

Figure 7-21. *Generic and specific run-time errors*

The second, specific error message, "The report definition for report 'zzCustomerEmail.rptCustomerEmail.rdlc' has not been specified," is more helpful for easily trapping the bug and getting the report to work.

Summary

In this chapter, we looked at how console applications can be used to produce Excel and PDF output without previewing the report. You also learned to automate the delivery of a report using a scheduler, and make use of inner exception handling to get to detailed error messages and troubleshoot issues quickly.

In the next chapter, we'll continue the same trend of automating report delivery with non-GUI clients. However, next, our client will be a Windows service.

CHAPTER 8

■ ■ ■

Reporting with a Windows Service

In Chapter 7, we produced reports with a console application; the console application is significant because it lacks a GUI. Now, let me introduce you to a host client that doesn't even have a text-based interface. You might be wondering how a user will communicate with a client that has no user interface. Well, our report's production will remain the same, but instead of live keyboard input, we'll make use of an automatic data feed using configuration files or another data source.

A Windows service application is versatile—it has the ability to start, stop, and pause according to user demand. Think of this: if you want to suspend the report production, all you need to do is stop the service.

Let's get started by building a Windows service application. After that, we'll work on the real-world practical reporting project.

This chapter covers

- "Windows Services 101," a step-by-step tutorial

- Producing a report in PDF format and sending it as an e-mail attachment

- Scheduling report delivery

Windows Services 101

How does a Windows service help users of client-side reporting? Like all the clients we've used in previous chapters, a Windows service has its own merits to qualify as a good client host. A Windows service application runs in the background as long as the operating system (Windows) is running, so a user can start, stop, or customize the service using the Control Panel.

A Windows service application with a timer control hosted inside it is a killer solution to produce and deliver time-sensitive reports. In such cases, delivering the report without requiring any human intervention is the key factor in increasing efficiency. There are a few choices of delivery: the report can be sent as an e-mail attachment, uploaded to an FTP site, or delivered in just about any way the business case demands.

A Windows service application can be installed on either an individual's PC or a server. If installed on a server, a single instance can service many different report delivery destinations based on settings provided to the application.

Creating a Windows Service Project

Please open Visual Studio, and use the following steps to create a Windows service application project; Figure 8-1 illustrates these steps:

1. Click File ➤ New ➤ Project, or press Ctrl+Shift+N.

2. In the "Project types" pane of the New Project dialog box, select Visual C# ➤ Windows.

3. In the Templates pane, select ➤ Windows Service.

4. Give the application a name; I've called the project RSWindowsService101. You may choose a different location for storing the application files according to your preference.

5. Click the OK button to finish the process. VS will create a new Windows service project.

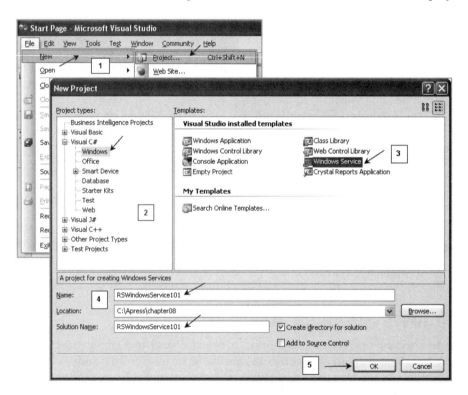

Figure 8-1. *Create a new Windows service project.*

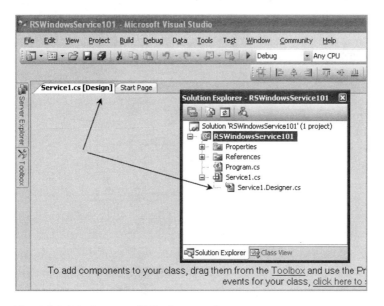

Figure 8-2. *Newly created Windows service*

Figure 8-2 shows the code and files produced inside Solution Explorer. As you may notice in Figure 8-2, a new class with the name Service1.cs is part of the project. Now, you can drag and drop different controls, like the timer control, from the toolbox on to the design surface.

Adding an Installer to the Windows Service Project

What is this installer? Well, each Windows service application needs some basic settings to run; for example, you might set how a service will run—via a user account or the local system account. Or you might dictate how a service should behave after booting Windows: should it automatically start, or must a user go to the service's Control Panel to manually start it?

We need to add an installer to our project for setting up these special parameters. Adding the installer is simple: right-click the open area inside the service designer, and select Add Installer. Figure 8-3 illustrates the steps for adding an installer.

A new file ProjectInstaller.cs is part of the project now. You'll also notice that two processes serviceProcessInstaller1 and serviceInstaller1 have become part of the ProjectInstaller design surface. What important properties should we know for both serviceProcessInstaller and serviceInstaller?

Let's begin with serviceProcessInstaller. Here, you need to define how your service will run, that is, which account to use. By default, the choice is User, but you can select anything from the available choices, shown in Figure 8-4, according to the demands of your business case.

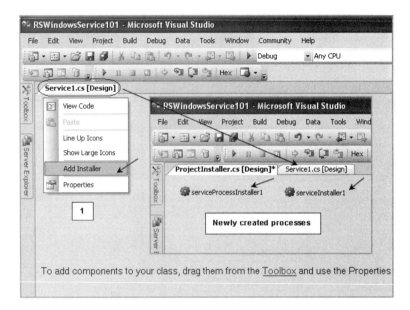

Figure 8-3. *Adding an installer to the project*

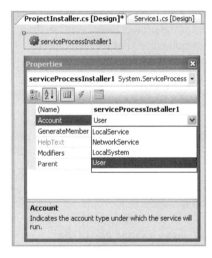

Figure 8-4. *Properties of serviceProcessInstaller*

Now, let's look at serviceInstaller1. Two important properties of serviceInstaller worth mentioning are DisplayName , which appears in the Windows service control to help identify the service, and StartType, which defines how the service should start when Windows is booted.

The default choice of StartType is Manual, but in most cases, you'll want to set it to Automatic. Setting it to Automatic guarantees that the service will run every time Windows runs. Figure 8-5 shows the available properties.

■**Note** You can set the Account property to User if the service is performing actions that need special security privileges, for example, to impersonate a domain account to access database resources.

Figure 8-5. *Properties of serviceInstaller*

Please make sure you set the properties as indicated in Table 8-1.

Table 8-1. *Properties Settings for the Windows Service Application*

Object	Property	Value
serviceProcessInstaller1		
	Account	LocalSystem
serviceInstaller1		
	DisplayName	RS Windows Service for Reports
	StartType	Automatic

Please check the following MSDN link for further information on project installers:

```
http://msdn.microsoft.com/library/default.asp?url=/library/➥
en-us/vbcon/html/vbtskAddingInstallersToYourServiceApplication.asp
```

User Interaction with a Windows Service

Typically, a Windows service application has no live user intervention through the keyboard or the mouse. The service starts to work in the background after its installation. To allow user input to the service, we have to use a text- or XML-based configuration file. Common data sources, such as MS Access or SQL Server, can also provide data as input to the service. Usually, a service produces logs for health or progress checks.

The Service class is inherited from the ServiceBase class, which provides the base for the service that is part of the Windows service application that calls the ServiceBase constructor of the derived class. This is done by making a call to the Start method when the service is started. Immediately after this, the OnStart method is called. In simple words, all the functions to handle the service are encapsulated within the ServiceBase class, leaving developers to focus on the function of the service application, not how to coordinate the service with the OS. You can find out more at this MSDN link:

```
http://msdn2.microsoft.com/en-us/library/➡
system.serviceprocess.servicebase_members.aspx
```

Let's examine the code that is produced after creating the project. You can switch to code view by right-clicking anywhere on the design surface and selecting View Code.

Typically, the OnStart and OnStop methods are key pieces of functionality for any Windows service application. The default code should look similar to the following:

```csharp
using System;
using System.Collections.Generic;
using System.ComponentModel;
using System.Data;
using System.Diagnostics;
using System.ServiceProcess;
using System.Text;

namespace RSWindowsService101
{
    public partial class Service1 : ServiceBase
    {
        public Service1()
        {
            InitializeComponent();
        }

        protected override void OnStart(string[] args)
        {
            // TODO: Add code here to start your service.
        }

        protected override void OnStop()
        {
            // TODO: Add code here to perform any tear-down necessary
            // to stop your service.
        }
    }
}
```

The default code produced for the project installer should look as follows:

```
using System;
using System.Collections.Generic;
using System.ComponentModel;
using System.Configuration.Install;

namespace RSWindowsService101
{
    [RunInstaller(true)]
    public partial class ProjectInstaller : Installer
    {
        public ProjectInstaller()
        {
            InitializeComponent();
        }
    }
}
```

Building the Project

All the clients we developed in the previous chapters had some default behavior when we ran them. However, Windows services are different; we can build the project, but we cannot immediately run it within the VS IDE to watch the behavior.

The code used in this tutorial doesn't do much. I've just shown you how you can build a skeleton Windows service. When we start with the reporting project later, you'll see that we can write code using the timer control to produce the report and automate its delivery.

For now, let's just get our Windows service application ready for client-side reporting. You can build a Windows service by selecting Build ➤ Build Solution from Visual Studio's main menu. If you press F5 on the keyboard, as you usually can to build projects, you will get an error that says, "Cannot start service from the command line or a debugger . . ."

If all goes well, your project should compile without any issues, and you should be able to see the Windows service application executable RSWindowsServer101.exe in the bin folder of the project, as shown in Figure 8-6.

Figure 8-6. *The project's bin folder contents after the build*

Installing the Windows Service Application

As I mentioned to you already, we cannot run a Windows service executable by double-clicking it or running from the command prompt. You'll need to make use of the utility installutil.exe, which is part of the .NET framework 2.0.

So, what is this installutil.exe? This tool ships with the .NET framework to perform the tasks of installing and uninstalling server resources. This tool automatically finds all the installer components from a given assembly and executes them. Recall that we added ProjectInstaller in our project (see Figure 8-3)? This information will be used later on by this tool to add or remove our service application. You can get more information on this utility here: http://msdn2.microsoft.com/en-us/library/50614e95(vs.71).aspx.

I assume that the service file RSWindowsService.exe is inside the folder C:\myservice. I'm using this short folder name to keep it simple; please replace it with the name of the folder containing the file on your machine when you try this example. Use the following steps to install the service and check the status:

1. Click Start ➤ Run ➤

   ```
   C:\WINDOWS\Microsoft.NET\Framework\v2.0.50727\InstallUtil.exe ➥
    c:\myservice\RSWindowsService101.exe
   ```

2. Check if the service is installed correctly by clicking Start ➤ Control Panel ➤ Administrative Tools ➤ Services.

3. Your service should be in the Service dialog box with name RS Windows Service for Reports, and your screen should look similar to the one shown in Figure 8-7.

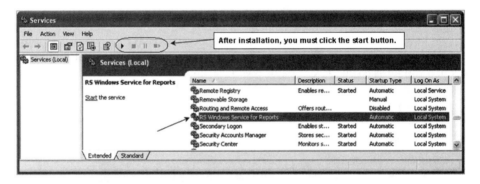

Figure 8-7. *Newly created service inside the service control panel*

Uninstalling a Windows Service Application

It is important to know how to uninstall a service, in case you need to uninstall the existing service to install a new version. It is common for a developer to develop several builds and several unit tests for each build; in that case, the developer needs to install the new build and uninstall the previous one each time a new service is registered.

Use the following steps to uninstall the service and check the status:

1. Make sure to stop the Windows service: click Start ➤ Control Panel ➤ Administrative Tools ➤ Services, select the service name, and click the stop button. Close the Windows Service dialog box once the service is stopped.

2. Click Start ➤ Run ➤

```
C:\WINDOWS\Microsoft.NET\Framework\v2.0.50727\InstallUtil.exe /u ➡
  c:\myservice\RSWindowsService101.exe
```

■**Note** We use `InstallUtil.exe` to both install and uninstall Windows services—you need to use the switch `/u` before the service name to uninstall.

Creating the New Complaints Report

Assume that you're working for Home Decorations, Incorporated as a developer, and you have the task of developing a report that must run as a Windows service every ten minutes. The report should list new complaints and e-mail them to the customer complaints escalation administrator. It should group data by complaint level and source of the complaint. The report should meet all the characteristics described in Table 8-2 and its output, in PDF format, should match Figure 8-8.

Table 8-2. *Report Characteristics*

Characteristics	Value
Report title	New Complaints Report (Header, aligned center)
Company title	Home Decorations Inc. (Header, aligned center)
Logo	No
Print date	Yes (Header, aligned center)
Data source	Complaints
Columns to report	ComplaintID, CreateDate, CustomerName, ComplaintLevel, ComplaintSource, ComplaintType
Page size	Letter
Page orientation	Landscape
Page number	Page: n/n (Header, aligned left)
Page footer	No
Output format	PDF

New Complaints Report

Home Decorations Inc.

Print Date: 6/23/2007

Page: 1/6

Complaint ID	Create Date	Customer Name	Complaint Type
Level:High			
Source:Phone			
11021	6/20/2007	Destiny Wilson	Damage Shipment
11041	6/20/2007	Amanda Carter	Billing
11063	6/20/2007	Angela Murphy	Wrong Product
11065	6/20/2007	Jessica Henderson	Billing
Source:E-mail			
11015	6/20/2007	Chloe Young	Billing
11037	6/20/2007	Chloe Garcia	Billing
11049	6/20/2007	Carol Rai	Damage Shipment
11083	6/20/2007	Alyssa Cox	Billing
Source:Web			
11013	6/20/2007	Ian Jenkins	Wrong Product
11023	6/20/2007	Seth Edwards	Damage Shipment
11078	6/20/2007	Gina Martin	Wrong Product
Level:Low			
Source:Phone			
11000	6/20/2007	Jon Yang	Damage Shipment
11036	6/20/2007	Jennifer Russell	Missing Operating Manual

Figure 8-8. *The New Complaints report*

Business Case

Keeping existing customers happy before finding new ones is a common successful business strategy. Usually, transactions between customers and a company are good. However, at times, an unhappy customer may complain. It is important for businesses to take complaints seriously and provide resolutions as soon as possible.

When a complaint arises, its severity decides the urgency of action needed. A complaint that a product is defective when it arrives is more severe than a missing sales invoice. Businesses must track all logged complaints, and this New Complaints report will just do that. This report will be automatically generated and make sure that administrators get proper notifications for swift complaint resolution.

A complaint can be received through any channel: A customer can log it online or a customer service representative can create one. Automating the extraction of all the new complaints helps administrators prioritize serious complaints. Since the output is in PDF format, the information can be easily shared and delivered as an e-mail attachment.

Getting the Windows Service Ready

Now it's your turn to practice getting a Windows service client ready. You may make use of the solution RSWindowsService101 as a template for this project or create the client from scratch. It is good idea to create the new application from scratch; you can always refer to the previous solution if you get stuck.

Use the following steps to create a Windows service project:

1. Click File ➤ New ➤ Project, or press Ctrl+Shift+N.

2. In the "Project types" pane of the New Project dialog box, select Visual C# ➤ Windows.

3. In the Templates pane, select ➤ Windows Service.

4. Give the application a name; I've called the project Complaint. You may choose a different location for storing the application files according to your preference.

5. Let's add the Installer to the project by right-clicking the open area inside the service designer and selecting Add Installer (see Figure 8-3). Please make sure to use LocalSystem as the Account and Automatic as the StartType.

6. Click the OK button to finish the process. VS will create a new Windows service project with the name Complaint.

Please add a new dataset to the project, and name it dsComplaint. Before continuing, please make sure your solution looks similar to Figure 8-9.

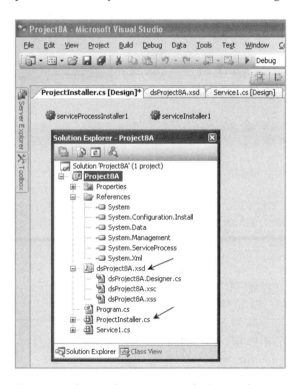

Figure 8-9. *The Windows service, Solution Explorer view*

Step 1: Creating a Data Table

We've already added the dataset to the project; now, its time to add the data table to it. The data table should have six columns, which are identified in the report characteristics in Table 8-2.

Use the following steps to add the data table inside the dataset:

1. You can go to the dataset designer in either of the usual two ways: double-click dsComplaint inside Solution Explorer or right-click the dsComplaint node and select View Designer.

2. Add the data table by right-clicking the design surface and selecting Add ➤ DataTable.

3. Click the header of the newly created data table, and name it dtComplaintList. Start adding columns to dtComplaintList by right-clicking the data table and selecting Add ➤ Column.

4. Add the following columns into the data table; your data table should look like the one shown in Figure 8-10:

- ComplaintID (System.String)

- CreateDate (System.DateTime)

- CustomerName (System.String)

- ComplaintLevel (System.String)

- ComplaintSource (System.Int32)

- ComplaintType (System.String)

Figure 8-10. *The final look of the dtComplaintList data table*

■**Note** If you face any issues with adding the dataset or data table, please refer to Chapter 3 for a walk-through.

Step 2: Designing the Report Layout

All right, we have our dataset in place with its data table and all the necessary columns. We're all set to start designing the report layout. Add the report by selecting the project in Solution Explorer, right-clicking it, and selecting Add ➤ New Item. Select Report from the Add New

Item dialog box, and name the report `rptComplaint.rdlc`. Click the Add button to add a new report to the project and open it in the report designer.

Adding the Header

Let's add the header to the report (recall that we don't need a footer in this report). As usual, adding the header is simple: right-click the open area inside the report designer, and select Page Header. After completing the action, your report design surface should look similar to the one shown in Figure 8-11. You may also notice that I've resized the Header and Body bands suitably.

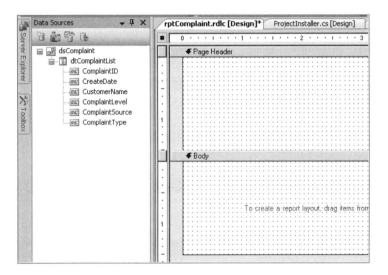

Figure 8-11. *The report designer with header and body sections*

Setting Up the Page

Now, let's set up the page. We need to make sure the report is letter size and has a landscape page orientation. Right-click the open area on the design surface, and select Properties; you may wish to put your name in the Author field and describe the report in Description. I'd advise you to let all other choices stay at their defaults.

■**Note** Please make sure to set Page Width to 11in and Page Height to 8.5in for a letter-size, landscape report.

Designing a Page Header

Now that we have the header and body sections added to our report, let's work on the header first, as we always do. Please drag and drop the following report items inside the header section:

- A text box for the report title

- A text box for the company title

- A text box for the print date

- A text box for the page number

Let's drag and drop four text boxes onto the design surface and arrange them according to the report's needs. Next, let's take care of setting properties of the report items as usual.

Report item properties are changed by selecting the report item, right-clicking it, and selecting Properties or by accessing general properties toolbox.

Select each text box, and specify the values according to Table 8-3.

Table 8-3. *Report Item Properties for Header*

Report Item	Property	Value
textbox1		
	Name	txtReportTitle
	Value	New Complaints Report
textbox2		
	Name	txtCompanyTitle
	Value	Home Decorations Inc.
textbox3		
	Name	txtPrintDate
	Value	="Print Date: " & Today
textbox4		
	Name	txtPageNumber
	Value	="Page: " & Globals!PageNumber & "/" & Globals!TotalPages
line1		
	Name	lineHeader
	LineWidth	1pt

After you're finished with the header section, your report design surface should look similar to Figure 8-12.

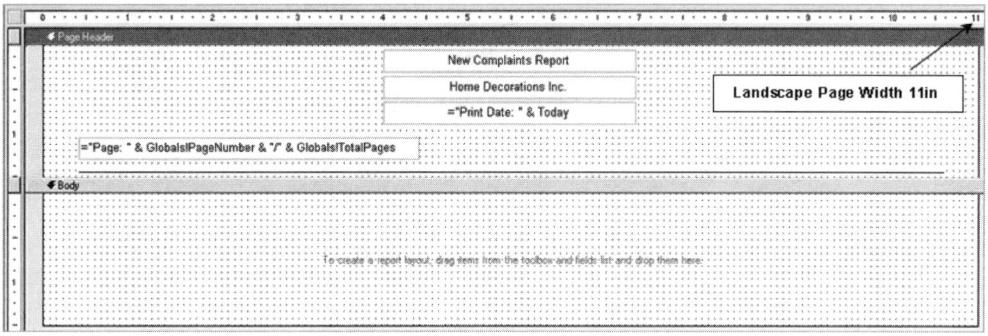

Figure 8-12. *Header section with landscape page orientation*

Designing the Body Section

Let's start working on the body section by dragging Report Items ➤ Table from the toolbox and dropping it inside the body section of the report designer. A new table item is created with the default name table1. Since we are going to group the complaint level and complaint source data, we only need four columns inside the table. To add one more column to table1, right-click the right-most column header on the table, and select Insert Column to the Right. You may adjust the width of column according to your data size.

Now, we have a total of four columns inside the table. You may choose your favorite method to map the data table columns to the text box report items—type an expression or drag and drop from the data source.

Let's drag and drop: select Data Source ➤ dsComplaint ➤ ComplaintID and drop it inside the first column of the table's detail section. Repeat the task for the rest of the columns from dsComplaint.

As you know, we need to add two data groups to this report; this type of data grouping is also called nested grouping. In other words, you can say a child group is nested within a parent group. In this example, complaint level is a parent group and the source of the complaint is child group. With nested grouping, the complaint administrator can see the breakdown of complaint by level and then source.

Adding grouping to the table is simple: all you need to do is to select the detail row, right-click the selected row, and select Insert Group. Your "group on" expression must be Fields!ComplaintLevel.Value. Since we don't need the group footer, you can uncheck Include Group Footer. Repeat the same action for the Complaint Source group. You can refer to Figure 7-9 for an illustration of how to add a data group. Please make sure your report design surface looks like the one shown in Figure 8-13.

Figure 8-13. *The report designer with nested data grouping*

Please make sure you've correctly added all columns inside the table; use Figure 8-13 and Table 8-4 to confirm.

Table 8-4. *Table Item Properties*

Report Item	Property	Value
textbox1	Value	Complaint ID
textbox2	Value	Create Date
textbox3	Value	Customer Name
textbox10	Value	Complaint Type
ComplaintID	Value	=Fields!ComplaintID.Value
CreateDate	Value	=Fields!CreateDate.Value
CreateDate	Format	d
CreateDate	TextAlign	Left
CustomerName	Value	=Fields!CustomerName.Value
ComplaintType	Value	=Fields!ComplaintType.Value
table1	DataSetName	dsComplaint_dtComplaintList
table1.TableRow1	RepeatOnNewPage	True (To display columns header on every page)
ComplaintLevel	Value	="Level:" & Fields!ComplaintLevel.Value
ComplaintLevel	BorderStyle	None, , , , Dotted
ComplaintSource	Value	="Level:" & Fields!ComplaintSource.Value
ComplaintSource	BorderStyle	None, , , , Solid

Adding a Timer Control to the Service

We need to add the timer control to this service—we want to know when ten minutes has elapsed. So according to that business rule, the service must scan the database to find out fresh complaints with a severity level of three. All such complaints must go as a report to complaint administrators by e-mail for prompt and swift resolution.

Adding the timer control to the service is simple: drag Toolbox ➤ Timer and drop it on the `Service1.cs` surface (see Figure 8-14).

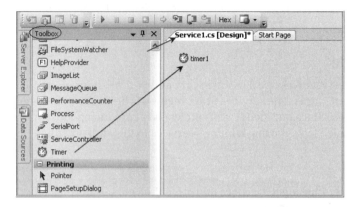

Figure 8-14. *Adding a timer control to the service*

Adding the Settings File to the Project

What is a settings file? The settings file stores the user input and lets Windows services use it. It's a bad idea to hard-code ten minutes' delay for the service; instead, we can specify it in the settings file. Imagine if the business later decides to use five minutes' delay; in that case, all we need to change is the settings file, instead of making code changes to the service.

Add the settings file by selecting the project in Solution Explorer, right-clicking it, and selecting Add ➤ New Item. Select Settings File from the Add New Item dialog box. Please name the settings file `SettingsComplaint.settings`, and click the Add button to complete the process.

Next, let's add two settings by going to the settings designer, which is visible to you after add the settings file. All you need to do is click the Name column and start inputting the necessary settings. You'll need `TimerDelay` and `EmailTo` as two entries. Please make sure your settings look similar to Figure 8-15.

Name	Type	Scope	Value
TimerDelay	string	Application	600000
EmailTo	string	Application	abcxyz@abcxyz123.com

Figure 8-15. *The settings file*

Beautification

Let's add solid borders at the top and bottom of the table1 header. As you may notice, we have a CreateDate column with a DateTime data type. Please make sure to change the format of this column to d.

Step 3: Writing C# Code

We'll need to write code inside Service1.cs. We'll use the Start and Stop methods of the service and the Tick method of the timer. The service's Start method is best suited for code to read configuration information. Since our focus in this project is on producing the report and e-mail, we won't take a detailed look at using Windows services to their full potential.

Adding the Reference

Start adding the reference by right-clicking References under the Project node and selecting Add Reference under the .NET tab in the Add Reference dialog box. Next, scroll down and select Microsoft.ReportViewer.WinForms; you need to click the OK button to complete the action. You'll see the newly added reference in Solution Explorer. Please see Figure 7-11 for an illustration of all the steps needed to add a reference to a project.

Please make sure code inside Service1.cs looks like the following:

```csharp
using System;
using System.Collections.Generic;
using System.ComponentModel;
using System.Data;
using System.Diagnostics;
using System.ServiceProcess;
using System.Text;
using System.IO;
using System.Data.SqlClient;
using Microsoft.Reporting.WinForms;
using System.Net.Mail;

namespace Complaint
{
    public partial class Service1 : ServiceBase
    {
        public Service1()
        {
            InitializeComponent();
        }
```

```csharp
        protected override void OnStart(string[] args)
        {
            try
            {
                //setup timer interval from settings file
                timer1.Interval =➥
Convert.ToInt32(SettingsComplaint.Default.TimerDelay);

                //generate report first time before calling
                //according to time interval
                generateReport();

                timer1.Enabled = true;
                timer1.Start();

                using (StreamWriter sw = new StreamWriter(@"c:\ServiceStart.txt"))
                {
                    sw.WriteLine("service start");
                }
            }
            catch (Exception ex)
            {
                using (StreamWriter sw = new StreamWriter(@"c:\ServiceError.txt"))
                {
                    sw.WriteLine(ex.Message);
                }
            }
        }

        protected override void OnStop()
        {
            //notify via email if service is stopped
            //SendMail("SMTPserver", "Complaint", ➥
            // SettingsComplaint.Default.EmailTo, "Service Stopped!", ➥
            // "Contact IT support","");
        }

        private void timer1_Tick(object sender, EventArgs e)
        {
            generateReport();
        }

        public void generateReport()
        {
            LocalReport rpvComplaint = new LocalReport();
```

```
            //declare connection string
            string cnString = "Data Source=(local);Initial➥
Catalog=RealWorld;Integrated Security=SSPI;";

            //declare Connection, command and other related objects
            SqlConnection conReport = new SqlConnection(cnString);
            SqlCommand cmdReport = new SqlCommand();
            SqlDataReader drReport;
            DataSet dsReport = new dsComplaint();

            try
            {
                //open connection
                conReport.Open();

                //prepare connection object to get the data
                //through reader and populate into dataset
                cmdReport.CommandType = CommandType.Text;
                cmdReport.Connection = conReport;
                cmdReport.CommandText = "Select * FROM Complaint➥
ORDER BY ComplaintLevel, ComplaintSource, ComplaintID";

                //read data from command object
                drReport = cmdReport.ExecuteReader();

                //load data directly from reader to dataset
                dsReport.Tables[0].Load(drReport);

                //close reader and connection
                drReport.Close();
                conReport.Close();

                //provide local report information to viewer
                rpvComplaint.ReportEmbeddedResource =➥
"Complaint.rptComplaint.rdlc";

                //prepare report data source
                ReportDataSource rds = new ReportDataSource();
                rds.Name = "dsComplaint_dtComplaintList";
                rds.Value = dsReport.Tables[0];
                rpvComplaint.DataSources.Add(rds);

                Warning[] warnings;
                string[] streamids;
                string mimeType;
                string encoding;
                string filenameExtension;
```

```
                byte[] bytes = rpvComplaint.Render(➥
"PDF", null, out mimeType, out encoding, out filenameExtension,
                    out streamids, out warnings);

                using (FileStream fs = new ➥
FileStream(@"c:\output.pdf", FileMode.Create))
                {
                    fs.Write(bytes, 0, bytes.Length);
                }

                //send newly created pdf file as email attachment
                //SendMail("SMTPserver", "Complaint",➥
SettingsComplaint.Default.EmailTo, "Service Stopped!",➥
"Contact IT support", "output.pdf");
            }
            catch (Exception ex)
            {
                string strInitialError = "Initial Error Message: " + ex.Message;

                string FinalErrorMessage = string.Empty;
                Exception innerError = ex.InnerException;
                while (!((innerError == null)))
                {
                    FinalErrorMessage += innerError.Message;
                    innerError = innerError.InnerException;
                }

                //write the error message to text file
                using (StreamWriter sw = new ➥
StreamWriter(@"c:\ServiceError.txt"))
                {
                    sw.WriteLine(strInitialError);
                    sw.WriteLine("-------------------");
                    sw.WriteLine(FinalErrorMessage);
                }
            }
            finally
            {
                //check if connection is still open then
                //attempt to close it
                if (conReport.State == ConnectionState.Open)
                {
                    conReport.Close();
                }
            }
        }
```

```csharp
        public void SendMail(string mailServerName,➥
string mailFrom, string MailTo, string subject, string body,➥
string fileName)
        {
            try
            {
                //MailMessage represents the e-mail being sent
                using (MailMessage message = new MailMessage(mailFrom,
                        MailTo, subject, body))
                {
                    message.IsBodyHtml = true;
                    message.Attachments.Add(new Attachment(fileName));
                    SmtpClient mailClient = new SmtpClient();
                    mailClient.Host = mailServerName;
                    mailClient.UseDefaultCredentials = true;
                    mailClient.DeliveryMethod =➥
SmtpDeliveryMethod.PickupDirectoryFromIis;
                    //Send delivers the message to the mail server
                    mailClient.Send(message);
                }
            }
            catch (SmtpException ex)
            {
                throw new ApplicationException
                    ("Smtp error sending mail: " + ex.Message);
            }
            catch (Exception ex)
            {
                throw ex;
            }
        }
    }
}
```

Apart from the regular ADO.NET code we use to gather the data and bind it to report, there are two important code sections here. The first section renders the PDF output using a call to the Render method. This method returns bytes of an array that we use to write the PDF file by calling the Write method on the I/O file stream.

The second key section uses e-mail to deliver the PDF report. I'm using a custom SendMail function to do the job. This function makes use of MailMessage from the System.Net.Mail namespace. You need to have access to an SMTP mail server to check this part of the function. Since a Windows service doesn't have any interactive user interface, I'm using the StreamWriter to write the logs in a text file.

Building the Project

Since this project is a Windows service, we cannot launch it from within the VS 2005 IDE, so we cannot build and run it by pressing F5 on the keyboard. Let's build the solution by selecting Build ➤ Build Solution from the main menu (you can also use the keyboard shortcut Ctrl+Shift+B).

If the program compiles without any errors, the VS IDE will generate Complaint.exe based on your build choice (debug or release); Figure 8-16 shows the location of the generated Windows service executable.

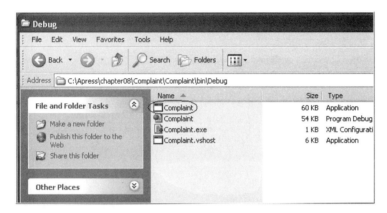

Figure8-16. *Complaint.exe's location on the local drive*

Now, to see our report in action, you need to install this service. You can install the service by making use of installutil.exe, as you learned earlier in the "Windows Services 101" tutorial. Click Start ➤ Run ➤

```
C:\WINDOWS\Microsoft.NET\Framework\v2.0.50727\InstallUtil.exe➥
 c:\Apress\chapter08\Complaint\Complaint\bin\Debug\Complaint.exe
```

(note that your path to the service may differ). This command will install the service, which you can start by clicking the Start button inside the Control Panel; refer to Figure 8-7 to see the Windows service Control Panel.

After you install and run the service, it will immediately produce the first report PDF output. After that, depending on your interval selection, the service will generate reports for all newly logged complaints—providing your complaint administrators an easy way to automate the reporting of sensitive data without any manual intervention.

Summary

In this chapter, you learned how to use a Windows service as a client to generate a report in PDF format. You also learned how to make use of a Windows service to schedule automated report delivery based on a desired time interval.

In the next chapter, you'll see how we can use SharePoint as a report delivery vehicle by generating reports using web parts.

CHAPTER 9

■■■

Reporting with Web Parts

In Chapter 8, we produced reports and learned how to deliver a report with a Windows service. Now, let me introduce you to one more report delivery platform—SharePoint. Excited? SharePoint is gaining popularity as an information delivery vehicle across the board to different business users.

So, how can we take advantage of SharePoint to host our reports? Well, it is not as complicated as you might be thinking. All you have to do is to develop reports using web parts and later host the web parts with SharePoint.

I'd like to mention here that hosting web parts in a SharePoint environment is a topic far beyond the reach of this book; I'll only show you how you can develop a report with web parts using Visual Studio 2005. You can go through Microsoft's help files to learn more about Share-Point technologies.

We'll start by building your knowledge of web parts applications. After that, we'll work on a real-world practical reporting project.

This chapter will cover

- "Web Parts 101," a step-by-step tutorial

- A brief examination of the web parts' framework

- Producing a report with the ReportViewer hosted inside a web part

Web Parts 101

In Chapter 5, you learned to host reports with ASP.NET web applications. Would you be surprised if I told you that we'll use the same approach in this chapter too? However, there is a difference, and that difference is the use of web parts. So, what are web parts? Well, in simple words, web parts empower users to customize the site content according to their preferences. Users can decide what information to display on a page and where that information looks best on the page. Many of the most popular web sites are beginning to provide such customization; sites like My MSN and My Yahoo are examples. Web parts were newly introduced with ASP.NET 2.0 in Visual Studio 2005.

Creating a web parts application is the same as creating ASP.NET Web Forms. You'll need to start with creating an ASP.NET web project; however, you'll notice that we'll use Report-Viewer inside a web part.

Creating a Web Site Project

Open Visual Studio, and use the following steps to create a web site project; Figure 9-1 illustrates these steps:

1. Click File ➤ New ➤ Web Site.

2. In the Templates pane of the New Web Site dialog box, select ASP.NET Web Site.

3. From the Language drop-down, select Visual C#.

4. Name this web site; I've called it RSWebParts101. You may choose a different location for storing the application files if you prefer. Please see Figure 9-1 for graphical presentation of the naming.

5. Click the OK button to finish the process. After you click the OK button, VS will create a new ASP.NET web site. Figure 9-2 shows the code produced and the files inside Solution Explorer.

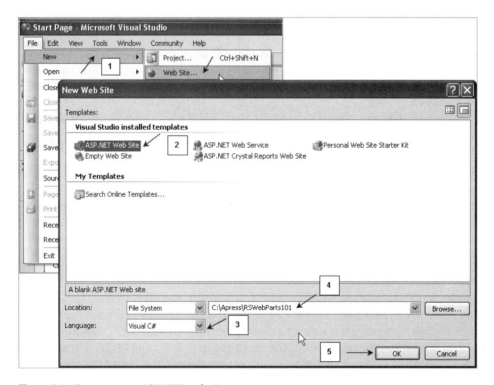

Figure 9-1. *Create a new ASP.NET web site.*

As you will notice in Figure 9-2, the web site project contains the App_Data folder and default.aspx page. As you know, a web site can have many pages. However, I'll keep it simple and make use of the default.aspx page for this project. Refer to Chapter 5 for the detailed walk-through of creating an ASP.NET web site project.

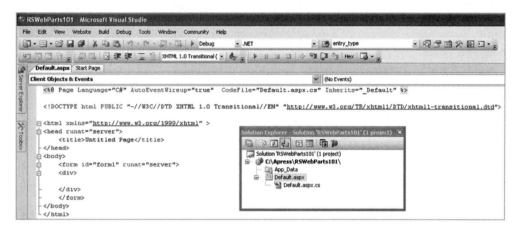

Figure 9-2. *The newly created web site*

Adding Web Parts to the default.aspx Page

Before we start to add web parts on the page, let's take a brief look at the web part framework. The framework consists of the following items:

- The WebPartManager control
- Zones
- Editors
- Catalogs

The job of the WebPartManager control is to enable page customization. Zones define the sections of the page that a user can customize. In this book, I'll only talk about the web part framework features needed to host our reports. Please check the following MSDN link for more information on the web part framework:

`http://msdn2.microsoft.com/en-us/library/ms379628(VS.80).aspx.`

Please use the following steps to customize `default.aspx`; Figure 9-3 illustrates adding web part functionality to the page:

1. Switch to design mode.

2. Drag WebParts ➤ WebPartManager from the toolbox, and drop it onto the design surface.

3. Drag WebParts ➤ WebPartZone from the toolbox, and drop it onto the design surface.

WebPartManager plays a dual role here. First, it provides the ability to customize the page. Second, it supports the personalization of the ASP.NET application. Personalization information is stored in an SQL Server database, which is produced when the application is built for the first time.

Note Please make sure to add the WebPartManager control on the page before adding any of the web parts.

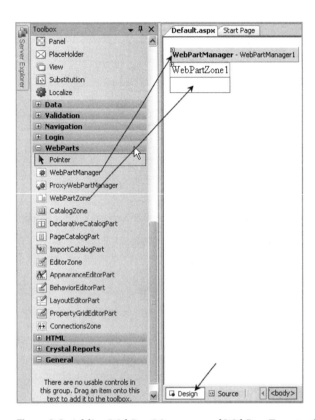

Figure 9-3. *Adding WebPartManager and WebPartZone to the project*

Add the ReportViewer Control to the WebPartZone

You might be wondering, now that we have the web part functionality all set up on the page, how the web part will show the report. Well, all we have to do is to get help from the Report-Viewer control. Let's add ReportViewer using drag and drop; from the toolbox, drag Data ➤ ReportViewer and drop it under the WebPartZone title (circled in Figure 9-4).

You may notice that after you drop the ReportViewer control, the WebPartZone size will change to accommodate the ReportViewer. You may need to adjust the size to show maximum report view. Please make sure your page looks similar to Figure 9-4.

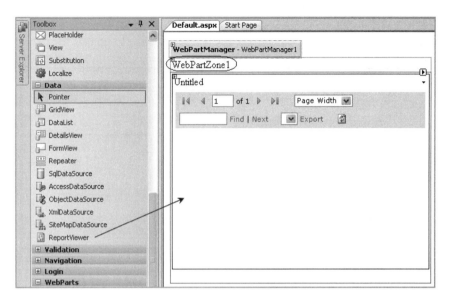

Figure 9-4. *Adding the ReportViewer to the WebPartZone*

Please make sure you set the properties outlined in Table 9-1.

Table 9-1. *Property Settings for the Web Site*

Object	Property	Value
WebPartZone1		
	HeaderText	Web Part 101 Report
	Width	800px
Reportviewer1		
	Width	800px

You can also add the WebPartManager control in the page source view by adding the following tag after <open>:

```
<asp:webpartmanager id="WebPartManager1" runat="server" />
```

After changing the properties, your page should look similar to the one shown in Figure 9-5.

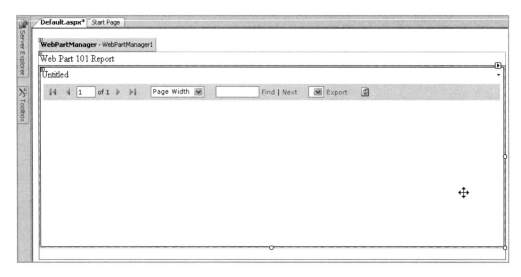

Figure 9-5. *Page layout with the web part in place*

If you look at the source for this page, you'll notice all the tags that we dropped onto the page.

```
<%@ Page Language="C#" AutoEventWireup="true"  CodeFile="Default.aspx.cs" ➥
 Inherits="_Default" %>

<%@ Register Assembly="Microsoft.ReportViewer.WebForms, Version=8.0.0.0, ➥
 Culture=neutral, PublicKeyToken=b03f5f7f11d50a3a" ➥
    Namespace="Microsoft.Reporting.WebForms" TagPrefix="rsweb" %>

<!DOCTYPE html PUBLIC "-//W3C//DTD XHTML 1.0 Transitional//EN" ➥
 "http://www.w3.org/TR/xhtml1/DTD/xhtml1-transitional.dtd">

<html xmlns="http://www.w3.org/1999/xhtml" >
<head runat="server">
    <title>Untitled Page</title>
</head>
<body>
    <form id="form1" runat="server">
    <div>
        <asp:WebPartManager ID="WebPartManager1" runat="server">
        </asp:WebPartManager>

    </div>
        <asp:WebPartZone ID="WebPartZone1" runat="server" ➥
HeaderText="Web Part 101 Report"
            Width="800px">
            <ZoneTemplate>
```

```
                    <rsweb:ReportViewer ID="ReportViewer1" runat="server" ➥
    Height="271px" Width="800px">
                    </rsweb:ReportViewer>
                </ZoneTemplate>
            </asp:WebPartZone>
        </form>
    </body>
</html>
```

Building the Project

The build part is always exciting, right? After all, this is the time we can see our hard work in action. Building a web site with web parts is similar to building a simple ASP.NET site. However, there are some minor considerations needed, which I'll discuss as we build the project.

Now, let's build it. As you know, you can build a project by clicking the small, green play button in the main toolbox or pressing F5 on the keyboard to start the application in run-time mode. If you're building the project for the first time in debug mode, click on the OK button in the "debug not enabled" information dialog box. This action will put debug-related settings in the Web.config file.

As I mentioned earlier, your first build will create an SQL Server personalization database. So, depending on your computer's speed, you'll notice a delay in loading the site into the browser. If all goes well, your project should compile without any issues, and you should be able to see the web site in your default browser. Your browser output should be similar to Figure 9-6.

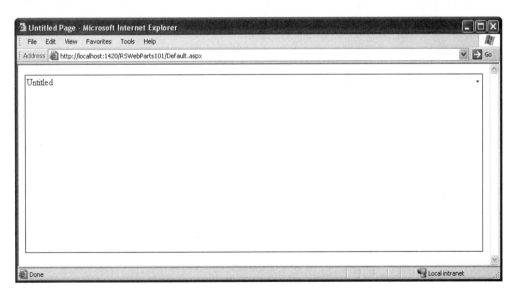

Figure 9-6. *Web site output in a browser window*

Hooray! Congratulate yourself for successfully creating a web site and hosting Report-Viewer using a web part. I know the output is just a blank web part, but you'll see a chart report in action in the reporting project that's coming up next.

Before we move on to our reporting project, though, let me show you what happened to the SQL Server personalization database, ASPNETDB. This database is store inside the App_Data folder after the first build. Just refresh the App_Data folder inside Solution Explorer to see the ASPNETDB.mdf file (shown in Figure 9-7). The personalization database is for the internal use of the web site, to store information related to web parts.

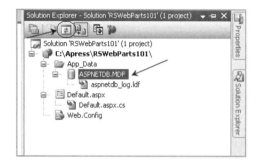

Figure 9-7. *Solution Explorer with the personalization database*

Creating the Branch Sales Performance Chart

You're working for Home Decorations, Incorporated as a developer. You have the task of developing a series of reports primarily for use by upper management, and one of the reports should produce a pie chart with the current fiscal year's sales information. This report will help management to compare across branches; it should meet all the characteristics described in Table 9-2, and the report output should match Figure 9-8.

Table 9-2. *Report Characteristics*

Characteristics	Value
Report Title	Branch Sales Performance Chart (Detail section—Center aligned)
Company Title	Home Decorations Inc. (Detail section—Right aligned)
Logo	Yes (Detail section—Left aligned)
Print Date	Yes (Detail section—Right aligned)
Data Source	Manually populate DataSet
Columns to Report	Branch, YearEndSalesTotal
Page Size	Letter
Page Orientation	Portrait
Layout Design	No Header and Footer, all information should be in Body section

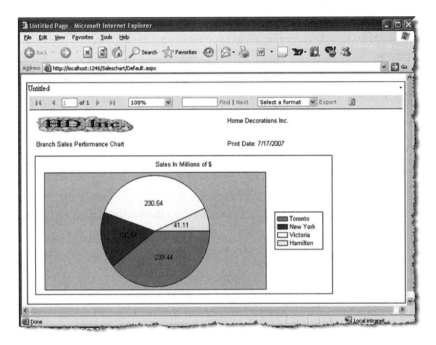

Figure 9-8. *Branch Sales Performance Chart report*

Business Case

We know how important healthy sales figures are at the end of a fiscal year, and these figures become even more interesting in a business with several branches or profit centers. A sales performance chart is one of the most common reports sought by upper management, because this report also highlights any underperforming branch that needs attention. You'll routinely see reports like this appear in boardroom presentations and publications sent to all stakeholders.

Getting the Web Site Ready

As you've already learned how to create an ASP.NET web site earlier in this chapter, now it's your turn to practice that and get the client ready. You may make use of the RSWebParts101 solution as a template for this project or create the client from scratch. It is good idea to create the new application from scratch; as usual, you can always refer to the steps mentioned in the tutorial if you get stuck.

Please use the following steps to create a web site project (see Figure 9-1):

1. Click File ➤ New ➤ Web Site.

2. In the Templates pane of the New Web Site dialog box, select ASP.NET Web Site.

3. From the Language drop-down, select Visual C#.

4. Name this web site; I've called it Saleschart. You may choose a different location for storing the application files if you prefer. Please see Figure 9-1 for a graphical presentation of the naming.

5. Click the OK button to finish the process. After you click the OK button, VS will create a new ASP.NET web site with the name Saleschart.

Please use the following steps to customize the default.aspx page:

1. Switch to design mode.

2. Drag WebParts ➤ WebPartManager from the toolbox, and drop it onto the design surface.

3. Drag WebParts ➤ WebPartZone from the toolbox, and drop it onto the design surface.

4. Drag Data ➤ ReportViewer from the toolbox, and drop it inside the WebPartZone control.

Please add a new dataset to the project, and name it dsSaleschart. You'll notice that VS IDE will ask you to put the dataset inside the App_Code folder; go ahead and click the Yes button. Click the Cancel button in the Table Adapter wizard dialog box; we'll create the data table later. Please make sure your solution looks similar to the one shown in Figure 9-9.

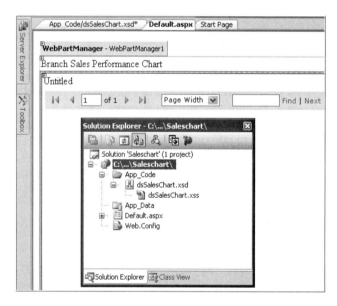

Figure 9-9. *The web site in Solution Explorer view*

Step 1: Creating a Data Table

Since we've already added the dataset to the project, it's time to add the data table to it. The data table should have the two columns identified in Table 9-2 (Branch and YearEndSalesTotal):

Please use the following steps to add the data table inside the dataset:

1. You can go to the dataset designer in two ways: double-click dsSaleschart inside Solution Explorer, or right-click dsSaleschart node and select View Designer.

2. Add the data table by right-clicking the design surface and selecting Add ➤ DataTable.

3. Please click the header of the newly created data table, and name it dtSaleschart. Start adding columns to dtSaleschart by right-clicking DataTable ➤ Add ➤ Column.

4. Please add the following columns to your data table, which should look like the one shown in Figure 9-10.

   - Branch (System.String)

   - YearEndSalesTotal (System.Double)

Figure 9-10. *Final look of the dtChart data table*

■**Note** If you face any difficulties with adding the dataset or data table, please refer to Chapter 3 for a walkthrough.

Step 2: Designing the Report Layout

All right, we've got our dataset in place with its data table and all the necessary columns, so we're all set to start designing the report layout. Let's begin by adding the report: select the project in Solution Explorer, right-click it, and select Add ➤ New Item. Next, select Report from the Add New Item dialog box. Please name the report rptSaleschart.rdlc. Click the Add button to complete the process; a new report is added to the project and opened in the report designer.

If you notice, the last item in Table 9-2 tells you that this report will have only one page, and won't have a header or footer; all information will appear in the body section. You might be wondering at a report with no header and footer! Sure, why not? This is one reporting project where you can use the body section to mange the report logo, title, and detail data. The report output consists of only one page; therefore, the information that would otherwise be part of header and footer can easily be placed in the body section.

Setting Up the Page

Let's set up the page according to the needs for the report; we need a letter-size report with a portrait page orientation. Right-click an open area on the design surface, and select Properties; you may wish to put your name in the Author field and any information about the report in the Description field. I'd advise you to leave all other choices at their defaults.

Designing the Body Section

This report is a perfect example of a freestyle report. It is interesting to see how different pieces of information are part of the body section instead of divided among header, footer, and body sections. How controls are placed is important in this report; it should not look crowded with report items. Please drag the following report items from the toolbox and drop them inside the body section:

- TextBox item for Report Title

- TextBox item for Company Title

- TextBox item for Print Date

- Image item for Logo

- Chart item

After adding the report items to the design surface, we need to set their properties to give them the look the report needs. Report item properties are changed by right-clicking the report item and selecting Properties or accessing the general properties toolbox.

Let's start changing properties; after selecting each text box, specify the values according to Table 9-3.

Table 9-3. *Report Item Properties*

Report Item	Property	Value
textbox1		
	Name	txtReportTitle
	Value	Branch Sales Performance Chart
textbox2		
	Name	txtCompanyTitle
	Value	Home Decorations Inc.
textbox3		
	Name	txtPrintDate
	Value	="Print Date: " & Today
image1		
	Name	imageLogo
	Source	Embedded

After you're finished setting the properties, your report design surface should look something like the one shown in Figure 9-11.

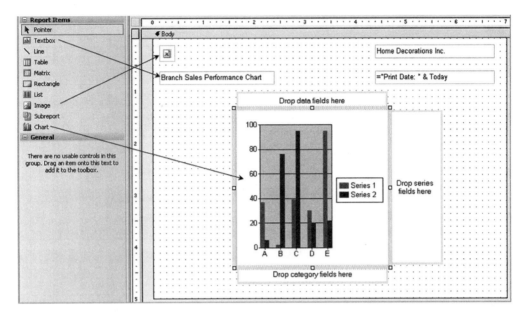

Figure 9-11. *The body section in the report designer*

Customizing the Chart Report Item

When you drag and drop the chart report item, it defaults to a column chart type, and you're guided to drag and drop data for chart plotting. In this example, we have the two pieces of data to plot.

Let's start by dragging Data Source ➤ dsSaleschart ➤ Branch and dropping it in the "Drop category fields here" box. Do the same for YearEndSalesTotal, but this time, drop it in the "Drop data fields here" box. Please make sure your report design surface looks like Figure 9-12 after you plot the chart item's data.

Though we now have the data plotted, the chart in Figure 9-12 still isn't a pie chart. So, how we can change the chart from the current column format to pie? Well, the chart report item has properties like any other report item. Therefore, right-click the chart, select Properties, and change the report type to Pie (and change any other settings you like). Figure 9-13 shows the Properties dialog box.

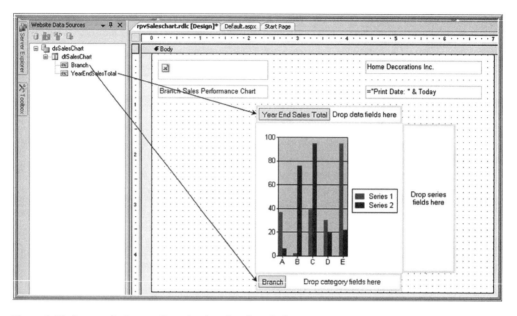

Figure 9-12. *Report designer after plotting the chart's data*

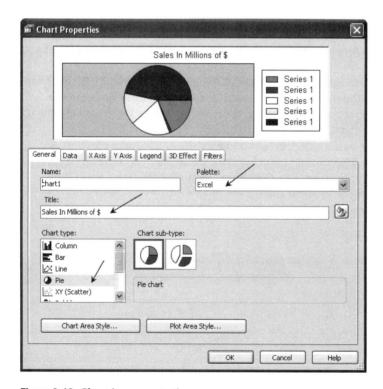

Figure 9-13. *Chart item properties*

Let's display sales figures on individual pie slices. You can do this by selecting the Data tab in the Chart Properties dialog box. Once inside the Data tab, select Value, and click the Edit button to open the Edit Chart Value dialog box. Select the Point Labels tab; check Show Point Labels, and set "Data label" to =Fields!YearEndSalesTotal.Value. Figure 9-14 illustrates the steps required to display the figures on the pie slices.

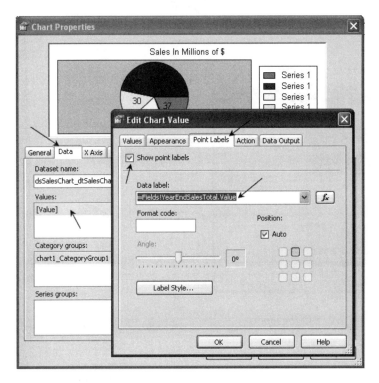

Figure 9-14. *Adding the sales amount as a label in the chart item's properties*

Handling Embedded Images

As you can see in Figure 9-8, we have a company logo to display in this report. We're going to embed the company logo in the report by setting the EmbeddedImages property of the report. All you need to do is browse to the physical path of the image and embed it within the report. Embedding images is simple: Select the report properties by right-clicking anywhere inside the empty report design surface. Click the embedded image properties collection. This will open the Embedded Images dialog box. Click the New Image button in the dialog box, and select the image you want to embed from your project folder. After you finish this process, you'll see that the image is added to the report, ready for use.

After you embed the image in the report, just set the Value property of the image report item to the image name, which is part of the report now. See Figure 9-15 for an illustration of the steps to add an image.

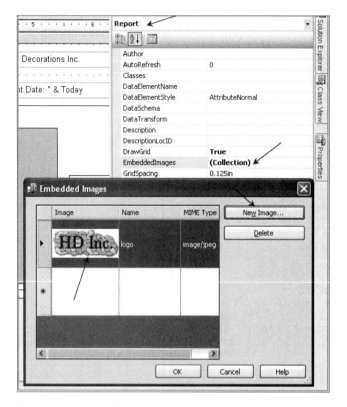

Figure 9-15. *Embedding the logo image in the report*

Beautifying the Report

To improve the look of the report, add a border to Chart1, and adjust the width and height to fill the available space of the report's design surface. You may also like to change the color or font of the report title or company name. Please see Figure 9-16 for the final look of the report designer before we move on to writing the code (you may revisit Chapter 4 to review formatting the report item).

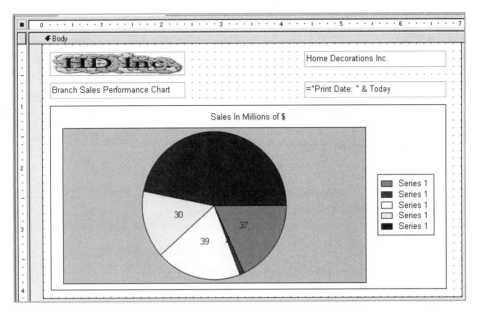

Figure 9-16. *The final look of the report*

Step 3: Writing the C# Code

We'll need to write code for the page load event. Please make sure code inside the default.aspx page looks like the following:

```csharp
using System;
using System.Data;
using System.Configuration;
using System.Web;
using System.Web.Security;
using System.Web.UI;
using System.Web.UI.WebControls;
using System.Web.UI.WebControls.WebParts;
using System.Web.UI.HtmlControls;
using Microsoft.Reporting.WebForms;

public partial class _Default : System.Web.UI.Page
{
    protected void Page_Load(object sender, EventArgs e)
    {
        try
        {
            // get reference of typed DataSet
            dsSalesChart dsChart = new dsSalesChart();
```

```
            // get row information from typed DataSet
            dsSalesChart.dtSalesChartRow dtChart;

            // add four rows to DataSet
            dtChart = dsChart.dtSalesChart.NewdtSalesChartRow();
            dtChart.Branch = "Toronto";
            dtChart.YearEndSalesTotal = 239.44;

            dsChart.dtSalesChart.AdddtSalesChartRow(dtChart);

            dtChart = dsChart.dtSalesChart.NewdtSalesChartRow();
            dtChart.Branch = "New York";
            dtChart.YearEndSalesTotal = 100.54;

            dsChart.dtSalesChart.AdddtSalesChartRow(dtChart);

            dtChart = dsChart.dtSalesChart.NewdtSalesChartRow();
            dtChart.Branch = "Victoria";
            dtChart.YearEndSalesTotal = 230.54;

            dsChart.dtSalesChart.AdddtSalesChartRow(dtChart);

            dtChart = dsChart.dtSalesChart.NewdtSalesChartRow();
            dtChart.Branch = "Hamilton";
            dtChart.YearEndSalesTotal = 41.11;

            dsChart.dtSalesChart.AdddtSalesChartRow(dtChart);

            // Specify report path
            ReportViewer1.LocalReport.ReportPath = "rpvSaleschart.rdlc";
            ReportDataSource rds = new ReportDataSource();

            rds.Name = "dsSalesChart_dtSalesChart";
            rds.Value = dsChart.Tables[0];
            ReportViewer1.LocalReport.DataSources.Add(rds);
        }
        catch (Exception ex)
        {
            // write error output on page
            Response.Write(ex.Message);
        }
    }
}
```

You might be wondering why no data connectivity was used in this project code. That is because I decided to show you one more way to bind data with the report—that is, to manually create rows in a typed dataset.

When we create a dataset and data table, the Visual Studio IDE writes some cool code for us to manage the input and output of data in the dataset. In this reporting project, I made use of this code to add branch-related data to the data table.

With the help of the `NewdtChartRow()` method, I created an empty row for the data table. After that, I set the values of each column inside the data table like this: `dtChart.Branch = "Toronto"`. Finally, I called method `AdddtChartRow()` to add the newly created row to the data table. This is one cool benefit we get by using a typed dataset (revisit Chapter 3 to review typed datasets).

Building the Project

This report is simple in nature; all it does is manually add report plotting data to a typed dataset and bind it to the report. As usual, you can build a project in a couple of ways (recall that if you have just one project in a solution, building the solution and building the project are the same): you can click the small, green play button in the main toolbox or press F5 on the keyboard to start the application in run-time mode.

If all goes well, you should see the page in the default browser with a nice pie chart. The output should match Figure 9-8.

Summary

In this chapter, we looked at how to use web parts to host reports to share them with a Share-Point portal. We also looked at how to use a chart item to produce a pie chart. Instead of pulling data from a database, in this chapter, we used the functionality of typed datasets to manually provide data to report.

In the next chapter, we'll make use of non–SQL Server data sources to produce reports. You'll see how easy it is to gather data from Microsoft Access, XML, and Oracle to produce reports using client-side RS.

■ ■ ■

CHAPTER 10

Reporting on Other Data Sources

So far, we have done all our reporting projects using SQL Server data. But let me ask you a question here; can we only develop reports using SQL Server data? I'm sure your answer is "No" if you recall one of my notes from Chapter 1. There, I mentioned that it is a common misconception that RS can only use SQL Server data.

All right, if SQL Server data is not the only data source available to us, which other data sources can we use? In this chapter, we'll explore those other data sources, and we will develop reporting projects using data sources other than SQL Server.

In this chapter, you will

- Learn about data sources other than SQL Server

- Develop a report using Microsoft Access data

- Develop a report using XML data

- Develop a report using Oracle data

Exploring Other Data Sources

In real-life business scenarios, we have to deal with all sorts of different data sources. No matter if you are a small- or medium-sized company or a corporate giant, chances are you deal with more than one data source. In such a challenging environment, you need a tool versatile enough to seamlessly report from all available data sources. The good news is that client-side RS does just that.

You might be wondering how client-side RS does the job. Well, the answer is as simple as the following statement: RS can use and report on data from any source that ADO.NET can access.

Many different data sources qualify. Trust me, the list is exhaustive. Some are generic, and some are proprietary. Covering every other data source that ADO.NET can connect to is beyond the reach of this book. So, to illustrate reporting on other data sources, I picked three of the most common ones:

- Microsoft Access

- XML

- Oracle

It is good to know that even though the data sources are different, the report development process stays the same; you'll only need to tweak the C# code according to the type of data source you are using. Once the dataset is ready with data, every other step to develop reports stays the same.

Before we start developing our reporting projects, I'd like to encourage you to learn the techniques from this chapter and then try them with your favorite data source. So, if you have a question like, "Can I report on data from a MySQL database?" Then my answer to you is, "Yes." Please check the following link for instructions to access MySQL with ADO.NET:

```
http://dev.mysql.com/tech-resources/articles/dotnet/index.html#ADO.NET
```

Reporting with MS Access Data

Let's start with developing a simple tabular format report using MS Access data. Many small applications still use this database as a data repository. It is also a favorite choice for temporary storage while further processing data gathered from large databases.

For the benefit of readers who have no knowledge of this software, Access is a relational database management system from Microsoft. It was a stand-alone product in the beginning, and later, it started to appear packaged with Microsoft Office. It combines the Jet relational database engine with a graphical interface. The development environment provides productivity-enhancing features for both advanced developers and beginning users. Please check the following link for more information:

```
http://office.microsoft.com/en-ca/access/default.aspx
```

■**Note** JET stands for Joint Engine Technology. It is also referred as Microsoft JET Engine or simply Jet.

So, what report would you like to develop using MS Access data? Well, the easy choice is to use the famous NorthWind sample that comes with Access. So here is the deal—to make this section interesting, we'll mimic the Alphabetical List of Products report, shown in Figure 10-1. If you've worked with MS Access previously, this is your chance to see how to develop the same report using client-side RS.

So, the challenge is to produce a report that is similar to the one in Figure 10-1. Before we move on to develop the client and report, let's get hold of the NorthWind sample database. You can download the sample database from here:

```
http://www.microsoft.com/downloads/details.aspx?FamilyID=➥
    C6661372-8DBE-422B-8676-C632D66C529C&displaylang=EN
```

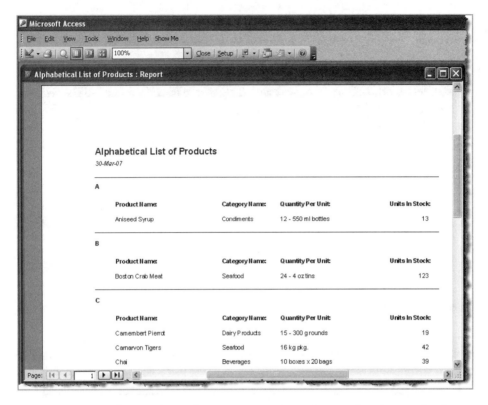

Figure 10-1. *The Alphabetical List of Products report from the sample MS Access database*

■**Note** You'll need MS Access if you would like to see the report in Figure 10-1 in action.

Creating a Windows Forms Project

Please open Visual Studio, and use the following steps, illustrated in Figure 10-2, to create a Windows application project:

1. Click File ➤ New ➤ Project, or press the hot keys Ctrl+Shift+N.

2. In the "Project types" pane of the New Project dialog box, select Visual C# ➤ Windows.

3. In the Templates pane, select Windows Application.

4. Please give the application a name; I've called the project AccessReport. You may choose a different location for storing the application files according to your preference.

5. Click the OK button to finish the process. After you click OK, Visual Studio will create a new Windows application project. You'll also notice that a new form with the name Form1 is part of the project.

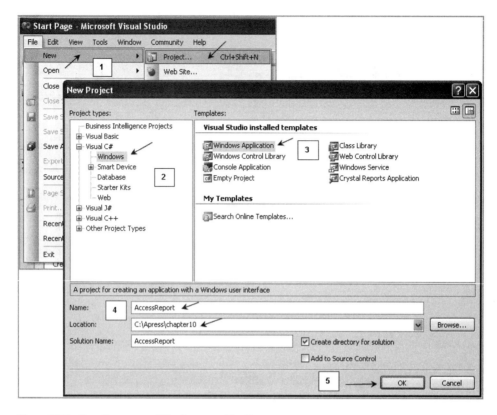

Figure 10-2. *Creating a new Windows application*

If you have difficulty creating a Windows Forms project, then I'd advise you to revisit Chapter 4 for detailed instructions. Let's move on and add the dataset and ReportViewer to the project. Let's start by selecting the project in Solution Explorer; right-click it and select Add ➤ New Item ➤ DataSet. Please name the dataset dsAccess. Before you add the ReportViewer, please make sure Form1 is open in designer. Now, let's add the ReportViewer to the project from the drag and drop toolbox by selecting Data ➤ ReportViewer.

Please make sure you set the properties listed in Table 10-1. After you specify all the properties, your Form1 should look similar to Figure 10-3.

Table 10-1. *Property Settings for the Access Project*

Object	Property	Value
Form1	Text	Reporting on MS Access Data
Form1	Size	790, 500
reportViewer1	Dock	Fill

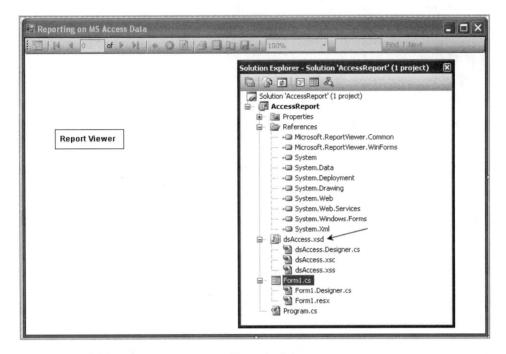

Figure 10-3. *The project after adding the dataset and ReportViewer*

Step 1: Creating a Data Table

Since we already have the dataset in the project, it's time to add a data table to it. Please use the following steps to add a data table inside the dataset:

1. You can go to the dataset designer in two ways: double-click dsAccess inside Solution Explorer, or right-click the dsAccess node and select View Designer.

2. Let's add the data table by right-clicking the design surface and selecting Add ➤ DataTable.

3. Click the header of the newly created data table, and name it dtAccess. Let's start adding columns to dtAccess by right-clicking the data table and selecting Add ➤ Column.

4. Please add the following columns into the data table, which should then look similar to Figure 10-4:

   • ProductName (System.String)

   • CategoryName (System.String)

   • QuantityPerUnit (System.String)

   • UnitsInStock (System.Int32)

Figure 10-4. *Final look of the dtAccess data table*

Step 2: Designing the Report Layout

Before we start with the layout design for the report, let's take a moment to analyze the MS Access report layout in Figure 10-1. What type of report items do you find in this report? Well, as you know, there are different approaches to developing the report. I think we can replicate this report by using a text box for the header, and for the body section, we can use a table. If you have a different idea, give it a try after you practice this exercise.

All right, we have our dataset in place, with the data table and all necessary columns. We're all set to start working on designing the report layout. Add the report by selecting the project in Solution Explorer and right-clicking it; select Add ➤ New Item, and select Report from the Add New Item dialog box. Please name the report rptAccess.rdlc. Click the Add button to complete the process and make the new report part of the project. You'll also notice that a new toolbox called Data Sources is available with our dataset information inside.

Adding a Header

Let's add the header to the report; although the MS access report in Figure 10-1 also has a footer, we'll skip it in our report. As usual, adding a header is simple: right-click the open area inside the report designer and select Page Header. Your report design surface should look similar to Figure 10-5.

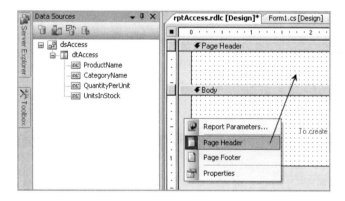

Figure 10-5. *The report design surface with header and body sections*

Setting Up the Page

According to the report's needs, let's set up the page. We need to make sure the report is letter-sized and has a portrait page orientation. Right-click the open area inside the design surface, and select Properties, where you may wish to put your name as the Author and add any information about the report in Description. I'd advise you to let all other choices stay at the defaults.

■**Note** Please make sure to set the properties Page Width to 8.5 inches and Page Height to 11 inches for a letter-sized, portrait report.

Designing the Page Header

Now, we have added the header and the body sections to our report. As usual, you may start to work on either of them first, but as we always do in this book, let's work on the header first. Please drag and drop the following report items inside the header section:

- A text box item for the report title

- A text box item for the report date

Report item properties are changed in one of the following two ways: by selecting the report item, right-clicking it, and selecting Properties or by accessing the general properties toolbox. Let's change the properties; select each of the text box items in turn, and specify the values for each report item's properties according to Table 10-2.

Table 10-2. *Report Item Properties for the Header*

Report Item	Property	Value
textbox1		
	Name	txtReportTitle
	Value	Alphabetical List of Products
	Font	Normal, Arial, 10pt, Bold
textbox2		
	Name	txtDate
	Value	=Today
	Format	dd-MMM-yy

Designing the Body Section

Let's start working on this section by selecting Toolbox ➤ Report Items ➤ Table and dragging and dropping it inside the body section in the report designer. A new table item is part of the report now, and it has the default name of table1. To add one more column, right-click the right-most column header on the table item, and select "Insert Column to the Right".

You may choose your favorite method to map the data table's column to the text box's report item(s): type an expression or drag and drop from the data source. Select Data Source ➤ dsAccess ➤ ProductName and drag and drop it inside the first column of the table item's detail section. Repeat this task for the rest of the columns in dsAccess. Make sure your report design surface looks similar to the one in Figure 10-6.

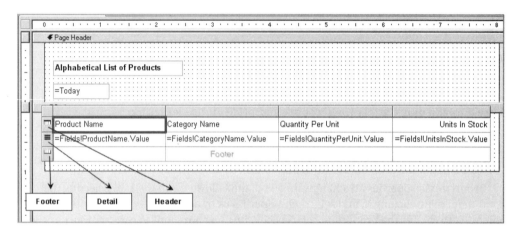

Figure 10-6. *The report designer after adding the header and body sections*

Even after adding the table item, we haven't quite finished mimicking the MS Access report. If you look at Figure 10-1 carefully, you may notice that the alphabetical list is reported with the help of data grouping in the ProductName column. You'll also notice that the column headers are repeated with every new letter of the alphabet.

So, now is the time to test the versatility of the table report item. We have to perform a series of steps to change the table so it'll mimic the output in Figure 10-1. Let's begin by adding a group. Select the Detail row, right-click it, and select Insert Group; the Grouping and Sorting Properties dialog box will appear. Please make sure to select the General tab, and type the following into the Expression field: **=LEFT(Fields!ProductName.Value,1)**. Please see Figure 10-7 for an illustration of these steps.

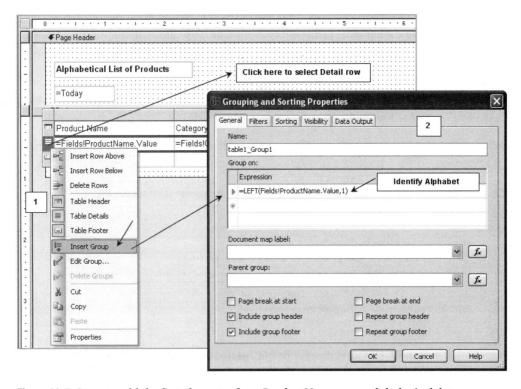

Figure 10-7. *Steps to add the first character from ProductName as an alphabetical data group*

To match our desired report output, we need to remove a few rows from the table item and introduce a few too. First, let's talk about getting rid of rows. Because of the Insert Group action, a group header and footer are part of the table now. Look at Figure 10-8; we need to copy the content of the row labeled "a" to the row labeled "b," because we want to repeat the column headers with each new letter of the alphabet when the group change occurs. After the copy, you'll notice that a new group header is inserted with the same content as row "a".

Next, select rows "a," "d," and "e," and delete them.

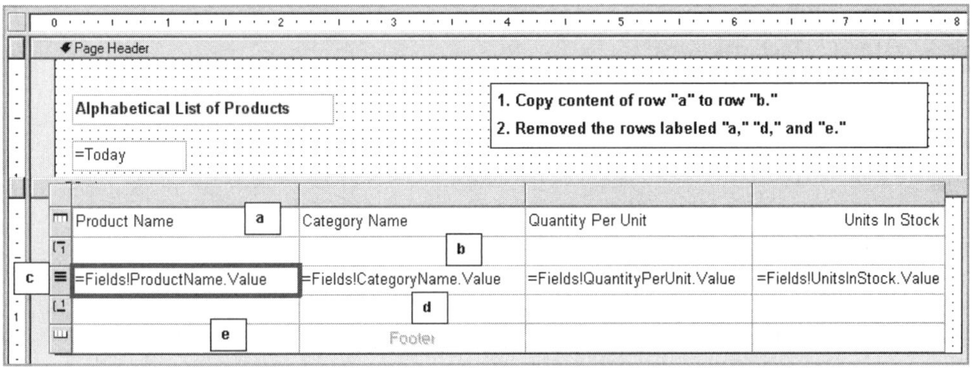

Figure 10-8. *Steps to add and remove the rows from the table report item*

A group can have more than one header and footer row. If you look at the MS Access report, each letter of the alphabet displays as a group title. To replicate in our report, we need to add the title to the group's first row. Click the first cell of the first row, and type the following in the Expression field: **=UCASE(LEFT(Fields!ProductName.Value,1))**. You may also notice that this is the same expression we used to group the data. The only difference here is the use of the UCASE() function to convert the output to uppercase letters. Figure 10-9 shows how to add a title to a group header and verify that you've removed unwanted rows.

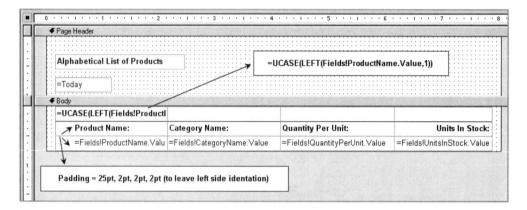

Figure 10-9. *Steps to add the title to the group's row header and verify the removal of rows*

If you look at the title's header expression, it is very simple. It takes the first character of ProductName, by using the LEFT() function, and converts it to uppercase with the help of the UCASE() function. To left indent the ProductName column, you'll need to set the padding as shown in Figure 10-9. I've also changed the font to make sure our output looks 100 percent the same as the Access report.

Step 3: Writing the C# Code

Well, that's all we need on the front end of the report design. Now, let's add the following code behind Form1.cs to get data and see if we managed to mimic the report:

```
using System;
using System.Collections.Generic;
using System.ComponentModel;
using System.Data;
using System.Drawing;
using System.Text;
using System.Windows.Forms;
using System.Data.OleDb;
using Microsoft.Reporting.WinForms;

namespace AccessReport
{
    public partial class Form1 : Form
    {
```

```csharp
public Form1()
{
    InitializeComponent();
}

private void Form1_Load(object sender, EventArgs e)
{
    // connection string
    string cnString = @"Provider=Microsoft.Jet.OLEDB.4.0; Data ➥
        Source=C:\Apress\chapter10\nwind.mdb;User Id=admin;Password=;";

    // string builder for query text
    StringBuilder sb = new StringBuilder();

    sb.Append("SELECT  Products.ProductName, Categories.CategoryName, ➥
        Products.QuantityPerUnit, Products.UnitsInStock ");
    sb.Append("FROM Categories INNER JOIN Products ON ➥
        Categories.CategoryID = Products.CategoryID ");
    sb.Append("ORDER BY Products.ProductName");

    OleDbConnection conReport = new OleDbConnection(cnString);
    OleDbCommand cmdReport = new OleDbCommand();
    OleDbDataReader drReport;

    DataSet dsReport = new dsAccess();

    try
    {
        // open connection
        conReport.Open();

        cmdReport.CommandType = CommandType.Text;
        cmdReport.Connection = conReport;

        // get query string from string builder
        cmdReport.CommandText = sb.ToString();

        // execute query and load result to dataset
        drReport = cmdReport.ExecuteReader();
        dsReport.Tables[0].Load(drReport);

        // close connection
        drReport.Close();
        conReport.Close();

        // prepare report for view
        reportViewer1.LocalReport.ReportEmbeddedResource ➥
```

```
                        = "AccessReport.rptAccess.rdlc";
                  ReportDataSource rds = new ReportDataSource();
                  rds.Name = "dsAccess_dtAccess";
                  rds.Value = dsReport.Tables[0];
                  reportViewer1.LocalReport.DataSources.Add(rds);

                  // preivew the report
                  reportViewer1.RefreshReport();
            }
            catch (Exception ex)
            {
                  MessageBox.Show(ex.Message);
            }
            finally
            {
                  if (conReport.State == ConnectionState.Open)
                  {
                        conReport.Close();
                  }
            }
        }
    }
}
```

■Note I used `Source=C:\Apress\chapter10\nwind.mdb` in the connection string; please change this to the correct path of `nwind.mdb` on your local drive.

This code is almost the same as we've used in past reporting projects. However, the main difference here is the use of `System.Data.OleDb`. ADO.NET uses this connectivity to get data from the Access database. You'll also notice the use of `StringBuilder`, which I used to break the large `SELECT` statement into smaller segments. This approach is preferred to improve the string concatenation efficiency. Please check the following Web site for more on `StringBuilder`:

```
http://msdn.microsoft.com/library/default.asp?url=/library/➥
   en-us/cpref/html/frlrfsystemtextstringbuilderclasstopic.asp
```

Building the Project

It's time to build the project now. You can click the small, green Play button in the main tool-box or press F5 on the keyboard to start the application in run-time mode. If the program compiles without any errors, you will see the form with the report in preview mode. Please make sure the report looks similar to Figure 10-10.

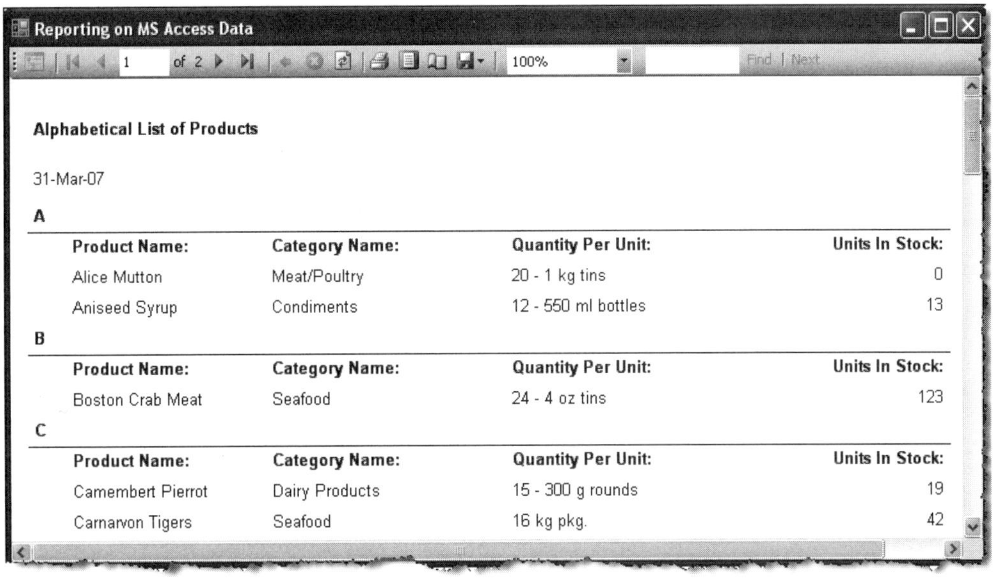

Figure 10-10. *Our report in preview mode*

There you go. Feel free to compare the outputs of our report to the Access report in Figure 10-1; the only difference is in the format of the date in the report header. I kept it normal instead of in italics, just for a change. If you've worked with Access reports in the past, I hope this exercise will give you some hints as to how a similar report is developed using RS.

Let's continue with the quest of exploring the other data sources; next in line is XML data.

Reporting with XML Data

I'm sure you had fun with reporting on the Access data; let's make life even more interesting. It is time to report on the XML data. The XML data type is no secret to developers today; even if you never used the XML before, I'm confident that you heard of it.

What is XML? In simple words, XML (Extensible Markup Language) is a World Wide Web Consortium (W3C) initiative that allows information and services to be shared. It has an easy structure that both humans and computers can understand and is used widely for the exchange of information. The information stored in the XML format can work on cross-platform scenarios. For example, if you have information in the XML format, it is easy to share between the UNIX and the Windows platforms. XML is an extensive topic; you can get more information on the subject from the following web site:

http://msdn2.microsoft.com/en-us/xml/default.aspx

Before we start to work on our reporting project, let's take a quick look at the XML data that we'll use. I'm using a standard XML file called books.xml. You can download the file from the following location:

http://msdn2.microsoft.com/en-us/library/ms762271.aspx

Here is a partial listing from the file:

```
<?xml version="1.0"?>
<catalog>
   <book id="bk101">
      <author>Gambardella, Matthew</author>
      <title>XML Developer's Guide</title>
      <genre>Computer</genre>
      <price>44.95</price>
      <publish_date>2000-10-01</publish_date>
      <description>An in-depth look at creating applications
      with XML.</description>
   </book>
   <book id="bk102">
      <author>Ralls, Kim</author>
      <title>Midnight Rain</title>
      <genre>Fantasy</genre>
      <price>5.95</price>
      <publish_date>2000-12-16</publish_date>
      <description>A former architect battles corporate zombies,
      an evil sorceress, and her own childhood to become queen
      of the world.</description>
   </book>
```

The content of the XML file is nothing but a books catalog. You can think of this XML file as a data table. Notice that the file content, catalog, is the name of the table, and id, author, title, genre, price, publish_date, and description are the data columns. So how many rows of data does the XML partial list have? Well, if your answer is "two," you're right. Now, all we have to do is to transform this XML information into a data table using the C# code.

Let's take this plain-looking XML file and convert it into a jazzy looking books catalog report. We'll use the three report items—text box, list, and image—to do the job. At the end of this exercise, the report should resemble Figure 10-11.

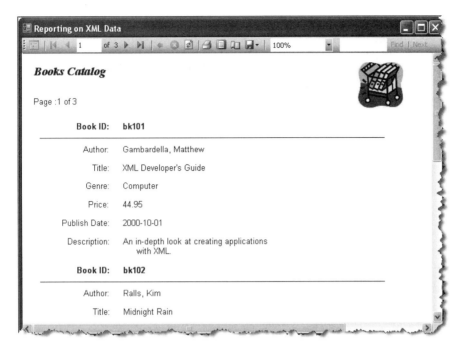

Figure 10-11. *The Books Catalog report using the XML data*

Creating a Windows Forms Project

Open Visual Studio, and use the following steps to create a Windows application project; please refer to Figure 10-2 from the Access report exercise for an illustration of this process:

1. Click File ➤ New ➤ Project, or you can press the hot key Ctrl+Shift+N.

2. In the "Project types" pane of the New Project dialog box, select Visual C# ➤ Windows.

3. In the Templates pane, select Windows Application.

4. Please give a name to the application; I've called the project XMLReport. You may choose a different location for storing the application files according to your preference.

5. Click the OK button to finish the process. Visual Studio will create a new Windows application project. You'll also notice that a new form with the name Form1 is part of the project.

Let's add the dataset and ReportViewer to the project. Select the project in Solution Explorer, right-click it, and select Add ➤ New Item ➤ DataSet. Please name the dataset dsXML. Before you add the ReportViewer, please make sure Form1 is open in designer. Now, let's add the ReportViewer to the project by dragging and dropping Data ➤ ReportViewer from the toolbox.

Set the properties as listed in Table 10-3.

Table 10-3. *Property Settings for the XML Project*

Object	Property	Value
Form1		
	Text	Reporting on XML Data
	Size	790, 500
reportViewer1		
	Dock	Fill

Step 1: Creating a Data Table

Since we already have the dataset in the project, it's time to add the data table to it. Please use the following steps to add a data table inside the dataset:

1. You can go to the dataset designer in two ways: double-click dsXML inside Solution Explorer, or right-click the dsXML node and select View Designer.

2. Add a data table by right-clicking the design surface and selecting Add ➤ DataTable.

3. Click the header of the newly created data table, and name it dtXML. Start adding the columns to dtXML by right-clicking the data table and selecting Add ➤ Column.

4. Please add the following columns into the data table; your data table should look like Figure 10-12:

   - id (System.String)

   - author (System.String)

   - title (System.String)

   - genre (System.String)

   - price (System.String)

   - publish_date (System.String)

   - description (System.String)

Figure 10-12. *Final look of the data table dtXML*

Step 2: Designing the Report Layout

Let's look at the XML report layout in Figure 10-11. The layout is simple; we have to deal with only the header and body sections. The header section contains the report title, page number, and logo image. The report is using the list report item to display the book information, and the book information is separated with a line report item.

Now that we have our dataset in place with a data table and all the needed columns, we can start working on designing the report layout. Add the report by selecting the project in Solution Explorer, right-clicking it, and selecting Add ➤ New Item. Next, select Report from the Add New Item dialog box, and name the report rptXML.rdlc. Click the Add button to complete the process and make the new report part of the project.

Adding a Header

Let's add the header to the report. Again, all you have to do is right-click the open area inside the report designer, and select Page Header. Refer to Figure 10-5 from the previous example if you need help with adding a header.

Setting Up the Page

Make sure that the report is letter-sized and has a portrait page orientation. Right-click the open area on the design surface, and select Properties. You may wish to put your name as Author and include information in the Description field. I'd advise you to let all other choices stay as the defaults.

Designing the Page Header

We'll start working on the header now. Please drag and drop the following report items inside the header section:

- A text box item for the report title

- A text box item for the page number

- An image item for the logo image

Let's change the properties; select each of the text box items, and specify the values for each report item's properties according to Table 10-4.

Table 10-4. *Report Item Properties for the Header*

Report Item	Property	Value
textbox1		
	Name	txtReportTitle
	Value	Books Catalog
	Font	Italic, Times New Roman, 14pt, Bold
textbox2		
	Name	txtPageCount
	Value	="Page :" & Globals!PageNumber & " of " & Globals!TotalPages
image1		
	Source	External
	Sizing	FitProportional
	Value	file:C:\Apress\chapter10\XMLReport\books.jpg

■**Note** Please remember to add file: in front of the image path if the image source is external.

Designing the Body Section

Let's start by dragging Report Items ➤ List from the toolbox and dropping it inside the Body section of the report designer; a new list item with the default name of list1 is part of the report now. As the name suggests, a list item is used to present details. To present details with a list item, we need to use the text box report item.

As you can see in Figure 10-13, we've added seven pieces of information to the list; therefore, we'll need to drag and drop fourteen text box items (one text box will act like a label and another text box will hold the value of each piece of information). To set up the text boxes, drag Report Items ➤ TextBox from the toolbox and drop it inside the list item. Lay out all fourteen text boxes as you see them in Figure 10-13, so that each piece of book information is a column presented vertically, instead of in the usual horizontal presentation. Therefore, you need to name the columns and map the text boxes to the corresponding data table column.

You may choose your favorite method to map the data table columns to the text box report items: type an expression or drag and drop from the data source. Let's drag and drop in our example. Select Data Source ➤ dsXML ➤ id; drag it, and drop it inside the second text box. Repeat this task for the rest of the columns from dsXML. Please make sure your report design surface looks similar to the one shown in Figure 10-13.

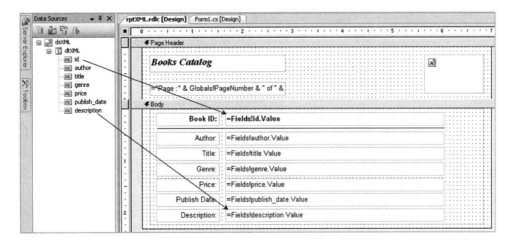

Figure 10-13. *The report designer after adding the header and the body*

That's all we need for the report design. Now, it's time to move on and write some C# code to report on XML data.

Step 3: Writing the C# Code

Let's add the following code behind `Form1.cs` to get XML data and produce the report output:

```csharp
using System;
using System.Collections.Generic;
using System.ComponentModel;
using System.Data;
using System.Drawing;
using System.Text;
using System.Windows.Forms;
using Microsoft.Reporting.WinForms;

namespace XMLReport
{
    public partial class Form1 : Form
    {
        public Form1()
        {
            InitializeComponent();
        }

        private void Form1_Load(object sender, EventArgs e)
        {
            DataSet dsReport = new dsXML();
```

```
                    // create temp dataset to read XML information
                    DataSet dsTempReport = new DataSet();

                    try
                    {
                        // using ReadXml method of DataSet to read
                        // XML data from books.xml file
                        dsTempReport.ReadXml(@"C:\Apress\Chapter10\XMLReport\books.xml");

                        // copy XML data from temp dataset to our typed dataset
                        dsReport.Tables[0].Merge(dsTempReport.Tables[0]);

                        // prepare report for view
                        reportViewer1.LocalReport.ReportEmbeddedResource➥
                          = "XMLReport.rptXML.rdlc";

                        // Setting this is important if you are using
                        // external image source.
                        reportViewer1.LocalReport.EnableExternalImages = true;

                        ReportDataSource rds = new ReportDataSource();
                        rds.Name = "dsXML_dtXML";
                        rds.Value = dsReport.Tables[0];
                        reportViewer1.LocalReport.DataSources.Add(rds);

                        // Preview the report.
                        reportViewer1.RefreshReport();
                    }
                    catch (Exception ex)
                    {
                        MessageBox.Show(ex.Message);
                    }
                }
            }
        }
```

■**Note** I used `C:\Apress\Chapter10\XMLReport\books.xml` as the path to the XML file. Please change this to the correct path of the XML file on your local drive.

The code used with this example is small compared with other exercises. The reason for this is that we didn't need to make use of any special data-access clients. We read the XML file directly into the dataset using the native ReadXml() method.

Building the Project

Let's build the project now. As usual, you can click the small, green Play button in the main toolbox or press F5 on the keyboard to start the application in run-time mode. If the program compiles without any errors, you will see the form with the report in preview mode. Please make sure the report looks similar to Figure 10-11.

As the exercise shows, that plain-looking XML data we started with can be converted into our jazzy looking report within minutes. I'd encourage you to try out other XML files. If you could not produce the output, please go through all the steps and check to be sure you haven't missed any.

All right, we are finished with two additional data sources, Access and XML, so let's move on to report on the third and last data source, Oracle.

Reporting with Oracle Data

Let's get ready for another fun-filled challenge—reporting on Oracle data. It doesn't matter if you are new to Oracle or already working with it; this exercise will introduce you to reporting on Oracle data using the client-side RS.

Oracle, like SQL Server, is a popular relational database management system. As we use ADO.NET with `SqlClient` to access SQL Server data, we can use `OracleClient` to do the same for Oracle data. You may wish to visit the official Oracle site to get more information:

`http://www.oracle.com/index.html.`

For both the Access and the XML data, we connected to physical files. Are we going to do the same with the Oracle? Well, no. Oracle is much like SQL Server in that both run as Windows services, which are different than file-based databases, such as Access. To develop our reports, Oracle has to be installed properly, and you must be able to query the database using the Oracle connectivity. Oracle comes in different versions. For this example, I'm using Oracle 10g Express Edition (XE). Oracle 10g Express is similar to Microsoft's SQL Server 2005 Express Edition. Both express versions are lightweight releases of their full-featured counterparts, and both offer excellent opportunities for developers to design solutions without the need of full-featured versions.

The good news is that Oracle XE is free to use in most cases (please check the licensing agreement). That means if you don't have access to the Oracle database already, you can download and try out this exercise with ease. You can download the installation package from the following link:

`http://www.oracle.com/technology/software/products/database/xe/index.html`

■Note If you are interested in the English version only, download `OracleXE.exe`. If you have a slow connection, be patient, as the download is large, about 165MB.

The installation package comes with a good set of documentation to get you started with Oracle XE. If you already know Oracle, the process will be simple. If you are new to Oracle, please read the help documents carefully. Oracle XE comes with a sample schema of a fictional human resources firm. We'll query the database for employee information and see how we can report on it with client-side RS. Please see Figure 10-14 for the results of the query we'll use to develop our report.

■**Note** Please make sure to unlock the human resources sample schema before you run the Oracle report. You can unlock the schema using the Administrative tool provided with 10g XE installation. Please consult the Oracle help documentation for more information.

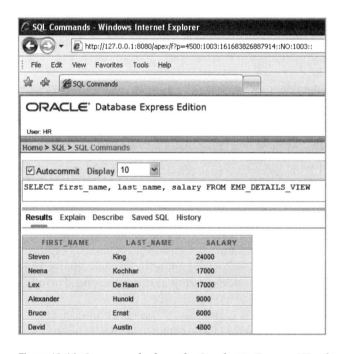

Figure 10-14. *Query results from the Oracle 10g Express HR schema*

As you can see in Figure 10-14, I'm selecting the three columns from the view EMP_DETAILS_VIEW. We'll send the same query from our Windows Forms client and develop a simple report to list all employees' names and salary information. When we finish the report, the output in the preview mode should look similar to the report shown in Figure 10-15.

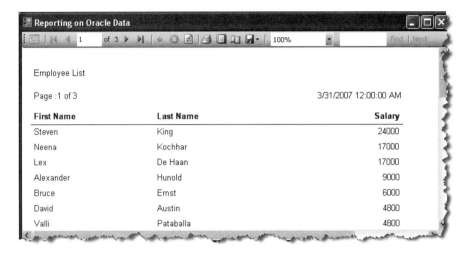

Figure 10-15. *The Employee List report using Oracle data*

Creating the Windows Forms Project

Please open Visual Studio, and use the following steps to create a Windows application project; refer to Figure 10-2 for an illustration of these steps:

1. Click File ➤ New ➤ Project, or you can press the hot key Ctrl+Shift+N.

2. In the "Project types" pane of New Project dialog box, select Visual C# ➤ Windows.

3. In the Templates pane, select Windows Application.

4. Please give the application a name; I've called the project OracleReport. You may choose a different location for storing the application files according to your preference.

5. Click the OK button to finish the process; Visual Studio will create a new Windows application project. Also notice that a new form with name Form1 is part of the project.

Let's next add the dataset and ReportViewer to the project. Select the project in Solution Explorer, right-click it, and select Add ➤ New Item ➤ DataSet. Please name the dataset dsOracle. Before you add the ReportViewer, make sure Form1 is open in designer. Now, add the ReportViewer to the project by selecting Data ➤ ReportViewer and dragging and dropping it onto the design surface.

Please set the properties in Table 10-5.

Table 10-5. *Property Settings for the Oracle Project*

Object	Property	Value
Form1		
	Text	Reporting on Oracle Data
	Size	790, 500
reportViewer1		
	Dock	Fill

Step 1: Creating a Data Table

Since we already have the dataset in the project, it's time to add a data table to it. Please use the following steps to add a data table inside the dataset:

1. You can go to the dataset designer in two ways: double-click dsOracle inside Solution Explorer, or right-click dsOracle node and select View Designer.

2. To add the data table, right-click the design surface, and select Add ➤ DataTable.

3. Click the Header of the newly created data table, and name it dtOracle. Add columns to dtOracle by right-clicking DataTable and selecting Add ➤ Column.

4. Add the following columns into data table; your data table should look like Figure 10-16:

   • first_name (System.String)

   • last_name (System. String)

   • salary (System.Double)

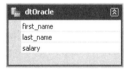

Figure 10-16. *Final look of the data table dtOracle*

Step 2: Designing the Report Layout

If you look at the Oracle report layout in Figure 10-15, what you'll find is a simple Employee List report. In this report, we have to deal with only the header and body sections. The header section contains the report title, page number, and print date. We'll use the table report item to display employee details.

We have our dataset in place with the data table and all the needed columns, so we're all set to start designing the report layout. Add the report by selecting the project in Solution Explorer, right-clicking it, and selecting Add ➤ New Item. Select Report from the Add New Item dialog box, and name the report rptOracle.rdlc. Click the Add button to complete the process; a new report is now part of the project.

Adding a Header

Let's add the header to the report, as usual, by right-clicking the open area inside the report designer and selecting Page Header (refer to Figure 10-5).

Setting Up the Page

As in the other projects in this chapter, make sure the report is letter-sized and has the portrait page orientation: right-click the open area inside the design surface, and select Properties. As usual, you may wish to put your name as Author and fill in the Description field.

Designing the Page Header

We'll start working on the header now. Please drag and drop the following report items inside the header section:

- A text box item for the report title
- A text box item for the page number
- A text box item for the print date

Report item properties can be changed in the same ways as the previous examples. Select each of the text box items in turn, and specify the values for each report item's properties according to Table 10-6.

Table 10-6. *Report Item Properties for the Header*

Report Item	Property	Value
textbox1		
	Name	txtReportTitle
	Value	Employee List
textbox2		
	Name	txtPageCount
	Value	="Page :" & Globals!PageNumber & " of " & Globals!TotalPages
textbox3		
	Name	txtPrintDate
	Value	=Today

Designing the Body Section

As before, drag a table from the toolbox and drop it inside the Body section to add a new table item named table1 to the report. By default, we get the three columns with the table item, and that is all we need for this report.

Let's again map the data table columns to the text box report items by selecting Data Source ➤ dsOracle ➤ first_name, dragging and dropping it inside the first column of the table's detail section. Repeat the task for the rest of the columns in dsOracle. Please make sure your report design surface looks similar to Figure 10-17.

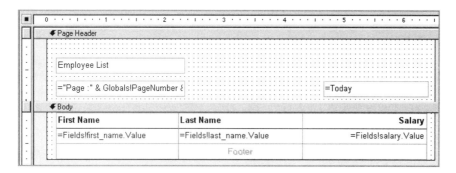

Figure 10-17. *The report designer after adding the header and body*

That's it for this report's design. You'll notice that I made the column headings bold. Feel free to try out any other formatting you may wish to apply. Now, it's time to move on and write some C# code to report on Oracle data.

Step 3: Writing the C# Code

Before we start with code, we need to add a reference to the Oracle client. We'll use the Oracle client that is installed with Oracle XE. Add the Oracle client reference by selecting References under this project in Solution Explorer, right-clicking it, and selecting Add Reference. Select the .NET tab in the Add Reference dialog box, scroll down to Oracle.DataAccess, and click the OK button. Please see Figure 10-18 for an illustration of these steps.

■Note Oracle may also use the System.Data.Oracle client that ships with Framework 2.0. However, you need to install the Oracle client on your machine.

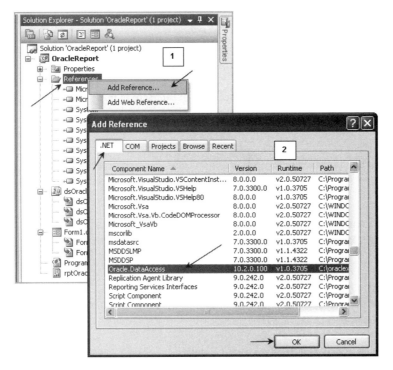

Figure 10-18. *Steps needed to add the Oracle client reference to the project*

As usual, add the following code behind `Form1.cs` to get to the Oracle data and produce the report output:

```
using System;
using System.Collections.Generic;
using System.ComponentModel;
using System.Data;
using System.Drawing;
using System.Text;
using System.Windows.Forms;
using Microsoft.Reporting.WinForms;
using Oracle.DataAccess.Client;

namespace OracleReport
{
    public partial class Form1 : Form
    {
        public Form1()
        {
            InitializeComponent();
        }
```

```csharp
private void Form1_Load(object sender, EventArgs e)
{
    // connection string
    string cnString = "User Id=hr;Password=hr;Data Source=XE";

    OracleConnection conReport = new OracleConnection(cnString);
    OracleCommand cmdReport = new OracleCommand();
    OracleDataReader drReport;

    DataSet dsReport = new dsOracle();

    try
    {
        // open connection
        conReport.Open();

        cmdReport.CommandType = CommandType.Text;
        cmdReport.Connection = conReport;
        cmdReport.CommandText = "SELECT first_name, last_name, salary ➥
                FROM EMP_DETAILS_VIEW";

        // execute query and load result to dataset
        drReport = cmdReport.ExecuteReader();
        dsReport.Tables[0].Load(drReport);

        // close connection
        drReport.Close();
        conReport.Close();

        // prepare report for view
        reportViewer1.LocalReport.ReportEmbeddedResource➥
          = "OracleReport.rptOracle.rdlc";
        ReportDataSource rds = new ReportDataSource();
        rds.Name = "dsOracle_dtOracle";
        rds.Value = dsReport.Tables[0];
        reportViewer1.LocalReport.DataSources.Add(rds);

        // Preivew the report.
        reportViewer1.RefreshReport();
    }
    catch (OracleException ex)
    {
        MessageBox.Show(ex.Message);
    }
    finally
    {
        if (conReport.State == ConnectionState.Open)
```

```
                    {
                        conReport.Close();
                    }
                }
            }
        }
}
```

■**Note** I used `cnString = "User Id=hr;Password=hr;Data Source=XE` as the connection string. If you used a different password than `hr` while unlocking the account, please make sure to change it in the code.

In the past, we used `SqlClient` and `OledbClient`; to work with Oracle data in this exercise, we use the `Oracle.DataAccess.Client` reference. The rest of the procedure to initiate a connection, that is, sending the query through a command, should be familiar. You may also notice that instead of trapping `Exception`, the code here traps specifically `OracleException`.

Building the Project

Again, build the project by clicking the small, green Play button in the main toolbox or pressing F5. If the program compiles without any errors, then you will see the form with the report in preview mode. Please make sure the report looks similar to Figure 10-15. If it doesn't, please check all the steps to make sure you didn't miss anything. If you see any errors related to the report, please consult the troubleshooting section in Chapter 4.

Summary

In this chapter, we discussed how client-side RS can make use of data sources other than SQL Server. We first connected to Microsoft Access data and then to XML data; both Access and XML are file-based data repositories. Finally, we reported on data from Oracle, which is a server-based repository.

In the next chapter, we'll discuss the remote processing mode. We'll also look at accessing a server-side report with the Windows Forms client.

CHAPTER 11

Integrating Server-Side Reports

In previous chapters, you learned to develop reports using different clients. In each chapter, we developed the reports with clients using Visual Studio. In a typical organization, though, you may find reports with server-side implementation. The question is, therefore, can you integrate this server-side report with your local client? To do so, will you need to rewrite the report for the client side?

Well, there's nothing to worry about—you don't need to rewrite the report. You can easily host server-side reports with your favorite client, just as you do reports built on the client side, and you can make use of server-side reports hosted with corporate reporting portals. We use the Report Manager for server-side reports; client-side RS brings power to all lines of business applications to access these server-side reports and provide a good user experience.

In this chapter, you will

- Explore the remote processing mode

- Learn to access server-side reports with a Windows Forms client

Remote Processing Mode

So far, you've set the report processing mode to Local for all the reporting projects. In this chapter, you'll set the processing mode to Remote for the first time. I suspect questions might be popping up in your mind: What is the real difference between these modes? Will ReportViewer show reports differently in remote mode?

ReportViewer will show the reports in the same way for both local and remote modes. However, there is a subtle difference in how report processing happens. In remote processing mode, the control brings back a fully processed report from server-side RS. If you use the report mode for the ReportViewer control, the control serves two purposes: it is used as a viewer, and it provides support for interacting with a report. I mean to say, if a report has parameters, users can specify values for those parameters within ReportViewer.

Unlike in local mode, all remote-mode data processing and rendering is done on the report server and only the output is produced for viewing. A report must be published before you can access it with the client, and you can get the report from a stream or by specifying the URL of the report address.

Note You cannot use .rdlc files in remote processing mode. If you want to publish your .rdlc files on the server side, you must first convert them to .rdl format. For detailed steps for converting .rdlc files to .rdl and vice versa, please check the following MSDN link: http://msdn2.microsoft.com/en-us/library/ms252109(vs.80).aspx.

How Server-Side Reporting Works

Server-side processing of reports is easy compared with the client-side report processing. As you know, for a client-side report, we need to collect the data. We also need to make sure a proper user interface is available for passing the information as parameters. For server-side reports, we don't have to worry with all of that, because the report server takes care of the data collection and processing, and the user interface to supply report parameters comes as part of the report preview. The important characteristics for accessing a server-side report at the client side follow:

- The processing mode

- The report server URL

- The report path

You'll need to specify these three characteristics with the ReportViewer control. As usual, you can set these properties using the Properties window (see Figure 11-1) or C# code.

As you can see in Figure 11-1, you'll need to start with setting the processing mode to Remote. Next, you'll need to specify the report server URL. The report server URL can be local or remote. For example, if RS is part of your development box, the typical path is http://localhost/reportserver. Finally, you'll need to specify the report path, which consists of the folder and report names.

Let's move on to access a server-side report with the Windows Forms client now. Developing server-side reports is beyond the reach of this book, so instead, we'll use samples provided by Microsoft. You can use reports built with the AdventureWorks database or the sample reports pack.

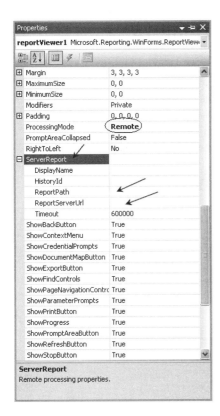

Figure 11-1. *ReportViewer Properties window for server-side reports*

For the example used in this chapter, I'm going to use the Trial Balance report from the Accounting Reports Pack. Please check the following Microsoft resource to download and install the SQL Server 2005 Report Pack for Financial Reporting:

```
http://www.microsoft.com/downloads/details.aspx?familyid= ➥
D81722CE-408C-4FB6-A429-2A7ECD62F674&displaylang=en
```

■**Note** Remote processing mode requires a licensed copy of SQL Server 2005 Reporting Services.

Server-Side Reports with the Windows Forms Client

Accessing server-side reports is easy—and why shouldn't it be, since the report is ready, with the design and data connectivity, on the server side? All the client application has to do is access the report with help of the ReportViewer control. Now, before we access our Trial Balance report, please see Figure 11-2 for a view of the Report Manager window with the report output. Later, we'll compare this output with output produced by the Windows Forms client.

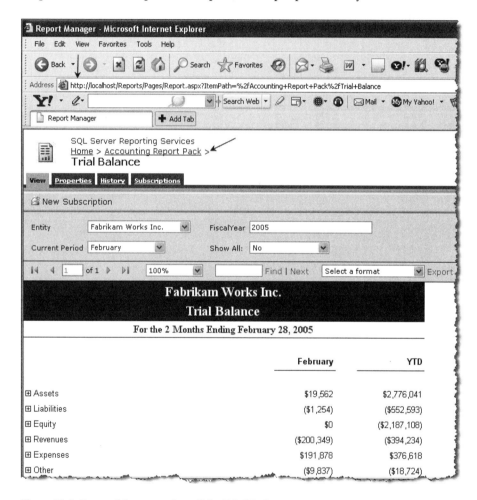

Figure 11-2. *Report Manager view of the Trial Balance report*

Creating a Windows Forms Project

Open Visual Studio, and use the following steps to create a Windows application project; Figure 11-3 illustrates these steps:

1. Click File ➤ New ➤ Project, or press the hot key Ctrl+Shift+N.

2. In the "Project type" pane of the New Project dialog box, select Visual C# ➤ Windows.

3. In the Templates pane, select Windows Application.

4. Please give the application a name; I've called the project WinServerSide. You may choose a different location for storing the application files according to your preference.

5. Click the OK button to finish the process. Visual Studio will create a new Windows application project as well as a new form with the name Form1.

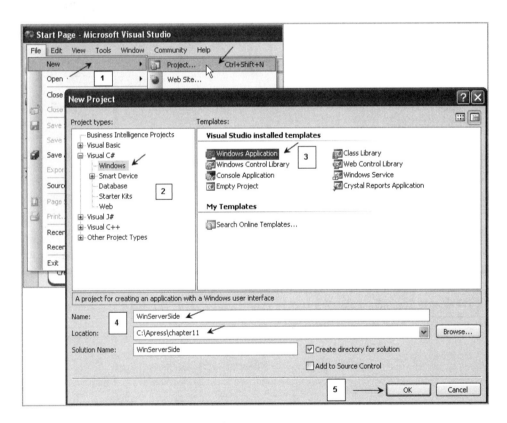

Figure 11-3. *Create a new Windows Application project.*

If you face difficulty creating the Windows Forms application project, revisit Chapter 4 for detailed instructions on creating a Windows Forms client.

Adding the ReportViewer Control

As I mentioned before, if you'd like to view the server-side report with minimal effort on the client side, all you need is the ReportViewer. So, let's add that to the project. Select Toolbox ➤ Data ➤ ReportViewer, and drag and drop the ReportViewer onto Form1, as shown in Figure 11-4. After you add the ReportViewer to Form1, you can go on to specify server-side report access information by clicking the Tasks button (circled in Figure 11-4).

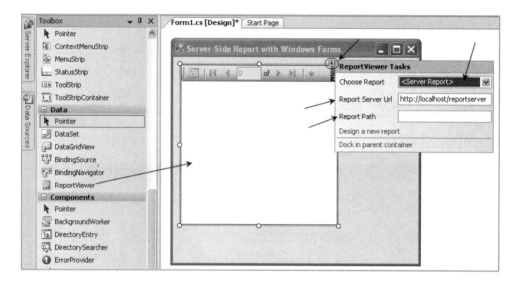

Figure 11-4. *Add the ReportViewer to the project.*

Please make sure you set the properties in Table 11-1. After you specify all properties, your Form1 should look similar to Figure 11-5.

Table 11-1. *Property Settings for the Web Site*

Object	Property	Value
Form1		
	Text	Server-Side Report with Windows Forms
	Size	750, 530
reportViewer1	Dock	Fill

Figure 11-5. *Form1 after setting properties*

Setting Up the ReportViewer Properties

All right, we've got Form1 ready with ReportViewer. All we need now is to set properties that will help the ReportViewer to display our Trial Balance report. You can set up properties in three different ways: First, you could use the Properties window, shown in Figure 11-6.

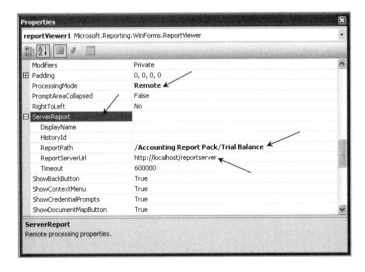

Figure 11-6. *Setting up ReportViewer using the Properties window*

Your second choice is to use the ReportViewer task. After you drop the ReportViewer control onto Form1, the ReportViewer Tasks pop-up dialog will appear, and you can specify properties using this task dialog (see Figure 11-4). The third choice is to write the C# code to set up the report properties. If you decide to write the code, please make sure that the code behind Form1.cs looks like the following:

```
using System;
using System.Collections.Generic;
using System.ComponentModel;
using System.Data;
using System.Drawing;
using System.Text;
using System.Windows.Forms;
using Microsoft.Reporting.WinForms;

namespace WinServerSide
{
    public partial class Form1 : Form
    {
        public Form1()
        {
            InitializeComponent();
        }

        private void Form1_Load(object sender, EventArgs e)
        {
            // set processing mode to remote
            reportViewer1.ProcessingMode = ProcessingMode.Remote;

            // specify report URL
            // please make sure to replace localhost with server name if needed
            reportViewer1.ServerReport.ReportServerUrl = new ➥
    Uri(@"http://localhost/reportserver");

            // specify report path, Folder = Accounting Report Pack
            // Report = Trial Balance
            reportViewer1.ServerReport.ReportPath = ➥
    @"/Accounting Report Pack/Trial Balance";

            // show the report
            this.reportViewer1.RefreshReport();
        }
    }
}
```

Server-Side Reports, At Your Service

Now, let's build the project. As you know, you can build a project by clicking the small, green Play button in the main toolbox or pressing F5 on the keyboard to start the application in run-time mode.

I assume that you've properly set all three important properties in ReportViewer, as we discussed earlier in this chapter. If all goes well, your project should compile without any issues, and you should be able to see the Trial Balance report in action; your output should look similar to Figure 11-7.

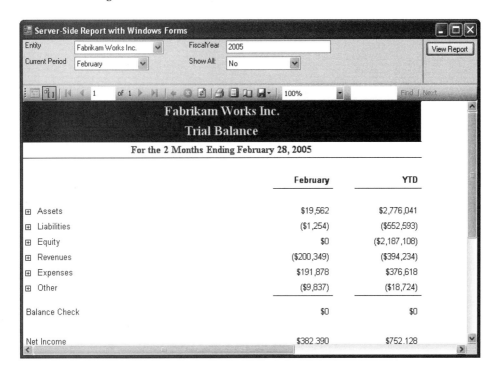

Figure 11-7. *A server-side report in action*

If your report looks similar to Figure 11-7, you've done it. That's all you need to embed the sever-side report at client-side. You may also like to compare the output of Figure 11-7 with the output of Figure 11-2; almost everything is the same except how the report is accessed.

Summary

This chapter discussed the remote processing mode. We did a hands-on exercise to access a server-side report with a Windows Forms client. As you can see, developers can take advantage of the server-side reporting portals to bring server-side reporting potential to client-side business applications.

In the next chapter, we'll look at ways to help you move on from Crystal Reports and enjoy the benefits provided by client-side RS.

■■■

CHAPTER 12

Moving from Crystal Reports to Reporting Services

I'm sure that you enjoyed the versatility of the client-side RS with various reporting projects we've done so far. Now, my question to you is, "What was report development like before the client-side RS in VS 2005?" Well, I'm sure the majority of developers would say that they worked with Crystal Reports (CR). I'm also included in this majority; I've used CR extensively with various commercial projects so far.

Although CR and RS are two different technologies, they produce the same result—a report. My rationale behind including this chapter in this book is to help you move toward the RS platform from CR. If you haven't used CR in the past, this chapter will help you to get to know some facts about CR, and you'll also see how report output similar to RS's can be produced using another technology.

This chapter will cover

- A side-by-side comparison of RS and CR

- Developing reports using both RS and CR

Which tool is preferable for developing reports, RS or CR? Tough one, right? Both the tools come as out-of-the-box solutions with VS 2005 for reporting on a variety of data sources. As with any competitive tools, each contains features that aren't in the other. I'd like to remind you, though, that our discussion is based on the client-side capabilities of both technologies. In my personal opinion, two choices are always better than one. However, I find it much easier to work with RS. One of the highlights that most motivates me to use RS is the free hand given to developers on the report's design surface. I can have a chart and a table at the same time inside the body section; imagine that! RS has brought a whole new functionality for developers, who can design reports just like they design Windows or Web Forms—just pick the report item, and place it where you want; it's that simple.

Before we continue our discussion further, if you are new to CR, you should know that CR is a reporting tool produced by Business Objects that has been an integral part of the Visual Studio series, including the 2005 release. CR can gather data and design reports from a wide range of data sources, such as SQL Server, Oracle, and spreadsheets like Microsoft Excel. You can get more information on CR here:

```
http://www.businessobjects.com/products/reporting/crystalreports/net/vsnet.asp
```

You might wonder why Microsoft is still shipping CR with Visual Studio. Well, since much development exists for CR, Microsoft would like to support it. At the same time, by introducing RS on the client side, Microsoft is empowering developers to be more productive using this new reporting tool. By including both tools, Microsoft gives developers the ability to choose for themselves which platform suits them best. As for long-term commitment, I've seen both CR and RS as report development tools shipped with the Visual Studio 2008 release.

And why a side-by-side reporting project? I think this way you can feel how easy it is to develop the report using RS. Instead of just telling you that creating reports using RS is easy, let me show you with the help of this exercise.

Comparing RS and CR Side by Side

The reporting project in this chapter differs from the reporting projects you've done so far. Why? Because, you'll see the same report output from two different tools side by side. So, if you're familiar with CR development, you can see how to leverage your existing skills and learn the RS equivalent. If you've not yet developed any CR reports, this is your chance to see the CR in action.

Let's develop a simple, tabular Books Year to Date Sales report for a publisher. This report will have a standard header and footer. Year-to-date sales information will be part of the body section. As Figure 12-1 shows, we'll see two different report previews. Although the report content will look the same, you'll see how reporting is made easy in VS 2005 with these two out-of-the-box solutions.

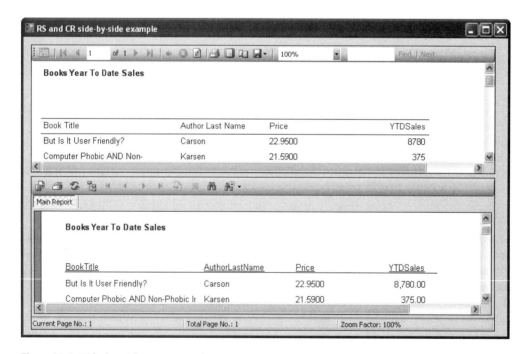

Figure 12-1. *Side-by-side report preview*

Creating the Windows Forms Project

Please open Visual Studio, and use the following steps to create a Windows application project; see Figure 12-2 for an illustration of these steps:

1. Click File ➤ New ➤ Project, or press Ctrl+Shift+N on the keyboard.

2. In the "Project types" pane of the New Project dialog box, select Visual C# ➤ Windows.

3. In the Templates pane, select Windows Application.

4. Let's give a name to the application; I've called the project RSandCR. You may choose a different location for storing the application files according to your preference.

5. Click the OK button to finish the process; VS will create a new Windows application project. You'll also notice that a new form with the name Form1 is part of the project.

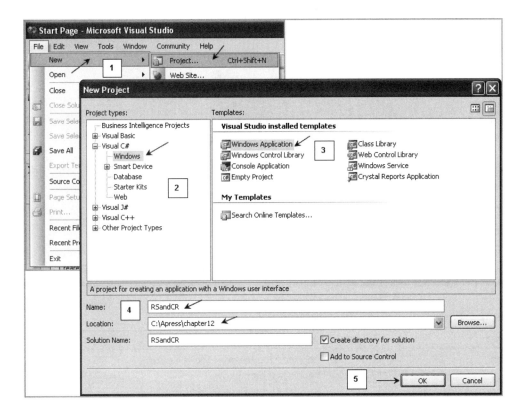

Figure 12-2. *Create a new Windows application.*

Let's move on and add the dataset and the ReportViewer to the project. So, as we have two different reports here, do we need the two datasets? Well, no, we can use the same dataset for both the reporting engines. Let's start by selecting the project under Solution Explorer; right-click it, and select Add ➤ New Item ➤ DataSet. Let's name the dataset dsRSandCR.

As you know, we use the ReportViewer to display the report output for RS. Similarly, we need to add the CrystalReportViewer to display the report output of CR. Add the ReportViewer to the project by dragging Data ➤ ReportViewer from the toolbox and dropping it onto the design surface. Similarly, add the Crystal ReportViewer by dragging Crystal Reports ➤ CrystalReportViewer from the toolbox and dropping it onto the design surface. Please see Figure 12-3 for the illustration of these steps.

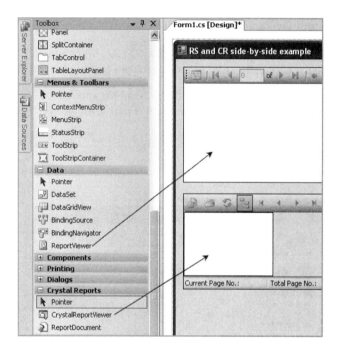

Figure 12-3. *Project after adding the dataset and ReportViewers*

Please make sure you set the properties in Table 12-1. After you specify all the properties, your Form1 should look similar to the Figure 12-4.

Table 12-1. *Property Settings for the Project*

Object	Property	Value
Form1	Text	RS and CR side-by-side example
Form1	Size	790, 500
reportViewer1	Size	750, 200
crystalReportViewer1	Size	750, 240

Figure 12-4 shows the references used by the RS and CR ReportViewers. These references are automatically added to the project when ReportViewers are placed in Form1.

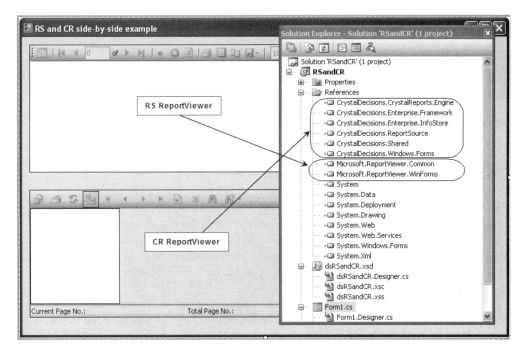

Figure 12-4. *Form1 with RS and CR ReportViewers*

Step 1: Creating a Data Table

Since we already have the dataset in the project, it's time to add a data table to it. Please use the following steps to add a data table inside the dataset:

1. You can go to the dataset designer in two ways: double-click dsAccess inside Solution Explorer, or right-click the dsRSandCR node and select View Designer.

2. Right-click the design surface, and select Add ➤ DataTable.

3. Click the header of the newly created data table, and name it dtRSandCR. Let's start adding columns to dtRSandCR by right-clicking DataTable and selecting Add ➤ Column.

4. Add the following columns into the data table; your data table should look like the one shown in Figure 12-5:

   - BookTitle (System.String)

   - AuthorLastName (System.String)

   - Price (System.String)

   - YTDSales (System.Double)

Figure 12-5. *Final look of the dtRSandCRs data table*

Step 2: Designing the Report Layout

Before we start designing the report, let's take a moment to analyze the report layout in Figure 12-1. Although the output of both reports looks the same, we need to use different approaches to report design. You'll use the table report item for the RS part of this exercise.

How about CR? Do we have the table report item in the CR design tool set also? I know many questions like these might be going through your mind, but hold on to them for now. As we go through each step of the report development, you'll see the different approaches to producing the same report unfold.

All right, we've got our dataset in place with a data table and all the necessary columns. We're all set to start working on designing the report layout. As you know, we need two reports: one each for RS and CR. The process to add reports in CR is similar to one we use for RS; the only difference is to select the proper report type.

Let's start adding the RS report by selecting the project under Solution Explorer. Right-click it, and select Add ➤ New Item. Next, select Report from the Add New Item dialog box (shown in Figure 12-6). Please name the report `rptRS.rdlc`. Click the Add button to complete the process.

Let's add the CR report now. Again, select the project under Solution Explorer, right-click it, select Add ➤ New Item, and then select Crystal Report from the Add New Item dialog box. Please name the report `rptCR.rdlc`. Click the Add button to complete the process.

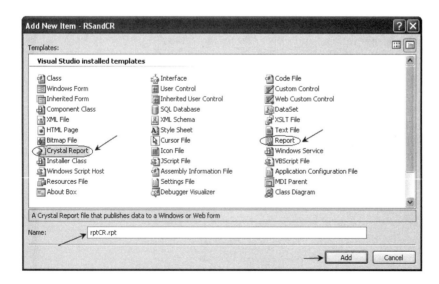

Figure 12-6. *Adding the new RS and CR reports*

As soon you add the CR report to the project, you'll notice that the Crystal Reports Gallery dialog box will greet you. Please make sure to select the As a Blank Report radio button, and click the OK button, as shown in Figure 12-7.

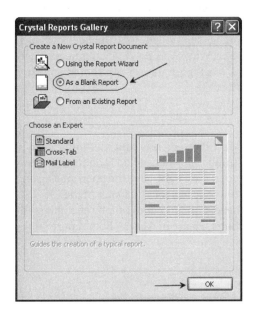

Figure 12-7. *CR report selection*

Notice that the two new reports are part of the project now and that a new toolbox called Data Sources is available with our dataset information inside RS. Similarly, a new toolbox called Field Explorer is available with the information needed to design in CR. Now, we're ready to move on to the design phase. Figure 12-8 shows the initial default design layout for RS and CR.

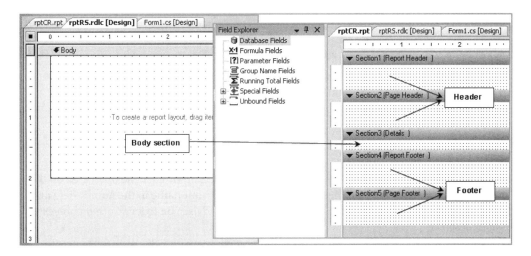

Figure 12-8. *Initial default report layout for RS and CR*

As you can see in Figure 12-8, both the RS and CR reports are open in design mode initially. You might be wondering why the CR version looks more complete, and the RS version is just a body section. Well, the RS approach is free form in nature, so you can add the sections that you need. In CR, even if you don't need headers and footers, they are there inside the report by default. So we need to add the header and footer only to the RS report.

Another observation about CR is it has two sets of headers and footers. Unlike RS, CR has a report header and footer and a page header and footer. Why? Well, if a developer needs a section to appear only one time at the beginning, or end, of a report, this section should appear in the report header, or report footer.

Adding the Header and Footer

Since we don't need to add the header and footer to the CR report, let's continue with the RS report. As usual adding the header and the footer is simple: all you need do is right-click the open area inside report designer and select Page Header; then right-click the open area again, and select Page Footer. Since we'll make use of only the page header and footer of the CR report, we can easily adjust the height of the report header and footer to zero by changing the properties or dragging the edges of the header and footer. Please make sure both reports look similar to Figure 12-9.

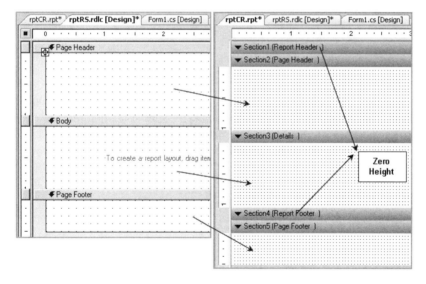

Figure 12-9. *Report layout in RS and CR with headers and footers*

Setting Up the Page

Let's work on the page setup now. As in previous RS projects, right-click the open area on the design surface, and select Properties; you may wish to put your name in the Author field and information about the report to the Description field. I'd advise you to let all other choices stay at their defaults.

Now, the question is, "How can we do a similar page setup for CR?" Well, the steps are simple: right-click inside a blank area of the header, footer, or body of the design surface, and

select Design ➤ Page Setup or Printer Setup. Page Setup is used to set page margins. Page size
and orientation are set using the Printer Setup option. Figure 12-10 shows how to access page
and printer setup options.

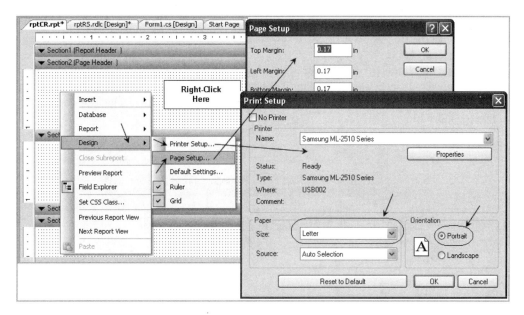

Figure 12-10. *CR report page and printer setup*

Designing the Page Header and Footer

Now that we've added all the necessary sections to our report, let's work on the header and
footer. Drag one Textbox item, and drop it inside the header and add another one inside the
footer section. As previously, report item properties are changed by selecting the report item,
right-clicking it, and selecting Properties or by accessing general properties toolbox.

Selecting each text box, and specify the values for each report item's properties according
to Table 12-2.

Table 12-2. *Report Item Properties for the Header and Footer*

Report Item	Property	Value
textbox1		
	Name	txtReportTitle
	Value	Books Year To Date Sales
	Font	Normal, Arial, 10pt, Bold
textbox2		
	Name	txtPageNumber
	Value	="Page " & Globals!PageNumber & " of " & Globals!TotalPages

Now, it's the CR report's turn for header and footer design. We'll have the same report title and page number for the CR report. This time, we need to use the text object (instead of the TextBox option) by selecting Crystal Reports ➤ Text Object and dragging and dropping it inside the header section. After you drop the object, you can type the report title inside the text object; please make sure to type the report title as **Books Year To Date Sales**. Similar to the way we change the properties in the RS text box, please change the Font property of the text object to Normal, Arial, 10pt, Bold.

The page number is treated as special field in CR. As you know, in RS, we can create special field equivalents by using expressions. Let's add the page number to the CR report by right-clicking inside the page footer section, and selecting Insert ➤ Special Field ➤ Page N of M; see Figure 12-11.

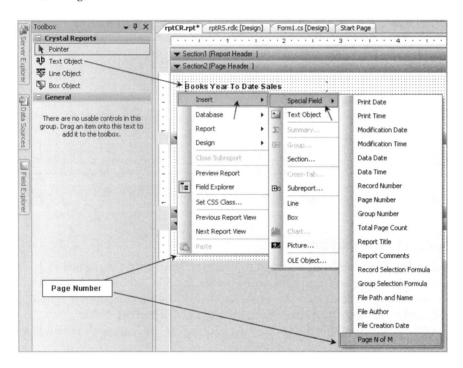

Figure 12-11. *The CR Text object and Page Number special field*

Designing the Body Section

Both of our reports have the header and the footer properly set now, so let's focus on the design of the body section. For the RS report, we'll make use of the table report item. Let's start by dragging Report Items ➤ Table from the toolbox and dropping it inside the body section in the report designer. A new table item is part of the report now, and it'll have a default name of table1. We need to add one more column, so right-click the rightmost column header and select "Insert Column to the Right".

As usual, you could choose to map the data table columns to the text boxes by either typing an expression or dragging and dropping from the data source. Let's drag Source ➤ dsRSandCR ➤ Book Title and drop it inside the first column of the table item detail section.

Repeat the task for the rest of the columns from dsRSandCR. Let's set the table row's top and bottom borders to solid lines, as we've done in the past. Please make sure your report design surface looks like Figure 12-12.

Page Header			
Books Year To Date Sales			
Body			
Book Title	Author Last Name	Price	YTDSales
=Fields!BookTitle.Value	=Fields!AuthorLastNam	=Fields!Price.Value	=Fields!YTDSales.Va
	Footer		
Page Footer			
="Page " & Globals!PageNumber & " of " & Globals!TotalPages			

Figure 12-12. *The RS report after adding header, footer, and body sections*

Let's work on the details (body) section of CR report now. As you know, with RS, we don't have to do anything special to reference the typed dataset. However, in CR, we need to make reference to it. Making reference is easy: right-click inside any section, and select Database ➤ Database Expert. A new Database Expert dialog box will appear. Expand Node ➤ Project Date ➤ ADO.NET DataSets, and move dsRSandCR to the Selected Tables section on the right side. Please see Figure 12-13 for an illustration of these steps.

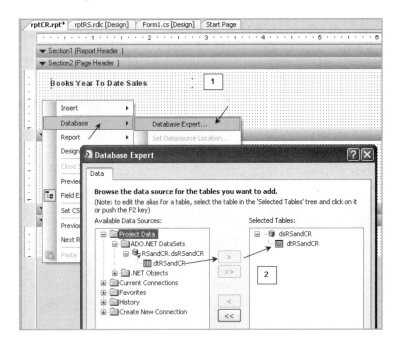

Figure 12-13. *Making reference to the typed dataset with CR report*

Mapping the newly referenced fields with the details section is easy too. As soon the reference to the typed dataset is set up with CR report designer, the Field Explorer pane gets refreshed. Select Field Explorer ➤ dtRSandCR ➤ Book Title, and drag and drop it inside the first column of the details section. Repeat the task for the rest the fields. You'll notice that, as soon you drop the field, the respective column header automatically appears in the page header section. Please see Figure 12-14 for an illustration of adding fields to the details section.

As with RS, you can select different report objects in CR and move them across to make objects look pretty. You can also access an individual object's property and set it according to your needs.

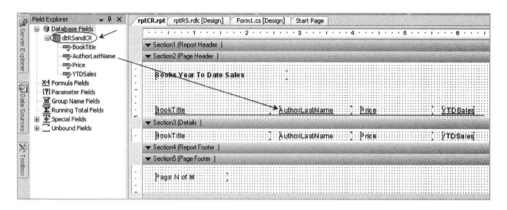

Figure 12-14. *The CR report after adding the header, footer, and body sections*

Step 3: Writing the C# Code

Well, that's all we need on the report design front. Let's add the following code to get data and see the RS and CR reports in action side by side:

```csharp
using System;
using System.Collections.Generic;
using System.ComponentModel;
using System.Data;
using System.Drawing;
using System.Text;
using System.Windows.Forms;
using System.Data.SqlClient;
using Microsoft.Reporting.WinForms;

namespace RSandCR
{
    public partial class Form1 : Form
    {
        public Form1()
        {
            InitializeComponent();
        }
```

```csharp
private void Form1_Load(object sender, EventArgs e)
{
    //declare connection string, please substitute
    //DataSource with your Server name
    string cnString = "Data Source=(local);Initial Catalog=RealWorld;
                            Integrated Security=SSPI;";

    //declare Connection, command and other related objects
    SqlConnection conReport = new SqlConnection(cnString);
    SqlCommand cmdReport = new SqlCommand();
    SqlDataReader drReport;
    DataSet dsReport = new dsRSandCR();

    try
    {
        //open connection
        conReport.Open();

        //prepare connection object to get the data through
        //reader and populate into dataset
        cmdReport.CommandType = CommandType.Text;
        cmdReport.Connection = conReport;
        cmdReport.CommandText = "Select * FROM ➥
BooksInfo Order By BookTitle";

        //read data from command object
        drReport = cmdReport.ExecuteReader();

        //load data directly from reader to dataset
        dsReport.Tables[0].Load(drReport);

        //close reader and connection
        drReport.Close();
        conReport.Close();

        //provide local report information to viewer
        reportViewer1.LocalReport.ReportEmbeddedResource =
                            "RSandCR.rptRS.rdlc";

        //prepare report data source
        ReportDataSource rds = new ReportDataSource();
        rds.Name = "dsRSandCR_dtRSandCR";
        rds.Value = dsReport.Tables[0];
        reportViewer1.LocalReport.DataSources.Add(rds);

        //load report viewer
        reportViewer1.RefreshReport();
```

```
                // prepare and load crystal reports viewer
                rptCR reportCR = new rptCR();

                // add typed dataset as data source
                reportCR.SetDataSource(dsReport.Tables[0]);

                // hide group tree which is visible by default for full view of
                // report
                crystalReportViewer1.DisplayGroupTree = false;

                // bind report instance with crystal report viewer for user display
                crystalReportViewer1.ReportSource = reportCR;
            }
            catch (Exception ex)
            {
                //display generic error message back to user
                MessageBox.Show(ex.Message);
            }
            finally
            {
                //check if connection is still open then attempt to close it
                if (conReport.State == ConnectionState.Open)
                {
                    conReport.Close();
                }
            }
        }
    }
}
```

This code is almost the same as the code we've used in past reporting projects. The main difference here is the use of two different ReportViewers. As you can see, in the case of CR, we need to instantiate the rptCR object and set a reference to its data source with our typed dataset table[0]. This code also hides the group tree of the CR ReportViewer to show the full report view, as no data group is applied for this report.

Building the Project

It's time to build the project now. You can click the small, green play button in the main tool-box or press F5 on the keyboard to start the application in run-time mode. If the program compiles without any errors, you will see the form with the report in preview mode. Please make sure the report looks similar to the one shown in Figure 12-1.

There you go; now you can see same report side by side using two different tools. The example we just did does not use the full potential of either RS or CR; the idea was to show you how to create a simple report using the two out-of-the-box solutions provided with Visual Studio.

Summary

In this chapter, I showed you how you can report the same set of data using client-side RS and CR. Finally, I gave you the C# code and saw both the reports in action.

In the next chapter, we'll take your RS report design skills to new heights, and I'll show you an example using third-party report items.

CHAPTER 13

∎∎∎

Using Third-Party Tools and Having Fun with RS

In past chapters, we used the capabilities provided by RS to create a variety of reports, and you've seen how we can take advantage of different clients to deliver reports. So are we finished with RS now? Well, there is always room for improvements and new ideas keep popping up for making use of this wonderful tool.

I decided to add this chapter to cover what else can be done with RS. Before this chapter, we used different features of client-side RS to develop reports, and in the majority of cases, we managed to do the job without any major concerns or issues. Now, if I ask you to develop a report to print a barcode as part of the report output, what then? We don't have any report item called barcode that comes with RS. So, what can be done here? Well, not to worry, third-party tools will come to the rescue.

How about making use of RS for fun? Well, why not? If you recall, in the introduction of this book, I promised to create a personal information dashboard using RS. Well, the time is right for me to fulfill that promise and show you how you can get to your own personal information dashboard.

This chapter will cover

- Integrating third-party tools with RS

- Reporting for fun—a personal dashboard

Integrating Third-Party Tools with RS

Simply out, third-party tools extend your existing tool set. For example, if you want more sophisticated graphs and charting capabilities, you can buy these from Dundas Software (http://www.dundas.com/Products/Chart/RS/index.aspx).

I'm confident that I don't need to give you an introduction to barcodes. After all, we deal with barcodes all the time. Used in tasks from buying groceries to filing important paperwork, barcodes are commonly used unique identifiers of products or services. Therefore, I thought it would be useful to demonstrate the integration of third-party tools by developing a report that has barcodes in it.

Barcode Professional from Neodynamic

After I decided to make use of a barcode report, I started the search for a third party that provides the barcode component. My search ended with Neodynamic. The folks at Neodynamic are generous enough to allow me to showcase their Barcode Professional component for this chapter. You can find more information about them here: `http://www.neodynamic.com`.

To demonstrate the use of this component, we'll create a Barcode Product List report. This report will show the barcode representation of a `ProductID`, together with the name and the product description.

Where do I get this barcode control? How do you use it? Well, before we start developing the report using this control, I'll show you how to get this tool up and running.

I'm using the trial download of this tool, which stands at version 4.0. It is quite possible that by the time the book reaches you, Neodynamic might release an update to this version. Nevertheless, our example should work with current and future versions. If you are not using version 4.0, I'd advise you to consult the Neodynamic web site for the most current information. You can download of the trial version here (you have to send a request to Neodynamic): `http://www.neodynamic.com/ND/Downloads.aspx?tabid=79&prodid=7`.

After you get the trial copy, installation is very simple. It is similar to a typical Windows production installation with a wizard-based interface. Please complete the installation according to the instructions provided by the wizard.

The next important step is to register the Neodynamic Barcode assembly to the GAC. In case you've never heard of the GAC before, it's the global assembly cache—a machinewide storage location used to hold assemblies that are intended to be shared by several applications on the machine. You can learn more about the GAC here:

```
http://msdn2.microsoft.com/en-us/library/yf1d93sz(vs.71).aspx
```

Why do we have to register the assembly related to this tool into the GAC? Well, since we will make reference to its functionality from within the report, the report will look for it in the GAC.

So, how do we register this assembly into the GAC? It is simple; you need to start by clicking Start ➤ All Programs ➤ Microsoft Visual Studio 2005 ➤ Visual Studio Tools ➤ Visual Studio 2005 Command Prompt. At the prompt, please type a command like the following one:

```
C:\Program Files\Microsoft Visual Studio 8\VC>gacutil➥
/i "C:\Program Files\Neody namic\Barcode Professional for Reporting Services\➥
v4.0\Bin\For SSRS 2005\Neodynamic.ReportingServices.Barcode.dll"
```

An alternate method is to drag and drop the assembly from the file system to the GAC. As you will notice, the utility that does the job of registering is called `gacutil`, and it takes /i and the path to the assembly name as command-line inputs. This code will work for you if you selected all default options during the installation of the tool. If you have selected any other path, make sure you make change to the command prompt appropriately. All right, we have enough information to go ahead and develop the barcode report.

Creating the Barcode Product List Report

You're working for AdventureWorks, Incorporated as a developer. You have the task of developing a Product List Barcode report. The report should be the graphical representation of data stored as product ID and provide interactive sorting capabilities for the user on the Product Name column. The report should meet all the characteristics described in Table 13-1, and the report output should match Figure 13-1.

Table 13-1. *Report Characteristics*

Characteristics	Value
Report title	Barcode Product List
Company title	AdventureWorks Inc.
Logo	No
Data source	`tblBarcode`
Page size	Letter
Page orientation	Portrait
Layout design	Header and body sections

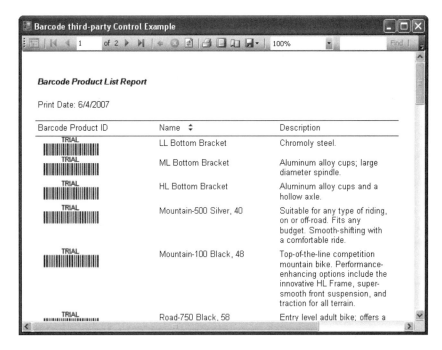

Figure 13-1. *Output of the Barcode Product List report*

Business Case

A barcode is most commonly used in areas that make use of 12-digit UPCs (Universal Product Codes). The UPC is assigned to retail merchandise to identify both the product and the vendor who sells it. Typing this rather long 12-digit number to identify every item is surely more effort than letting a scanner do the job. Barcodes convert the UPC to machine-readable format.

Barcodes consist of black lines such that the width of each black line and the white space between lines coincides with the numbers of the UPC. In this report, the UPC is the data contained inside the `ProductID` column from table `RealWorld.tblBarcode`.

Creating a Windows Forms Project

Please open Visual Studio, and use the following steps, illustrated in Figure 13-2, to create a Windows application project:

1. Click File ➤ New ➤ Project, or press the hot keys Ctrl+Shift+N.

2. In the "Project types" pane of the New Project dialog box, select Visual C# ➤ Windows.

3. In the Templates pane, select Windows Application.

4. Please give the application a name; I've called the project Barcode. You may choose a different location for storing the application files according to your preference.

5. Click the OK button to finish the process. After you click OK, Visual Studio will create a new Windows application project. You'll also notice that a new form with the name `Form1` is part of the project.

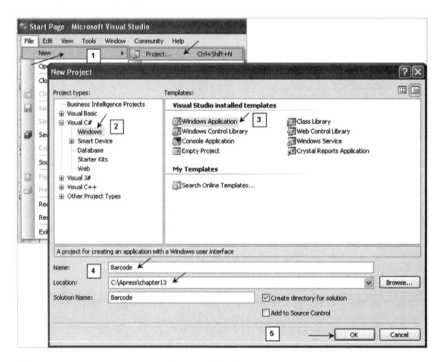

Figure 13-2. *Create a new Windows application.*

If you face difficulty creating the Windows forms application project, then I'd advise you to revisit Chapter 4 for detailed instructions. Let's move on and add the dataset and ReportViewer to the project. Let's start by selecting the project in Solution Explorer, right-clicking it, and selecting Add ➤ New Item ➤ DataSet. Please name the dataset `dsBarcode`.

Before you add the ReportViewer, please make sure Form1 is open in the designer. Now, let's add the ReportViewer to the project by dragging Data ➤ ReportViewer from the toolbox and dropping it onto the form.

Please make sure you set the properties in Table 13-2. After you specify all the properties, your Form1 should look similar to Figure 13-3.

Table 13-2. *Property Settings for the Barcode Project*

Object	Property	Value
Form1	Text	Barcode third-party control example
Form1	Size	790, 500
reportViewer1	Dock	Fill

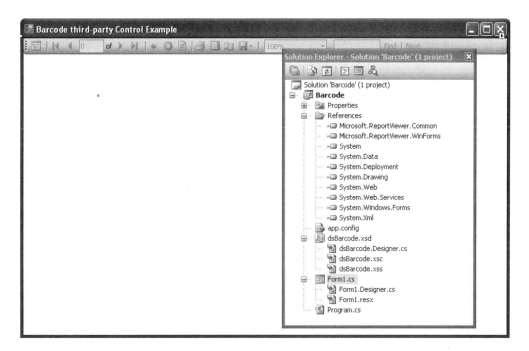

Figure 13-3. *The project after adding the dataset and ReportViewer*

Step 1: Creating a Data Table

Since we already have the dataset in the project, it's time to add a data table to it. Please use the following steps to add a data table inside the dataset:

1. You can go to the dataset designer in two ways: double-click dsBarcode inside Solution Explorer, or right-click the dsBarcode node and select View Designer.

2. Let's add the data table by right-clicking the design surface and selecting Add ➤ DataTable.

3. Click the header of the newly created data table, and name it dtBarcode. Let's start adding columns to dtBarcode by right-clicking the data table and selecting Add ➤ Column.

4. Please add the following columns into the data table, which should then look similar to Figure 13-4:

   - ProductID (System.Int32)

   - Name (System.String)

   - Description (System.String)

Figure 13-4. *Final look of the data table dtBarcode*

Step 2: Designing the Report Layout

Let's take a moment to analyze the report layout shown in Figure 13-1. The report lists information in three different columns. What makes this report interesting is the first column; instead of a numeric ProductID, we will see sophisticated barcode. The second interesting feature of this report is the interactive sorting ability on Product Name column.

We're all set to start working on designing the report layout. Let's add the report by selecting the project in Solution Explorer, right-clicking it, and selecting Add ➤ New Item. Next, select Report from the Add New Item dialog box. Please name the report rptBarcode.rdlc. Click the Add button to complete the process and make a new report part of the project.

Adding the Header

Let's add the Header to the report. As usual, adding a header is as simple as right-clicking the open area inside the report designer and selecting Page Header. After completing the action your report design surface should look similar to the one shown in Figure 13-5.

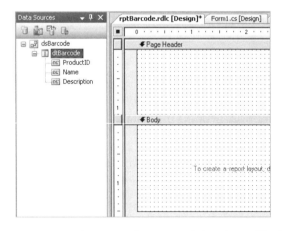

Figure 13-5. *The report designer with header and body sections*

Setting Up the Page

According to the business case needs, let's set up the page. We need to make sure the report is letter sized and has portrait page orientation. Right-click the open area inside the design surface, and select Properties; you may wish to put your name in the Author field and add information to the Description field.

Designing the Page Header

Now, we have the header and the body sections added to our report. Though you may decide to work on any of them first, as we always do, let's start with the header. Please drag and drop the following report items from the toolbox and drop them inside the header section:

- TextBox item for the report title

- TextBox item for the report date

Recall that report item properties are changed by right-clicking the report item and selecting Properties or by accessing the general properties toolbox. Let's change the properties now; after selecting each text box, specify the value for each according to Table 13-3.

Table 13-3. *Report Item Properties for the Header*

Report Item	Property	Value
textbox1		
	Name	txtReportTitle
	Value	Barcode Product List Report
	Font	Italic, Arial, 10pt, Bold
textbox2		
	Name	txtDate
	Value	= "Print Date: " & Today

Designing the Body Section

Let's start working on the body section by dragging Report Items ➤ Table from the toolbox and dropping it inside the body section on the report designer. A new table item is part of the report now, and it has the default name of table1. Since we have three columns in this table, which are added by default, we don't need to add additional columns for this report.

As usual, you can take care of mapping data table columns to text boxes by typing an expression or dragging and dropping from the data source. Let's select Data Source ➤ dsBarcode ➤ ProductName and drag and drop it inside the second column of the table's detail section. Please repeat this step to fill the Description column. I know what you are thinking, "What happened to first column?" Well, I want you to drag Image from Toolbox ➤ Report Items and drop it into the first column. Please make sure your report design surface looks similar to the one shown in Figure 13-6.

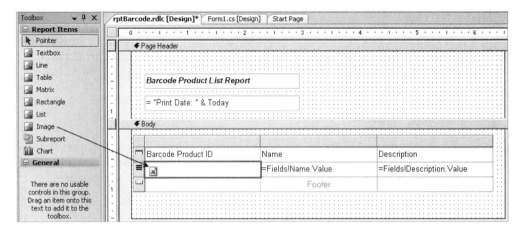

Figure 13-6. *The report designer after adding the header and body and table*

You are probably thinking, "What is this image item doing inside the first column of `table1`?" Well, since a barcode is nothing but an image generated by Neodynamic's tool, we need the image item to display the equivalent of `ProductID` as that barcode image. It might sound complex to you now, but wait until you see the property settings and code involved. You'll be amazed at how simple it is to generate barcodes.

Before we proceed, set the properties of the image item according to Table 13-4.

Table 13-4. *Image Item Properties for the First Column (ProductID)*

Property	Value
Source	`Database`
Sizing	`AutoSize`
MIMEType	`Image/Png`
Value	`=Code.GetBarcode(Fields!ProductID.Value.ToString)`

So, you might be wondering what this MIMEType property is. The barcode tool generates results in different graphical formats. For this report, we're going to use the `.png` image format. To display the barcode correctly, we have to tell the image item to handle graphics of this type. The Value property is a call to the Neodynamic assembly that takes our `ProductID` as input and returns its barcode equivalent.

All right, are we ready to write some C# code now? Well, not yet. We still have to perform one important setting. That is, to make reference to the Neodynamic assembly and write a `GetBarcode` function.

Adding reference to the barcode assembly is easy; see Figure 13-7 for an illustration of the steps:

1. Right-click an open area in the report designer, and select Properties.

2. In the Properties dialog box select the References tab, and click the add assembly button (the button is labeled with two dots).

3. In the Add Reference dialog box, select Assembly Neodynamic Barcode Professional 4.0.

4. Click the Add button.

5. Click the OK button to finish the process.

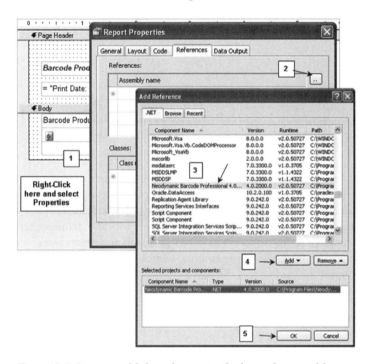

Figure 13-7. *Steps to add the reference to the barcode assembly*

After you finish adding the assembly reference, you will be redirected to the Report Properties dialog box, where you'll notice that the Neodynamic assembly is properly referenced in the report. Now, we need to create an instance of the barcode tool and name it objBarcode. The class reference should be Neodynamic.ReportingServices.Barcode. Please make sure your final report properties look similar to the ones shown in Figure 13-8.

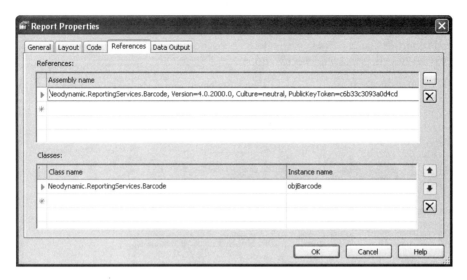

Figure 13-8. *Final look of report references properties*

As you can see in Figure 13-8, we need to make reference to the barcode assembly to start the integration. Once a reference is established, we need to know which class to use for barcode generation. In this case, we are going to use the Neodynamic.ReportingServices.Barcode class. Before we make a call to this class, we need to instantiate it with the name objBarcode.

All right, with the reference setup complete now, let's go ahead and create our custom function GetBarcode, which we need to allow our report to interact with the barcode tool. You can write custom code under the Code tab of the Report Properties dialog box (see Figure 13-9). Please add the following code into the Report Properties Code section:

```
Public Function GetBarcode(ByVal code As String) As Byte()
    'Set the value to encode
    objBarcode.Code = code
    'Set the Industrial 2 of 5 Barcode Symbology
    objBarcode.Symbology = Neodynamic.ReportingServices.Symbology.Industrial2of5
    'Set the Bar's height to 20 px
    objBarcode.BarHeight = 0.2
    'Hide the value to encode in the barcode image
    objBarcode.DisplayCode = False
    'Generate the barcode image
    Return objBarcode.GetBarcodeImagePng()
End Function
```

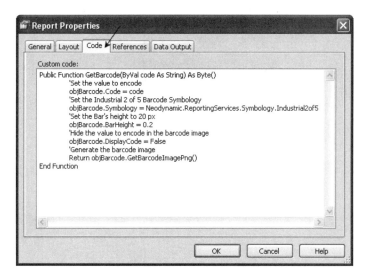

Figure 13-9. *Custom code to interact with the barcode assembly*

You might be wondering why the code in Figure 13-9 is inside the report instead of in Form1. The reason is simply that we are making a call to the barcode generation assembly dynamically during the rendering of the report—notice that our custom code calls the GetBarcodeImagePng() method from the assembly to return the barcode image in .png format.

Let's move on to introduce interactive sorting to the second column, that is, Name. Setting interactive sort is simple; just use the following steps, illustrated in Figure 13-10:

1. Right-click the Name column header, and select Properties.

2. In the Properties dialog box, select the Interactive Sort tab.

3. Click the "Add an interactive sort action on this textbox" check box.

4. In the "Sort expression" field, please select =Fields!Name.Value from the list.

5. Click the OK button to finish the process.

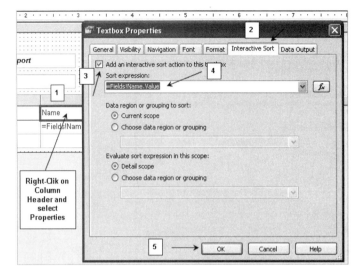

Figure 13-10. *Steps to add interactive sorting*

Step 3: Writing the C# Code

Well, that's all we need on the report design front, so add the following code behind Form1.cs to see the barcode report in action:

```csharp
using System;
using System.Collections.Generic;
using System.ComponentModel;
using System.Data;
using System.Drawing;
using System.Text;
using System.Windows.Forms;
using System.Data.SqlClient;
using Microsoft.Reporting.WinForms;

namespace Barcode
{
    public partial class Form1 : Form
    {
        public Form1()
        {
            InitializeComponent();
        }
```

```
private void Form1_Load(object sender, EventArgs e)
{
    //making Neodynamic assembly trusted
    this.reportViewer1.LocalReport.AddTrustedCodeModuleInCurrentAppDomain(
        "Neodynamic.ReportingServices.Barcode,➥
         Version=4.0.2000.0,Culture=neutral,➥
        PublicKeyToken=c6b33c3093a0d4cd");

    // connection string
    string cnString = @"Data Source=(local);Initial Catalog=RealWorld;➥
        Integrated Security=SSPI;";

    SqlConnection  conReport = new SqlConnection(cnString);
    SqlCommand cmdReport = new SqlCommand();
    SqlDataReader drReport;

    DataSet dsReport = new dsBarcode();

    try
    {
        // open connection
        conReport.Open();

        cmdReport.CommandType = CommandType.Text;
        cmdReport.Connection = conReport;

        // get query string from string builder
        cmdReport.CommandText = "SELECT * FROM tblBarcode";

        // execute query and load result to dataset
        drReport = cmdReport.ExecuteReader();
        dsReport.Tables[0].Load(drReport);

        // close connection
        drReport.Close();
        conReport.Close();

        // prepare report for view
        reportViewer1.LocalReport.ReportEmbeddedResource➥
            = "Barcode.rptBarcode.rdlc";
        ReportDataSource rds = new ReportDataSource();
        rds.Name = "dsBarcode_dtBarcode";
        rds.Value = dsReport.Tables[0];
        reportViewer1.LocalReport.DataSources.Add(rds);
```

```
            // preivew the report
            reportViewer1.RefreshReport();
        }
        catch (Exception ex)
        {
            MessageBox.Show(ex.Message);
        }
        finally
        {
            if (conReport.State == ConnectionState.Open)
            {
                conReport.Close();
            }
        }
    }
  }
}
```

This code is almost the same as the code we've used in past reporting projects. However, one point I want to make here involves the use of `this.reportViewer1.` `LocalReport.AddTrustedCodeModuleInCurrentAppDomain`.

We need to call this method to ensure that our application fully trusts the barcode assembly, which we registered in the GAC earlier. If we don't mention this in the code behind `Form1`, we'll get a run-time error displaying the assembly trust complaint.

Building the Project

It's time to build the project now. You can click the small, green play button in the main tool-box or press F5 on the keyboard to start the application in run-time mode. If the program compiles without any errors, you will see the form with the report in preview mode. Please make sure the report looks similar to the one in Figure 13-1.

Did you notice upward- and downward-facing arrow icons next to the Name column in the report preview? These are the result of enabling the interactive sort on this column. Feel free to click them to see how report output is sorted in ascending and descending order.

■**Note** You'll notice the word "trial" appears with each barcode image. This is because I'm using the trial version of the software. If you buy the full version, this message will disappear.

Creating a Personal Dashboard

Who doesn't like fun? So far we have used client-side RS to create serious business reports. But RS can be used for fun too. Let's put together a quick dashboard that will show you how. I'm sure the word dashboard is familiar to all of us: basically, a dashboard is a collection of information that is put together in one place for a quick glance.

So, in this section, I'll show you how to create a report that will act as a dashboard for you. This report will consist of a live news feed; you can take it from there and create your own masterpiece. In this example, you will see how to use a custom page setup and RSS news feeds. Are you ready? OK, let's move on and put our dashboard into action.

My Dashboard

A dashboard layout is a personal choice that varies from user to user, so the best report style to use for a dashboard is the free-form style. We're going to make use of one Rectangle report item in this example, which will hold a jazzy logo, and a List report item for the RSS news feed from Yahoo. We will make this dashboard a Windows Forms application sitting on your desktop. You can click it as often you want to get the latest news headlines. When you are finished with this example, your dashboard should look similar to the one shown in Figure 13-11.

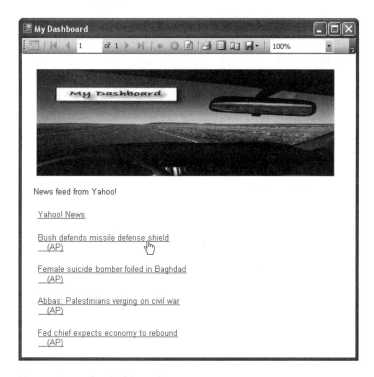

Figure 13-11. *The dashboard*

Getting the Windows Forms Application Ready

Please open Visual Studio, and use the following steps to create a windows application project; Figure 13-2 illustrates these steps:

1. Click File ➤ New ➤ Project, or press the hot keys Ctrl+Shift+N.

2. In the "Project types" pane of the New Project dialog box, select Visual C# ➤ Windows.

3. In the Templates pane, select Windows Application.

4. Please give the application a name; I've called the project MyDashboard. You may choose a different location for storing the application files according to your preference.

5. Click the OK button to finish the process. After you click OK, Visual Studio will create a new Windows application project. You'll also notice that a new form with the name Form1 is part of the project.

As usual, let's add the dataset and ReportViewer to the project. Let's start by selecting the project in Solution Explorer, right-clicking it, and selecting Add ➤ New Item ➤ DataSet. Please name the dataset dsDashboard. Before you add the ReportViewer, please make sure Form1 is open in the designer. Now, add the ReportViewer to the project by dragging Data ➤ ReportViewer from the toolbox and dropping it onto the design surface. Please make sure you set the properties mentioned in Table 13-5.

Table 13-5. *Property Settings for the MyDashboard Project*

Object	Property	Value
Form1	Text	My Dashboard
Form1	Size	790, 500
reportViewer1	Dock	Fill

Step 1: Creating a Data Table

Since we already have the dataset in the project, it's time to add a data table to it. Please use the following steps to add a data table inside the dataset:

1. You can go to the dataset designer in two ways: double-click dsDashboard inside Solution Explorer, or right-click dsDashboard node and select View Designer.

2. To add the data table, right-click the design surface, and select Add ➤ DataTable.

3. Click the header of the newly created data table, and name it dtDashboard. Add columns to dtDashboard by right-clicking DataTable and selecting Add ➤ Column.

4. Add the following columns into the data table; your data table should look like Figure 13-12:

   • NewsTitle (System.String)

   • NewsLink (System.Double)

Figure 13-12. *Final look of the data table dtDashboard*

Step 2: Designing the Report Layout

We're all set to start designing the report layout. Let's start by adding the report: select the project in Solution Explorer, right-click it, and select Add ➤ New Item. Then, select Report from the Add New Item dialog box. Name the report rptDashboard.rdlc, and click the Add button to complete the process and add a new report to the project.

Setting Up the Page

So far in this book, we have used the letter-size page and either a landscape or portrait page orientation. For this report, we will use a custom page setup. Instead of using our regular letter size, we will use a page setup that is 5 × 4 inches. Let's set up the page: Right-click the open area inside the design surface, and select Properties. Under the Layout tab of the Report Properties dialog box, set the page width and height to 4 and 5 inches, respectively. I'd also like you to set the top, bottom, left, and right margins to zero. Please make sure your page layout settings looks similar to the ones shown in Figure 13-13.

Figure 13-13. *Our custom page setup*

Designing the Body Section

As you can see in the design shown in Figure 13-14, all report items are inside the body section. Let's start with the rectangle item, which holds our logo. Start by dragging Report Items ➤ Rectangle from the toolbox and dropping it inside the body section on the report designer. Next, drag and drop an image item inside the rectangle item.

Let's take care of the RSS news feed section. For this section, we need two text box items and one list item. First, drag and drop the text box item, and add the list item. Once the list item is on the design surface, drag and drop the second text box item inside the list item.

Please set the properties of the various report items according to values specified in Table 13-6.

Table 13-6. *Report Item Properties for the Body Section*

Report Item	Property	Value
image1		
	MIMEType	image/jpeg
	Sizing	Fit
	Font	Italic, Times New Roman, 14pt, Bold
	Source	External
	Value	file:C:\Apress\chapter13\MyDashboard\MyDashboard\ dashboard.jpg
Textbox1		
	Value	News feed from Yahoo!
List1		
	DataSetName	dsDashboard_dtDashboard
NewsTitle		
	Value	=Fields!NewsTitle.Value
	Color	Blue
	TextDecoration	Underline

Please make sure your final design looks similar to Figure 13-14.

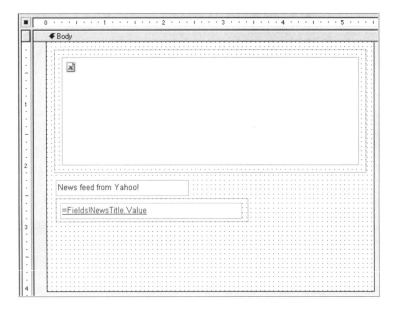

Figure 13-14. *The report designer with all report items for the dashboard*

Did you notice, in Figure 13-14, that the news title from the RSS feed looks like a link that we can click? Well, to achieve this, we need to do two steps. The first step is to set the TextDecoration property of the text box to Underline.

The second step is to instruct the text box to jump to the underlying resource when the user clicks it. This is simple to do; you select the NewsTitle text box and right-click it to access the Properties window. Once inside the Properties window, select the Navigation tab (see Figure 13-15), and select the Jump to URL radio button. Next, either type or select =Fields!NewsLink.Value (the link to the actual news item from the Yahoo web site) as the value for that option.

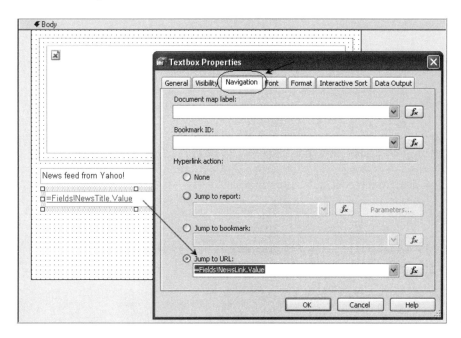

Figure 13-15. *Setting up the Jump to URL property of the text box item*

Step 3: Writing the C# Code

Well, that's all we need on the front end of the report design. Let's add the following code behind Form1.cs to make our dashboard work:

```
using System;
using System.Collections.Generic;
using System.ComponentModel;
using System.Data;
using System.Drawing;
using System.Text;
using System.Windows.Forms;
using System.Xml;
using Microsoft.Reporting.WinForms;
```

```
namespace MyDashboard
{
    public partial class Form1 : Form
    {
        public Form1()
        {
            InitializeComponent();
        }

        private void Form1_Load(object sender, EventArgs e)
        {

            System.Uri uri = new Uri(@"http://rss.news.yahoo.com/rss/topstories");

            XmlDocument doc = new XmlDocument();
            using (XmlReader reader = XmlReader.Create(uri.ToString()))
            {
                doc.Load(reader);
                reader.Close();
            }

            XmlNodeList title = doc.GetElementsByTagName("title");
            XmlNodeList link = doc.GetElementsByTagName("link");

            // get reference of typed DataSet
            dsDashboard dsRSS = new dsDashboard();

            // get row information from typed DataSet
            dsDashboard.dtDashboardRow dtRSS;

            // add four rows to DataSet
            for (int i = 1; i < 6; ++i)
            {
                dtRSS = dsRSS.dtDashboard.NewdtDashboardRow();
                dtRSS.NewsTitle = title[i].InnerText;
                dtRSS.NewsLink = link[i].InnerText;
                dsRSS.dtDashboard.AdddtDashboardRow(dtRSS);
            }

            // Specify report path
            reportViewer1.LocalReport.ReportEmbeddedResource =➥
                "MyDashboard.rptDashboard.rdlc";
            ReportDataSource rds = new ReportDataSource();

            reportViewer1.LocalReport.EnableExternalImages = true;
            reportViewer1.LocalReport.EnableHyperlinks = true;
```

```
            rds.Name = "dsDashboard_dtDashboard";
            rds.Value = dsRSS.Tables[0];
            reportViewer1.LocalReport.DataSources.Add(rds);
            reportViewer1.RefreshReport();
        }
    }
}
```

Before we start to build our project, let's take a quick look at the code. The code here will look a little different, as it has a section that deals with the interaction with the RSS feed, which comes in an XML format. We begin by establishing the link to the Yahoo site to get the feed and storing it as XMLDocument.

Once we have XMLDocument ready, we need to extract the XML nodes that we're interested in, which are title and link. Using the for loop, we store the first four news items from the feed into the dataset. You'll notice that the loop starts with 1 (instead of being zero referenced), because the first link from the feed is not the actual news item; it is just the header. After getting the dataset ready, all that's left is to bind the dataset and render the report.

However, I'd like to mention the following two lines of code:

```
            reportViewer1.LocalReport.EnableExternalImages = true;
            reportViewer1.LocalReport.EnableHyperlinks = true;
```

The first line will allow the image control to access the external image. The second line enables the hyperlinks, so that a user can click the news item to see the selected news item from the Yahoo site in a browser window.

Building the Project

It's time to build the project now. You can click the small, green play button in the main toolbox or press F5 on the keyboard to start the application in run-time mode. If the program compiles without any errors, you will see the form with the report in preview mode. Please make sure the report looks similar the one shown in Figure 13-11.

Summary

In this chapter, you learned how to integrate third-party controls with client-side RS and how we can make use of RS to create a free-form report with live RSS feeds.

Starting with the next chapter, we will dip into the world of Visual Studio 2008. We'll develop a report using the Windows Forms and Web Forms applications.

CHAPTER 14

■■■

Reporting with Visual Studio 2008 Windows Forms

In the past 13 chapters, you saw RS in action with a variety of different clients and learned various techniques for developing cool reports. Chapter 13 concluded our discussion of client-side RS, but there is one last topic we still have to look into—developing reports with Visual Studio 2008 (yes, the release after VS 2005).

"Orcas" was the codename for the upcoming release of Visual Studio. As I was working on this book, VS 2008 was still in community preview, and stable client-side RS functionality was provided in the beta 1 release of VS 2008. Therefore, I decided to include two chapters to let you know how VS 2008 interacts with client-side RS.

I'm sure many questions might be popping up in your mind now. How different is report development in VS 2008 compared with VS 2005? Can I use the knowledge from the past 13 chapters to my advantage and develop similar reports with VS 2008? Not to worry! The good news is almost all the reports we developed so far can be created with VS 2008 in a similar fashion. To prove it, I'll show you how to develop VS 2008 reports with Windows Forms in this chapter, and in the last chapter of this book, you'll learn to develop reports with VS 2008 using ASP.NET Web Forms.

This chapter will cover

- Developing VS 2008 reports using Windows Forms

- Developing reports using Report Wizard

Developing VS 2008 Reports Using Windows Forms

The steps needed to create a Windows Forms client with VS 2008 are similar to those for creating with one with VS 2005. Sure, there will be some product enhancements in VS 2008. However, both the IDEs are much the same when it comes to developing the client-side reports. One cool addition to VS 2008 is Report Wizard; the next section of this chapter shows Report Wizard in action!

Product Profitability Report

You're working for AdventureWorks, Incorporated as a developer. You have the task of developing a Product Profitability report. Along with product pricing details, you also need to show profit on each product as an individual pie chart. The report should meet all the characteristics described in Table 14-1, and the report output should match Figure 14-1.

Table 14-1. *Report Characteristics*

Characteristics	Value
Report title	Product Profitability Report
Company title	AdventureWorks Inc.
Print date	Yes
Page number	Yes (Page: n/n)
Data source	`tblProductProfit`
Columns to report	`ProductName, ListPrice, CostPrice, ProfitAmount`
Page size	Letter
Page orientation	Portrait
Layout design	Header and body sections

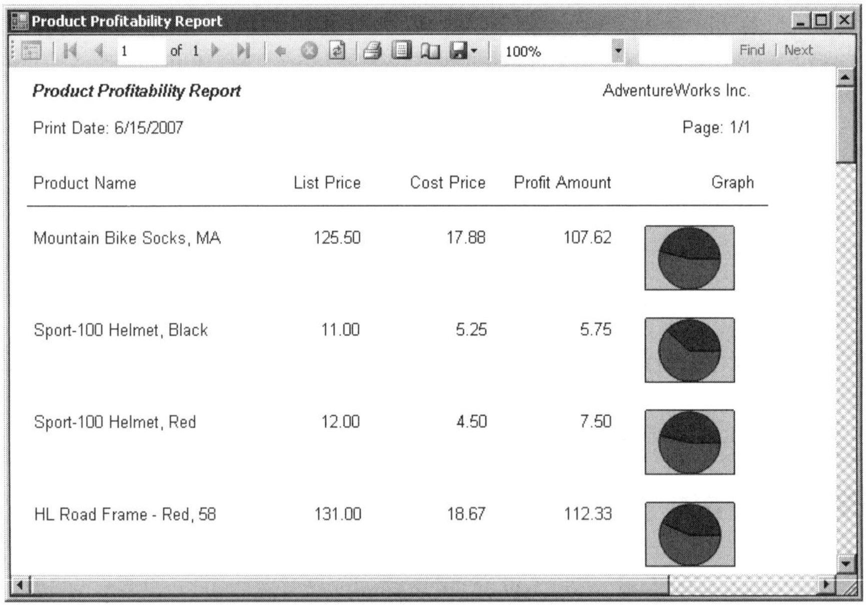

Figure 14-1. *The Product Profitability report*

Business Case

We know the prime objective of business is to make a profit. Every product has a base cost, which is the cost of the purchase, the cost of the manufacturing, or both. Businesses must set a list price for the product that includes the profit markup on top of the cost.

Folks in sales and marketing departments especially look for reports like the Product Profitability report to check on how much profit margin each product contributes. This report also helps them to make important decisions, like adjusting the list price for big orders to attain a suitable profit.

Getting the Windows Forms Application Ready

Please open Visual Studio, and use the following steps, illustrated in Figure 14-2, to create a Windows application project:

1. Click File ➤ New ➤ Project, or press the hot keys Ctrl+Shift+N.

2. In the "Project types" pane of the New Project dialog box, select Visual C# ➤ Windows.

3. In the Templates pane, select Windows Forms Application.

4. Please give the application a name; I've called the project ProductProfit. You may choose a different location for storing the application files according to your preference. Visual Studio 2008 lets you choose your target .NET Framework; I want you to select .NET Framework 2.0, as we have used this framework through this book (it is OK to choose 3.0 or 3.5 also if you wish to create the Windows Forms application).

5. Click the OK button to finish the process. After you click OK, Visual Studio will create a new Windows Forms application project. You'll also notice that a new form with the name Form1 is part of the project.

Similar to the way we did in the past reporting projects, its time to add the dataset and ReportViewer. Let's start by selecting the project in Solution Explorer, right-clicking it, and selecting Add ➤ New Item ➤ DataSet. Please name the dataset dsProductProfit. Before you add the ReportViewer, please make sure that Form1 is open in the designer. Now, add the ReportViewer to the project by dragging Data ➤ ReportViewer from the toolbox and dropping it onto the design surface.

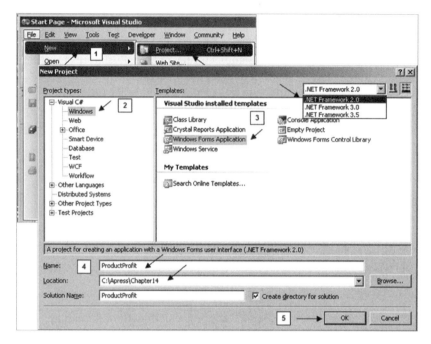

Figure 14-2. *Creating a new Windows application*

Please make sure you set the properties in Table 14-2. After you specify all the properties, your Form1 should look similar to Figure 14-3.

Table 14-2. *Property Settings for ProductProfit Project*

Object	Property	Value
Form1	Text	Product Profitability Report
Form1	Size	790, 500
reportViewer1	Dock	Fill

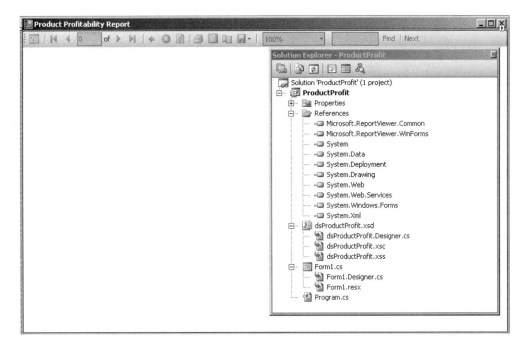

Figure 14-3. *The project after adding the dataset and ReportViewer*

Step 1: Creating a Data Table

Since we already have the dataset in the project, it's time to add a data table to it. Please use the following steps to add a data table inside the dataset:

1. You can go to the dataset designer in two ways: double-click dsProductProfit inside Solution Explorer, or right-click the dsProductProfit node and select View Designer.

2. Let's add the data table by right-clicking the design surface and selecting Add ➤ DataTable.

3. Click the header of the newly created data table, and name it dtProductProfit. Let's start adding columns to dtProductProfit by right-clicking the data table and selecting Add ➤ Column.

4. Please add the following columns into the data table, which should then look similar to Figure 14-4:

   - ProductName (System.String)

   - ListPrice (System.Double)

   - CostPrice (System. Double)

   - ProfitAmount (System. Double)

Figure 14-4. *Final look of the data table dtProductProfit*

Step 2: Designing the Report Layout

Before we start with the layout design for the report, let's take a moment to analyze the report layout shown in Figure 14-1. The report lists information consisting of four different columns. What makes this report interesting are the individual pie charts showing the profit ratio for each of the products.

We're all set to work on designing the report layout. Let's start adding the report by selecting the project in Solution Explorer, right-clicking it, and selecting Add ➤ New Item. Select Report in the Add New Item dialog box. Please name the report rptProductProfit.rdlc. Click the Add button to complete the process and add a new report to the project.

Adding a Header

Let's add the header to the report. As usual, adding a header is simple; all you have to do is right-click the open area inside the report designer and select Page Header. After completing the action, your report design surface should look similar to the one shown in Figure 14-5.

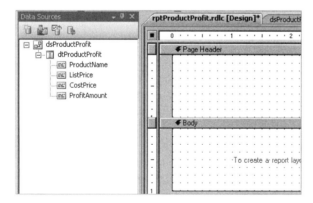

Figure 14-5. *The report designer with header and body sections*

Setting Up the Page

According to the report's needs, let's set up the page. We need to make sure the report is letter size and has a portrait page orientation. Right-click the open area inside the design surface, and select Properties; you may wish to put your name in the Author field and information about the report in the Description field.

Designing the Page Header

Now, we have the header and the body sections added to our report. As usual, you may decide to work on any of them first; but as we do always, let's work on the header first. Please drag the following report items from the toolbox and drop them inside the header section:

- TextBox item for the report title

- TextBox item for the company title

- TextBox item for the report date

- TextBox item for the page number

- TextBox item for the product name heading

- TextBox item for the list price heading

- TextBox item for the cost price heading

- TextBox item for the profit amount heading

- TextBox item for the graph heading

Report item properties are changed by right-clicking the report item and selecting Properties or by accessing the general properties toolbox. Let's start changing the properties; after selecting each of the text boxes, please specify the values for each according to Table 14-3.

Table 14-3. *Report Item Properties for the Header*

Report Item	Property	Value
textbox1		
	Value	Product Profitability Report
	Font	Italic, Arial, 10pt, Bold
textbox2		
	Value	AdventureWorks Inc.
	TextAlign	Right
textbox3		
	Value	= "Print Date: " & Today
textbox4		
	Value	="Page: " & Globals!PageNumber & "/" & Globals!TotalPages
	TextAlign	Right
textbox5		
	Value	Product Name
textbox6		
	Value	List Price
textbox7		

Continued

Table 14-3. *Continued*

Report Item	Property	Value
	Value	Cost Price
textbox8		
	Value	Profit Amount
textbox9		
	Value	Graph
	Format	N
textbox6 to textbox9		
	TextAlign	Right
textbox6 to textbox8		
	Format	N

Designing the Body Section

A table report item is the usual choice for tabular reports like this. However, this time, I'll show you how you can use a list report item for a tabular format report. Let's start by dragging Report Items ➤ List from the toolbox and dropping it inside the body section on the report designer to add a new list item with the default name of list1 to the report.

When you use a list item, all you get is a container into which you can drop other report items for the list. Therefore, to display a list of products and prices, we need a text box inside the newly added list. As you did for this report header, drag and drop four text boxes inside list1. Please make sure to align them according to their headings, which we already put in the header section. Your report design should look similar to the one shown in Figure 14-6.

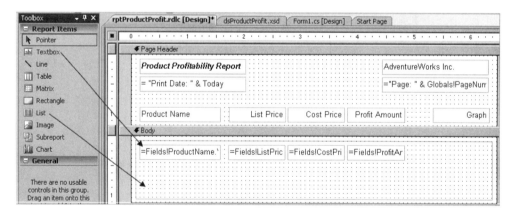

Figure 14-6. *The report designer after adding the list and its text boxes*

You're probably wondering where the pie chart is. Well, in the next section we are going to add the pie chart. First, let's properly set all properties of the text boxes inside list1. Please make sure all text box values match those in Table 14-4.

Table 14-4. *Text Box Values Inside list1*

List Detail Textbox	Value
Product Name	=Fields!ProductName.Value
List Price	=Fields!ListPrice.Value
Cost Price	=Fields!CostPrice.Value
Profit Amount	=Fields!ProfitAmount.Value

Add a Chart Report Item to list1

Adding chart items is easy and is the same as adding the text boxes. So, let's drag and drop a chart item inside list1. The first time you drop the chart item, it will increase the size of the Detail section, and it will have a Column type setting. You can change the type by right-clicking the chart item and selecting Chart Type ➤ Pie ➤ Simple Pie.

We need both the List Price and Profit Amount columns' data as plot data for our pie chart. Let's start by dragging Data Source ➤ dsProductProfit ➤ ListPrice from the toolbox and dropping it at the "Drop data fields here" prompt. Please repeat for the ProfitAmount column; make sure your report design surface looks like the one shown in Figure 14-7 after you drop the plotting data on the chart item.

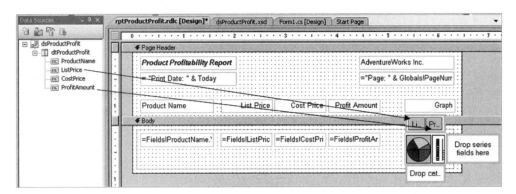

Figure 14-7. *The report designer after specifying plot data on the chart*

When we add the chart item, the legend appears automatically. For this report, we don't need the legend, as the size of chart is small. We can hide the legend by right-clicking the chart item and selecting Properties. Next, select the Legend tab, uncheck "Show legend," and click OK to complete the process. Please see Figure 14-8 for an illustration of these steps.

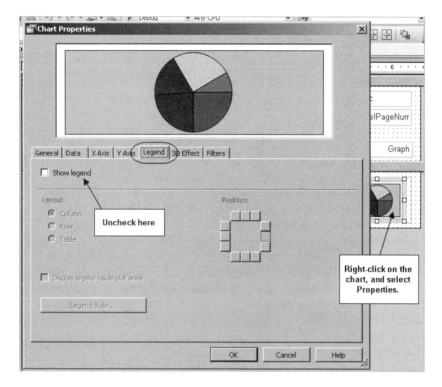

Figure 14-8. *Steps needed to hide the legend*

The last step remaining in the report design is setting up the data grouping for list1. Why do we need grouping here? We need a data group for our chart item, because we are using a data region inside the list report item (so RS needs the group expression). Each row of data from the list will be passed, as a single item from the group, onto a chart for plotting. If you don't set the group, you'll get a run-time error saying, "The Chart chart1 is in a list that has no group expression defined for it." Adding a group to a List Item is simple; the steps are illustrated in Figure 14-9:

1. Right-click the list1 list item, and select Properties.

2. Click the "Edit details group" button.

3. In the Grouping and Sorting Properties dialog box, select the General tab. In the "Group on" section, select =Fields!ProductName.Value for the Expression.

4. Click the OK button to finish the process, and click the OK button once more to close the List Properties dialog box.

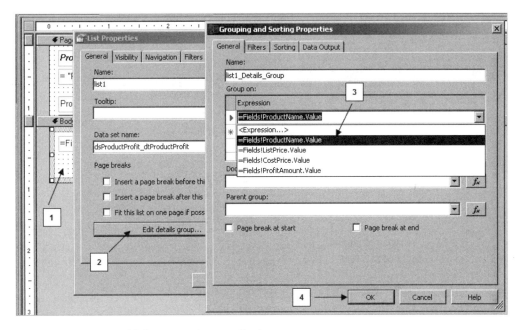

Figure 14-9. *Steps to add data grouping to a list item*

Step 3: Writing the C# Code

Well, that's all we need on the report design front. Let's add the following code behind
Form1.cs to get data and see if we managed to mimic the report:

```
using System;
using System.Collections.Generic;
using System.ComponentModel;
using System.Data;
using System.Drawing;
using System.Text;
using System.Windows.Forms;
using System.Data.SqlClient;
using Microsoft.Reporting.WinForms;

namespace ProductProfit
{
    public partial class Form1 : Form
    {
        public Form1()
        {
            InitializeComponent();
        }
```

```csharp
private void Form1_Load(object sender, EventArgs e)
{
    // connection string
    string cnString = @"Data Source=(local);➥
  Initial Catalog=RealWorld;Integrated Security=SSPI;";

    SqlConnection  conReport = new SqlConnection(cnString);
    SqlCommand cmdReport = new SqlCommand();
    SqlDataReader drReport;

    DataSet dsReport = new dsProductProfit();

    try
    {
        // open connection
        conReport.Open();

        cmdReport.CommandType = CommandType.Text;
        cmdReport.Connection = conReport;

        // get query string from string builder
        cmdReport.CommandText = "SELECT * FROM tblProductProfit";

        // execute query and load result to dataset
        drReport = cmdReport.ExecuteReader();
        dsReport.Tables[0].Load(drReport);

        // close connection
        drReport.Close();
        conReport.Close();

        // prepare report for view
                        reportViewer1.LocalReport.ReportEmbeddedResource =➥
            "ProductProfit.rptProductProfit.rdlc";
        ReportDataSource rds = new ReportDataSource();
        rds.Name = "dsProductProfit_dtProductProfit";
        rds.Value = dsReport.Tables[0];
        reportViewer1.LocalReport.DataSources.Add(rds);

        // preview the report
        reportViewer1.RefreshReport();
    }
    catch (Exception ex)
    {
        MessageBox.Show(ex.Message);
    }
```

```
        finally
        {
            if (conReport.State == ConnectionState.Open)
            {
                conReport.Close();
            }
        }
    }
}
```

The code in this example is similar to what you have seen in past chapters. The only difference here is the SQL statement to connect to the table inside the real-world database.

Building the Project

You can click the small, green play button in the main toolbox or press F5 on the keyboard to start the application in run-time mode. As usual, if the program compiles without any errors, you will see the form with the report in preview mode. Please make sure the report looks similar to the one shown in Figure 14-1.

Did you notice that each profit ratio is neatly present in graphical form? The pie chart has two sets of data plotted—the bigger the Profit Amount plot is, the better the chart looks, right? After all, we do business to generate profit!

Developing a Report Using Report Wizard

One of the new features of the client-side reporting in VS 2008 is Report Wizard. The client-side Report Wizard works just like its server-side RS counterpart. Both beginner and professional developers can benefit from this wizard. For beginners, it is an easy tool to generate reports and later study them. Professional-level developers can use the wizard as a quick way to generate a report based on a template and later change it to suit their needs.

If I was in your seat, I'd be wondering how the wizard is invoked and how to use it. To use the wizard, you have to create a specific new project type, Reports Application project, which will let you develop a report using Report Wizard. This project type also creates a Windows Forms client to test the report. Now, let's create a report in VS 2008 using Report Wizard.

The Report Wizard in Action!

Please open VS 2008, and use the following steps, which are illustrated in Figure 14-10, to create a Reports Application project:

1. Click File ➤ New ➤ Project, or press Ctrl+Shift+N.

2. In the "Project types" pane of the New Project dialog box, select Visual C# ➤ Database.

3. In the Templates pane, select Reports Application.

4. Please name the application; I've called the project ReportWizard. You may choose a different location for storing the application files, if you prefer. VS 2008 lets you choose the target .NET Framework, so select .NET Framework 2.0.

5. Click the OK button to finish the process; VS 2008 will create a new Reports Application project.

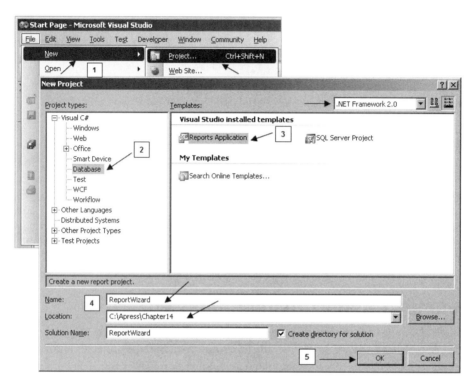

Figure 14-10. *Creating a new Reports Application project*

As soon as you click the OK button to create the Reports Application project, Report Wizard will automatically launch. Like any other wizard you have seen in Microsoft products, this wizard starts with a welcome dialog box (see Figure 14-11).

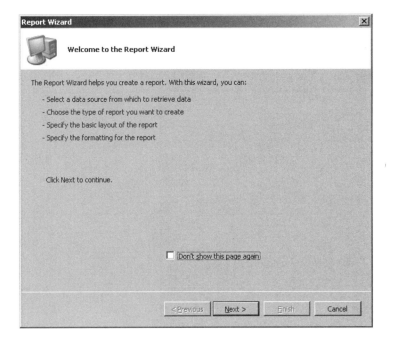

Figure 14-11. *The Report Wizard welcome dialog box*

The Report Wizard's welcome screen has buttons to navigate, complete, and cancel the wizard. It also lists the actions to create a report: setting up the data source, selecting the report type, specifying the layout, and formatting the report. It also has a check box to tell the wizard not to show the welcome page.

■**Note** If you click the Cancel button on the welcome dialog box of the wizard, this action will add an empty report to the project. It is your responsibility, as the developer, to further design this empty report.

Let's move ahead. Click the Next button on the welcome screen of the wizard to progress to specifying the data source; this step is needed for the wizard to know what type of data to gather and where the data is. Your wizard screen should look similar to the one shown in Figure 14-12.

Figure 14-12. *The Report Wizard data source dialog box*

■**Note** You can navigate among wizard screens by clicking on the Previous and the Next buttons.

Which data source should we use here? To keep it simple, we'll use the same tblProductProfit data source that we used earlier in this chapter. In this example, I'm showing you how to connect to a SQL Server data source, but you can also connect to non–SQL Server data sources.

Click the Add Data Source button shown in Figure 14-12. You can select Database, Web Service, or Object as the data source type. Select Database, as shown in Figure 14-13, and click the Next button to move forward.

The next screen in the wizard will ask you to choose your data connection. Please perform the following steps, illustrated in Figure 14-14, to add a new data connection:

1. Click the New Connection button.

2. Select the appropriate server name; in my case I've selected localhost. If your server is not local, you need to set up the connection to your remote SQL instance.

3. Click the "Select or enter the database name" radio button, and use the drop-down list to select your database or type its name in the field. I've selected RealWorld as the database. At this time, you can click the Test Connection button to see if your connection works.

4. Click the OK button to finish adding the data connection.

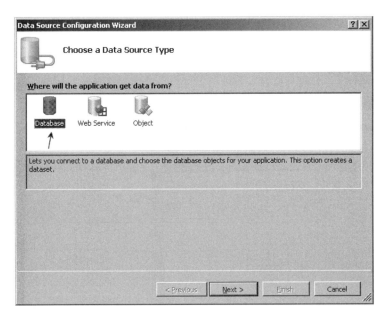

Figure 14-13. *Report Wizard's Choose a Data Source Type screen*

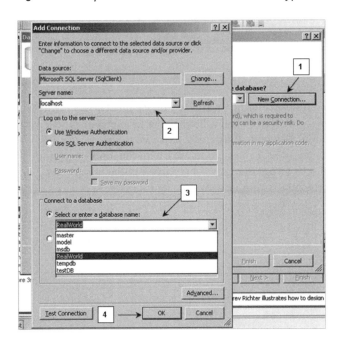

Figure 14-14. *Using Report Wizard to choose a new data connection*

Select the newly created data connection, and click the Next button. The next screen will ask you to save the connection string that you created in the last step. Give a meaningful name to the connection string; I've called it RealWorldConnectionString. Click the Next button to move forward.

This action will take you to the last screen of Report Wizard to manage the data source. This screen is asking you to select the database object that will be used to generate the report. Please select `tblProductProfit` from the Tables section, and click the Finish button to complete the process; see Figure 14-14.

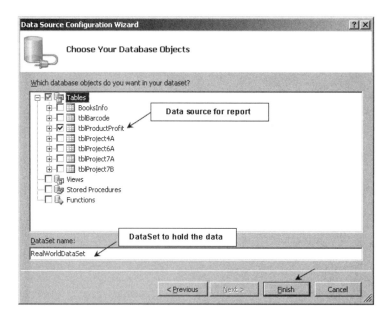

Figure 14-15. *Using Report Wizard to choose database objects*

Now, to move forward and work with the report type and layout, we must select the data source and click the Next button (see Figure 14-16). You will see that a dataset will appear with the data table inside, like when we manually create the dataset and data table.

All right, we have the data source ready. Let's move on to work with the report type and report layout. Report Wizard lets you select from two types of reports: Tabular and Matrix. To keep it simple, let's select Tabular as the report type, as shown in Figure 14-17.

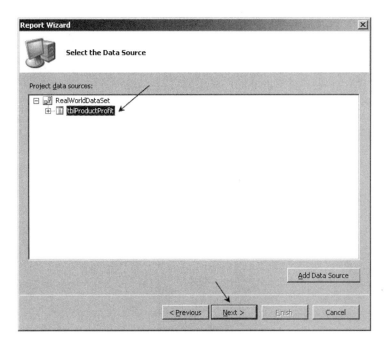

Figure 14-16. *Selecting the newly created data source*

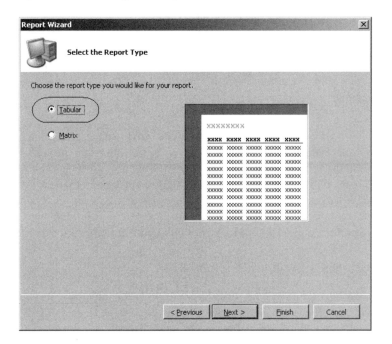

Figure 14-17. *Selecting the report type*

After you select the report type, the next wizard screen will ask you to lay out the data from the data source `tblProductProfit`. I'm using `ProductModel` to group the rest of the information as details. This section of the wizard will let you make use of as many fields as you like from the table on the report design surface. As Figure 14-18 shows, I moved `ProductModel` to the group section; this will create a group inside the table report item. Similarly, all the fields that are moved to the details section will appear as detail rows inside the report.

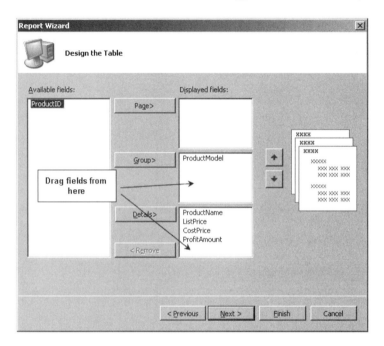

Figure 14-18. *Placing fields from the data table*

After the wizard takes care of assigning the fields from the table into the page, group, and details sections, it is time to work on the table layout. You have two options to select the layout: Stepped and Block. Most of the reports we have done so far have use a stepped layout; that means group output appears with related details inside the group header and footer. Block layout is similar to stepped layout functionally. However, they differ in the output. If you select the block layout, the group and related details appears as a block surrounded by borders. You can toggle between the Stepped and Block layout radio buttons to see dummy previews.

Select the Block layout, and check the "Include subtotals" check box to add subtotals to this report, as shown in Figure 14-19.

After taking care of the table layout, the wizard turns its attention to the table style. As you can see in Figure 14-20, the wizard offers six types of styles. You can go through them and pick the one best suited to your preference; the dummy preview will change as you select each table style. I've selected Corporate as the style for this sample report. Please make a style selection, and click the Next button to move forward.

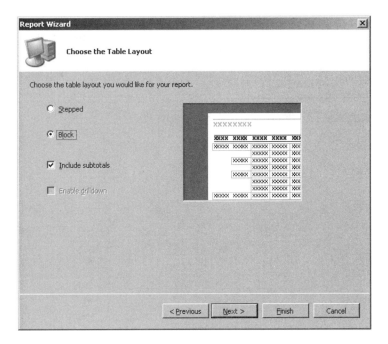

Figure 14-19. *Setting up the table layout*

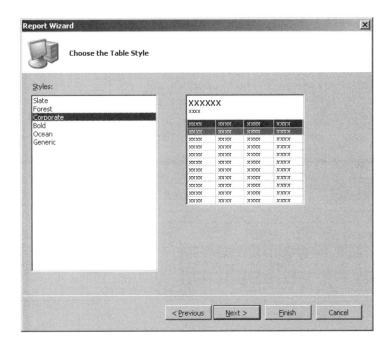

Figure 14-20. *Choosing the table style*

Finally, we have come to the end of the wizard. This last screen is a summary of actions the wizard is performing to generate the report. In this screen, the wizard asks the developer to provide the name of the report. I've given the report the name Sample Report by Wizard. After you set the report name, click the Finish button to complete the wizard. Please see Figure 41-21 for an illustration of the final steps.

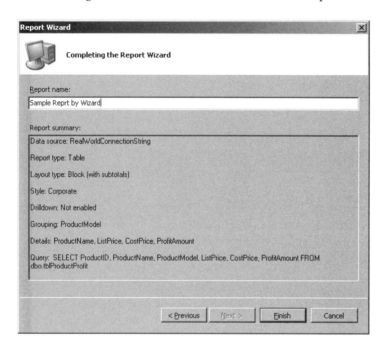

Figure 14-21. *The last screen of the wizard with the report name*

You'll notice that as soon as you click the Finish button, Visual Studio 2008 does some processing to generate the report application. Let's take a look at the report generated by the process; see Figure 14-22.

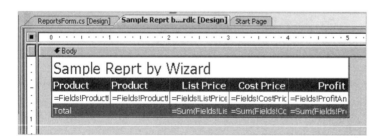

Figure 14-22. *The report in design mode*

As you can see, the wizard has taken all our selections and generated the report. For example, you can see the Corporate style. All the data has the border style set according to our block table layout, which we also selected with the wizard. If you open the report in the report designer and study it, you will see that proper grouping was done on ProductModel.

All right, the report design looks good. How about the other components that this wizard generated? Well, not to worry, the wizard generates everything that is needed to give life to this report—that includes a Windows Forms application with ReportViewer, a dataset, and the related ADO.NET code to query and gather data. In fact, you don't have to write a single line of code or do any tweaking to run this report.

All you need to do now is to build this newly generated report application. You already know how to build, right? You can press F5 on the keyboard or click the green play button in the main toolbar. The application should build successfully, and your output should look similar to Figure 14-23.

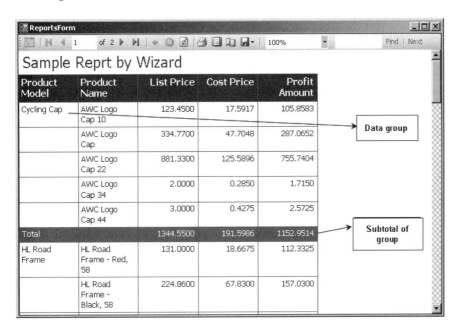

Figure 14-23. *Report output*

As Figure 14-23 shows, the report output has the proper data grouping on ProductModel. You'll also notice that automatic subtotals are available for each group. Since we selected the block table layout, all data appears with blocks with all the borders (top, bottom, right, and left) set. What if you would like to change the color or size of the borders? Well, feel free to modify this report as you do normally. Once the wizard is finished with its process, the ball comes back to your court. You can fine tune the report's look and content according to your requirements.

Summary

In this chapter, you learned how to develop a report with the Visual Studio 2008 Windows Forms client. You also practiced using the new Report Wizard feature to generate reports. Report Wizard is very helpful for generating a report as a template that can be modified with the report designer according to your needs.

In the next chapter, you'll see how you can use Visual Studio 2008 to develop an ASP.NET web site and host reports with it.

CHAPTER 15

■ ■ ■

Reporting with Visual Studio 2008 Web Forms

In Chapter 14, you learned to develop reports using Visual Studio 2008 with Windows Forms. In this chapter, we will look at how to develop the report using Visual Studio 2008 with ASP.NET web forms. Developing VS 2008 reports with web forms is not hugely different from developing VS 2005 Web Forms reports, so you will see similarities between this chapter and Chapter 5, in which you saw VS 2005 Web Forms in action.

As we are developing reports for the new client here, let me also show another reporting technique of RS—the drill-down feature of RS. You'll see how certain parts of a report can be toggled to hide and unhide based on a user's choice. So, what are we waiting for? Let's start.

This chapter will cover creating Visual Studio 2008 reports with ASP.NET web forms by developing a drill-down report.

Product Drill-Down by Category Report

Assume you're working for AdventureWorks Incorporated as a developer. You have the task of developing a Product Drill-Down by Category report. Initially, the report should only show the product categories and the total number of products belonging to each category. Once the user drills down, the report should show a list of products by subcategory. The report should meet all the characteristics described in Table 15-1, and the report output should match Figure 15-1.

Table 15-1. *Report Characteristics*

Characteristics	Value
Report title	Product Drill-down by Category Report
Company title	AdventureWorks Inc.
Page number	Yes (Current Page: n, Total Pages: n)
Data source	ProductDrilldown
Columns to report	ProductNumber, ProductName, CategoryName, SubCategoryName, ListPrice
Page size	Letter
Page orientation	Portrait
Layout design	Header and body sections

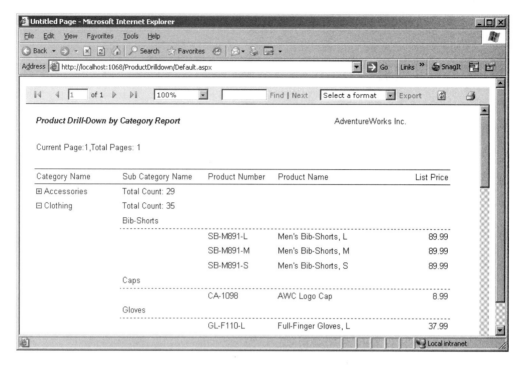

Figure 15-1. *The Product Drill-Down by Category report*

Business Case

A product drill-down report is a common report requested by various departments in organizations. The beauty of a drill-down report is the ability to empower the user to see only the needed information from the output. The other highlight of this report is the ability to show the count of products belonging to each product category.

A user can expand or collapse the group sections to find more details as needed. You might be wondering how it works. Well, with drill-down reports, detail rows are simply hidden and become visible only when a user toggles them.

This is similar to the tree view structure you are familiar with in software commonly in use today (we use this a lot while mapping data columns from the data source). You can toggle a tree node by clicking either the plus (+) or minus (−) symbol on the node to view or hide the underlying details, respectively. In Figure 15-1, a plus sign (+) is displayed to the left of the product category. A user can click the icon, and as a result, the Hidden property of the details row is toggled between true and false.

▪**Note** If you decide to export the drill-down report, it will only work in Excel format. PDF format doesn't support this; the output in the PDF file will be the last state of the report in preview mode, either expanded or collapsed.

Getting the ASP.NET Web Site Ready

Please open Visual Studio, and use the following steps, illustrated in Figure 15-2, to create an ASP.NET Web Site:

1. Click File ➤ New ➤ Web Site.

2. In the Templates pane, select ➤ ASP.NET Web Site.

3. In the Templates pane, select language ➤ Visual C#.

4. Please give the application a name; I've called the project ProductDrilldown. You may choose a different location for storing the application files according to your preference. Also make sure to select .NET Framework 2.0.

5. Click the OK button to finish the process. After you click OK, Visual Studio will create a new ASP.NET Web Site. You'll notice that a new page with the name `Default.aspx` is added to the solution. Please see Figure 15-3 for generated code and a view of Solution Explorer.

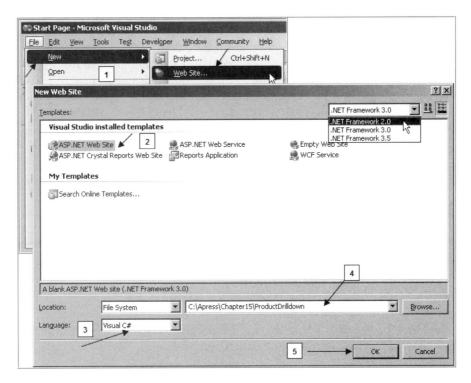

Figure 15-2. *Create a new ASP.NET Web site*

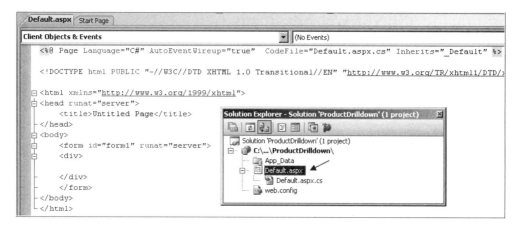

Figure 15-3. *Generated code and view of Solution Explorer*

It's time to add the dataset and ReportViewer. Let's start by selecting the project in Solution Explorer, right-clicking it, and selecting Add ➤ New Item ➤ Dataset. Please name the dataset dsProductDrilldown. You'll notice that Visual Studio will ask you to put the dataset inside the App_Code folder; go ahead and click the Yes button.

Before you add the ReportViewer, please make sure that the Default.aspx page is open in the designer and that HTML source mode is selected. Now, let's add the ReportViewer to the project by dragging Data ➤ ReportViewer from the toolbox and dropping it between the <div> tags. As a result of this action, you'll notice that ReportViewer1 is added to the Default.aspx page, and the generated code will look like the following:

```
<html xmlns="http://www.w3.org/1999/xhtml">
<head runat="server">
    <title>Untitled Page</title>
</head>
<body>
    <form id="form1" runat="server">
    <div>
        <rsweb:ReportViewer ID="ReportViewer1" runat="server" Width="100%">
        </rsweb:ReportViewer>
    </div>
    </form>
</body>
</html>
```

You'll also notice that I've set Width="100%" to make sure the ReportViewer takes the maximum space available on the page to display the report.

Step 1: Creating a Data Table

Use the following steps to add a data table inside the dataset:

1. You can go to the dataset designer in two ways: double-click dsProductDrilldown inside Solution Explorer, or right-click the dsProductDrilldown node and select View Designer.

2. Let's add the data table by right-clicking the design surface and selecting Add ➤ data table.

3. Click the header of the newly created data table, and name it dtProductDrilldown. Let's start adding columns to dtProductDrilldown by right-clicking the data table and selecting Add ➤ Column.

4. Please add the following columns into the data table, which should then look similar to Figure 15-4:

   - ProductNumber (System.String)

   - ProductName (System.String)

   - CategoryName (System.String)

   - SubCategoryName (System.String)

   - UnitsInStock (System.Double)

Figure 15-4. *Final look of the dtProductDrilldown data table*

Step 2: Designing the Report Layout

You must be thinking designing a drill-down report will be a daunting task! Well, although it might looks like one, the process is simple—as simple as adding a few data groups and setting up a few properties.

As you can see in Figure 15-1, the report shows the product category as a tree view that is ready for the user to toggle. Underlying this hidden view is the product subcategory and other information related to the products. Another interesting point here is the use of the Count() function to count the number of products for each product category.

Add the report by selecting the project inside Solution Explorer and right-clicking it; select Add ➤ New Item, and select Report from the Add New Item dialog box. Please name the report rptProductDrilldown.rdlc. Click the Add button to complete the process and make the new report part of the project. You'll also notice that a new toolbox called Data Sources is available with our dataset information inside.

Adding a Header

Let's add the header to the report. As usual, adding a header is simple: right-click the open area inside the report designer and select Page Header. Your report design surface should look similar to Figure 10-5.

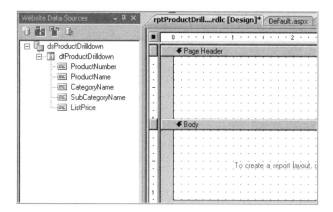

Figure 15-5. *The report design surface with header and body sections*

Setting Up the Page

According to the requirements defined earlier, let's set up the page. We need to make sure the report is letter sized and has a portrait page orientation. Right-click the open area inside the design surface, and select Properties; you may wish to put your name in the Author field and fill in the Description field.

Designing the Page Header

Now, we have the header and the body sections added to our report. Next, please drag and drop the following report items inside the header section:

- Textbox item for the report title

- Textbox item for the company title

- Textbox item for the page number

Report item properties are changed in one of the following ways: you need to select the Report Item, right-click it, and select Properties or access the general properties toolbox. Let's start changing the properties; after selecting each of the text boxes, please specify the values for each report item's properties according to Table 15-2.

Table 15-2. *Report Item Properties for the Header*

Report Item	Property	Value
textbox1		
	Value	Product Drill-Down by Category Report
	Font	Italic, Arial, 10pt, Bold
textbox2		
	Value	AdventureWorks Inc.
	TextAlign	Right
textbox3		
	Value	="Current Page: " & Globals!PageNumber & "," & "Total Pages: " & Globals!TotalPages

Designing the Body Section

Since we need two data groups for this report, we will make use of the table report item. Let's start working on this section by dragging Report Items ➤ Table from the toolbox and dropping it inside the body section in the report designer. A new table item is part of the report now, and it has the default name of table1. To add two more columns, right-click the right-most column header on the table item, and select "Insert Column to the Right". Make sure you have a total of five columns inside table1.

As usual, after adding a table you may choose your favorite method to map the data table's columns to the text box report items: type an expression or drag and drop from the data source.

Drag Data Source ➤ dsProductDrilldown ➤ ProductNumber and drop it inside the third column of the table item's detail section. Why start mapping with the third column? Well, as you can see in Figure 15-1, we are going to use the first two columns only as headers for the product category and subcategory.

Repeat the data mapping task for the rest of the columns in dsProductDrilldown.

As you know, we need to add two data groups to table1. Let's insert the group by selecting the entire detail row (TableRow3) of table1. Once the row is selected, right-click it, and select Insert Group. For the "group on" expression, select or type =Fields!CategoryName.Value. Since we don't need the group footer, please make sure to uncheck the Include Group Footer check box (you may revisit Chapter 4 to learn more about how to work with the table report item). Repeat the same steps to add the product subcategory group. However, this time, for the "group on" expression select or type =Fields!SubCategoryName.Value.

All right, we added the two necessary groups; however, we have not yet set the drill-down behavior of the report, which we need to hide the product subcategory and related production information. Therefore, while creating the group for the product subcategory, we also have to make sure to go to the Visibility tab of the Grouping and Sorting Properties dialog box to set the "Initial visibility" option to Hidden. Check the "Visibility can be toggled by another report item" check box, and select or type textbox9 (a placeholder for the data column of the product category) in the "Report item" field. Please see Figure 15-6 for an illustration of these steps.

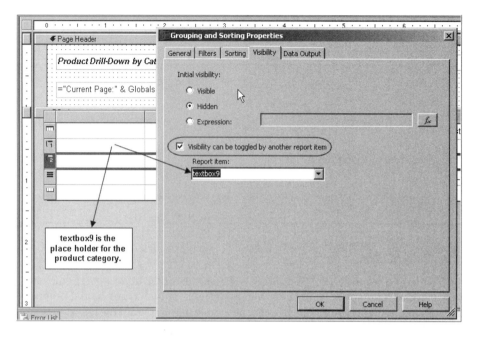

Figure 15-6. *Toggle visibility on the product category to create a drill-down effect.*

That's it; that is what we need to create a drill-down effect. Now, let's move on and take care of headings for the product category and subcategory. Select Data Source ➤ dsProductDrilldown ➤ CategoryName and drag and drop it inside the first column of group header 1. When you drag and drop, the default name of the text box gets changed to the data column name. Therefore, in this case, make sure to change the text box name from CategoryName back to textbox9. This action will also add the group header Category Name automatically. It is your choice to accept it or change the group header according to your needs. Repeat the step to target TableRow3 and the second column for SubCategoryName.

As you know, one of the requirements for the report is the count of products for each product category. We can easily achieve this by specifying the following expression in the second column of TableRow2:

```
="Total Count: " & Count(Fields!SubCategoryName.Value, "table1_Group1")
```

As you can see, we are using the Count() function to include all the subcategories falling under the data group table1_Group1. Please make sure your report design surface looks similar to the one shown in Figure 15-7.

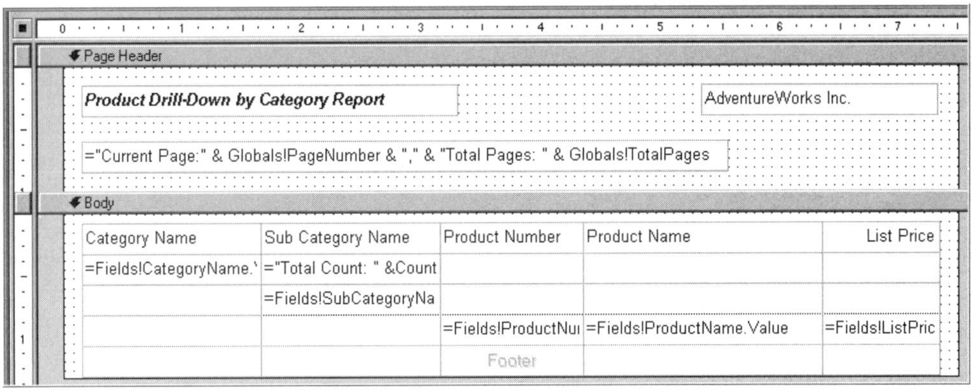

Figure 15-7. *The report designer after adding the header and body sections*

Please make sure all items inside table1 are properly set to property values matching those in Table 15-3.

Table 15-3. *Items Property Values Inside table1*

Item	Property	Value
textbox26	Value	Category Name
textbox4	Value	Sub Category Name
textbox6	Value	Product Number
textbox13	Value	Product Name
textbox16	Value	List Price
textbox16	TextAlign	Right
textbox9	Value	=Fields!CategoryName.Value
textbox14	Value	="Total Count: " & Count(Fields!SubCategoryName.Value, "table1_Group1")
SubCategoryName	Value	=Fields!SubCategoryName.Value
ProductNumber	Value	=Fields!ProductNumber.Value
ProductName	Value	=Fields!ProductName.Value
ListPrice	Value	= Fields!ListValue.Value
ListPrice	Format	N
TableRow1	BorderStyle	None, , , Solid, Solid

Step 3: Writing the C# Code

Well, that's all we need on the front end of report design. Let's add the following code behind the Default.aspx.cs:

```csharp
using System;
using System.Data;
using System.Configuration;
using System.Web;
using System.Web.Security;
using System.Web.UI;
using System.Web.UI.WebControls;
using System.Web.UI.WebControls.WebParts;
using System.Web.UI.HtmlControls;
using System.Data.SqlClient;
using Microsoft.Reporting.WebForms;

public partial class _Default : System.Web.UI.Page
{
    protected void Page_Load(object sender, EventArgs e)
    {
        //Declare connection string
        string cnString = "Data Source=(local);Initial Catalog=RealWorld;➥
                Integrated Security=SSPI;";

        //Declare Connection, command and other related objects
        SqlConnection conReport = new SqlConnection(cnString);
        SqlCommand cmdReport = new SqlCommand();
        SqlDataReader drReport;
        Dataset dsReport = new dsProductDrilldown();

        try
        {
            conReport.Open();

            cmdReport.CommandType = CommandType.Text;
            cmdReport.Connection = conReport;
            cmdReport.CommandText = "Select * FROM dbo.ProductDrilldown ➥
              order by CategoryName,SubCategoryName,ProductNumber";

            drReport = cmdReport.ExecuteReader();
            dsReport.Tables[0].Load(drReport);

            drReport.Close();
            conReport.Close();

            //provide local report information to viewer
            ReportViewer1.LocalReport.ReportPath = "rptProductDrilldown.rdlc";
```

```
            //prepare report data source
            ReportDataSource rds = new ReportDataSource();
            rds.Name = "dsProductDrilldown_dtProductDrilldown";
            rds.Value = dsReport.Tables[0];
            ReportViewer1.LocalReport.DataSources.Add(rds);
        }
        catch (Exception ex)
        {
            //display generic error message back to user
            Response.Write(ex.Message);
        }
        finally
        {
            //check if connection is still open then attempt to close it
            if (conReport.State == ConnectionState.Open)
            {
                conReport.Close();
            }
        }
    }
}
```

The C# code we use in this example is the same ADO.NET interface we have used so far. We connect to the database and execute the query to gather the data. Once data is collected inside the dataset, we bind the dataset to the report. Finally, with the help of the ReportViewer, we have shown the report output to the report user.

Building the Project

Now, it's time to build the project. You can click the small, green play button in the main tool-box or press F5 on the keyboard to start the application in run-time mode. If the program compiles without any errors, you'll see the form with the report in preview mode. Please make sure the report looks similar to Figure 15-1.

Did you notice that each product category is displayed initially, and when you toggle any product category by clicking the plus sign, all the related, hidden product information appears? When you click the minus sign, the product information should disappear again. This form of interactivity helps developers provide a better user experience.

Summary

In this chapter, we looked at two topics. First, we learned how to make use of the Visual Studio 2008 ASP.NET web forms to deliver a report to various clients. Second, we looked at how we can use the drill-down feature of RS to create an interactive report.

I wish I could say, "In next chapter you will learn . . ." However, we have reached the last chapter. I sincerely hope that the material covered in this book helps you to become champion of client-side RS. Happy reporting!

■■■

The Visual Studio 2005 IDE

Although I mentioned in the introduction that a working knowledge of the Visual Studio 2005 IDE is essential for this book, I strongly believe in including a quick walkthrough of it for reference to benefit beginner-level readers. You can go through this appendix to get a refresher on the essentials of the VS 2005 IDE. As you read through this appendix, you'll notice that the menus, toolbars, and windows making up the development interface workspace represent the common UI approach from Microsoft.

Covering every aspect of the IDE is beyond the reach of this book. Therefore, I'm discussing the frequently used aspects that will matter most while developing reports. So, let's get started!

Launching the Visual Studio 2005 IDE

First things first, you need to know how to launch the VS 2005 IDE. You can start by clicking the Windows Start button ➤ All programs ➤ Microsoft Visual Studio 2005. Next, click the Microsoft Visual Studio 2005 icon; the VS 2005 IDE will start.

If you recall, the first time you launched the IDE, you were asked to select the default environment settings. If you selected Visual C# Development Settings, your IDE should look similar to Figure A-1.

As you can see in Figure A-1, the IDE consists of the menus, toolbars, and various Windows. As you use different features of IDE, you'll come across different windows and toolbar choices.

Note If you are starting the IDE for the first time, select Visual C# Development Settings when you're prompted to select default environment settings.

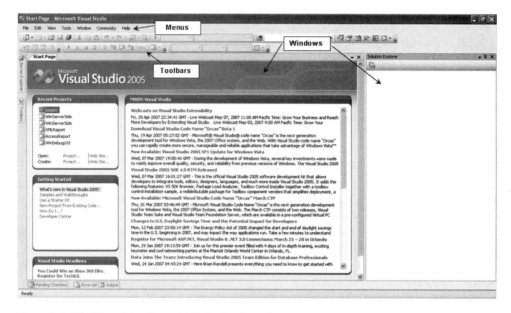

Figure A-1. *The Visual Studio 2005 IDE after launch*

The Structure of the Visual Studio 2005 IDE

The structure of the VS 2005 IDE consists of various components. I'll discuss the three most important ones:

- Menus

- Toolbars

- Windows

When you launch the VS 2005 IDE, the default menu structure is composed of the following seven options (the number varies if your default language is not C#): File, Edit, View, Tools, Window, Community, and Help. The physical location of the menu bar is fixed in the top right-hand corner, unless you dock a toolbar adjacent to it (see Figure A-1).

As you create different clients using the IDE, the menu will dynamically change according to the client selection. Like menus, toolbars have a dynamic nature—they also change according to the choice of the client project you're developing. Additionally, toolbars are not static like menus; you can arrange them and add or remove items from them according to your preference and convenience.

Finally, you'll notice several different windows as you go on developing various reports. Some windows are always part of the project, and some are available only in certain situations. For example, all projects should have the Solution Explorer window (Figure A-1 shows a blank Solution Explorer window). As you know, the structure of IDE changes according to the project; let's look at the basics of the IDE now.

The Basic IDE Structure

Let's explore the basics of the IDE structure using a Windows Forms application project. Please use the following steps to create a Windows application project:

1. Click File ➤ New ➤ Project, or press Ctrl+Shift+N.

2. In the "Project types" pane of the New Project dialog box, select Visual C# ➤ Windows.

3. In the Templates pane, select ➤ Windows Application.

4. You may name the project or leave the default suggestion provided by the IDE (I'm keeping it at the default, WindowsApplication1). Click the OK button to finish the process. Visual Studio 2005 will create a new Windows Forms application project. You'll also notice that a new form with name Form1 is part of the project. Your IDE should look similar to Figure A-2.

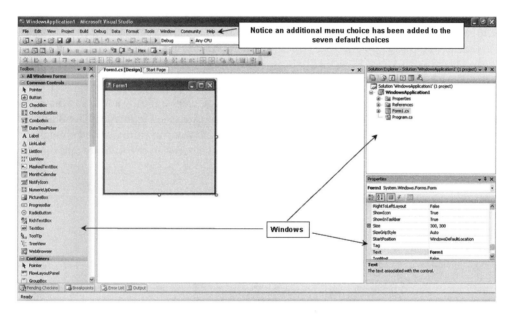

Figure A-2. *The VS 2005 IDE after creating the Windows application project*

Menus

As you can see, the first launch of the IDE has seven menu choices. After we create the Windows Forms project, we get five more choices—12 in total. So, what are those five extra menu options? Well, before we look into them, let's quickly glance at the default seven menu choices.

The File menu consists of choices to manage the various project development activities, like creating a project, opening an existing project, and saving a project.

The Edit menu, as the name suggests, has the choices to manage common editing actions, such as Copy, Cut, Paste, and Undo.

The View menu has the choices to manage the presentation of various components of the IDE. For example, you can hide or unhide a window. You can also have the choice to switch between the design and the code windows.

The most often used choice in the Tools menu is Options, though you also have other selections that allow you to perform activities such as customizing the IDE, working with add-ins, and accessing macros.

The Window menu gives you the facility to manage the various windows in the IDE.

The Community and Help menus are there to help you with your development efforts. The Help menu connects to the online help, to make you more productive. Developers can also interact with others in the community by discussing issues or asking for the help using the Community menu.

Please go through the official Microsoft help documents to learn more details about each of the menu choices.

■**Note** Menu choices change dynamically based on the design-time and run-time mode of IDE.

The five extra menu choices are specific to the Window Forms project. The Project menu choice has the options to manage the project; if you were building a web site instead of a Windows Forms application, this menu would be Website (see Figure A-3). The Build menu is used to make builds of the project, and Debug lets you run through the debugging process. Please see Figure A-3 for the differences in menus between the web site and the Windows Forms projects.

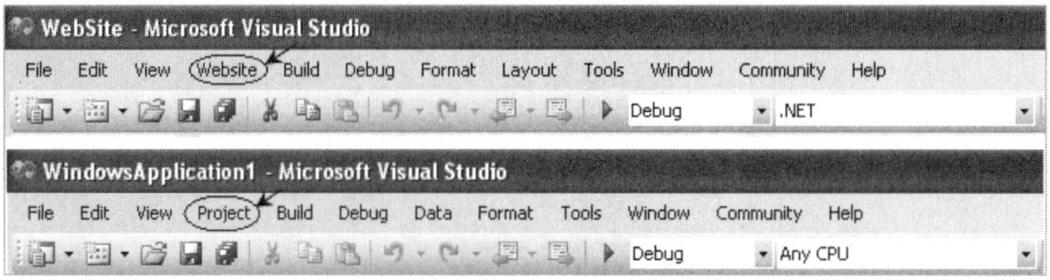

Figure A-3. *Menu choices for web site and Windows Forms projects*

Toolbars

Toolbars provide shortcut methods to perform tasks. For example, if you don't want to click the File menu and then click the Save option, you can do the same task by simply clicking the toolbar icon with a picture of a little blue floppy disk.

When it comes to using the IDE, we all have our own ways. You might like to work with the keyboard best, or you might prefer to use the mouse to the max. Using the toolbars, though, is the most common method to do various tasks during both design time and run time. Almost all common development tasks have a toolbar choice available to improve the user experience.

Toolbars are not static in position like the menus. The most common place for toolbars is immediately under the menu choices, but they can be moved to positions along the right, left, or bottom edges of the IDE. Toolbars can also float. Figure A-3 shows the default position of the standard toolbar.

How you want to place your toolbars is purely your choice. Feel free to adjust them inside the IDE to suit your preference. Toolbars change dynamically based on the mode of the IDE, that is, whether you are working in design-time or run-time mode. Please consult with Microsoft help for more information on the toolbars. Please see Figure A-4 for a typical look of the IDE with various toolbars available to streamline the development process.

Figure A-4: *Three more toolbars in addition to the standard toolbar*

Windows

The Visual Studio 2005 IDE consists of many windows. All windows have specific roles to play: some are active and helpful while in design-time; others are available only in run-time mode. Covering every window available in the IDE is beyond the reach of this book. Therefore, I'll discuss the three most common and important ones here:

- Solution Explorer

- Toolbox

- Properties

In Figure A-2, the Toolbox window is docked on the right side of the IDE, and both the Solution Explorer and the Properties windows are docked on the left side. Before we look inside each window in detail, let's look at the generic characteristics that are common to all the windows. The look of a window generally differs because of its content; for example, the contents of the Toolbox Window are different than the content of the Properties window. What is common among the windows is they way they blend into the IDE.

Let me ask you a question here: do you think that windows have a fixed position inside the IDE? I'm sure your answer is, "No."

Like toolbars, windows can be placed according to your individual preference. For instance, you can shuffle the position of the Solution Explorer and the Toolbox windows. If you want, you can keep the windows floating or auto-hide them, which means you hide the content of the window and just display the window icon. Figure A-5 shows various options for windows' positions and points out the auto-hide option.

At times, you need more space to work with on the IDE's design surface. In such situations, auto-hide is a handy feature. If you auto-hide a window, as soon as you move the mouse over the window's icon, the window becomes visible again.

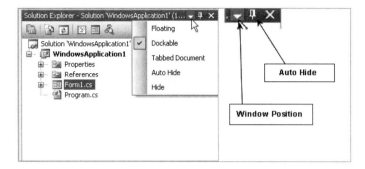

Figure A-5. *A window's position and auto-hide options*

■**Note** You can use the View menu choice to set up commonly used windows. For example, if you've hidden the Properties window, you can make it visible by clicking the View menu and selecting the Properties menu option.

In addition to hiding a window and making it visible, you can keep a window's position floating or dock it. I always like to see the Toolbox window on the left-hand side of the IDE, so I dock it there. Docking a window is simple: You just drag the window by holding the blue title area. As you drag, you will see a guideline to dock either on the left, right, top, or the bottom position. A guideline showing all four directions allows you to show the window as a tab choice inside the IDE designer. Figure A-6 shows docking in action.

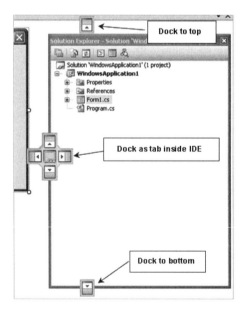

Figure A-6. *Docking a window*

Solution Explorer

Solution Explorer is the location for all the information to manage the solution and one or more associated projects; you can manage individual projects and their related files here. If you take a look Figure A-7, you'll notice that the solution WindowsApplicaton1 is presented in the tree structure format. The hierarchy of the information trails from the solution to the projects and ends with the individual files. Often, the individual files are further separated by putting them inside the folders.

Have you noticed the different icons in the tree structure? I'm sure you have. These images help you to identity each file type and section. You can click on the plus (+) and minus (–) symbols in Solution Explorer to hide or expand any section.

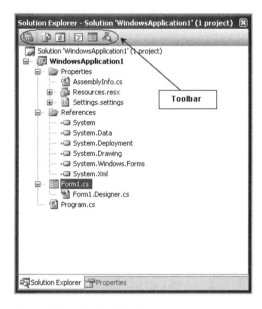

Figure A-7. *Solution Explorer*

As you can see, the top section of the Solution Explorer window has six icons. Consider them as six different commands that you can perform from within this window; they all have important roles to play. As you can see in Figure A-7, the first command helps you to probe the property of any selected file. The second command is to show all the files; this means to show Bin and Obj folders in the tree, which are hidden by default (see Figure A-8).

Next in line is the Refresh command; you can click this button to refresh the Solution Explorer window. As you add or remove files from Solution Explorer, the VS 2005 IDE automatically refreshes the window content to its most current status.

The next three buttons on the Toolbar help you to quickly access various aspects of selected files. From the left to the right, they display the code window, the designer associated with the file, and the class diagram.

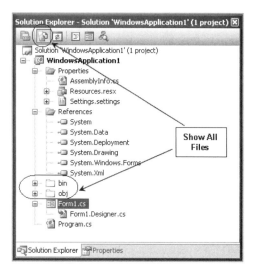

Figure A-8. *Solution Explorer (showing all files)*

Toolbox

As you can see in Figure A-2, the Toolbox window is docked on the left side of the IDE. Like the Solution Explorer window, this window is also often used by developers; it contains various elements that you can add to the project.

The content of this window depends on the type of project. In Figure A-9, you have standard Windows Forms controls. If the project is a web site, then the content will reflect that project selection.

The elements are separated into different tabs, such as Common Controls, Containers, and Data. You can also create your own tab to host third-party or custom controls.

Figure A-9. *The Toolbox window*

Properties

The third window that I'd like to discuss in this section is Properties. As you can see in Figure A-2, the Properties window is docked on the right side of the IDE with the Solution Explorer window. You can use the Properties window to access the individual characteristics related to specific elements of the project; the element could be a form, file, class, or control.

As Figure A-10 shows, all associated properties of Form1 are displayed as content in this window. You can set the properties' values inside the window.

You can view properties according to their categories or sort them alphabetically. In Figure A-10, properties are alphabetically sorted. Which is better, sorting by category or sorting alphabetically? Well, that choice is different from developer to developer. I personally like the alphabetically sorted view. But if you like to see all the appearance-related properties, such as color and fonts, together, the categorized view is best for you.

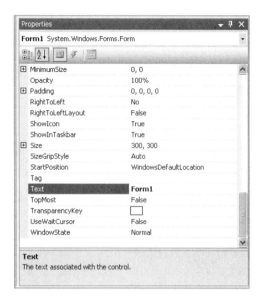

Figure A-10. *The Properties window*

The first two buttons in the Properties window toolbar are used to toggle between the categorized and alphabetically sorted views. The next two buttons on the toolbar are used to toggle between viewing properties or events (the lightening bolt icon). The events view is similar to the properties view in that you can sort events either alphabetically or by group. The last button on the toolbar displays the property pages associated with the currently selected item. If the item does not have property pages, this button will be disabled.

■**Note** The Properties window is smart. If you select an item that has no event, the events button will be disabled.

The bottom of the Properties window has a section for the description of the currently selected property. In Figure A-10, the text property is described. You can hide the description pane if you want to use the space occupied by it by right-clicking anywhere in the window and unchecking the description setting.

You can change properties in one of the two ways. Certain properties can be changed by clicking on the property name. For example, the enabled property has a true/false value. If you click this property, you will toggle the value to either true or false. Some properties, like text, you can simply select and type in the value.

Working Space

All right, you have seen the important windows that are used to manage the solution, work with properties, and access project elements. Now, what about the actual work itself? I mean to say, where do you design your form and write code?

Well, as Figure A-11 shows, all available space in the IDE aside from the windows is actual workspace for you to manage project content. You'll notice in Figure A-11 that we have three open tabs: one is the form designer; another has code behind it, and the third is the Start Page tab, which is the welcome page of the Visual Studio 2005 IDE.

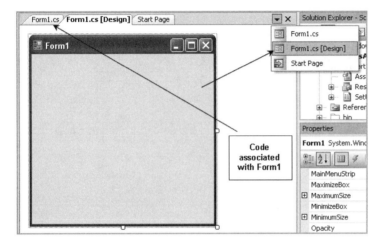

Figure A-11. *Working space*

So, as you go on working with the project, if you open new files, they will be added to this working space as tabs. You can switch to a new tab by clicking the downward facing arrow icon next to the "X" sign (see Figure A-11).

■**Note** An asterisk (*) will appear on a tab to indicate that the contents of the tab (either the form or the code) have changed and are not yet saved.

Other Windows Within the IDE

In addition to all the windows we discussed so far, the IDE contains a few other useful windows. Many things in the IDE are contextual; they differ depending on the current mode. That means certain windows are only meaningful in design-time mode and others in run-time mode.

For example, as Figure A-12 shows, if your code results in some error, the error will appear in the Error List window. Another example is the Output window, which will show the most recent output of the last performed action of the IDE.

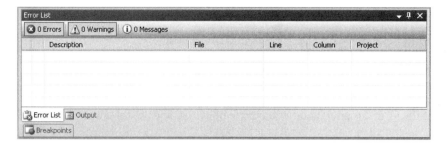

Figure A-12. *The Error List window*

If you need more information on the IDE, you can find details here: `http://msdn2.microsoft.com/en-us/library/h8w79z10(VS.80).aspx`.

Index

You Need the Companion eBook

Your purchase of this book entitles you to buy the companion PDF-version eBook for only $10. Take the weightless companion with you anywhere.

We believe this Apress title will prove so indispensable that you'll want to carry it with you everywhere, which is why we are offering the companion eBook (in PDF format) for $10 to customers who purchase this book now. Convenient and fully searchable, the PDF version of any content-rich, page-heavy Apress book makes a valuable addition to your programming library. You can easily find and copy code—or perform examples by quickly toggling between instructions and the application. Even simultaneously tackling a donut, diet soda, and complex code becomes simplified with hands-free eBooks!

Once you purchase your book, getting the $10 companion eBook is simple:

❶ Visit **www.apress.com/promo/tendollars/**.

❷ Complete a basic registration form to receive a randomly generated question about this title.

❸ Answer the question correctly in 60 seconds, and you will receive a promotional code to redeem for the $10.00 eBook.

eBookshop

2855 TELEGRAPH AVENUE | SUITE 600 | BERKELEY, CA 94705

Offer valid through 3/08.